ETHICS AND
ENTERTAINMENT

W9-ACF-569

ETHICS AND ENTERTAINMENT

Essays on Media Culture and Media Morality

Edited by Howard Good *and*
Sandra L. Borden

McFarland & Company, Inc., Publishers
Jefferson, North Carolina, and London

Library of Congress Cataloguing-in-Publication Data

Ethics and entertainment : essays on media culture and media
   morality / edited by Howard Good and Sandra L. Borden.
      p.   cm.
   Includes bibliographical references and index.

   ISBN 978-0-7864-3909-6
   softcover : 50# alkaline paper ∞

   1. Mass media — Moral and ethical aspects.   2. Broadcasting —
Moral and ethical aspects.   I. Good, Howard, 1951–   II. Borden,
Sandra L., 1963 –
P94.E77   2010
174 — dc22   2009046359

British Library cataloguing data are available

Cover image ©2010 Shutterstock

Manufactured in the United States of America

*McFarland & Company, Inc., Publishers
   Box 611, Jefferson, North Carolina 28640
   www.mcfarlandpub.com*

For my father, Samuel Good
— H.G.

For my children, Katie and Zach
— S.B.

Table of Contents

PART IV: ENTERTAINMENT AND AUTHORSHIP

PART V: ENTERTAINMENT AND DIGNITY

Introduction

Let's get something straight from the start. The title of this book may prominently feature the word "ethics," but the co-editors have no interest in self-righteous moralizing. Our aim isn't to add more voices to the large chorus lamenting the perceived shortcomings of media entertainment, but to provide useful guidelines and perspectives for examining the ethical issues confronting entertainment producers and consumers. Such an examination has perhaps never been more important than now. "During the 20th century," ethicists Philip Patterson and Lee Wilkins point out, "the predominant use of the media shifted from the distribution of information to entertainment and the popularization of culture."[1] If anything, the shift has only accelerated in the first decade of the 21st century.

Plato famously said, "When the mode of music changes, the walls of the city shake."[2] The oft-repeated proverb contains much truth. Throughout the modern era, the emergence of new forms of media entertainment—movies, comic books, television, rock 'n' roll, video games—has repeatedly unnerved the custodians of traditional culture. In 1916 psychiatrist Hugo Munsterberg devoted practically an entire book to outlining the potential negative effects of movies on audiences. "The sight of crime and of vice," he warned in *The Photoplay: A Psychological Study,* "may force itself on the consciousness with disastrous results.... The possibilities of psychical infection and destruction cannot be overlooked."[3] His concerns would be echoed over the following decades, not just about movies, but about all kinds of entertainment. For example, Frederic Wertham argued in his 1954 bestseller, *Seduction of the Innocent,* that the violent, sexed-up imagery in comic books undermined mental health, literacy, and respect for authority among teenagers. He noted darkly that comic books were found in the rooms of teen suicides.[4]

To be sure, some media scholars and commentators perceive violent entertainment as socially constructive. "Repeated illustrations of violence and immorality are necessary to impart ethical lessons to the citizenry just as 'hellfire and brimstone' are used in sermons to emphasize the frightening prospects of hell," Lawrence Jarvik wrote.[5] Former comic book writer Gerard Jones claims that violent entertainment offers children and teenagers an opportunity for catharsis, a way of working through difficult emotions.[6] But there's a difference between the modern frequency of TV or movie viewing and the infrequent attendance at the ancient Greek tragedies that Aristotle thought capable of providing catharsis. "The Athenian could not go to the theatre every day," Hamilton Frye points out in the introduction to his translation of Aristotle's *Poetics*. "That would be emotional dysentery. He took his purge regularly twice a year."[7]

Media critics are, in fact, increasingly alarmed over the sheer volume of entertainment being produced and consumed today, often invoking images of natural disaster to describe it. Thus Dolf Zillmann refers to a "media avalanche," while F. Miguel Valenti observes that "we are drowning in a veritable sea of media."[8] Both recognize that, quite apart from issues of content, push-button access to entertainment raises its own set of ethical concerns. And we aren't referring to how easily kids can sneak peeks at the Playboy Channel.

Entertainment was once something you had to go out of your way to find — in Valenti's phrase, "a diversion from the everyday world."[9] It required special effort to attend a movie or concert or ball game. But technology has changed all that. Now movies, music, sports, and more are available night and day in your car, at home, on your laptop, and over your cell phone.[10] Entertainment is no longer a diversion from the everyday world; it *is* the everyday world.

The entertainment industry may well be the most powerful force in American life today. As media critic Neil Postman says, politics, news, religion, and education have all become "adjuncts of show business."[11] How else to explain the existence of Court TV, *Sesame Street*, and televangelists, or the fact that former Sen. Fred Thompson announced his candidacy for the 2008 Republican presidential nomination not at a Washington press conference, but while a guest on *The Tonight Show with Jay Leno*?

And yet for all the anxiety over contemporary media technology, and for all the hand-wringing over contemporary media content, the basic issues haven't changed greatly over the past 50 years. It's with a disconcerting sense of *déjà vu* that one reads a series of questions posed by sociologist Ernest van den Haag in 1960: "Does our society foster personal relationships, 'individuality,' and 'privacy,' or marketability, out-directedness, and pseudo-personalizations parasitically devouring the genuine personalizations of those who assume them? Could Jesus go into the desert today to contemplate? Wouldn't he be followed by a crew of *Life* photographers, cameramen, publisher agents, etc.? What of the gossip columns, of people's interest in other people's private lives ... don't these phenomena suggest a breakdown of reserve, vicarious living, indeed, pseudo-life and experience?"[12]

Well, yeah. But just because the answer to these questions is obvious doesn't mean anything else about the media is. The world of media entertainment has grown so vast and various that it's increasingly difficult to view it whole. Only one thing seems certain: As that world goes round and round, it'll continue to spin off new technologies, programming, and controversies.

It'd take a library to adequately cover all the ethical issues that media entertainment raises. Unfortunately, the editors couldn't compile a library, just a book. *Ethics and Entertainment* nonetheless manages to address a wide range of issues. The book is divided into five parts, each dealing with a major ethical concern voiced by critics about media entertainment.

Part I, "Entertainment and Celebrity," examines the quintessential example of "pseudo-life and experience" in our age: the obsession with celebrity. The traditional role of the hero—famous for his or her great deeds—has been replaced by the celebrity who is famous sometimes just because of his or her appearance in the media. "The creation of 24-hour news coverage and the Internet means there are more places for celebrities to be seen by their public," Philip Drake of Paisley University in Scotland points out. "The process of becoming a celebrity has become quicker."[13] Psychologist James Houran speculates that in a secular society like ours, the need for ritualized idol worship can be displaced onto celebrities. Unreligious people tend to be more interested in celebrity culture, he has found. For them, celebrity fills some of the same roles that religion fills for believers, such as the desire to admire the powerful and the drive to fit into a community of people with shared values.[14]

In the opening chapter of Part I, "The Ethics of Speaking Out," Wendy N. Wyatt and Kristie Bunton propose a four-step test to determine when, if ever, celebrities are ethically justified to speak out on an issue of social or political concern. Nikki Usher and Janel S. Schuh offer in their chapter, "'I'm Sorry, Oh, So Sorry: Celebrity Apologies and Public Ethics,'" a set of criteria for judging whether an apology for bad public behavior by a Mel Gibson or a Britney Spears is ethical. Meanwhile, Kyle F. Reinson uses the sad cases of Kitty Genovese and Terry Schiavo to explore in his chapter, "Quasars: Silent Celebrities, Ethical Implications," the ethics of turning news subjects into silent stars—the "quasars" of the title—that come to symbolize whatever the news media decide they should.

Part II deals with "Entertainment and Children." According to one study, about 90 percent of American children under age 2—and as many as 40 percent under 3 months—are regular watchers of television, DVDs, and videos. Another recent study found that 75 percent of children up to age 6 watch TV every day, typically in their own bedrooms.[15] Still other researchers reported that children ages 8 to 18 devote, on average, six hours and 21 minutes a day to recreational media use, including watching TV; listening to CDs, MP3s, or the radio; going online; and playing video games.[16] Fifty years ago, Aldous Huxley warned in *Brave New World Revisited* that the media foresaw immense profits if they could enlist children at an early age into the army of consumers.[17] It's a warning few parents seem to have heard or, at least, heeded.

Erin L. Ryan and Keisha L. Hoerrner, however, have taken Huxley's warning seriously in their chapter 5, "The Diaper Demographic." They enlist the help of Immanuel Kant, John Stuart Mill, and John Rawls to investigate the ethics of Baby Einstein and Brainy Baby using entertainment to turn infants into lifelong consumers. Before that, in chapter 4, Marie Hardin and Thomas F. Corrigan take a look at another ubiquitous form of media in the lives of older children. Their chapter, "'Sportainment' Meets High School Sports," argues that sports coverage is more than just the presentation of scores, recaps, and highlights, and advocates a communitarian lens for viewing the relationship among "sportainment," youths, education, and culture. In his chapter, "*Superbad*: A Twisted and Touching Ethical Mess of a Movie," Joseph C. Harry takes on the teen comedy. Drawing on John Dewey's version of pragmatism, he explains how the 2007 film "achieves an ethical stance by casting the characters' drunken fun and uncommitted sex within an emergent, ever-wider moral perspective of mutually respectful love, trust, and commitment."

Contributors to Part III delve into the murky area of "Entertainment and Factuality." One of the defining characteristics of postmodern culture is the hybridization of media. The term refers not only to converged technologies—the fact that you can now watch a movie on your cell phone or read a newspaper on your PC—but also to the conflation of once-distinct genres. We speak glibly about docudramas, nonfiction novels, reality TV, and infotainment as if the meaning of such hybridization were self-evident. It's not. Cynthia M. King and Deni Elliott note in their chapter, "Tall Tales: Exploring the Ethics of Storytelling in the Age of Infotainment," that infotainment and similar hybrids blur the boundaries between fact and fiction by definition; they outline a voluntary disclosure system to assist storytellers and audiences in distinguishing fantasy from reality in the infotainment age.

Other chapters in the section also explore the ethics of hybridity. Steve Lipkin examines ethical questions related to both the content and form of the 9/11 docudrama *United 93* in "This Time It's Personal." Mike Dillon asks larger questions about the harms of packaging politics as just another form of entertainment in "Bread and Circuits: Politics in an Entertainment Culture." In "The *Common Morality* of Interviewers: Evaluating Moral Guidelines of Non-Journalists," David Charlton looks at the ethics of Jon Stewart or David Letterman conducting political interviews in a comedy talk-show setting. Jack Breslin discusses the conflicts that ensue from the mixing of journalistic techniques and entertainment imperatives in such reality crime shows as *America's Most Wanted* and *COPS* in "Cops and Reality TV: Public Service or Public Menace?"

In recent years, the line between author and audience has eroded no less than that between fact and fiction, and some of the credit — or blame — for this belongs to the influence of deconstructionist philosophy. Deconstructionism calls into question the traditional Western belief in the unique authorial self, approaching texts as neither discrete nor original. "There is naturally a desire, for whoever speaks or writes, to sign in an idiomatic, that is, irreplaceable manner," Jacques Derrida, perhaps the best-known deconstructionist, said. "But as soon as there is a mark, that is, the possibility of a repetition, as soon as there is language, generality has entered the scene and the idiom compromises with something that is not idiomatic: with a common language, concepts, laws, general norms."[18]

Part IV, "Entertainment and Authorship," explores the responsibilities of authorship. The very concept of authorship — and the related notion of intellectual property — is under assault, as much lately from YouTube and Facebook as from the metaphysical implications of French deconstructionism. At the same time, there is a fresh demand for authenticity in the age of Twitter and reality TV, which has seen the cultural authority of the detached, objective voice long associated with media credibility severely diminished. In "Documentary Tradition and the Ethics of Michael Moore's *SiCKO*," Sandra L. Borden uses virtue theory to establish that Moore's work, despite receiving loud and frequent criticism for bending the facts, exhibits coherence, continuity, and creativity within the documentary tradition. Howard Good, in his chapter "'Just a Cartoonist': The Virtuous Journalism of Joe Sacco," recovers a forgotten concept of virtuous journalism to make the case that lowly comic book artist Joe Sacco represents the highest ideals of journalism. In "Whose Tube Is It Anyway?" John Chapin writes on the potential of YouTube videos for infusing the marketplace of ideas with more voices while leaving us vulnerable to covert persuasion by authors in disguise. Bill Reader rounds out this section by searching for authenticity in "The Enlightenment Ethics in DIY [Do It Yourself] Culture."

There is probably not a media ethics course in the country that doesn't introduce its students to the Second Formulation of Kant's Categorical Imperative (and if there is, it should immediately disband), also sometimes called the "humanity principle": "Act so that you treat humanity, as much in your own as in the person of every other, always at the same time as an end and never merely as a means." That is, people, no matter what their circumstances (rich or poor, black or white, Democrat or Republican, fat or thin), possess moral worth by virtue of their common humanity and, therefore, deserve dignity and respect. If taken seriously, the "humanity principle" would mean radical changes in the nature of entertainment. The media would no longer treat audiences solely instrumentally — as means to the ends of greater profits — and audiences would be more discriminating in their choice of media fare, shunning entertainment that exploited sex for titillation, violence for escape, and racial stereotypes for laughs.

In Part V, contributors tackle issues related to "Entertainment and Dignity." K. Maja Krakowiak claims in "Fictionalized Torture: Jack Bauer's War on Terrorism" that Fox's hit TV series *24* has legitimized government use of torture to combat terrorism. Elizabeth K. Hansen and Angela F. Cooke-Jackson discuss the ethical problems caused by the media-driven image of the people of Appalachia as lazy, ignorant, and toothless in "Hillbilly Stereotypes and Humor: Entertaining Ourselves at the Expense of the Other." Trin Turner and Joshua D. Upson, in "Epistemic Freedom, Science Fiction, and Ethical Deliberation," experiment with science fiction as a vehicle for attaining moral clarity about abortion and gay-friendly schools. And Berrin A. Beasley argues in "Weight Watching: The Ethics of Commodifying Appearance for Profit" that weight loss/makeover TV shows — *The Biggest Loser, Celebrity Fit Club,* and so on — are teaching Americans that their appearance is unacceptable and that they need this product or that service to improve themselves.

Regardless of the section in which their chapters appear, the contributors all go beyond mere description of ethical dilemmas to provide concrete criteria for analyzing, and perhaps resolving, them. And as should be apparent by now, the dilemmas generated by media entertainment — or what some have called "mass culture" — are many and various and not without existential repercussions. "The total effect of mass culture," Van den Haag wrote, "is to distract people from lives which are so boring that they generate obsession with escape. Yet because mass culture creates addiction to prefabricated experience, most people are deprived of the remaining possibilities of autonomous growth and enrichment, and their lives become ever more boring and unfulfilled."[19]

In other words, the entertainment served up by the media may look good and even taste good, but it's full of empty calories and doesn't intellectually, spiritually, or otherwise nourish us. This kind of skepticism about the value of entertainment has been around for centuries. Seneca condemned gladiatorial games in ancient Rome for making spectators *"crudelior et inhumane"* ("more cruel and inhumane").[20] The Puritans prohibited attending plays, dancing around the maypole, bowling on the green, and shuffleboard as sinful.

"Every age," the great social critic Christopher Lasch said, "develops its own peculiar forms of pathology, which express in exaggerated form its underlying character structure."[21] There's no certainty that media entertainment is one of our age's peculiar forms of pathology, but there's no certainty that it isn't. If it is, we might do well to do as this book suggests— think more often and more deeply about the ethics of how we entertain others as well as ourselves.

NOTES

1. Philip Patterson and Lee Wilkins, *Media Ethics: Issues and Cases*, 6th ed. (Boston: McGraw Hill, 1997), 266.

2. Despite a scrupulous search, we haven't been able to locate the original source of the quotation, only secondhand attributions to the ancient Greek philosopher.

3. Quoted in Steven Starker, *Evil Influences: Crusades Against the Mass Media* (New Brunswick, NJ: Transaction, 1989), 100.

4. Stephen Weiner, *Faster Than a Speeding Bullet: The Rise of the Graphic Novel* (New York: Nantier Beall Minoustchine, 2003), 8.

5. Quoted in Sissela Bok, *Mayhem: Violence as Public Entertainment* (Reading, MA: Addison-Wesley, 1998), 34.

6. Gerard Jones, *Killing Monsters: Why Children Need Fantasy, Super Heroes, and Make-Believe Violence* (New York: Basic, 2002).

7. Quoted in Bok, *Mayhem*, 167.

8. Dolf Zillmann, "The Coming of Media Entertainment," in *Media Entertainment: The Psychology of Its Appeal*, ed. Dolf Zillmann and Peter Vorderer (Mahwah, NJ: Lawrence Erlbaum, 2000, 15; F. Miguel Valenti, *More Than a Movie: Ethics in Entertainment* (Boulder, CO: Westview, 2000), 4.

9. Valenti, *More Than a Movie*, 34.

10. Or, as Andrew Keen rather wryly put it, "There was a time, not long ago, when, if we wanted to watch television, we'd turn on our television sets. Now, we turn on our computers, flip open our cell phones, switch on our TiVos, or plug into our video iPods." *The Cult of the Amateur: How Today's Internet Is Killing Our Culture* (New York: Doubleday, 2007), 123–24.

11. Neil Postman, *Amusing Ourselves to Death: Public Discourse in the Age of Show Business* (New York: Viking, 1985), 4.

12. Ernest van den Haag, "A Dissent from the Consensual Society," in *Mass Culture Revisited*, ed. Bernard Rosenberg and David Manning White (New York: Van Nostrand, 1971), 88.

13. Sarah Cassidy, "Celebrity obsession is turning nasty, academics warn," The Independent, http://www.independent.co.uk/news/uk/this-britain/celebrity-obsession-is-turning-nasty-academics-warn-506466.html (accessed 16 June 2009).

14. Ernest van den Haag, "A Dissent from the Consensual Society," in *Mass Culture Revisited*, ed. Bernard Rosenberg and David Manning White (New York: Van Nostrand, 1971), 88.

15. "Too Many Babies Are Teeny TV Watchers," MSNBC.com. http://www.msnbc.com/id/18539759/ (accessed 8 May 2007).

16. Associated Press, "Kids Hooked on the Media," *Poughkeepsie* (NY) *Journal*, March 10, 2005, 10A.

17. Quoted in Bok, *Mayhem*, 52.

18. Jacques Derrida, "There Is No One Narcissism," www.units.muohio.edu/technologyandhumanities/eng495/derrida.htm (accessed June 15, 2009).

19. Van den Haag, "A Dissent from the Consensual Society," 92.

20. Quoted in Bok, *Mayhem*, 19.
21. Christopher Lasch, *The Culture of Narcissism: American Life in an Age of Diminishing Expectations* (New York: Warner, 1979), 87–88.

WORKS CITED

Bok, Sissela. *Mayhem: Violence as Public Entertainment*. Reading, MA: Addison-Wesley, 1998.
Derrida, Jacques. "There is No One Narcissism," www.units.muohio.edu/technologyandhumanities/eng495/derrida.htm (accessed June 15, 2009).
Jones, Gerard. *Killing Monsters: Why Children Need Fantasy, Super Heroes, and Make-Believe Violence*. New York: Basic, 2002.
Keen, Andrew. *The Cult of the Amateur: How Today's Internet Is Killing Our Culture*. New York: Doubleday, 2007.
Lasch, Christopher. *The Culture of Narcissism: American Life in an Age of Diminishing Expectations*. New York: Warner, 1979.
Patterson, Philip, and Lee Wilkins. *Media Ethics: Issues and Cases*, 6th ed. Boston: McGraw Hill, 1997.
Postman, Neil. *Amusing Ourselves to Death: Public Discourse in the Age of Show Business*. New York: Viking, 1985.
Starker, Steven. *Evil Influences: Crusades Against the Mass Media*. New Brunswick, NJ: Transaction, 1989.
Valenti, F. Miguel. *More Than a Movie: Ethics in Entertainment*. Boulder, CO: Westview, 2000.
Van den Haag, Ernest. "A Dissent from the Consensual Society." In *Mass Culture Revisited*. Ed. Bernard Rosenberg and David Manning White. New York: Van Nostrand, 1971.
Weiner, Stephen. *Faster Than a Speeding Bullet: The Rise of the Graphic Novel*. New York: Nantier Beall Minoustchine, 2003.
Zillmann, Dolf. "The Coming of Media Entertainment." In *Media Entertainment: The Psychology of Its Appeal*. Ed. Dolf Zillmann and Peter Vorderer. Mahwah, NJ: Lawrence Erlbaum, 2000, 15.

I. ENTERTAINMENT AND CELEBRITY

CHAPTER 1

The Ethics of Speaking Out

Wendy N. Wyatt *and* Kristie Bunton

"Just so you know, we're ashamed the president
of the United States is from Texas."

It's March 2003 — 10 days before the U.S. invasion of Iraq — and American country music star Natalie Maines, lead singer of the Dixie Chicks, utters these 15 words to a London concert audience. Almost immediately, Maines' words hit home. These are days when airplay of patriotic songs is on the rise; radio listeners are hearing Darryl Worley's "Have You Forgotten," Clint Black's "I Raq and Roll," Lee Greenwood's "God Bless the USA," and Toby Keith's "Courtesy of the Red, White and Blue."[1] Mere hours after Maines' remarks, she and the Dixie Chicks become a target of radio and concert boycotts, CD-smashing protests, verbal attacks by conservative pundits, politicians and citizens, and even death threats. Not every response is negative, however. Some people offer Maines their support, saying dissent is important to democracy. People in the public eye, they say, should "underscore the fact that America is a place filled with varying opinions about the government and its leaders."[2]

"George Bush doesn't care about black people."

Fast forward to September 2005. In the aftermath of Hurricane Katrina, NBC has organized an "NBC: We Are the World" telethon. Viewers tune in to watch Leonardo DiCaprio, Faith Hill, Hilary Swank, Harry Connick, Jr., and others raise money for hurricane victims. The live show progresses as planned until the appearance of Kanye West, the man with that day's best-selling album. Standing next to comedian Mike Myers, West veers from the script and — clearly nervous and emotional — claims that the government's relief efforts are racially biased. He criticizes the media's portrayal of African-Americans in New Orleans and then comments on the "shoot on sight" order given to the National Guard. One minute into his condemnation, as Myers

9

is returning to the script, West adds, "President Bush doesn't care about black people." NBC producers quickly cut to comedian Chris Tucker. By the time a recorded version of the telethon airs three hours later on the West Coast, West's remark about Bush has been deleted.

Like Natalie Maines' remarks two years earlier, word of West's remarks spreads quickly. Some 13.8 million viewers see the live telecast, but scores more see West's comments when they become one of the most widely circulated files on the Internet.[3] NBC quickly distances itself from the comment, issuing a statement that reads, "It would be most unfortunate if the efforts of the artists who participated tonight and the generosity of millions of Americans who are helping those in need are overshadowed by one person's opinion."[4] But one person's opinion has quite an effect on the public discourse surrounding the relief efforts. With his comments, West receives more attention from and access to the mainstream than any rapper since Chuck D, who in the late 1980s called rap music "the black CNN." While many observers on the right harshly criticize West, others say he has done Americans a service by explicitly "putting the issue on the table for national debate."[5]

"Let's face it, if mothers ruled the world, there would
be no goddamned wars in the first place."

Fast forward two more years to 2007. It's September 16, the night of the annual Primetime Emmy Awards, and Sally Field wins an Emmy for her role as the mother of an Iraq War veteran in the drama series *Brothers and Sisters*. After dedicating her award to the mothers of the world who "stand with an open heart and wait, wait for their children to come home from danger, from harm's way and from war," Field makes her own anti-war statement, declaring that "if mothers ruled the world, there would be no goddamned wars." While audience members in the theater hear Field's comments, TV viewers do not. Fox, the network airing the Emmys, quickly replaces the comment with several seconds of dead air. In a statement issued the day after the Emmys, Fox says, "Some language during the live broadcast may have been considered inappropriate by some viewers. As a result, Fox's broadcast standards executives determined it appropriate to drop sound during those portions of the show."[6] Many argue, however, that because the broadcast was delayed, Fox could have bleeped out Field's expletive rather than deleting the entire comment. The deletion leads critics to believe Fox was censoring political views rather than language.

Speaking Out

In the examples described, the Dixie Chicks, Kanye West, and Sally Field spoke out about an issue of social or political concern using their access to the public sphere — those real and virtual areas of informal public life where people can go to "talk about issues, get information, exchange ideas, and form opinions."[7] Although these entertainers certainly have a legal *right* to speak out — at least in the United States — this chapter focuses on the *ethics* of doing so. Were they ethically justified in using an entertainment venue to speak out about political topics? And can we identify general ethical guidelines or a decision-making process that will help guide other analyses of speaking out?

In this analysis, we focus on a specific kind of speaking out: an instance in which an entertainer, athlete, artist, or other famous person uses a public occasion designated for something else to express political or social views. These instances have an air of surprise about them. After all, concerts are for performing music, telethons for raising money, and award shows for celebrating top performances. Instances of speaking out catch the audience off guard and seem to defy the role expectations that audiences have for the people speaking out.

The Dixie Chicks, Kanye West, and Sally Field provide only a few examples of those who have recently spoken out. Consider musician Bono of U2; these days, we know him almost as well for his humanitarian work as for his music. Consider also Sean Penn, Bruce Springsteen, Angelina Jolie, Martin Sheen, Tim Robbins, and Susan Sarandon; each of these celebrities has used his or her status to get on a soapbox and speak out.

Speaking out isn't particularly a recent phenomenon. In 1973 debate raged around actor Marlon Brando when he refused an Oscar to protest Hollywood's treatment of American Indians. And actress Jane Fonda was famously nicknamed "Hanoi Jane" after her outspoken opposition to the Vietnam War. Speaking out isn't a phenomenon limited to entertainers either. During the 1968 Olympics in Mexico City, two black American sprinters — gold medalist Tommie Smith and bronze medalist John Carlos — bowed their heads and raised black-gloved fists during the medal ceremony in a protest against racism. Today the NBA's Etan Thomas and the NFL's Scott Fujita have spoken out on war, poverty, and racism,[8] and groups of Olympic and professional athletes have taken a stand against the genocide in Darfur.

Although instances of speaking out seem to rise in proportion to our growing fascination with celebrities, some celebrities deliberately pass on the opportunity. Comedian Steve Carrell, for instance, says he declines to speak publicly about his political views because "my voice is no more valuable, no less valuable than anyone else's."[9] Tennis champion Pete Sampras agrees: "It's not my place to tell you whom to vote for, to take any political stand, to tell you what religion to believe in. I'm an athlete. I can influence certain things, but when I see other athletes and celebrities telling you whom to vote for, I actually get a bit offended."[10]

Some of the most notable instances of speaking out have provoked vehement criticism. In response to the Dixie Chicks, some said the statement was unpatriotic. Others said it was inappropriate at a concert venue, particularly a concert out of the country. In a letter to the editor of *USA Today*, one reader said, "When traveling abroad, it is in poor taste for Americans to knock our country or its people, even the leaders with whom we may disagree."[11] Still others thought Maines and the Dixie Chicks should just "shut up and sing." A *St. Louis Post-Dispatch* opinion piece expressed this sentiment: "If the actors and singers and dancers want me to go to their movies and plays and concerts and pay to see them perform, they need to let me appreciate their talents for what they are, and they need to keep their political opinions to themselves."[12]

At the same time angry citizens were denouncing the Dixie Chicks as traitors, others offered support, claiming that freedom in a democracy means nothing without dissent. Another *USA Today* letter writer said, "It is very patriotic for a person or group of people who are in the public eye to underscore the fact that America is a place filled with varying opinions about the government and its leaders."[13]

The question then becomes: when — if ever — is speaking out ethically justified? If we were to gauge the justifiability of Natalie Maines', Kanye West's, or Sally Field's words based simply on negative responses, it might be tempting to suggest that speaking out is categorically unjustifiable. But such an attitude runs counter to one of our most cherished values: free expression. Any effort at regulating speech — even if from an ethical rather than a legal perspective — must be justified. A democratically organized public must have both freedom of inquiry and freedom to distribute the results of this inquiry; citizens in a democracy need a forum for articulating their views.

The Value of Expression

Perhaps, then, voices should be encouraged or — dare we say — even required. The democratic ideal depends on an active and educated citizenry. Participation is crucial to the entire endeavor. Entertainers, athletes, and artists — people we'll call simply celebrities — who have chosen to speak out are making an effort to join the public conversation. If nothing else, they can't be criticized for failing to participate. For such democratic theorists as John Dewey and Jürgen Habermas, the moral life is about being able to engage. Knowledge comes from the direct give-and-take that occurs when citizens opt into the public sphere. To paraphrase Dewey, we come to understand what we know and what we still need to learn only when we subject our preferences to the test of debate.[14]

The idea here is that a celebrity speaking out on an issue is only one side of the discursive equation. The opportunity to respond is always available, and as news articles attest, citizens don't hesitate to respond. Sometimes it comes in the form of language — letters to a newspaper or cheers and boos from an audience. At other times, the response is more symbolic — a radio boycott or even a CD "smash."

And sometimes even the celebrity targets of citizens' responses see value in the debate. Filmmaker Michael Moore is well-known for his political and social activism, but when he received the 2003 Academy Award for best documentary and used his acceptance speech to denounce the Iraq War, reaction was fast and fierce. The DVD for *Bowling for Columbine*, the film that won Moore the Oscar, includes a special feature in which he discusses his Oscar night speech. In it, he notes the power of audience response:

> Looking back on it now, what feels really great about it is that that's one of the wonderful things about living in a free society. That's the noise of democracy. That's the noise of a free people — people cheering something they agree with; people saying "no," I don't agree with that. It was one of those profound moments. You wish we had more of those in our society.[15]

The crucial value of free expression and the need for discourse in a democracy that Moore recognized may lead us toward the conclusion that speaking out should be categorically justifiable — that there should be no instances when it would be unethical. Before settling on that claim, however, we must consider a complicating factor.

The Concern Over Abuses of Power

Despite a sincere commitment to free expression, issues of speaking out raise a red flag in regard to power and the potential for its abuse. For celebrities, power is manifested in two distinct ways: the power of the celebrity to stand in for the people and the power of the celebrity to educate the people.

Celebrities as Stand-Ins

As Daniel Boorstin famously declared in *The Image*, "Our age has produced a new kind of eminence. This new kind of eminence is 'celebrity.'"[16] In addition to being given "a greater presence and a wider scope of activity and agency" than the rest of us, celebrities also gain discursive power.[17] In his book *Celebrity and Power*, P. David Marshall points out that "within society, the celebrity is a voice above others." While the rest of us are "constructed as a demographic aggregate," celebrities express themselves with an individual and idiosyncratic voice that is then "channeled into the media systems as being legitimately significant."[18] In short, while everyone in a democracy is supposed to have a voice, celebrities' voices—just by virtue of the person to whom they're attached—automatically get a hearing and automatically get to matter.

Marshall notes that because today's celebrities emerge from a legitimation process connected to the people rather than to merit or lineage, they become proxies for the people. In the public spectacle, they serve as stand-ins—as spokespersons—for political, social, and economic issues. Their activity, therefore, "can be seen as the site of agency and activity in a culture."[19] Whether deserved or not, this stand-in status gives celebrities an obligation to serve with integrity and to use their role as proxies to fairly represent others. Well-known for his activism aimed at ending the genocide in Darfur, actor George Clooney has noted that the best way he can help victims of the atrocities is simply to "make sure that cameras and lights follow" when he travels to Darfur or speaks out about it.[20]

Celebrities as Teachers

In *Beleaguered Rulers*, William May claims that celebrities, together with media professionals, have replaced both teachers and religious leaders as the most important educators of our time. We pay attention to the authoritative voice of celebrities just as we used to look to the academy or the church. Therefore, many celebrities who speak out about politically and socially serious issues are conscious of the corresponding responsibility to do so in a well-educated manner. For instance, when speaking about his advocacy for clean water in Africa, actor Matt Damon told a reporter, "'For a lot of actors, our biggest fear is that we're going to start talking about things we don't fully understand and sound like idiots.... In the long run, I'll do much more good if, when I open my mouth, I have something worth saying.'"[21] Because we have limited personal access to celebrities, however, the education they provide tends to take on more the form of a lecture than the kind of educative debate Dewey and Habermas advocate. Two-way discourse is replaced by a passive reliance on celebrities to provide our "views and cues."[22]

Whether celebrities deserve the power they hold is certainly a germane question and one that cultural studies scholars have addressed, but it is not particularly the point of this discussion. Rather, what matters here is that the power of the celebrity exists. As stand-ins for the public and educators of the public, celebrities always have the potential to abuse their power. To steer clear of this, they, first, must be cognizant of the power differential inherent in their relationships with the public and, second, must use their voices wisely and responsibly. This would suggest that not all instances of speaking out are morally justifiable, that the freedom to express oneself must be partnered with the responsible use of one's power.

What, particularly, does it mean to balance freedom and responsibility? Did Natalie Maines get it right? What about Kanye West or Sally Field? Because we can't assign categorical acceptability to the issue of speaking out, how can a celebrity know whether her inclination to do so is ethically justified, and equally important, how should the rest of us judge that person's actions? As with all things ethical, no formula can magically generate the answer; there's no avoiding the work — the sometimes gut-wrenching work — that ought to go into justifying a decision to speak out. But there are ways to ensure that the decision-making process is sophisticated, systematic, and thorough. Therefore, we offer a test to help determine the ethical justifiability of speaking out.

Our four-part test is designed specifically for instances of speaking out in which celebrities use a public occasion designated for something else to express political or social views. These instances often cause controversy because the celebrities speaking out catch their audiences "off guard," and they seem to defy the role expectations that audiences have for them. All four parts of the test must be satisfied to justify speaking out. It's important to reiterate that speaking out is not a legal issue, but an ethical one. We offer no argument for restricting free speech. Whether celebrities *can* speak out is not in dispute; we ask whether they *should*.

The Speaking-Out Test

1. What is the relationship of the celebrity to the issue he or she is speaking out about?
2. What is the motivation for speaking out?
3. What is the nature of any harm created?
4. Does speaking out promote dialogue?

1. What is the relationship of the celebrity to the issue he or she is speaking out about? The first step of the test asks for reflection on whether the celebrity is well suited to speak on the issue. Does the celebrity have a particular stake in the issue or particular expertise about it? Does the celebrity speak from an informed perspective with an understanding of the repercussions that may result from what he or she says? Has the celebrity shown a long-term commitment to the issue? Charles Taylor would call this *strong evaluation*. According to Taylor, strong evaluation "enables authentic moral choice."[23] Actions that have been strongly evaluated are well considered and consistent with prior actions.

Were Maines', West's, and Field's actions strongly evaluated? As U.S. citizens, they all have an understandable concern with American social and political issues. In fact, some democratic theorists would argue they have a moral obligation to participate in discussions on these issues. Beyond their citizenship, however, were Maines, West, and Moore particularly well suited to speak out? Maines is a Texan. Field said in her speech that she was speaking for the mothers, of which she is one. And though West's life as a celebrity is far removed from the reality of black Americans who lived through Hurricane Katrina, he is a black man with a particularly relevant perspective on the attitudes of the country's leadership toward black Americans. What's more, before his remarks about Bush, West used hip-hop lyrics to criticize other politicians for what he viewed as racist policies connected to drug addiction and HIV/AIDs treatment.

On the other hand, consider a case from June 2005 when actor Tom Cruise appeared on NBC's *Today* show to promote his upcoming film *War of the Worlds*. The interview with Matt Lauer turned into what the *The Washington Post* called a "full-bore assault on the psychiatric profession."[24] In addition to publicly criticizing actress Brooke Shields for seeking therapy and taking anti-depressants for postpartum depression, Cruise told Lauer that "there is no such thing as a chemical imbalance in a body" and that "psychiatry is a pseudoscience."[25] What made Cruise well-suited to speak about psychiatry generally, and postpartum depression specifically? Were his actions strongly evaluated? Cruise doesn't have formal training in psychiatry, though he claims to understand its history. What's more, as a man, Cruise can never fully understand postpartum depression or its ramifications. Cruise has, however, had a long-term commitment to Scientology, which rejects the tenets of the established medical community, so his attitude about psychiatry is consistent with his prior beliefs.

2. What is the motivation for speaking out? From a Kantian perspective, a fundamental consideration must be the intentions behind the action, and only those actions that stem from a good will are morally defensible. As Immanuel Kant described, a good will is the only thing that can be taken as good without qualification: "Intelligence, wit, judgment, and any other talents of the mind we may care to name, or courage, resolution, and constancy of purpose, as qualities of temperament, are without doubt good and desirable in many respects; but they can also be bad and hurtful when the will is not good."[26] A good will, for Kant, is "esteemed beyond comparison as far higher than anything it could ever bring about."[27] The consequences of speaking out, then, are of little importance to Kant. Even if the outcome is universally declared as good, speaking out is unjustifiable if the will — the motivation behind the action — is bad.

Although motivation is an important criterion in all instances in which an individual is making a moral judgment, it is particularly important for this test because a number of questionable motivations for speaking out readily present themselves. The most notable of those is speaking out in order to gain publicity — treating an issue or another person merely as a means for the celebrity's own end, which might include softening or rehabilitating an image. This kind of purely self-interested motivation for speaking out is problematic, even if the consequences turn out favorably for all.

Likewise, just as celebrities shouldn't use others merely as a means for garnering attention, they must be wary of being used themselves. The possibility exists for a celebrity to be used as the voice for a cause, particularly because of that celebrity's access to the public sphere. Therefore, in addition to checking their own motivations for speaking out, celebrities must always be wary of the intentions of others who encourage them to speak out.

Of course, judging someone else's motivations is risky business. Therefore, the second step of the speaking-out test can only truly be determined by the person doing the speaking. Was Maines speaking from her heart, or was she looking for a brouhaha? Did West plan his comment just to get his name in newspapers? Did Field create controversy just because she likes the attention? Only Maines, West, and Field can know for sure, but from our position as analysts, the three don't appear to contradict the motivation criterion.

What about the motivation of Cruise? Was he acting from a good will when he attacked psychiatry as pseudoscience on the *Today* show? Judging from Cruise's impassioned responses to Lauer's questions, he seemed to believe what he was saying. But we must question whether Cruise's commitment to Scientology has become so devout that he has become blind to the organization using him — someone with serious star power — as nothing more than a means to its own ends. And even if Cruise weren't being used by Scientology, if Scientologists saw Cruise as serving the religion's interests, we can still question his refusal to engage in real debate about the merits of psychiatry.

3. What is the nature of any harm created? The third step of the test deals with probable consequences. Of course, no one can predict with complete confidence what consequences will result from speaking out. But certain consequences can be anticipated, and if these consequences involve harm to others, the nature of that harm must be taken into consideration.

A helpful way to consider the nature of harms is by borrowing from philosopher Bernard Gert's work on morality. Gert defines a harm — what he calls an *evil*— as "something that you would always avoid for yourself or your friends unless you had some reason for not avoiding it."[28] For Gert, harms are death, pain, disability, loss of freedom, loss of pleasure, deception, promise-breaking, cheating, disobeying the law, and failing in one's duty. Gert sets these out as moral rules (i.e., Do not kill). Although the rules are universal, they are not absolute. It is the exceptions to these rules that become the point of reflection in the speaking-out test. In Kantian form, Gert maintains that exceptions must be part of the public system. "If you are going to break a moral rule, you have to be willing that everyone be publicly allowed to break the rule in the same circumstances."[29] This requirement, according to Gert, captures the kind of impartiality that morality requires.

Some of the harms on Gert's list are unlikely concerns for celebrities wishing to speak out. Their words rarely would cause death, disability, or loss of freedom. Likewise, most instances of speaking out do not involve cheating, disobeying the law, or deception (unless one is being deceptive about one's motivations, which is already prohibited by the second step of the test). But speaking out could be considered a breach of a tacit promise or a failure to perform one's duty if audiences expect behaviors that conform to a certain role. What's more, speaking out could cause pain, in the emotional sense, or loss of pleasure, and the nature of those harms cannot be dismissed.

Did Maines and West cause Bush emotional pain when they chastised him? The remarks must have stung — at least a little. But we could rationally argue that the nature of the harm is relatively benign, particularly for a public official whose job puts him in the spotlight for criticism, even when that criticism is sharp. An important consideration in this part of the test is whether speaking out victimizes the powerless — people who are least able to protect themselves. Bush, the explicit target of Maines' and West's remarks and an implicit target of Field's, was one of the most powerful men in the world, so none of the three celebrities enjoyed a power advantage over the subject of their critique. Bush had seemingly limitless access to the public sphere and could easily respond to critiques with a voice just as powerful — perhaps more so — than that of his critics. Of course, in these examples, Bush could not give an immediate response — he wasn't on site at the Dixie Chicks' concert, the Hurricane Katrina telethon, or the Emmy Awards — but if he wanted to respond, he certainly had the means to do so.

However, this may not always be the case. It's important to consider whether speaking out will bring harm to a vulnerable party. From a Rawlsian perspective, justice is achieved by protecting the interests of the most vulnerable.[30] Therefore, instances of speaking out that silence or rebuke a voiceless party cannot be ethically justified. For example, when Cruise attempted to discredit psychiatry on the *Today* show, psychiatrists feared that he would "undo decades of work to remove the stigma from mental illness and psychiatric treatment,"[31] thereby deterring people from getting the care they need and further silencing an already vulnerable group.

4. *Does speaking out promote dialogue?* This final step connects to the earlier discussion on the value of expression. In a democracy, public discourse is not only welcome, it is essential. If citizens do not weigh in on issues of

public concern, the democratic endeavor is lost. Therefore, the extent to which an instance of speaking out spurs such discourse becomes a valuable consideration.

Did West's brief comment during the Hurricane Katrina telethon help prompt a larger discussion on U.S. race relations? It's possible that some people who watched the telethon or who read about West's comment in the newspapers the next day talked not only about *him*, but also about the *claim* he was making. How about Maines? Many reactions focused not on her particular comment, but on patriotism and the duty of citizens during times of war. While some claimed that Americans must unquestionably support their leaders, others argued that dissent is, in fact, patriotic and a virtue in a democracy. And, finally, Field's acceptance speech created discussion not only her about anti-war message, but also about the motivations of the Fox network in censoring her.

In some cases, speaking out can even promote dialogue about celebrities' role in a culture obsessed with them. When celebrities are able to create a nationwide buzz with as few as seven words, conversations about that power can be fruitful from a media literacy perspective. Pausing to consider why celebrities' "advice is much more important than anybody else's around us"[32] can help us better understand the myth of the celebrity. It can illuminate that celebrities "in many ways are our projection of what's best and what's worst in humanity — a collective representation in the same way as the Greek gods were in the past."[33] And it can lead to more discerning consumption of media messages, a key goal of critical media literacy.[34]

However, speaking out can sometimes shut down dialogue rather than foster it. Depending on the power differential, celebrities' words can serve to silence others. Social psychologist Tara Burke said Cruise's outburst against psychiatry on the *Today* show was quite harmful. "It's one thing to say, 'There's a crisis in the world and we need to help' and it's another thing to say, 'Do what I do or you're stupid' or 'This is all in your head.'"[35] Cruise was widely criticized in the media for his remarks, and following his *Today* show appearance, several news organizations ran stories about postpartum depression that spoke of the importance of getting treated. However, the concern expressed by the American Psychiatric Association was that, for many, the damage was done.

Satisfying the Test

In our analysis, Natalie Maines, Kanye West, and Sally Field all satisfy the four steps of the speaking-out test. Their relationships to the issue are sufficiently well established. Their motivations are not questionable. The nature of the harm they inflicted is not serious because their comments were addressed toward someone who has more power and equal access to the public sphere to respond to the remarks. And, finally, each of the instances of speaking out spurred dialogue about issues of public importance. In contrast, Tom Cruise failed to satisfy at least two of the four steps: the relationship to the issue and the nature of harm. Even if Cruise's motivations were pure, and even if his remarks spurred more dialogue than they shut down, according to the test he must satisfy all four steps. His instance of speaking out is, therefore, ethically unjustifiable.

The Listener's Role in Speaking Out

We have focused on very specific examples of celebrities speaking out — those unexpected, often small moments that create big controversy. In our culture, there is no shortage of celebrities being used as rhetorical tools in social and political contexts. We encounter their voices serving as spokespeople for non-profit organizations or as UN ambassadors (Angelina Jolie speaking out on behalf of the world's refugees). We hear them testifying in front of Congress (Meryl Streep speaking out against the pesticide Alar). And, of course, we witness them endorsing political candidates (Oprah campaigning for Barack Obama on her TV show). Sometimes political and social messages even become intertwined with the products the celebrities create: the 2006 season of the hit television show *ER* included a recurring subplot about the genocide in Darfur. We believe the speaking-out test could be adapted to the full spectrum of venues through which celebrities share their beliefs about social and political issues.

Certainly, the speaking-out test suggests crucial ethical obligations for speakers, but we want to conclude by suggesting the test is futile if listeners don't also exercise their ethical obligations. For speaking out to create the kind of dialogue suggested by Dewey and Habermas, listeners must engage in the process, too. The public sphere succeeds only if both speakers and listeners are civil and open-minded about considering one another's claims. In today's increasingly fractured media landscape, it has become easy for listeners to simply seek out views that reinforce their own predispositions. When citizens hear celebrities express a view with which they agree, they may tuck it away as evidence of their own rightness. Conversely, if the view expressed is inconsistent with their views, citizens may dismiss it as evidence that the "other" side is full of baloney. In neither case, then, is the celebrity's speaking out actually spurring dialogue between people with competing views. What is required are listeners with open minds who are willing to enter a conversation that includes multiple views. Celebrities can begin the conversation by speaking out in justifiable ways, but listeners must continue it.

NOTES

1. Tim Cuprisin, "Patriotic Country Tunes Win Airplay," *Milwaukee Journal Sentinel*, March 28, 2003, Final Ed., 6B.

2. "Dixie Chicks Can Protest War, Too," *USA Today*, March 19, 2003, Final Ed., 14A.

3. Gail Werde and Bill Werde, "An Urban Music Industry Ponders a Rapper's Words," *Billboard*, September 17, 2005, 5–6.

4. Jim DeRogatis, "A Flood of Words: Context Is Required to Understand Kanye West's Latest Outburst — Criticizing President Bush on National TV During Telethon," *Chicago Sun-Times*, September 5, 2005, 35.

5. DeRogatis, "A Flood of Words," 35.

6. Edward Wyatt, "Fox Explains Censorship of Actors at Emmys," *The New York Times*, September 18, 2007, Late Ed., E1.

7. Patrick Plaisance, *Media Ethics: Key Principles for Responsible Practice* (Los Angeles: Sage, 2009), 218.

8. Dave Zirin, "Protesting from the Olympic Pulpit," (Minneapolis) *Star Tribune*, August 8, 2008, A13.

9. "10 Questions." *Time*, June 30, 2008, 6.

10. *Ibid.*, 8.

11. Cody Lyon, "Dixie Chicks' Remarks Abroad Were in Poor Taste," letter to the editor, *USA Today*, May 26, 2006, Final Ed.,10A.

12. John Sonderegger, "Celebrities Who Expound Their Views on Politics Just Succeed in Losing Fans," *St. Louis Post-Dispatch*, March 21, 2001, Five Star Late Lift Ed., 2.

13. "Dixie Chicks Can Protest," 14A.

14. John Dewey cited in Christopher Lasch. "Publicity and the Lost Art of Argument," *Gannett Center Journal* 4.2 (Spring 1990): 1.

15. Michael Moore (director and producer). DVD special feature: Michael Moore interview *Bowling for Columbine* [Film] (2002). MGM Home Entertainment.

16. Daniel Boorstin, *The Image*. (New York: Atheneum, 1962), 57.

17. P. David Marshall. *Celebrity and Power: Fame in Contemporary Culture* (Minneapolis: University of Minnesota Press, 1997), ix–x.

18. *Ibid.*

19. *Ibid.*, 244.

20. Caryn James, "Megastars Out to Save the World? Those Halos Can Tarnish in an Instant," *The New York Times*, November 13, 2006, 3E.

21. Dorinda Elliott, "Good Work Hunting," *Conde Nast Traveler*, September 2008, 68.

22. William May, *Beleaguered Rulers: The Public Obligation of the Professional*. (Louisville, KY: Westminster John Knox, 2001), 193.

23. Peggy Bowers, "Charles Taylor's Practical Reason," in eds. Sharon Bracci and Clifford Christians, *Moral Engagement in Public Life* (New York: Peter Lang, 2002), 37.

24. Richard Leiby, "A Couch Tom Cruise Won't Jump On," *Washington Post*, June 25, 2005, C01.

25. *Ibid.*

26. Immanuel Kant, *Groundwork on the Metaphysic of Morals*, H.J. Patton, trans. (New York: Harper Torchbooks, 1964), 61.

27. Kant, *Groundwork on the Metaphysic of Morals*, 62.

28. Bernard Gert, *Morality Versus Slogans* (paper presented to the Center for the Study of Ethics in Society, Western Michigan University, Kalamazoo, Michigan, 1989), http://aristotle.tamu.edu/~rasmith/Courses/251/gert-paper.html (accessed June 1, 2007), para. 17.

29. *Ibid.*, para. 40.

30. John Rawls, *A Theory of Justice*, rev. ed. (Cambridge, MA: Belknap, 1999).

31. Tracy Connor, "Tom a Pill on TV. Calls Lauer 'Glib,' Again Rips Brooke" (New York) *Daily News*, June 25, 2008, 3.

32. Diane Pacom cited in Wendy Warburton, "Star Power: Celebrities Are No Smarter

Than the Rest of Us. So Why Do We Take Their Advice?" *The Ottawa Citizen*, March 3, 2007, J1.

    33. Warburton, "Star Power," J1.

    34. Elizabeth Thoman, "Skills and Strategies for Media Education," in Los Angeles County Office of Education staff development materials, *Student as Media Evaluator* (1999).

    35. Warburton, "Star Power," J1.

Works Cited

Boorstin, Daniel. *The Image.* New York: Atheneum, 1962.

Bowers, Peggy. "Charles Taylor's Practical Reason." In *Moral Engagement in Public Life.* Ed. Sharon Bracci and Clifford Christians. New York: Peter Lang, 2002.

Connor, Tracy. "Tom a Pill on TV. Calls Lauer 'Glib,' Again Rips Brooke," *New York Daily News,* June 25, 2008, 3.

Cuprisin, Tim. "Patriotic Country Tunes Win Airplay," *Milwaukee Journal Sentinel,* March 28, 2003, 6B.

DeRogatis, Jim. "A Flood of Words: Context Is Required to Understand Kanye West's Latest Outburst — Criticizing President Bush on National TV During Telethon," *Chicago Sun-Times,* September 5, 2005, 35.

Elliott, Dorinda. "Good Work Hunting," *Conde Nast Traveler,* September 2008, 68.

Gert, Bernard. *Morality Versus Slogans* (paper presented to the Center for the Study of Ethics in Society, Western Michigan University, Kalamazoo, Michigan, 1989).

James, Caryn. "Megastars Out to Save the World? Those Halos Can Tarnish in an Instant," *New York Times,* November 13, 2006, 3E.

Kant, Immanuel. *Groundwork on the Metaphysic of Morals,* New York: Harper Torchbooks, 1964.

Leiby, Richard. "A Couch Tom Cruise Won't Jump On," *Washington Post,* June 25, 2005, C01.

Lyon, Cody. "Dixie Chicks Can Protest War, Too," letter to the editor, *USA Today,* March 19, 2003, 14A.

Marshall, P. David. *Celebrity and Power: Fame in Contemporary Culture.* Minneapolis: University of Minnesota Press, 1997.

May, William. *Beleaguered Rulers: The Public Obligation of the Professional.* Louisville, KY: Westminster John Knox, 2001.

Moore, Michael (director and producer). DVD special feature: Michael Moore interview *Bowling for Columbine* [Film] (2002). MGM Home Entertainment.

Plaisance, Patrick. *Media Ethics: Key Principles for Responsible Practice.* Los Angeles: Sage, 2009.

Rawls, John. *A Theory of Justice,* rev. ed. Cambridge, MA: Belknap, 1999.

Roloff, Dale. "Dixie Chicks' Remarks Abroad Were in Poor Taste," letter to the editor, *USA Today,* May 26, 2006, 10A.

Sonderegger, John. "Celebrities Who Expound Their Views on Politics Just Succeed in Losing Fans," *St. Louis Post-Dispatch,* March 21, 2001, 2.

Thoman, Elizabeth. "Skills and Strategies for Media Education." In Los Angeles County Office of Education staff development materials, *Student as Media Evaluator,* 1999.

Warburton, Wendy. "Star Power: Celebrities Are No Smarter Than the Rest of Us. So Why Do We Take Their Advice?" *The Ottawa Citizen* March 3, 2007, J1.

Werde, Gail, and Bill Werde. "An Urban Music Industry Ponders a Rapper's Words," *Billboard,* September 17, 2005, 5–6.

Wyatt, Edward. "Fox Explains Censorship of Actors at Emmys," *New York Times,* September 18, 2007, E1.

Zirin, Dave. "Protesting from the Olympic Pulpit," *Minneapolis Star Tribune,* August 8, 2008, A13.

CHAPTER 2

"I'm Sorry, Oh, So Sorry": Celebrity Apologies and Public Ethics

Nikki Usher *and* Janel S. Schuh

Celebrities often behave badly: Britney Spears going commando, Kid Rock trashing a Waffle House, Christian Bale losing it on the *Terminator Salvation* set. Their personal problems and antics have become regular parts of the cycle of media culture, from celebrity gossip websites to the evening news. So why is it that some celebrities are celebrated for breaking the rules—from legal offenses to norms of proper behavior — while others must face the media to utter shame-faced apologies?

Why and when celebrities must say they are sorry creates the opportunity to reflect upon the relationship between stars and public ethics. This chapter probes how the public knows stars have gone too far, when apologies by stars should be considered ethical, and what the missteps of stars reveal about society's ethical judgments. Although the public might relish the antics of bad girls and boys like Lindsay Lohan and Stephon Marbury, some celebrities do go too far. We argue that some ethical rules simply cannot be broken, especially when harm is done to others. In fact, celebrities, by the nature of their public status, should behave according to particular normative ethical standards. As this chapter explains, the public image people wish celebrities to maintain mirrors the public's aspirations for the ethical norms they would like to follow in their own lives.

Our focus is on one of the most significant breaches of celebrity ethics — when celebrities make discriminatory comments about race, religion, or sexual orientation. When celebrities espouse discriminatory views, they must issue a public apology or risk losing their careers. We argue, however, that celebrities have an *ethical obligation* to issue media-disseminated public apologies for their ethical violations, especially those as egregious as discriminatory statements.

Through three case studies of celebrity apologies for discriminatory remarks—*Seinfeld* comic Michael Richards's apology for his anti-black tirade, *Grey's Anatomy* actor Isaiah Washington's apology for anti-gay remarks, and Mel Gibson's apology for his anti–Semitic rant—this chapter explores the relationship between stars and apologies in public discourse. We begin by considering the idea of celebrity ethics and why discriminatory discourse by celebrities constitutes an ethical breach. Next, we discuss what constitutes an ethical apology from stars and use textual analysis to assess why these particular celebrities were compelled to issue public apologies and whether their apologies were, in fact, ethical. We close by considering what these celebrity apologies tell us about ourselves. Especially in societies that aspire to civil discourse in order to fulfill democratic potential,[1] discriminatory remarks by celebrities prompt serious reflections on people's moral shortcomings.

Celebrity Ethics

As individual citizens within a society, celebrities have the same obligations other citizens do to adhere to ethical norms of that society. But do these celebrated individuals also have an ethical obligation to act as exemplars of those norms—to act as role models? Some stars try to reject this notion, stating they are paid to be athletes/actors/models/etc., and not, in the words of retired professional basketball player Charles Barkley, "to raise your kids."[2] We argue, however, that celebrity practices and teleological theories of ethics when taken together suggest that celebrities *do* have an ethical obligation to act as exemplars of society's ethical norms.

First, stars actively seek media access to capture the public's attention. Celebrities are public figures, people with greater access to the media than private individuals.[3] Stars strategically and purposefully employ the media—usually with the help of publicists, managers, agents, and others—to achieve and maintain carefully crafted public images.[4]

Second, celebrities willingly participate in publicity activities designed to capture public attention and encourage the emotional and financial involvement of audience members.[5] This media publicity encourages audience consumption of celebrity-related products by paralleling the celebrities' "real" selves with their performance selves: A romantic lead might relay her own dating woes; a rebellious basketball player might brag about his rebellious nature off the court; and a singer might relate the lyrics of a popular song to her own life. Celebrity publicity promotes consumption by portraying celebrities as both ordinary—which fosters audience identification with celebrities—and extraordinary—which invites audiences to admire celebrities.

In general, audiences are well aware there actually is an "ordinary" human being behind each celebrity.[6] The media reinforce this fact with stories about celebrities doing everyday activities. *Us* magazine, for example, has a regular feature titled "Just Like Us" that showcases celebrities doing ordinary things, such as buying groceries and going on family walks. As often as not, celebrities are willing participants in media stories about their private lives. Their "self-disclosure," a regular aspect of celebrity publicity,[7] mimics the self-disclosure people practice in their own personal relationships.[8] As a result, audiences come to view celebrities as down-to-earth, ordinary people and may develop parasocial relationships with them wherein they feel they can relate to stars in somewhat the same way they relate to people in their everyday lives.[9]

Yet the mass media, together with the "celebrity publicity machine,"[10] also portray stars as having unique, natural, and indefinable star qualities— stars are extraordinary. The media imply that celebrities are famous (and rich, successful, etc.) because they are intrinsically superior to ordinary people, and thus worthy of emulation.[11]

Third, celebrities act as if they *believe* they have the potential to influence people. Celebrities intend to use their fame and prominence to influence audiences to invest in anything with which celebrities are associated, from albums and sports tickets to clothes and cars to charities and political agendas. The ultimate goal of celebrity publicity practices is simple: influence.

Indeed, celebrities seem to be influential in shaping people's actions and behaviors. Research suggests that the greater the identification with a celebrity, and the greater the desire to emulate that celebrity, the more likely audiences are to financially invest in products and services,[12] and even causes,[13] with which the celebrity is associated, as well as to learn from and adopt attitudes and behaviors consistent with that celebrity's image.[14]

It seems, then, that celebrities not only aim to influence the public, but do indeed influence them—for good or for bad. Accordingly, we argue that despite Barkley's denial, celebrities *do* have ethical responsibilities to society beyond those of the average individual. Consistent with teleological perspectives on ethics, celebrities have an ethical obligation to maximize the potential for positive consequences and minimize the potential for negative consequences[15] by acting as exemplars of social norms—by behaving as the public believes all human beings in contemporary society *should* behave.[16]

However, celebrities are likely to fall short of these norms. Like all people, stars are bound to misbehave and make mistakes. Indeed, some celebrities build their images around chronic misbehavior. In some cases, however, the miscues are too egregious, as when celebrities make discriminatory

remarks. Such remarks stigmatize people as different — usually with the implication of inferiority — potentially reifying stereotypes and encouraging prejudice and discrimination. The offense dehumanizes individuals and groups,
an effect that can only be compounded by the mass media's dissemination of
the celebrity offense.[17]

Discriminatory remarks violate ethical principles from a number of perspectives. From a utilitarian perspective, which falls within the teleological
paradigm, the key to serving the public good is maximizing positive outcomes while minimizing negative outcomes.[18] The potential harm of discriminatory remarks from celebrities far outweighs any gains associated with their
freely expressing discriminatory views. The deontological paradigm, on the
other hand, emphasizes duties; within this paradigm, Immanuel Kant, among
others, argues that ethical behavior should be universally applicable.[19] Consistent with this perspective, Willard Enteman noted that "the very nature of
stereotyping, prejudice, and discrimination is that they convert real persons
into artificial persons and, as a consequence, treat human beings as objects,"
thereby stripping people of their innate dignity.[20] Accordingly, we argue everyone has an ethical obligation to refrain from expressing discriminatory views
and using slurs or similar derogatory speech — and celebrities are no exception. Moreover, as role models, celebrities cannot ignore their obligation to
deliver ethically sound apologies when they do make discriminatory remarks
or otherwise fail to exemplify the ethical norms to which they are held.

The Ethics of Celebrity Apologies

In people's private lives, theorist Aaron Lazare explains, apologies are
intended to restore broken relationships. For the offended, apologies can heal
humiliated egos and eliminate grudges, remove the imperative for revenge,
and create opportunities for forgiveness for the offended.[21] For the offender,
apologies can dull the guilt and shame that comes with having committed an
offense.[22]

A public apology, however, is a distinct apology from one to many. The
offender is a public figure or political/public entity whose regret is expressed
to a wider audience through the mass media.[23] Public apologies function on
a broader scale than do private apologies, and they compel their own set of
normative, ethical, and rhetorical exigencies. Celebrity apologies constitute
one subset of public apologies.

Keith Hearit and Sandra Borden offer criteria for judging the ethics of
apologetic decision-making by public individuals and organizations.[24] They
offer an "ideal" public *apologia*[25] by which to compare others. Based on their

criteria and applied specifically to celebrities, an ideal ethical celebrity apology would:

1. address the offended and other stakeholders.
2. be performed in an appropriate context (e.g., in public and/or private).
3. be delivered in a manner that is truthful, sincere, timely, and voluntary.
4. explicitly acknowledge and accept responsibility for any offense.
5. express regret and empathy for the offended.
6. seek forgiveness from and reconciliation with the offended.
7. fully disclose information about the offense, including, as applicable, any explanation (but *not* with the intent to defend the offense).
8. And offer appropriate corrective action/compensation (not necessarily financial).[26]

Hearit and Borden argue that an apology need not meet all the criteria to be considered ethically acceptable. Indeed, there are often conflicting responsibilities—such as those to the offended, the public, and other stakeholders (employees, co-stars, producers, etc., in the case of celebrities)—that make an ideal apology impossible.[27] In this next section, we examine three public apologies by celebrities for discriminatory remarks and compare them to the standards for an ideal celebrity apology.

Michael Richards and "Nigger"

The Offense

Seinfeld's Cosmo Kramer, played by Michael Richards, may be one of the most comical and loveable characters in American television history. After the long-running sitcom ended, Richards returned to his roots as a stand-up comic. His actions at a comedy club, however, suggested Richards did not share his sitcom character's loveable nature.

Heckled by a few African-Americans in the audience at the Laugh Factory in Los Angeles on November 17, 2006, Richards began a racist rampage captured on the cell phone video camera of one of the hecklers, Kyle Doss. Richards began his tirade by screaming, "Fifty years ago we'd have you upside down with a fucking fork up your ass." He continued amid titters from the audience members, "You can talk, you can talk, you're brave now, motherfucker. Throw his ass out. He's a nigger! He's a nigger! He's a nigger! A nigger, look, there's a nigger!"[28] The tirade lasted three minutes until most in the audience had left. The video Doss captured was available almost instantly on the Web, and news of the tirade quickly spread to mainstream media outlets.

The Apology

Richards needed to apologize to have hopes of retaining any public face. He likely felt pressure from *Seinfeld*'s spin agents to restore his long-cultivated *Seinfeld* image, especially given the forthcoming release of the seventh season of *Seinfeld* on DVD. Jerry Seinfeld was scheduled to appear on David Letterman's *The Late Show* to promote the release just a few days after the tirade, and he arranged for a satellite video conference so Richards could apologize.[29] Richards appeared visibly confused as he rambled on for more than seven minutes, attempting to apologize for his rant:

> I lost my temper on stage.... I got heckled and took it badly, and I went into a rage and said some pretty nasty things to some Afro-Americans, a lot of trash talk.... I'm really busted up over this, and I'm very sorry to those in the audience — the blacks, the Hispanics, the whites, everyone who took the brunt of that anger — [for] how it came through, and I am concerned about more hate and anger coming through ... not just towards me but towards a black/white conflict ... for me to be at a comedy club and to flip out and say this crap, I'm very very sorry.... I'll get to the force-field of this hostility.... I'm not a racist, that's what's so insane about this. But it's said, and it came through, and it fires out through me.... I just have to do personal work.[30]

As compared with the ideal ethical celebrity apology, Richards's apology lacked ethical viability, in part because his apology was not delivered in a manner consistent with an ethically sound apology. Richards did not mention delivering a private apology to the individuals he offended. He only broadly acknowledged the comedy club audience and made a vague allusion to blacks in the United States, but did not engage the private individuals he harmed. Indeed, his reference to "some Afro-Americans" suggests he failed to make a true effort to connect with offended audience members.

Although the apology was timely and apparently truthful, Richards' monotone delivery made his sincerity questionable. The circumstances of the apology suggest it may not have been voluntary: His appearance during Jerry Seinfeld's visit to *The Late Show* to promote *Seinfeld* could be interpreted as a command performance from his former boss, someone who stood to suffer financially from Richards' tirade. Further, the late night talk show, which is characterized by humor and witty banter, was an entirely inappropriate context for a serious apology. The audience laughed intermittently during the first few minutes of Richards' apology until Seinfeld scolded them into silence.

The content of Richards' apology was likewise ethically inadequate. Tellingly, Richards' apology lacked any sense of empathy for the individuals he offended or for others he offended in the broader society. Richards asked for neither forgiveness from nor reconciliation with those he offended. By citing the heckling, Richards seemed to be trying to shift blame to the individuals he offended.

Richards claimed to regret his actions, but downplayed his racist speech by blaming the "nasty things" he said on "rage," thereby failing to take full responsibility for his offense. Richards blatantly denied the racism his words implied and only alluded to the hatred associated with those words. Although he did acknowledge the broader "black-white" conflict, Richards failed to adequately address how using the word "nigger" itself reflects a legacy of racism in the United States. Nor did he offer any corrective action or compensation for the offense (although, to be fair, one might ask if there was anything he could have offered that would have rectified the offense).

A media cycle, from tabloids to talk shows, vilified Richards for being a racist.[31] Black leaders condemned him. Al Sharpton, for example, argued Richards' apology failed to address the "continual problem of racism in this country."[32] Richards' words also threatened to harm the *Seinfeld* brand: Jesse Jackson urged a boycott against the *Seinfeld* seventh-season DVD box set.[33]

Richards did eventually reach out to members of the African-American community. He appeared on Jackson's nationally syndicated radio program for another apology, both to black Americans and to the two black men he originally offended. Later, he indicated he had attempted reparations and reconciliations with the two men. But these efforts, which came only as negative media coverage continued, were not enough to compensate for Richards' racist tirade or the ethical deficiencies of his original apology.

By 2007, Richards had all but disappeared from public view, announcing he had "retired" from stand-up comedy to focus on spiritual healing.[34] Although he has since done some voice work for animated films, Richards would need to do major image repair if he had any hopes of launching or starring in another project. But *Seinfeld*— the television show in which Richards was part of an ensemble cast led by the more famous Seinfeld — remains popular in reruns and on DVD ... and Richards still receives his residual payments. Richards' case suggests that the practice of aligning celebrity images with performances can shield stars from utter ruin when they make discriminatory comments.

Isaiah Washington and "Faggot"

The First Offense and Apology

Grey's Anatomy has been one of the most popular medical dramas on American network television in the past decade, with more than 20 million regular viewers at its height of popularity in 2006.[35] But it has not been without controversy. In October 2006, actor Isaiah Washington, who played surgeon Dr. Preston Burke, became embroiled in a controversy over homophobia that eventually cost him his job on the show.

Reports surfaced that Washington and lead actor Patrick Dempsey (Dr. Derek Shepherd) had been quite literally at each other's throats over Washington's use of the word "faggot" to refer to castmate T.R. Knight (Dr. George O'Malley), whose homosexuality had not previously been disclosed to the public.[36] A few weeks later, Washington issued a public statement in *People* magazine: "I sincerely regret my actions and the unfortunate use of words during the recent incident on-set.... I have nothing but respect for my coworkers ... and have apologized personally to everyone involved."[37]

Washington's statement fulfilled only a few of the criteria for an ideal ethical celebrity apology. The public apology seemed reasonable and context-appropriate, as did his decision to apologize privately to "everyone involved." However, Washington did not specifically address his castmates or the gay and lesbian community at large. Indeed, Washington only implicitly acknowledged the offense, expressing regret for his "unfortunate use of words" rather than admitting use of a homophobic slur.

However anemic, the apology seemed to suffice, and the controversy appeared to blow over. The Gay and Lesbian Alliance Against Defamation (GLAAD) issued no statement reprimanding Washington. In this instance, one hateful homophobic word was not enough to provoke a strong public reaction, perhaps because the offense occurred in a relatively private setting (on stage at a film studio) and was not recorded. Show creator Shonda Rhimes told the press that the scuffle was "four and a half seconds of one day in three years. I feel like we've already moved on."[38]

The Second Offense and Apology

At the January 2007 Golden Globes, however, Washington reopened the wound. During broadcast press interviews, he responded to a question about the offstage incident by stating, "No, I did not call T.R. a faggot. Never happened, never happened," thereby compounding the initial offense by using the inflammatory word in the process of denying its earlier use.[39] Unlike on a closed set, homophobic remarks made at a televised media event constituted a clear violation of social norms. This time Washington's comments received immediate and intense media attention. Knight and other cast members criticized the comments on talk shows and in interviews,[40] and the controversy overshadowed the show's Best TV Drama win at the Golden Globes.[41] Neil Giuliano of GLAAD told the press that Washington's comments "feed a climate of hatred and intolerance that contribute to putting our community in harm's way."[42]

Media scrutiny and pressure from ABC forced Washington to issue a formal public apology four days later. Via a network publicist, he announced:

I apologize to T.R., my colleagues, the fans of the show and especially the lesbian and gay community for using a word that is unacceptable in any context or circumstance…. By repeating the word Monday night, I marred what should have been a perfect night for everyone who works on *Grey's Anatomy*. I can neither defend nor explain my behavior. I can also no longer deny to myself that there are issues I obviously need to examine within my own soul, and I've asked for help…. I know the power of words, especially those that demean. I realize that by using one filled with disrespect I have hurt more than T.R. and my colleagues. With one word, I've hurt everyone who has struggled for the respect so many of us take for granted. I welcome the chance to meet with leaders of the gay and lesbian community to apologize in person and to talk about what I can do to heal the wounds I've opened.[43]

This apology by Washington closely matches the ideal ethical celebrity apology in terms of content. He directly addressed Knight, his colleagues, fans, and the gay and lesbian community, explicitly acknowledged and accepted full responsibility for repeated use of "a word that is unacceptable in any context or circumstance," and fully disclosed information about the offense without defending his use of the anti-gay slur. Further, Washington expressed regret for using the slur and demonstrated empathy for Knight and other gays and lesbians through his acknowledgement of the pain he caused and recognition of the "power of words." He noted he sought reconciliation with the gay and lesbian community (although, interestingly, not with Knight) and indicated steps to take corrective action, explaining he was seeking help to examine his internal "issues." By acknowledging the broader social context of his offense, Washington recognized the legacy of hatred, prejudice, and discrimination toward gays and lesbians.

However, Washington's second apology fell short in terms of the manner of delivery. Although a public apology was clearly necessary, there was no mention of any private apology to Knight. The statement was relatively timely, but — taken in context with the first incident, the remarks at the Golden Globes, and a statement by ABC Entertainment, which produced *Grey's Anatomy*, indicating that Washington's actions were "being addressed"[44] — is hard to accept as truthful, sincere, or voluntary. Thus, the apology cannot be considered ethically acceptable.

ABC enrolled Washington in corporate sensitivity training (referred to as "gay rehab" in some media stories),[45] and Washington agreed to do a public service announcement on behalf of GLAAD, which aired in May 2007 during the show's third season finale. Nonetheless, suspicions remained high that his apology was prompted by corporate executives who hoped to retain a positive image of openness toward gay and lesbian viewers. In June 2007, after ABC opted not to renew his contract,[46] Washington made comments, including "There's no rehab for homophobia — that was just some crap being put out by the network"[47]—that seemed to confirm suspicions his apology was well-choreographed but insincere.

Interestingly, Washington seems to have suffered no major career setbacks because of his repeated use of an anti-gay slur and his subsequent firing. Shortly after he was let go from *Grey's Anatomy*, he was picked up by the same network for a role on *Bionic Woman* (a show cancelled halfway through its first season) and has had several roles since then. Washington's case would seem to suggest that, despite multiple offenses and unethical apologies, celebrities can weather negative media attention and public outcry over discriminatory comments and suffer few lasting consequences.

Mel Gibson: "Fucking Jews" and "Sugar Tits"

The Offense

Megastar actor and director Mel Gibson issued a public apology after a drunken tirade during a July 2006 DUI arrest in Malibu, California, when he made anti–Semitic and sexist remarks. Gibson, a "recovering" alcoholic, was caught speeding with an open bottle of tequila in the car and a blood alcohol level of .12 (the legal limit in California is .08).[48] An arrest report obtained by the gossip site TMZ.com revealed that Gibson launched into a hateful rant audiotaped by the arresting officer.[49] Among other things, Gibson said, "Fucking Jews.... The Jews are responsible for all the wars in the world," asking the officer, "Are you a Jew?"[50] During booking, he also yelled, "What do you think you're looking at, sugar tits?" at a female police sergeant.

TMZ's scoop on Gibson's arrest and remarks became news across national and international media outlets.[51] Gibson had gone beyond misbehavior: His drunk driving was coupled with discriminatory speech. Although his offensive comments targeted both Jews and women, his anti–Semitic remarks garnered the most attention in the ensuing public discourse. Not helping Gibson's image was residual anger among Jewish leaders about the portrayal of Jews in his 2004 blockbuster, *The Passion of the Christ*.

The Apology

Gibson's apology had three phases: two public statements and a two-part sit-down interview with Diane Sawyer. Gibson began with a public statement issued the day after his arrest that focused primarily on his behavior toward the arresting officer:[52]

> After drinking alcohol on Thursday night, I did a number of things that were very wrong and for which I am ashamed. I drove a car when I should not

have, and was stopped by the LA County Sheriffs. The arresting officer was just doing his job and I feel fortunate that I was apprehended before I caused injury to any other person.... I have battled alcoholism for all of my adult life and profoundly regret my horrific relapse.

Although timely and apparently sincere and voluntary, Gibson's apology was not completely truthful; he did not disclose fully details regarding either his anti–Semitic and sexist comments or his arrest for drunken driving. Gibson acknowledged the potential consequences of his drunken driving, but did not indicate any understanding of the ramifications of his discriminatory speech. Also, Gibson did not seem to accept responsibility for his offenses: By offering his history of alcoholism as an explanation, he seemed to be using it as an excuse.

A public statement seemed appropriate given the offenses, but Gibson's apology was not directed to the individuals he had personally offended, nor did it include any mention of any private apology to the officers. Although Gibson did express regret, saying he was "deeply ashamed of everything" in his first apology, he indicated no empathy for the offended and made no request for forgiveness.[53] Nor did he offer any means of trying to compensate for his drunken driving or discriminatory speech. Ultimately, this apology met very few of the criteria for an ethically sound apology.

Predictably, Jewish leaders expressed dissatisfaction with Gibson's first apology.[54] Given the media's attention to his anti–Semitic remarks, Gibson released a more extensive second apology five days later to *People* magazine, one that, although imperfect, was more ethically sound than his initial apology.[55]

There is no excuse, nor should there be any tolerance, for anyone who thinks or expresses any kind of anti–Semitic remark. I want to apologize specifically to everyone in the Jewish community for the vitriolic and harmful words that I said to a law enforcement officer the night I was arrested on a DUI charge.

I am a public person, and when I say something, either articulated and thought out, or blurted out in a moment of insanity, my words carry weight in the public arena. As a result, I must assume personal responsibility for my words and apologize directly to those who have been hurt and offended by those words....

But please know from my heart that I am not an anti–Semite. I am not a bigot. Hatred of any kind goes against my faith.

I'm not just asking for forgiveness. I would like to take it one step further, and meet with leaders in the Jewish community, with whom I can have a one on one discussion to discern the appropriate path for healing....

This is not about a film. Nor is it about artistic license. This is about real life and recognizing the consequences hurtful words can have. It's about existing in harmony in a world that seems to have gone mad.[56]

In this apparently empathetic public statement, Gibson acknowledged the harm his anti–Semitic comments may have caused and recognized they represented a dramatic departure from social mores. Expressing appropriate attitudes of humility and regret, he asked for forgiveness and offered to take steps to repair his relationship with the Jewish community, including reparations and corrective action. Shortly after issuing the statement, Gibson dramatically disappeared from the public eye for alcohol rehabilitation.

Whereas the first apology did not acknowledge Jews at all, this second apology appears specifically crafted to appease the Jewish community. Gibson again made no mention of any private apology to individuals he personally offended. Nor did he even acknowledge the sexist comment he made. As such, his motives for releasing this second public statement are suspect. If his apologies were sincere, why not apologize for all his offensive remarks, including sexist ones, not just those that received the most media attention? Further, why did he not express these sentiments in his initial apology?

Gibson's claim to "assume personal responsibility" was likewise suspect. He denied any bigotry, pleading with the public to "know from my heart that I am not an anti–Semite. I am not a bigot." He stated there was "no excuse" for his anti–Semitic remarks, but shifted blame for "a moment of insanity" by bringing attention to his alcoholism. The power of Gibson's apology is diluted by his reliance on his strategy of denial.

Although flawed, this second apology met many of the criteria for an ideal ethical apology. In addition, Gibson's statement included two elements that bolstered its ethicality. It contained an explicit acknowledgment of his status as a "public person" with words that "carry weight in the public arena." Thus, Gibson acknowledged his potential influence over and responsibility to society. Also, the apology ended with an unequivocal rejection of the notion that the statement was merely a ploy to ensure the success of his next film, *Apocalypto,* scheduled for release just months later. Taken as a whole, Gibson's second apology can be judged as ethically acceptable, although imperfectly so because it still stands as manufactured within a celebrity media machine and forced by an inadequate first apology. Thus it appears insincere and unconvincing to many hurt by his remarks, especially given his previous history.

For four months, Gibson refused media interviews. Despite occasional rumors about Gibson engaging in conversations with Jewish entertainment industry leaders, Disney dropped Gibson's proposed mini-series on the Holocaust, an improbable project in light of the Malibu incident.[57] But Gibson could stay in the shadows for only so long, especially with the upcoming release of *Apocalypto.* He emerged to give a third apology in a two-part interview with Diane Sawyer on *Good Morning America.*[58]

In the first interview, Gibson talked at length about his battle with alcoholism, revealing he continued to drink the night of his arrest while talking to his children about the incident. He appeared remorseful, saying, "It sounds horrible. And I'm ashamed of that. That came out of my mouth.... That's not who I am, you know." Sawyer revisited Gibson's words in a second interview, asking whether it was possible to say anti–Semitic things and not be anti–Semitic. Gibson responded:

> I don't know.... Because one changes from day to day and there are different forces exercised on you that may or may not, and people every day say things they don't mean and mean things they don't feel. They may feel them temporarily. I mean, we're, we're all broken.

He ended his interview with a plea not to be taken for a "monster."

This apology was flawed, especially in manner. The timeliness of this apology is questionable, as he gave the interview four months after his arrest and just a few weeks before the release of *Apocalypto.* Although the interview seemed voluntary, it is important to consider the interview within the context of the Hollywood production system — would Gibson have given this interview if he and others were not invested in a blockbuster movie they wanted people to see?

The apology did address stakeholders: He apologized to Jews (but, again, not to women) and begged not to be seen as a monster. But Gibson did not choose to televise a meeting with Jewish leaders in which he humbly apologized and asked for reconciliation. His third apology was conducted in a highly manufactured context — a sit-down broadcast interview — no doubt managed by a public relations team. Thus, the sincerity of Gibson's apology is suspect, which makes it hard to categorize it as ethically acceptable.

Just weeks after the two-part interview, *Apocalypto* opened to generally positive reviews[59] and grossed a respectable $15 million its opening weekend.[60] For several years, Gibson remained behind the scenes, executive producing or producing various projects, but was set to re-emerge on the screen as the lead in the 2009 film *Edge of Darkness.* Beyond those first few months, it seems that Gibson suffered few negative ramifications of his discriminatory speech. His case would support the conclusion that celebrity status can be a particularly effective shield for major stars.

Celebrity Ethics and Reflecting Upon Ourselves

Celebrities hold a curious position in modern societies: Most have no official power or authority, but they are able to influence people. As we noted, publicity practices encourage audiences to form parasocial relationships with celebrities. Stars are simultaneously portrayed as extraordinary beings, rightfully living in a world most people cannot occupy, and as ordinary people whom audiences come to "know" intimately through revealing interviews and regular media coverage. Celebrities exploit these relationships to influence audiences. Thus, whether they choose to acknowledge their responsibilities as role models or not, celebrities have an ethical obligation to minimize the negative consequences of their behaviors, including delivering ethically sound apologies when they fail to live as exemplars of societal ethical norms.

In this chapter, we have explored three instances in which celebrities violated celebrity ethics and publicly apologized for using discriminatory speech, an egregious violation of social norms. Throughout, the Hearit and Borden criteria proved useful in assessing the ethical acceptability of each apology. However, when apologizing for an offense as rank as making discriminatory remarks, an apology's ethical acceptability ultimately seemed to come down to one criterion: sincerity.

The public is right to demand, through the mass media, some sort of an apology from stars for their discriminatory remarks. In a way, the media act as an arbiter of ethics, first conveying the offense to the wider public and then conveying the apology. The mass media take on an ethical role when they take on the indignation of the offended and frame discriminatory remarks by celebrities as requiring an apology.

But many celebrity apologies are not ethical, having been constructed with the goal of preserving a celebrity image rather than reaching a true reconciliation. By conveying these insincere apologies to the public and moving on to different stories, the media seem to fail to serve the public interest and perpetuate a cycle of insincere apologies. For their part, the public generally seem to either accept the apologies at face value or allow the apology to become a running joke.

What does it tell us about society when celebrity apologies are insincere and the public nonetheless seems to accept them and move on? The fact that the public often allows celebrity apologies to operate as image repair reveals the shortcomings of their relationships with celebrities. The public holds celebrities to high expectations for ethical behavior because they are extraordinary. Yet when they fall short of these expectations, the public fails to hold them accountable because they are ordinary people who, like everyone else, make mistakes.

If the public's expectations for celebrities do mirror society's aspirations for ethical behavior, then perhaps their failures mirror the public's own ethical failures. Perhaps people continue to buy into the aura of celebrity and are willing to forgive when celebrities misbehave — even when stars make discriminatory remarks and fail to provide sincere apologies — because it is too uncomfortable for people to face their own ethical shortcomings. After all, as Gibson said, "We're all broken."

NOTES

1. Jurgen Habermas, *The Theory of Communicative Action,* Vol 1. (Cambridge, England: Polity, 1985).
2. Nike Air, "I Am Not a Role Model." Television advertisement. Wieden & Kennedy, 1993, http://www.youtube.com/watch?v=nMzdAZ3TjCA, accessed March 29, 2009.
3. Johan Retief, *Media Ethics: An Introduction to Responsible Journalism* (Cape Town, South Africa: Oxford University Press, 2002), 155.
4. Josh Gamson, *Claims to Fame: Celebrity in Contemporary America* (Berkeley: University of California Press, 1994), 57–125; Graeme Turner, *Understanding Celebrity* (Thousand Oaks, CA: Sage, 2004), 29–85; Graeme Turner, Frances Bonner and P. David Marshall, *Fame Games: The Production of Celebrity in Australia* (Melbourne, Australia: Cambridge University Press, 2000), 60–159.
5. Gamson, *Claims to Fame,* 57–78, 101, 124; Turner, *Understanding Celebrity,* 34–35.
6. David C. Giles, "Parasocial Interaction: A Review of the Literature and a Model for Future Research," *Media Psychology* 4 (2002): 279–305.
7. Turner, Bonner, and Marshall, *Fame Games,* 126–140.
8. Donald Horton and Richard R. Wohl. "Mass Communication and Para-social Interaction: Observations on Intimacy at a Distance," *Psychiatry* 19 (1956): 215–229.
9. *Ibid.,* 215–229.
10. Gamson, *Claims to Fame,* 46.
11. *Ibid.,* 15–54.
12. Michael Basil, "Identification as a Mediator of Celebrity Effects," *Journal of Broadcasting and Electronic Media* 40 (1996): 478–495; David H. Silvera and Benedikte Austad, "Factors Predicting the Effectiveness of Celebrity Endorsement Advertisements," *European Journal of Marketing* 38 11/12 (2004): 1509–1526.
13. William Brown, Michael Basil, and Mihai Bocarnea, "The Influence of Famous Athletes on Health Beliefs and Practices: Mark McGwire, Child Abuse Prevention, and Androstenedione," *Journal of Health Communication* 8 (2003): 41–57; Peter Cram, A. Mark Fendrick, John Inadomi, Mark Cowen, Daniel Carpenter, and Sandeep Vijan, "The Impact of a Celebrity Promotional Campaign on the Use of Colon Cancer Screening: The Katie Couric Effect," *Archives of Internal Medicine* 163.13 (2003): 1601–1605.
14. Brown, Basil, and Bocarnea, "The Influence of Famous Athletes on Health Benefits and Practices," 41–57; William Brown, "Mediated Involvement with a Celebrity Hero: Responses to the Tragic Death of Steve Irwin" (paper presented at the annual conference of the International Communication Association, San Francisco, CA, October 24, 2006).
15. Retief, *Media Ethics,* 7–8.
16. For more on normative ethics, see, for instance, Kant's Categorical Imperative in the *Groundwork of the Metaphysics of Morals* (San Francisco: Wilder, 2008).
17. Retief, *Media Ethics,* 193–203.
18. *Ibid.*
19. *Ibid.*
20. Willard Enteman, "Stereotyping, Prejudice, and Discrimination," in *Images That Injure: Pictorial Stereotypes in the Media,* eds. Paul Lester and Susan Ross, 15–22 (Westport, CT: Praeger, 2003).
21. Aaron Lazare, *On Apology* (New York: Oxford University Press, 2004), 1.
22. *Ibid.*
23. Benoit, William L. *Accounts, Excuses, and Apologies: A Theory of Image Restoration Strategies* (New York: State University of New York Press, 1995), 9–31.
24. Keith Hearit and Sandra Borden, "Apologetic Ethics," in *Crisis Management by Apology: Corporate Response to Allegations of Wrongdoing,* Keith Hearit, 58–78 (Mahwah, NJ: Lawrence Erlbaum, 2006).
25. Although Hearit specified that apologia describes expressions of regret and responsibility with a focus on defense [Keith Hearit, *Crisis Management by Apology,* vii], the term

is often used to describe the public utterances of apologies, see B.L. Ware, and Wil A. Linkugel. "They Spoke in Defense of Themselves: On the Generic Criticism of Apologia," *Quarterly Journal of Speech* 59 (1973): 273–84.

26. Interestingly, many of these criteria are consistent with those used to describe an effective apology (i.e., one that is likely to result in forgiveness and reconciliation). For example, according to Aaron Lazare, an effective apology consists of four elements: an acknowledgement of the offense; an explanation; an expression of appropriate attitudes of remorse, forbearance, shame, humility and/or sincerity; and an indication of reparations or reconciliation with the injured party; Lazare, *On Apology* (New York: Oxford University Press, 2004), 4.

27. Hearit and Borden, "Apologetic Ethics," 56.

28. "'Kramer's' Racist Tirade — Caught on Tape," *TMZ*, 20 November 2006, http:// www.tmz.com/2006/11/20/kramers-racist-tirade-caught-on-tape/ (accessed February 20, 2009).

29. Bill Carter, "Richards Tries to Explain His Rant at Comedy Club," *New York Times*, November 22, 2006. http://www.nytimes.com/2006/11/22/arts/television/22rich.html (accessed February 20, 2009).

30. "Kramer" Apologizes on the Letterman Show, http://www.youtube.com/watch?v= 6hYrmPUwknk (accessed February 20, 2009).

31. Don Kaplan, "'Kramer' Shock Racist Tantrum: Old Pal Seinfield 'Sick' over Meltdown at Club," *New York Post*, November 21, 2006, http://www.nypost.com/seven/11212006/ news/nationalnews/kramer_shock_racist_tantrum_nationalnews_don_kaplan.htm (accessed February 20, 2009); "Kramer Kerfuffle: Racist or Mistake," *New York Post*, November 25, 2006, http://www.nypost.com/seven/11252006/postopinion/letters/kramers_kerfuffle__rac ist_or_a_mistake__letters_.htm (accessed February 16, 2009).

32. "Sharpton: Comedian's Apology Not Enough," *CNN*, 22 November 2006, www.cnn. com/2006/Showbiz/TV/11/22/sharpton.richard/index.html (accessed February 19, 2009).

33. Associated Press, "Jesse Jackson Urges Boycott of 'Seinfeld' DVD Box Set in Wake of 'Kramer's Racist Rant'" (November 28, 2006), www.fox.newsw.com/story/0,2933,2321 91,00.html (accessed February 19, 2009).

34. Charles Mcdermid, "Richards Finds Solace in Cambodia," *Los Angeles Times*, July 13, 2007, http://articles.latimes.com/2007/jul/13/entertainment/et-richards13 (accessed February 17, 2009).

35. Ann Oldenberg, "'Anatomy' Has All the Right Parts," *USA Today*, April 26, 2006, http://www.usatoday.com/life/television/news/2006-04-26-greys_x.htm (accessed February 16, 2009).

36. "Exclusive: Isaiah Washington Apologizes," *People*, October 25, 2006, http://www. people.com/people/article/0,26334,1550408,00.html (accessed February 20, 2009).

37. *Ibid.*

38. *Ibid.*

39. Natalie Finn, "Isaiah Apologizes for "Unacceptable" Remark," *E! Online*, January 18, 2007. http://www.eonline.com/news/article/index.jsp?uuid=51d8c103-9268-43a1-85f9- ea161477fe59 (accessed February 20, 2009).

40. Gina Serpe, "Grey's Stars Still Seeing Red Over Slur," *E! Online*, January 17, 2007, http://www.eonline.com/news/article/index.jsp?uuid=2335b61f-822a-4d64-b1bd-35f5a494 c2e3 (accessed February 17, 2009).

41. Finn, "Isaiah Apologizes for "Unacceptable" Remark."

42. *Ibid.*

43. Edward Wyatt, "Anatomy of an Insult: ABC Is Stung by an Actor's Anti-Gay Slurs," *New York Times*, January 22, 2007, http://www.nytimes.com/2007/01/22/arts/television/22 grey.html (accessed February 17, 2009).

44. Mike Bruno, "Washington Apologizes for Gay Slur," *Entertainment Weekly*, January 18, 2007, http://www.ew.com/ew/article/0,,20009105,00.html (accessed February 17, 2009).

45. "Washington Going to Some Gay Rehab, Not in the Juvenile Sense of Gay, Liter-

ally," *The Insider,* http://www.theinsider.com/news/24143_Washington_Going_to_Some_Gay _Rehab_Not_in_the_Juvenile_Sense_of_Gay_Literally (accessed February 17, 2009).

46. Serpe, "Grey's Stars Still Seeing Red over Slur."

47. Emily Fromm, "Isaiah Washington: 'There's No Rehab for Homophobia,'" *People,* June 28, 2007, http://www.people.com/people/article/0,,20044077,00.html (accessed February 17, 2009).

48. "California's 0.08% BAC Limit and Administrative License Suspension Laws Working to Deter Drunk Driving Accidents" (1997), http://dmv.ca.gov/about/profile/rd/resnotes/baclimit.htm.

49. TMZ Staff, "Gibson's Anti-Semitic Tirade — Alleged Cover Up," *TMZ.com,* July 28, 2006.

50. Other offenses by Gibson included breaking the law, disrespecting public officials, and making sexist comments toward a female deputy. Although these offenses all raise questions about the scope of celebrity ethics, they are beyond the scope of the present discussion about discrimination based on race, ethnicity, religious groups, and sexual orientation.

51. BBC, "Mel Gibson's Statement in Full," *BBC,* August 1, 2006; "Gibson: 'I Am Not an Anti-Semite': Actor in 'Ongoing Recovery' After Arrest on Suspicion of DUI," *CNN,* August 1, 2006; Alison Hope Weiner, "Mel Gibson Apologizes for Tirade After Arrest," *New York Times,* July 29, 2006.

52. TMZ Staff, "Gibson's Anti-Semitic Tirade — Alleged Cover Up."

53. *Ibid.*

54. Associated Press, "Experts: Mel Gibson's Apology Too Late," August 2, 2006, http://www.foxnews.com/story/0,2933,206716,00.html (accessed February 20, 2009).

55. Associated Press, "Gibson's Statement About Anti-Semitic Remark," *msnbc.com,* August 1, 2006. http://www.msnbc.msn.com/id/14135592/ (accessed June 1, 2009).

56. "Statement from Mel Gibson," CNN, August 1, 2006, http://www.cnn.com/2006/SHOWBIZ/Movies/08/01/gibson.statement/index.html (accessed February 20, 2009).

57. TMZ staff, "Mel Phones Jews—'I'm Really Sorry,'" *TMZ,* August 24, 2006.

58. Diane Sawyer, "GMA Exclusive: Diane Sawyer Interviews Mel Gibson," in *ABC Good Morning America* (ABC, 2006).

59. Lisa Schwarzbaum, "Apocalypto," *Entertainment Weekly,* December 6, 2006, http://www.ew.com/ew/article/0,,1567004,00.html (accessed February 21, 2009); Mick LaSalle, "Rape, Murder, Mayhem — There Goes the Civilization," *San Francisco Chronicle,* December 8, 2006. http://www.sfgate.com/cgi-bin/article.cgi?file=/c/a/2006/12/08/DDGSLM-PQNF15.DTL&type=movies (accessed February 21, 2009).

60. "Apocalypto," Box Office Mojo website, http://www.boxofficemojo.com/movies/?id =apocalypto.htm (accessed February 22, 2009).

WORKS CITED

Basil, Michael. "Identification as a Mediator of Celebrity Effects." *Journal of Broadcasting and Electronic Media* 40 (1996): 478–495.

Benoit, William L. *Accounts, Excuses, and Apologies: A Theory of Image Restoration Strategies.* New York: State University of New York Press, 1995.

Brown, William. "Mediated Involvement with a Celebrity Hero: Responses to the Tragic Death of Steve Irwin." Paper presented at the annual conference of the International Communication Association, San Francisco, CA, October 24, 2006.

_____, Michael Basil, and Mihai Bocamea. "The Influence of Famous Athletes on Health Beliefs and Practices: Mark McGwire, Child Abuse Prevention, and Androstenedione." *Journal of Health Communication* 8 (2003): 41–57.

Cram, Peter, A. Mark Fendrick, John Inadomi, Mark Cowen, Daniel Carpenter, and Sandeep Vijan. "The Impact of a Celebrity Promotional Campaign on the Use of Colon Cancer Screening: The Katie Couric Effect." *Archives of Internal Medicine* 163, no. 13 (2003): 1601–1605.

Enteman, Willard. "Stereotyping, Prejudice, and Discrimination." In *Images That Injure: Pictorial Stereotypes in the Media*. Eds. Paul Lester and Susan Ross. Westport, CT: Praeger, 2003, 15–22.

Gamson, Josh. *Claims to Fame: Celebrity in Contemporary America*. Berkeley: University of California Press, 1994.

Giles, David C. "Parasocial Interaction: A Review of the Literature and a Model for Future Research." *Media Psychology* 4 (2002): 279–305.

Habermas, Jurgen. *The Theory of Communicative Action, Vol. 1*. Cambridge, England: Polity, 1985.

Hearit, Keith, and Sandra Borden. "Apologetic Ethics." In *Crisis Management by Apology: Corporate Response to Allegations of Wrongdoing*, edited by Keith Hearit, 58–78. Mahwah, NJ: Lawrence Erlbaum, 2006.

Horton, Donald, and Richard R. Wohl. "Mass Communication and Para-social Interaction: Observations on Intimacy at a Distance." *Psychiatry* 19 (1956): 215–229.

Kant, Immanuel. *Groundwork of Metaphysics and Morals*. San Francisco: Wilder, 2008.

Lazare, Aaron. *On Apology*. New York: Oxford University Press, 2004.

Retief, Johan. *Media Ethics: An Introduction to Responsible Journalism*. Cape Town, South Africa: Oxford University Press, 2002.

Turner, Graeme. *Understanding Celebrity*. Thousand Oaks, CA: Sage, 2004.

_____, Frances Bonner, and P. David Marshall. *Fame Games: The Production of Celebrity in Australia*. Melbourne, Australia: Cambridge University Press, 2000.

CHAPTER 3

Quasars: Silent Celebrities, Ethical Implications

Kyle F. Reinson

I think I would have called the police to save Miss Genovese but I know that I did not save a beggar in Calcutta. Was my failing really so much smaller than that of the people who watched from their windows on Austin Street?[1]
— A.M. Rosenthal, *Thirty-Eight Witnesses* (1964)

This poor woman (Theresa Marie Schiavo) and this poor family are being used as a political football, and these guys will do anything to push the point that they think is important, that they will invade this family's privacy.[2]
— U.S. Rep. Jim McDermott (2005)

In March 1964, Catherine Susan Genovese was murdered near her apartment in the New York City Borough of Queens. In March 2005, Theresa Marie Schiavo died quietly at a hospice in Pinellas Park, Florida. Their lives have been eclipsed by two dramatic and entertaining narratives, myths that spoke up louder than their own private identities.

For Genovese, the narrative began when *The New York Times* reported that 37 neighbors watched and did nothing to save her despite her pleas for help; their apathy was the supposed embodiment of America's inclination not to care. For Schiavo, her family's long battle over the removal of her feeding tube suddenly resulted in three branches of the federal government intervening in her legal case — arguably, a political response to the electoral outcomes of 2004. Two women died, but one is remembered mostly because *everybody* got involved, and the other mostly because *nobody* did. Their names are invoked in public and private discussions about the value of human life and the quality of the human condition. Their identities have been oppressed within the cultural gap between the narratives surrounding them and the reality of who they were.

41

They held celebrity power. As scholar Philip Drake explains, this power is contingent on both the audience's and the media's investment in the nature of celebrity.[3] In *Celebrity and Power: Fame in Contemporary Culture*, P. David Marshall notes "celebrity draws its power from those elements outside tradition" and "exists above the real world, in the realm of symbols that gain and lose value like commodities on the stock market."[4] And yet, despite their celebrity, Genovese and Schiavo did not ride in limousines pursued by the paparazzi and granted no exclusive interviews to Barbara Walters. They did not appear on late-night talk shows to promote themselves. They neither commanded large fortunes and powerful positions, nor signed autographs for adoring fans.

A significant shift is in process, and the media landscape is no longer the sole domain of the major television networks, Hollywood studios, or newspapers of record. If anyone from nightly news anchor to blogger is a gatekeeper, then anyone can oppress or liberate identities with narratives. Ethical implications loom for anyone who creates or consumes narratives at a moment in history when *real-time revisionist history* is possible. If we are all gatekeepers, we must watch closely the cultural gaps between developing narratives and what actually might be happening. By turning a critical eye toward mediated communication, gatekeepers small and large can be advocates for protecting or even liberating oppressed identities from their connection to painful issues of the past. In the ethical consumption and creation of narratives lies the opportunity for Genovese, Schiavo, and so many others taken out of cultural context to truly rest in peace.

The World Outside

In his 1922 book, *Public Opinion,* Walter Lippmann reached back to Plato's *The Republic* to begin his examination of "The World Outside and the Pictures in Our Heads."[5] Lippmann, one of journalism's seminal voices, used the allegory of the cave to explain the oppressive hold that media can have on an audience or object. At times, all of us can become the prisoners he describes, shackled in the cave. We can only consume and process limited amounts of information, and depend on what we read, see, and hear to understand the world.

Ronald Steel notes that *Public Opinion* was a reaction to Lippmann's work with the Committee on Public Information, which spun the information stream into public support for the First World War. According to Steel, Lippmann's efforts "made him realize how easily public opinion could be manipulated, and how often the press distorted the news."[6] Prior to writing the book, Lippmann collaborated with his friend Charles Merz on a study of

The New York Times called "A Test of the News." Lippmann and Merz looked at three years in the newspaper's coverage of the Bolshevik revolution. They found, as Steel notes, that "the paper cited events that did not happen, atrocities that never took place, and reported no fewer than ninety-one times that the Bolshevik regime was on the verge of collapse."[7] Lippmann concluded that "public opinions must be organized for the press if they are to be sound,"[8] and he was taking into account not only the manipulation of journalism, but also the public's ability to understand complex issues.

The available cultural terrain for the liberation and oppression of identity has expanded exponentially since Lippmann's time. The terrain has been flooded with ways for people to find out what is going on around them, and in turn, ways for people to tell the world what they are doing through the Internet and mobile technology. In this environment of massive information exchange overload, news competes for our attention and requires packaging and selling to do so. In the point-and-click culture of the Internet, where content drives how Americans become engaged with information, news products tend to attract our attention best when they can also entertain us.

Journalism historian Michael Schudson points to the "newsification of popular culture," where "serious news institutions have been turning news into entertainment," but suggests "the larger trend is that entertainment has turned into news."[9] Echoing this notion, communication scholar W. Lance Bennett argues that commercial interests have helped fully shape news into an entertainment hybrid, which he calls "infotainment."[10] In this hybrid model of news, a compelling narrative must exist, and a central figure, or celebrity, is a key component to the story. "Media entrepreneurs," adds researcher Graeme Turner, "want celebrities involved with their projects because they believe this will help them attract audiences."[11] Although most celebrities willingly absorb this attention for their outstanding athletic prowess or their performances in blockbuster films, there is an ethical implication for entertaining news narratives— namely, publicity brought upon people who did not invite it.

Sometimes the stories we follow expose private persons whether they like it or not: the teen who goes missing on her high school senior trip to Aruba or the man who disappears climbing an Oregon mountain during a snowstorm. Narratives can live on for years, attached firmly to identities in the news. They reinforce the notion of the tragic victim, as evident in the case of missing teen Natalee Holloway.[12] Narratives can also anoint a hero, as reporters did in 2009, lauding the efforts of a U.S. Airways pilot who landed an airplane in New York's Hudson River without a single death.[13]

On occasion, tragic and heroic figures alike become more than names in the news; they become icons. The publicity surrounding them turns into a commodity others may trade for political or economic advantage. When figures in the news are unable to speak, others will gladly speak *for* and *about* them. We rely on these experts to put stories and identities into context and to further develop the narrative.

Schudson notes that Lippmann "saw the core of journalism's corruption ... in its own smug assurance of knowledge and its eagerness to assert opinion rather than provide facts.[14] In *Warp Speed: America in the Age of Mixed Media*, Bill Kovach and Tom Rosenstiel also lament that "so much of the news media culture today involves commenting on the news rather than reporting it that in follow-up coverage, especially on television, the principle of keeping fact separate from suspicion and analysis separate from agenda-setting is no longer clearly honored."[15] In this assertive storytelling process, where facts are omitted and style trumps substance, the voiceless in the news are oppressed, and even contributions from those with voices are reduced to what they can say in a brief quote or sound bite. At worst, voices are not heard; at best, they are fragmented.

With the emergence of Web spaces like Twitter and Facebook, the Internet is filled with headlines, speculation, and entertainment in real time from a multitude of sources and gatekeepers.[1] The 24-hour news cycle may have set the tone, but bloggers can break news even faster, with less oversight and fewer ethical checks and balances. Open-source software allows the creators of narrative to inexpensively disseminate information, sometimes through anonymous identities that are not easily held accountable for invasions of privacy or other ethical lapses.[17] As new gatekeepers emerge, the prospect for ethical communication grows ever more questionable.

The Quasar

In his 1978 book, *Celebrity*, film critic and educator James Monaco posits a compelling typology for understanding the phenomenon. Celebrity *heroes*, he suggests, glean their recognition mainly for achievement in science or the arts. Celebrity *stars* actively manage their personae by seeking opportunities to "be seen" or promote their work, often for their own political or economic advantage. Monaco also suggests there are silent celebrities, whom he calls *quasars*.

Monaco offers the saga of newspaper heiress Patty Hearst's kidnapping by the Symbionese Liberation Army (SLO) in the 1970s as the quintessential example of the quasar fascinating the news media and the public. He explains that quasars are largely victims of the media who gain importance due to news attention.[18] There were myriad quasars prior to Monaco's identification of this celebrity typology, but the proliferation of mass media and new media have made them more culturally relevant. They have become an accepted piece of the media landscape.

The news media, bloggers, pundits, academics, and even other celebrities can make meaning of quasars because their voices remain silent and oppressed. The public memory of a quasar no longer reflects the true self; their identities are brazenly linked to painful events. We know so little about these people, but our media culture demands that we use them to symbolize something greater. Eschewing a more complete understanding of these quasar identities, the storytellers widen the cultural gap further by expressing concern from a distance and placing these names deeper into the narratives.

Charles Krauthammer, a regular pundit across media platforms, wrote of Genovese in a 2007 piece for *Time*: "I've always been struck by the double injustice of her murder. Not only did the killer cut short her life amid immense terror and suffering, but he defined it. He — a stranger, an intruder — gave her a perverse immortality of a kind she never sought, never expected, never consented to." Krauthammer stopped short of implicating the news media in the process of making her immortal, but noted that Genovese, "surely thought that in her 28 years she had been building a life of joys and loves, struggle and achievement, friendship and fellowship. That and everything else she built her life into were simply swallowed up by the notoriety of her death, a notoriety unchosen and unbidden."[19] Today the amount of information dwarfs what was available in decades past, fertile ground for anyone, at nearly anytime, to become a quasar.

The Quasar in Myth

On March 14, 1964, *The New York Times* ran the headline: "Queens Woman Is Stabbed to Death in Front of Home." The page twenty-six story's first sentence explained, "A twenty-eight-year-old Queens woman was stabbed to death early yesterday morning outside her apartment house in Kew Gardens."[20] The newspaper reported who was killed, what happened, where it happened, and when it happened. The lead's indication that she was "stabbed to death" even answers the question of *why* she died. *The Long Island Press* the day before simply acknowledged "Woman, 28, Knifed to Death" in its March 13 headline.[21] This news was processed much like thousands of similar reports. Although murder is certainly newsworthy, the ethical implications of why the story was not forgotten after these published reports is worthy of consideration.

Had no further information surfaced, there is a good chance that Catherine Susan Genovese might have been afforded rest in peace. But a cultural gap was created by an oppressive narrative. In his 1964 book, *Thirty-Eight Witnesses*, A.M. Rosenthal outlines the rationale for not leaving the story alone. He personalizes a victim he never knew, saying she "was called Kitty by almost everyone in the neighborhood."[22] The 87-page book was a follow-up to *The New York Times* story of March that same year in which the news-paper attached *meaning* to the victim's identity. The narrative expanded inter-nationally. People everywhere who *did not live* in her neighborhood became familiar enough with Genovese to call her "Kitty."

Rosenthal had won a 1960 Pulitzer Prize for his "International Report-ing" in Poland, the same award Walter Lippmann would win in 1962 for his interview with Soviet Premier Nikita Khrushchev. Rosenthal was apparently told by then-New York Police Commissioner Michael Joseph Murphy that as many as 38 people witnessed the Genovese murder and did nothing to stop it. Overwhelmed by this news tip, the new Metro editor assigned Martin Gansberg to revisit the story because he saw in Gansberg "a sense of enthu-siasm," and he was "new enough not to resent dogged, difficult work." Besides, Gansberg was within his "line of vision."[23]

The resulting Gansberg article ran on the newspaper's front page on March 27 with the sobering headline, "37 Who Saw Murder Didn't Call the Police." Rosenthal upped the total to 38 for the book later that year. Even the packaging of *Thirty-Eight Witnesses* played up the shock Americans should have confronted, with a blurb on the book jacket teasing, "Her silent neigh-bors looked on while a young woman was stabbed to death in three separate attacks during 35 minutes...." A headshot of Genovese appeared in the book, and on the back cover, a professionally lit photo of gallant newspaperman Rosenthal behind a typewriter, a plume of smoke billowing out of his pipe. His left hand was outstretched, as if he were explaining New York City's most heinous tragedy of urban alienation to a cub reporter.

Rosenthal effectively shifted the focus away from the actual crime of Winston Mosely — who was convicted in the Genovese case and as of 2009 was still serving prison time for the cold-blooded murder and sexual assault — to the crime of 38 residents in the Kew Gardens section of Queens. They watched a murder unfold, hearing calls for help and doing nothing. The cul-tural gap widened to obscure the case further and to further oppress its vic-tim's identity within the narrative. With each discussion and expression of outrage over the decades, and with references to Genovese in popular song, entertaining television programs, and live theater referring to the crime of the "38 witnesses," her celebrity expanded. [24]

This same unsettling narrative continues, reified, to oppress the iden-tity of Genovese. On August, 26, 2008, more than 44 years after her murder, *Newsday* attempted to tell the story of a more recent tragedy. "In the last moments of her life, Ebony Garcia cried out for help — and no one in the Queens building where she died responded," reporter Rocco Parascandola wrote. "One resident thought the sounds she heard came from someone who was drunk. Another, visiting from Korea, heard cries but doesn't understand English. And two others say they didn't hear anything. The brutal College

Point stabbing death recalls the infamous 1964 case of Kitty Genovese, stabbed to death as she walked toward her Kew Gardens apartment house about 3 A.M.— while neighbors ignored her calls for help."[25]

In the pages of *Thirty-Eight Witnesses*, Rosenthal's imagistic prose puts the greater moral lesson of the tragedy into focus: "One person or two or even three or four witnessing a murder passively would have been an unnoticed symptom of the disease in the city's body and again would have passed unnoticed. But thirty-eight — it was like a man with a running low fever suddenly beginning to cough blood; his friends could no longer ignore his illness, nor could he turn away from himself."[26] The number became ingrained, even if the facts of the case never supported the total of eyewitnesses the story alleged.

The New York Times and the 1964 book's shocking account of what happened to Genovese has endured as a narrative surrounding her and the community of Kew Gardens where she lived. "The Genovese Syndrome," also known as the bystander effect, has been researched internationally. Rosenthal, Gansberg, and the *Times* indirectly launched academic study leading to conferences, Good Samaritan laws, and even the plotline for the final episode of the popular NBC sitcom *Seinfeld*.

When Queens lawyer and amateur historian Joseph De May, Jr., created a Web site called "A Picture History of Kew Gardens, NY," he addressed the cultural gap Rosenthal widened in the 1960s and continued to defend until his death. *The New York Times* admirably acknowledged De May's "More Complex View" of the case in a 2004 piece by Jim Rasenberger called "Kitty, 40 Years Later." Rasenberger stops far short of implicating the drama of the 1964 *Times* piece and follow-up book in the misconceptions about the case, but notes that "for all that has been said and written about Ms. Genovese's murder, important questions persist. Some Kew Gardens residents maintain, even now, that there were fewer than 38 witnesses and that many of them could not have seen much of the killing — in other words, that there was less cold-heartedness in Kew Gardens than has been commonly portrayed."[27]

The piece offered details of Genovese's life unrelated to her murder and afforded De May the public opportunity to dissent from the popular narrative. De May analyzed documents from the trial and found he could only account for two attacks and that far fewer than 38 residents could have been eyewitnesses.[28] De May "points out that a good number of the witnesses were elderly, and nearly all awoke from deep slumbers, their brains befogged, their windows shut to the cold." Rosenthal discounts the revisionist take by De May, explaining to Rasenberger, "In a story that gets a lot of attention, there's always somebody who's saying, 'Well, that's not really what it's supposed to be.'... There may have been 38, there may have been 39 ... but the whole picture, as I saw it, was very affecting."[29]

Scholarly circles have also embraced the original story largely without question until recently. Even in the fifth edition of his 2004 textbook, *Essentials of Sociology: A Down to Earth Approach*, James Henslin includes an excerpt from the 1964 *Times* article to illustrate the concept of alienation and community. "Urban dwellers live in anonymity...," writes Henslin, "they grow aloof from one another and indifferent to other people's problems—as did the neighbors of Kitty Genovese."[30] Meanwhile, British researchers Rachel Manning, Mark Levine, and Alan Collins draw "a clear distinction between the story itself and the research tradition that emerged as a response to it.... It does not matter to the bystander effect that the story of the 38 witnesses may be misconceived."[31] Interviewed by Larry Mcshane for an Associated Press story headlined "Genovese syndrome: Fact or fiction," Manning conceded, "Once such 'facts' become generally accepted ... they are often difficult to correct."[32]

The Quasar in Politics

Theresa Marie Schiavo was born Theresa Marie Schindler in the suburbs of Philadelphia on December 3, 1963.[33] She married Michael Schiavo in November 1984 in Southhampton, Pennsylvania. According to police reports, on February 25, 1990, Ms. Schiavo suffered cardiac arrest at her Florida home, "apparently caused by a potassium imbalance ... leading to brain damage due to lack of oxygen."[34] Schiavo was in a persistent vegetative state, unable to speak and nourished by a feeding tube. On the heels of the 2004 presidential and congressional elections, a heated national debate ensued over the legal battle between her guardian and husband, Michael Schiavo, and her parents, Robert and Mary Schindler. The Schindlers sought custody of their daughter to prevent the removal of her feeding tube and went through a lengthy process in the Florida courts, leading to news media and national interest.

Dramatic news coverage of the legal matter was ubiquitous and grew more intense as Congress debated the passage of "Terri's Law" to prevent the removal of her feeding tube. In stark contrast to the Genovese case narrative, Schiavo's death was neither sudden nor was she ignored by neighbors. Vigils were held by supporters on the Schindler side of the battle, and all three branches of the federal government were engaged in the outcome. While "The Genovese Syndrome" became shorthand for apathy in American life and the bystander effect, "Terri's Law" applied *only* to Terri Schiavo. The attention she received across media platforms from media producers and consumers points to the power of the quasar to engage the global village in the lives of others through distant media.

Media correspondent Terrance Smith, appearing on *The NewsHour with*

Jim Lehrer on PBS, explained that the Schiavo drama received "wall-to-wall coverage in newspapers, broadcast television, cable news, the Internet, across the board."[35] Her case also illustrates how news coverage grants the quasar a special locus of attention that can be traded in public matters. Schiavo was, in a sense, a commodity like any celebrity. Shortly after her death in March 2005, Republican Sen. Mel Martinez of Florida revealed that "a senior member of his staff had written an unsigned memorandum about the partisan political advantages of intervening in the case of Terri Schiavo."[36] After it became clear that Schiavo was about to die, the political utility of her celebrity was shifted to a public service message, with First Lady Laura Bush emphasizing the need for living wills.[37]

Contemporary quasars, in other words, embody a cause or a public education mission. They become operational shorthand for laws or personalize initiatives that seldom *require* such personification. One state Web site explains that "Megan's Law is named after seven-year-old Megan Kanka, a New Jersey girl who was raped and killed by a known child molester who had moved across the street from the family without their knowledge."[38] The public memory of the quasars links their identities to discussions they themselves could not have foreseen. It also moves public memory away from facts and into narrative fiction. There is oppression in a mediated culture that allows identities to exist only within the context of crime and tragedy.

From Oppression to Liberation

Slavko Splichal points to the changing conception of publicity in mass society. The communication of ideas and thoughts for debate, he writes, is being "overshadowed by 'the activity of making certain that someone or something attracts a lot of interest or attention from many people.'" He argues that "the control dimension of publicity embodied in the corporate freedom of the press should be effectively supplemented by actions toward equalizing private citizens in the public use of reason," adding that "reforms of political, economic and social regulatory practices are needed to open citizens' access to the public sphere and mass media, which can only be based on the legal recognition of the generic human right to communicate."[39]

However, citizens bear their own share of responsibility for the quasar phenomenon, especially in the Information Age. Viral attention on the Internet awaits the man who falls asleep at a New York Mets baseball game *and* his friends who record a video of themselves stacking beer cups on his head.[40] A "Star Wars Kid" suffers embarrassment as his creative dance moves attract more than 12 million views on *YouTube*.[41] The oppression of an identity takes more than a media environment that values entertaining narrative over fact-based reporting. Members of the public must accept the narrative as well, and each time they do, the quasar falls deeper into the cultural gap that has been created.

Watching the Gap

When people board trains at New York's Pennsylvania Station in Manhattan to ride the Long Island Railroad east toward Queens, they are reminded to "WATCH THE GAP." These three simple words are painted on the platforms, appear on the train tickets and are trumpeted through the speakers repeatedly by railroad personnel. This urgent command shows concern for the safety of passengers, reminding them they need to be careful getting on and off the train. In a swiftly changing media environment, we might all well benefit from a similar ethical reminder to create and accept narratives in a manner that liberates— not oppresses— identities. In the cultural gap, we must refrain from accepting what we think is the truth, or the "world outside."

It is likely passengers who speed by the Kew Gardens station, less than a block from where the murder of Catherine Susan Genovese occurred in 1964, will never consider it more than a stop on the Long Island Railroad route. For those who are aware of the connection, the challenge might be to forget Genovese's name and its association with the bystander effect. Those who choose to construct narrative might liberate Genovese from the cultural gap by leaving her name out of the story, by finding ways to explain social phenomena without implicating her memory.

Quasars are not always enduring figures. They need not always be victims of the media either. They are the object of attention and celebrity even as they do not seek fame. If dialogical communication cannot be realized with them, those who create media narratives must ethically account for their use. Quasars are, after all, human beings with identities. They are entitled to privacy and, above all, human dignity.

NOTES

1. A. M. Rosenthal, *Thirty-Eight Witnesses* (New York: McGraw-Hill, 1964), 86.

2. Sheryl Gay Stolberg, "Drawing Some Criticism, Legislators with Medical Degrees Offer Opinions on Schiavo Case." *The New York Times*, March 23, 2005, A14.

3. Philip Drake, "Who Owns Celebrity? Privacy, Publicity and the Legal Regulation of Celebrity Images," in *Stardom and Celebrity: A Reader*, ed. Sean Redmond and Su Holmes (Los Angeles: Sage, 2007), 219–229.

4. P. David Marshall, *Celebrity and Power: Fame in Contemporary Culture* (Minneapolis: University of Minnesota Press, 2004), 16–17.

5. Walter Lippmann, *Public Opinion* (New York: Free, 1922), 3.

6. Ronald Steel, *Walter Lippmann and the American Century* (Boston: Little, Brown, 1980), 172–73.

7. *Ibid.,* 172.

8. Lippmann, *Public Opinion,* 32.

9. Michael Schudson, *The Power of News* (Cambridge, MA: Harvard University Press, 1995), 179.

10. W. Lance Bennett. *News: The Politics of Illusion* (New York: Longman, 2003).

11. Graeme Turner. "The Economy of Celebrity," in *Stardom and Celebrity: A Reader,* ed. Sean Redmond and Su Holmes (Los Angeles: Sage, 2007), 193.

12. Bob Considine, "Journalist Claims to Crack Natalee Holloway Case," MSNBC, http://today.msnbc.msn.com/id/22949353.html (accessed September 1, 2008).

13. Ray Rivera, "A Pilot Becomes a Hero Years in the Making," *The New York Times,* January 16, 2009, http://www.nytimes.com/2009/01/17/nyregion/17pilot.html (accessed April 1, 2009).

14. Michael Schudson, "Lippmann and the News," *The Nation,* December 13, 2007, http://thenation.com/doc/200771231/schudson (accessed August 30, 2008).

15. Bill Kovach and Tom Rosenstiel, *Warp Speed: America in the Age of Mixed Media* (New York: Century Foundation, 1999), 21.

16. Twitter, a popular social networking Web site and micro-blog, requires its participants' posts to be 140 characters or less. For January 2009, Compete.com writer Andy Kazeniac noted that Twitter experienced more than 54 million visits. See http://blog.compete.com/2009/02/09/facebook-myspace-twitter-social-network/ and http://twitter.com (accessed May 20, 2009).

17. For an example of this troubling trend, see Jessica Bennett's piece in *Newsweek* May 4, 2009, available at http://www.newsweek.com/id/195073 (accessed May 20, 2009).

18. James Monaco, *Celebrity: Who Gets It, How They Use It, Why It Works* (New York: Dell, 1978), 11.

19. Charles Krauthammer, "The Fine Art of Dying Well," *Time,* March 5, 2007, http://www.time.com/time/magazine/article/0,9171,1595226,00.html (accessed August 30, 2008).

20. Rosenthal, *Thirty-Eight Witnesses,* 13.

21. "Woman, 28, Knifed to Death," *The Long Island Press,* 13 March 1964, 26.

22. Rosenthal, *Thirty-Eight Witnesses,* 32.

23. Rosenthal, *Thirty-Eight Witnesses,* 25.

24. Musician Phil Ochs based the first line of his hit 1967 song *Outside of a Small Circle of Friends* on the parable of the 38 witnesses. It can still be heard on YouTube at http://www.youtube.com/watch?v=ulTmmTIlM_o (accessed May 20, 2009). The 1975 CBS television Friday Night Movie *Death Scream* featuring celebrities like Art Carney, Raul Julia, Edward Asner and Cloris Leachman, was based on the Genovese murder. See more details at http://www.imdb.com/title/tt0072857/(accessed May 20, 2009). Even as recently as 2007, a J.R. Teeter stage play titled *The Witnesses of Kitty Genovese* was staged in Rochester, New York. See http://www.breadandwatertheatre.org/news.htm#Apathy%20the%20Target%20in%20The%20Witnesses%20of%20Kitty%20Genovese (accessed May 20, 2009).

25. Rocco Parascandola, "Woman Stabbed to Death; Cries for Help Unanswered," *Newsday,* August 26, 2008, http://dailypress.com/topic/ny-nynystab265816813aug26,0,2085460.story (accessed August 30, 2008).

26. Rosenthal, *Thirty-Eight Witnesses,* 75.

27. Jim Rasenberger, "Kitty, 40 Years Later," *The New York Times,* February 8, 2004, http://nytimes.com/2004/02/08/nyregion/kitty-40-years-later.html (accessed March 29, 2009).

28. Joseph De May, Jr., "Kitty Genovese: The Popular Account Is Mostly Wrong," http://oldkewgardens.com/ss-nytimes-3.html (accessed September 2, 2008).

29. Rasenberger, "Kitty, 40 Years Later."

30. James M. Henslin, *Essentials of Sociology: A Down-to-Earth Approach* (Boston, MA: Pearson, 2004), 406–7.

31. Rachel Manning, Mark Levine, and Alan Collins, "Kitty Genovese Murder and the Social Psychology of Helping: The Parable of the 38 Witnesses," *American Psychologist* (September 2007): 557.

32. Larry Mcshane, "Genovese Syndrome: Fact or Fiction?" *USA Today*, October 1, 2007, http://www.usatoday.com/tech/science/discoveries/2007-10-01-genovese-syndrome-ques tioned_N.htm (accessed March 29, 2009).

33. Kelley Benham, "From Ordinary Girl to International Icon," TampaBay.com, March 31, 2005, http://sptimes.com/2005/03/31/news (accessed February 4, 2006).

34. Kathy Cerminara and Kenneth Goodman, "Key Events in the Case of Theresa Marie Schiavo: A Timeline," http://www.miami.edu/ethics2/schiavo (accessed November 30, 2005).

35. PBS, *Online NewsHour: Online Focus*. March 24, 2005. http://www.pbs.org/news hour/bb/media/jan-june05/schiavo_3-24.html (accessed April 6, 2009).

36. David Kirkpatrick, "Schiavo Memo Is Attributed to Senate Aide," *The New York Times*, March 30, 2005, http://80proquest.umi.com.ezproxy.fau.edu/pqdweb?did=818283251 &sid=2&Fmt=3&clientld=3326&VName=PQD (accessed November 25, 2005).

37. Anne Kornblut, "First Lady Says She and President Have Living Wills," *The New York Times*, April 7, 2005, http://query.nytimes.com/gst/fullpage.html?sec=health&res=9503 EED8123FF933A05750C0A9639C8B63 (accessed April 6, 2009).

38. Edmund G. Brown, Jr., "Office of the Attorney General," 2009. http://www.megans law.ca.gov/homepage.aspx (accessed April 4, 2009).

39. Slavko Splichal, *Principles of Publicity and Press Freedom* (Lanham, MD: Rowman & Littlefield, 2002), xiv.

40. YouTube. September 14, 2008. http://video.google.com/videosearch?client=firefox-a&rls=org.mozilla:enUS:official&channel=s&hl=en&q=guy%20at%20baseball%20game%20 falls%20asleep&um=1&ie=UTF-8&sa=N&tab=wv# (accessed April 5, 2009).

41. Oliver Moore, "'Star Wars' Kid Named Most-Seen Clip on Net," *The Globe and Mail*, November 28, 2006. http://query.nytimes.com/gst/fullpage.html?sec=health&res= 9503EED8123FF933A05750C0A9639C8B63 (accessed April 6, 2009).

WORKS CITED

Benham, Kelley. "From Ordinary Girl to International Icon," TampaBay.com (March 31, 2005), http://sptimes.com/2005/03/31/news.
Bennett, W. Lance. *News: The Politics of Illusion*. New York: Longman, 2003.
Brown, Edmund G., Jr. "State of California Office of the Attorney General" (2009). http://www.meganslaw.ca.gov/homepage.aspx.
Cerminara, Kathy L., and Kenneth Goodman. "Key Events in the Case of Theresa Marie Schiavo: A Timeline" (2005). http://www.miami.edu/ethics/schiavo/terri_schiavo_time line.html.
De May, Jr., Joseph. "Kitty Genovese: The Popular Account Is Mostly Wrong" (2008). http://oldkewgardens.com/ss-nytimes-3.html.
Drake, Philip. "Who Owns Celebrity?: Privacy, Publicity and the Legal Regulation of Celebrity Images," in *Stardom and Celebrity: A Reader*. Sean Redmond and Su Holmes, eds. Los Angeles, CA: Sage, 2007.
Henslin, James M. *Essentials of Sociology*. Boston: Pearson, 2004.
Kovach, Bill, and Tom Rosenstiel. *Warp Speed: America in the Age of Mixed Media*. New York: Century Foundation, 1999.
Krauthammer, Charles. "The Fine Art of Dying Well." *Time* (March 5, 2007), http://www.time.com/time/magazine/article/0,9171,1595226,00.html.
Lippmann, Walter. *Public Opinion*. New York: Free, 1922.
Manning, Rachel, Mark Levine and Alan Collins. "Kitty Genovese Murder and the Social Psychology of Helping: The Parable of the 38 Witnesses." *American Psychologist* (September 2007).
Marshall, P. David. *Celebrity and Power: Fame in Contemporary Culture*. Minneapolis: University of Minnesota Press, 2004.
McShane, Larry. "Genovese Syndrome: Fact or Fiction? " *USA Today* (October 1, 2007),

http://www.usatoday.com/tech/science/discoveries/2007-10-01-genovese-syndrome-questioned_N.htm.

Monaco, James. *Celebrity: Who Gets It, How They Use It, Why It Works.* New York: Dell, 1978.

Moore, Oliver. "'Star Wars' Kid Named Most-Seen Clip on Net." *The Globe and Mail* (November 28, 2006), http://query.nytimes.com/gst/fullpage.html?sec=health&res=9503EED 8123FF933A05750C0A9639C8B63.

Rosenthal, A. M. *Thirty-Eight Witnesses.* New York: McGraw-Hill, 1964.

Schudson, Michael. "Lippmann and the News." *The Nation* (December 13, 2007), http://thenation.com/doc/200771231/schudson.

_____. *The Power of News.* Cambridge, MA: Harvard University Press, 1995.

Splichal, Slavko. *Principles of Publicity and Press Freedom.* Lanham, MD: Rowman & Littlefield, 2002.

Steel, Ronald. *Walter Lippmann and the American Century.* Boston: Little, Brown, 1980.

Stolberg, Sheryl Gay. "Drawing Some Criticism, Legislators with Medical Degrees Offer Opinions on Schiavo Case." *The New York Times* (March 23, 2005) A14.

Turner, Graeme. "The Economy of Celebrity," in *Stardom and Celebrity: A Reader.* Sean Redmond and Su Holmes, eds. Los Angeles, CA: Sage, 2007.

Chapter 4

"Sportainment" Meets High School Sports

Marie Hardin *and* Thomas F. Corrigan

Ryan Kelly, a senior at Ravenscroft High School in North Carolina, plays the double bass in his school's orchestra. He also plays on the school's basketball team. Until his junior year, the lanky forward hadn't received much attention outside Ravenscroft for either pursuit. That changed when Ryan sprouted from 6-foot-7 to 6-foot-9 in a matter of months. His 6:15 A.M. visits to the gym also began to pay off in a big way, and Ryan burst onto the national scene, getting the attention of ranking services, such as Scout.com, and of major college programs. It's easy to find him; a Google search turns up thousands of hits and YouTube sports videos of Ryan, both from the lens of videographers and from fans' cell phones.

After he was ranked, Ryan gave upwards of a hundred interviews—to reporters, bloggers, and writers for college booster publications. Many interviews occurred via phone calls that interrupted his studies each night. The questions were relentless: Had he made a decision about college, even though he hadn't yet completed his third year of high school? The questions were probing too, reflecting the level of attention on the young player. He had, for instance, moved up a college visit by a day — what did that mean? Whom did he meet? Ryan handled the questions well; the 17-year-old had received media training from a public affairs coordinator at his school.[1]

But his mother, Doreen Kelly, said Ryan finally reached fatigue — not from his hours on the basketball court, but from those on the phone. He told his parents, "'I really don't want to do this anymore,'" she recalls. They stepped in, she said. "We try to be polite and say, 'Ryan's got homework to do.'"[2] Still, Ryan couldn't avoid the media attention altogether; she and her son both came to accept it as part of the game. But "the mother in me aches," she said, when she thinks about the inordinate amount of media focus on a

17-year-old who still plays in his high school orchestra. She added, "There's something about the promotion and reporting of stars that negates the beauty of high school team sports."[3]

"Sportainment" at the High School Level

The promotion of young "star" athletes has grown exponentially during the past decade. In the process, high school sports coverage has evolved into what author, educator and former professional basketball player, John Gerdy, describes as "sportainment."[4] Long the norm for professional and college sports,[5] couching high school competition in terms of entertainment moves organized youth sports away from the values that made them cherished in U.S. culture, such as sportsmanship and character-building; instead, sportainment relies on a form of "marketplace ethics," where profitability takes precedence over emphasis on traditional sporting values.[6] HDTV telecasts, athlete press conferences, demographically targeted magazines, dedicated Web sites, and made-for-TV events are all part of this model. Gerdy writes that the effects devastate the redeeming qualities of athletic competition:

> We have trivialized sport. Those things that we have long valued in sport — its ability to promote good health, develop character, encourage sportsmanship, and bring people together — are simply no longer important.... It is about entertainment, money, ego, image, and getting on television.[7]

This chapter explores the trend and its implications, arguing that the Faustian bargain embedded in the pursuit of high school athletics as *sportainment* is one that violates the ideals justifying cultural support of youth sports. Sports coverage is more than just the presentation of scores, recaps, and highlights, and it cannot be viewed simply as a form of escapist entertainment. The narratives of sports coverage serve an important function in the democratic process by transmitting cultural values.[8] Manipulation of these cultural narratives in light of media producers' reliance on "marketplace ethics" has threatened the ideals of high school athletics.

As high school sports move toward a "big-time" model, media producers carry a social responsibility for coverage that does not ultimately harm community. We advocate a communitarian lens for viewing the relationship among sportainment, youths, education, and culture.

Communitarianism as an Ethical Paradigm

Communitarianism is a line of ethical and philosophical reasoning grounded in the notion that the individual depends on the group, or, more broadly, the community.[9] It has developed as one of two "general theoretical prisms"—the other being understood as libertarian—for the understanding of media in a democratic society.[10] In contrast with the libertarian paradigm, a communitarian framework requires that "the full self-realization of each individual, both as freedom loving beings *and as engaged members of a community* [emphasis ours], must be the underlying motive of all media policies."[11]

We define "community" for our purposes as a geographically interested/centered social web of relationships among individuals and groups in which the social welfare of children is considered a common interest and commitment.[12] This definition allows the geographic center of interest to be as small as Raleigh, North Carolina (the home of Ravenscroft High School), or as large as the United States. More importantly, this definition also necessarily implies awareness that, ultimately, the welfare of individuals within a community depends on the actions of others.[13] Decision-making on behalf of "self-interest," then, must also be decision-making that accounts for the good of the community.[14]

Communitarianism examines both the process and social effects of behavior. Ethical decisions are viewed as the impact of the sum of choices on society and in light of the "shadow of the future" they cast;[15] the rationale for "individual acts must be weighed against the normative standard of the goal of a more just society."[16] Communitarianism necessarily stresses the role of media in the context of the community, and the emphasis is as much on media responsibility as it is on (individualist-oriented) media freedom.[17] As Christians, Ferré, and Fackler suggest of a communitarian orientation, it asks that "choices of story coverage and advocacy not hinge on outcomes that advance individual gratification" but instead on those that advance social justice.[18] Patrick Lee Plaisance suggests that although certain forms of journalism, such as "public" or "civic" journalism, have incorporated elements of communitarianism, "a media truly informed by communitarian ideas would look radically different" than media forms today.[19] He adds: "It transcends, as it were, the current obsession with presentation and entertainment to the extent that such concerns limit media's ability to create opportunities for social interaction."[20]

Applied in a media setting, then, communitarianism requires that institutions and individuals consider, among other factors, the good of the community with the understanding that doing so is for their own good. Applied specifically to coverage of high school sports, we suggest that a communitarian lens would require considering how media coverage cultivates and protects the values that make scholastic sports integral to American education and community life. In doing so, we argue that the cultivation of a national "star system," along with the conceptualization of scholastics sports as filling the same entertainment interests as professional and college sports, should be halted.

High School Sports: Their Role in U.S. Culture

According to Poynter Institute ethics expert Bob Steele, sports may be as central to U.S. culture as politics and religion.[21] Sports are cultivated as communal; that is, they are seen as helping to forge relationships and unite people of all ages, across class and race boundaries, behind the "home team"— whether that is the U.S. Olympic team or a local high school squad. Furthermore, mediated sports have always been a site for escapist entertainment ("it's *only* a game"), the creation and maintenance of heroes, and the reinforcement of cultural values.

That sports reinforce such values as hard work, teamwork, fair play, discipline, and deference to authority has been the rationale for institutionalizing athletics in U.S. education.[22] Sports have been positioned as a venue in which youth learn the "morally unquestionable team ethic" and can establish enduring friendships, reach high levels of fitness, and attain competitive goals.[23]

An oft-touted value of high school sports is their power to bring people in schools and communities together, and the cohesive function of school sports is seen as an invaluable asset to educators and civic leaders.[24] Sports are viewed as a force that binds neighbors as they rally behind youngsters on a field or in a gymnasium; part of fandom for the home team involves participation in communal rituals and intergenerational traditions.[25] The power of scholastic sports to forge and represent a community, bridge racial divides, and even heal wounded familial relationships is the stuff of famous sports movies, such as *Hoosiers* and *Remember the Titans*.

However, John Gerdy has warned against blindly prioritizing sports as a tool for community-building. In his 2006 book, *Air Ball*, he concedes that athletics can "unify educational institutions and communities in ways that the English department cannot," but adds: "This belief drives much of the push toward increased commercialism, visibility, and national-level competition."[26]

Eminent sports sociologist Jay Coakley has also warned of a "performance ethic" that has become an unchallenged value in youth sports.[27] Performance, an outcome measured in individual statistics and win/loss records, often usurps educational values as "an indicator of the quality of the sport experience," Coakley writes.[28] Combined with unquestioned cultural beliefs about the necessity of competitive sports to build and unify communities as well as myths about the purity of sports competition, the performance ethic has enabled a sportainment model for media (re)presentations of youth sports to develop without proper scrutiny.[29]

Some activists, educators, and scholars, however, have argued that high school sports need more values-oriented oversight; they are "a pressing issue of the day" because of the growing role of commercialism and the power of state associations and leagues, which operate with little or no regulation.[30]

Other fears include the potential for steroid use by developing bodies[31] and the emergence of diploma-mills for athletes in pursuit of college eligibility.[32] Gerdy and Coakley have also speculated on the long-term health effects on a generation of young Americans oriented toward sports as activities for elite-level performance as opposed to activities for fit, healthy lifestyles.[33]

The pressure on elite high school athletes to excel and promote themselves is fierce; one trend is parents' hiring of agents, who construct video-laden Web sites on which they showcase the skills of young athletes.[34] College recruiting programs are reaching out to hoopsters as young as 14 and integrating product sponsors into recruiting efforts.[35] Commercial Web sites (many of which profit from organizing and sponsoring youth-sports events and related products) rank athletes as early as age 11.[36] Club sports have also emerged as year-round, high-pressure affairs that offer another way for youths to gain sports experience — if they can afford the high cost and are willing to commit to great time demands.[37]

High School Athletes in the Media Spotlight

High school sports have been a time-honored staple of small-town newspapers, Friday night play-by-play on AM radio, and local television news highlights. High school sports coverage can be among the most trafficked sections on newspaper Web sites; a 2006 study showed that athletes get up to eight times the coverage of academic all-stars.[38] Youth sports may be a "final frontier," so to speak, where access to athletes is not filtered by an agent or spokesperson, perhaps allowing for more spontaneity, expression of emotion and, ultimately, more authentic stories.[39]

Educators, coaches, students, and parents have welcomed the publicity, mostly for commercially related reasons.[40] Coverage on all media platforms (newspaper, magazine, Web, and broadcast) has increased; coverage is predicted to both *fragment*— simultaneously going hyper-local and national — and *expand*.[41] Justification for the surge includes more space for news and programming, thanks to the Web and the proliferation of cable regional sports networks, combined with what media producers say is a demand from high school and college fans interested in potential recruits. Another driver is the relatively low cost of producing and covering high school events. The talent is free, and the exorbitant rights fees that accompany college and professional sports are virtually nonexistent.[42]

Television as the Primary Conduit

Sports are not the only children's competitions that are televised, but other competitions do not compare with the regularity and ubiquity of sports coverage.[43] ABC's (now ESPN's) broadcast of the Little League World Series began in 1963, making it the longest-running relationship between a network and a major sports organization. In 2005 more than 500 media credentials were issued for the event.[44] Regional sports networks have capitalized on high school sports as cheap filler with local and regional appeal to advertisers. Fox Sports Net (FSN), a network of affiliate RSNs, has been one of the major players for development of scholastic sports programming, developing an invitational football bowl game, a magazine, and a national ranking for high school teams.[45]

ESPN has followed — with a national emphasis — the lead of FSN in focusing on high school athletics. The network made waves in 2002 when ESPN2 broadcast two St. Vincent-St. Mary's games that featured high school basketball star and future NBA player LeBron James. The games registered some of the highest ratings the network had in two years.[46] The ratings, the result of relentless promotion of James, prompted ESPN to pursue high school sports as a low-cost revenue stream, and some experts to point to the "LeBron factor" as initiating the unprecedented focus on high school athletes.[47]

ESPN, for its part, has moved far beyond the "LeBron factor" and demonstrated its commitment to cultivating many more high school stars and content. In 2008 it launched its multiplatform initiative to provide blanket coverage of prep sports. The initiative, called "RISE," includes Web sites, magazines, and events.[48] The network also announced it would add coverage of high school sports to its flagship program, *SportsCenter*, and to *ESPNews* and *College Football Live*.

Rankings to Cultivate Stars

Much of the appeal in high school sports coverage on the national scale is in the cultivation of stars at both the athlete and team level. ESPN and others have pursued this with a two-pronged approach: 1) rankings and 2) events that then showcase players and teams who have garnered top-ranked spots. An example of the way ranking and events work hand in hand is ESPN's promotion of a football game in fall 2007 between Southlake Carroll (Texas) and Miami Northwestern (Florida); the network marketed the game as a match-up of the country's top two teams.[49]

The major ranking services are not independent of the media institutions they serve, but are often owned by them.[50] As media coverage has increased, so has the number of rankings, mostly aimed at boys' football and basketball; these rankings both feed and justify intense media scrutiny of the players they highlight (such as Ryan Kelly, mentioned at the beginning of this chapter).[51] Doug Huff, a sports editor in Wheeling, West Virginia, who started the first national poll to be carried by national wire services in 1987, said rankings create a "mushrooming effect." He told *The New York Times*: "You create interest, and you get expanded print coverage. Then TV jumps on it.... If you'd told me 20 years ago that this stuff was going to be covered so widely, I wouldn't believe it."[52]

Rankings, whether generated by media producers or used by them, have introduced myriad ethical issues into high school sports that reflect questionable educational priorities.[53] Furthermore, just as they have been at the college level, rankings have been a headache for media organizations from the standpoint of credibility and ethics.[54] The pressure to produce up-to-the-minute updates and cultivate "in-the-know" sources about emerging high school stars—both determined by and determining of the rankings—has increased, creating a "feeding frenzy" around these athletes.[55]

Meanwhile, according to scholar William Law, sports are still mythologized as the "last unsullied territory in an otherwise corrupt landscape" by media producers who are "sitting in the starting blocks, behaving as if the revolution hadn't happened."[56] High school basketball games are scheduled to begin at or after 10 P.M. on a school night — at gymnasiums in high-crime, urban areas— to satisfy the demands of television producers.[57]

Media executives say they are sensitive to the values involved in high school sports and to the fragile egos of youngsters who are still maturing. An ESPN vice president, for instance, promised that Little League World Series games would be aired with "the purest of intentions" and that announcers for the event are encouraged to present the games as reflective of the league's emphasis on participation over competition.[58] Even so, ESPN ombudsman George Solomon, after the airing of a high school football game in August 2006, wrote that such coverage told "the world high school sports are about winning, big-time recruits and ratings— but not education."[59] Unsportsmanlike conduct exhibited in the games, such as face-mask violations, are part of players' performing for the camera in hopes of a *SportsCenter* highlight while commentators discuss their scholarship offers.[60] Not surprisingly, offshore sports books now take bets on these types of games.[61]

Robert Andrew Powell, author of *We Own This Game*, a book about the corruption in the football program at ESPN-promoted Miami Northwestern, said in a *Slate* column that he is "mortified" at the prospect of more school matches getting high-profile coverage. He added:

> After a decade of following prep sports, I can say with confidence: When a dynasty emerges in high school sports, there's probably something crooked going on.... Airing high-school games on national television provides tremendous incentive for principals, coaches, superintendents and high school associations to bend the rules and sacrifice academics in pursuit of high profiles and profits.[62]

A Communitarian Framework for Coverage of High School Sports

In the same *Slate* column, Powell argues that national coverage of high school sports contests should be stopped. Just because it is legal, he notes, "doesn't mean it's right. High-school football should be as local and as small-time as possible."[63]

We agree. But why? On what ethical grounds do we urge media producers, educators and communities to decide together to reject the transformation of youth sports into sportainment?

We do so on communitarian grounds. As noted previously, *communitarianism* is grounded in the notion that the individual depends on the group, or, more broadly, the community.[64] Since the welfare of individuals within a community — and, importantly, the welfare of children — depends on the actions of others,[65] decision-making on behalf of "self-interest" must also be decision-making that accounts for the good of the community.[66]

The central question for media producers, parents, and educators — all charged with making decisions in the best interest of the children within a community — is how a media model that aspires to present youth sports as sportainment would (or would not) benefit that community. Communitarianism forces all parties to ask: What "shadow of the future" is cast by different approaches to coverage of high school sports? How do these approaches safeguard (or not) the culturally shared values in sports that have ensured their place in secondary education? More plainly, how can the promotion of high school sports at the national level (complete with media creation of 16-year-old stars for commercial gain) create outcomes that serve our common vision of school sports? Does the sportainment model enhance or impede our teaching of all youths the value of fitness, fair play, discipline, and teamwork as a part of a broad academic agenda that seeks to promote the flourishing of individuals *and* community?

We understand that communitarianism as a guiding framework cannot provide the answers to nuanced, day-to-day questions media producers face in covering local youth sports (such as "How much attention should a key play, involving an error by an inexperienced player, get in the game recap?"). We do, however, believe that a communitarian lens is one that allows stakeholders (media, parents, educators, students and the community) to answer the big-picture questions we have presented by focusing on common values that have always justified the use of public dollars to support youth sports and physical education. As common values are pried apart from the distractions and illusion of big-time media coverage, the suggestion that scholastic sports should be as "local and small-time as possible" seems not only reasonable, but also necessary.

We realize that prying the common values we attach to scholastic sports apart from the distractions and illusions that come with the national spotlight for a young athlete will be difficult (as difficult as addressing such issues as the use of performance-enhancing drugs in sports at all levels). The individualistic outlook that prevails in American media and the wider American culture provides support for the "performance ethic" in scholastic and youth sports. The idea that the "NFL has filtered down" to the high school football field, for instance, is seen by some coaches, educators, and parents as a sign of progress.[67]

But these discussions must be had. Communitarianism calls for media producers to conceive and foster an "ethics of engagement" and for community members to participate in difficult decision-making about issues that affect their lives and the well being of the community as a whole.[68]

If community members around a high school football team consider the costs to pursue national media exposure (which must entail a national playing schedule and the requisite time and expense for the school, parents, and students), they must consider the impact on the school's budget and, subsequently, the education of all of students in its charge. They must consider what shared values are emphasized in such pursuit and which ones must be discarded. Should fitness, fair play, discipline, and teamwork — the values traditionally understood as crucial to the development of a community's model citizens — take a back seat to the sportainment model's production of powerhouses and marketing of star athletes? And, finally, they must also consider the payoff: What is gained (and who gains), and what is lost (and who loses)?

Such discussions will, by necessity, involve competing agendas. For instance, what about promising athletes who seek (along with their parents) publicity they believe will lead to a lucrative college scholarship? Communities, in truth, may be deeply fragmented; thus, the identification of "common problems" and, subsequently, "common goals," may be a prospect conceived in naiveté; however, the cultivation of "moral agency" in media-community discourse is a worthy, democratic objective.[69]

Considering Ryan Kelly

When we consider the implications of coverage on the values that put sports in the educational setting in the first place, we have no choice but to critically assess our approach and to redraw our path as one more supportive of our academic ideals, our sporting ideals, and our democracy. Where would such a path take us as we consider Ryan Kelly, the student-athlete discussed at the beginning of this chapter?

First, it would take us to conversations among media producers and a variety of citizens that examined the "shadow of the future" coverage of Kelly might cast. Primary to a communitarian approach is *a commitment to an "ethics of engagement" by media producers early in the decision-making process*; in truth, this element alone would produce the kind of "radical" difference in the media landscape Plaisance suggested springs from communitarianism. It would force media producers to move away from a "here today, gone tomorrow" mindset that encourages "outcomes that advance individual gratification."[70] The first step for ESPN, regional sports networks, newspaper editors, and bloggers who write for subscription-based Web sites, for instance, would be that of *community-focused* social interaction to explicate the values and goals understood as pursuant to the common good.

This commitment means a recognition by media producers of themselves as part of the *local* community but also as part of a *national* community that has embraced a core set of common values and visions concerning sports, youths, and education. This recognition would necessarily imply a responsibility on the part of media producers to support the values and visions of these communities.

A commitment to engagement that seeks to uncover and honor community values would, at its most basic level, require media producers to *identify all parties in a community* affected by the inclusion of organized athletics in education. Kelly is one voice among many, including his parents, siblings, teammates, teachers, coaches, and school administrators. Others should be his non-sporting classmates, their parents, and — ultimately — the members of the community who will be affected by the quality of citizens emerging from the education system. In general, educators, parents, and students all have a stake in coverage of Kelly and their right to engage as moral agents.

Another key element in a communitarian approach to coverage of Kelly would be *inclusive discourse* as both *precursor to* and *part of* coverage. This requires cooperation among educators, community leaders (including elected officials), coaches, and media producers to create the time and space for open public discussion that honors a variety of perspectives with the goal of identifying common values. (The difficulty of such pursuit has already been addressed in this chapter). A series of town-hall style meetings, for instance, could engage the perspectives of journalists, media producers, parents, athletes, and educators. Unifying principles that emerge from these conversations could serve as the springboard for decision-making concerning coverage of Ryan and of the athletes who come behind him.

Sacrifices in the interest of the common good would likely be expected of many stakeholders. For instance, young star athletes (and their parents) might have to accept that games will not be scheduled to meet "prime-time" network demands. Web, TV, and print reporters might have to accept that they should not call a 17-year-old athlete at home for interviews. (With a communitarian media model, can we envision the regular intrusions on homework time that Kelly faced?) Thus, priority can be properly placed on the values the community embraces in giving Kelly — and all athletes his age — the chance to play in the educational setting.

It is also likely that, as the conversation moves from situations such as Kelly's to the national community, another sacrifice would be the framing of high school sports along the lines of sportainment. We believe that national conversations about education, sports and values— and how those (do not) mesh with a system of high-pressure rankings and major media coverage, will result in the rejection of scholastic sports as big-time entertainment. As media producers embrace a communitarian model — one that includes educators, students, parents and citizens in conversations about coverage — it seems such a conclusion is not only desirable, but also inevitable.

NOTES

1. Doreen Kelly, personal interview, June 24, 2008.
2. *Ibid.*
3. *Ibid.*
4. John Gerdy, "Pro Sports as Show Business," *Professional Sports: Examining Pop Culture* (Greenhaven Press, 2003), 143.
5. Professional sports have always been presented in terms of public entertainment, and college sports— although conducted in an academic setting — have been conceptualized as such for decades. Harold Stoke, a president of two major American universities, wrote in a March 1954 article in *The Atlantic Monthly* that "of all the instrumentalities which universities have for entertaining the public, the most effective is athletics" ("College Athletics: Education or Show Business?" 46)
6. Gerdy, "Pro Sports as Show Business."
7. *Ibid.*, 146, 148.
8. Thomas P. Oates and John Pauly, "Sports Journalism as Moral and Ethical Discourse," *Journal of Mass Media Ethics* 22 (2007): 340.
9. Philip Patterson and Lee Wilkins, *Media Ethics: Issues and Cases*, 6th Ed. (Boston: McGraw Hill, 2008); Renita Coleman, "The Ethical Context for Public Journalism: As an Ethical Foundation for Public Journalism, Communitarian Philosophy Provides Principles for Practitioners to Apply for Real-World Problems," *Journal of Communication Inquiry* 24, no. 1 (2000): 41–66.
10. Patrick Lee Plaisance, "The Mass Media as Discursive Network: Building on the Implications of Libertarian and Communitarian Claims for News Media Ethics Theory," *Communication Theory* 15 (2005): 292.
11. Plaisance, "The Mass Media," 294.
12. We understand the difficulties we present in introducing the term "community," as this term carries what Philip Selznick has aptly termed "baggage." Plaisance ("The Mass Media," p. 306) also (rightly) suggests that the idea of community has been loaded "with more meaning than it is capable of carrying." Furthermore, our definition may not be sufficiently "inclusive" and "neutral," although we do not specify any interest beyond a common understanding among members that the welfare of children is a cultural responsibility. See Philip Selznick, *The Moral Commonwealth: Social Theory and the Promise of Community* (Los Angeles: University of California Press, 1992): 358.
13. James Carey, "Community, Public, and Journalism," *Mixed News: The Public/Civic/ Communitarian Journalism Debate* (Mahwah, NJ: Lawrence Erlbaum, 1997), 4; Sandra L.

Borden, *Journalism as Practice: MacIntyre, Virtue Ethics and the Press* (Hampshire, UK: Ashgate, 2007), 8.

14. Coleman, "The Ethical Context," 42.

15. Patterson and Wilkins, *Media Ethics: Issues and Cases,* 15.

16. Patterson and Wilkins, *Media Ethics: Issues and Cases,* 15.

17. John Merrill, "Communitarianism's Rhetorical War Against Enlightened Liberalism," *Mixed News: The Public/Civic/Communitarian Journalism Debate* (Mahwah, NJ: Lawrence Erlbaum, 1997), 55.

18. Clifford G. Christians, John P. Ferré, and P. Mark Fackler, *Good News: Social Ethics and the Press* (New York: Oxford University Press, 1993), 93.

19. Plaisance, "The Mass Media," 310.

20. Plaisance, "The Mass Media," 311.

21. Mark Jurkowitz, "Muckrakers in the Outfield," *The Phoenix,* April 5, 2006, http://thephoenix.com/Boston/News/8312-Muckrakers-in-the-outfield/?rel=inf (accessed April 27, 2006).

22. Anna Marie Frank, *Sports and Education: A Reference Handbook* (Santa Barbara, CA: ABC-CLIO, 2003) 82; Oates and Pauly, "Sports Journalism," 340.

23. Oates and Pauly, "Sports Journalism," 340; Frank, *Sports and Education,* 132–133.

24. Frank, *Sports and Education,* 133.

25. *Ibid.,* 133.

26. John Gerdy, *Air Ball* (Jackson: University Press of Mississippi, 2006), 43.

27. Jay Coakley, *Sports in Society: Issues and Controversies,* 8th ed. (New York: McGraw-Hill, 2004), 134.

28. *Ibid.,*133.

29. Marie Hardin and Thomas F. Corrigan, "Media and the Business of High School Sports," *Journal of Sports Media* 3, no. 2 (2008): 91.

30. Jay Weiner, "Reporting on the Business of Sports," *Real Sports Reporting* (Bloomington: Indiana University Press), 218.

31. Enrique Rangel, "HS Athletes Pass Steroids Test," *Lubbock Avalanche-Journal,* June 19, 2008, http://www.lubbockonline.com/stories/061908/loc_292671263.shtml (accessed August 29, 2008).

32. Duff Wilson, "School That Gave Easy Grades to Athletes Is Closing," *The New York Times,* December 24, 2005, http://www.nytimes.com/2005/12/24/sports/ncaafootball/24 schools.html (accessed August 29, 2008).

33. John Gerdy, *Air Ball,* 44; Coakley, *Sports in Society,* 150.

34. Alan M. Goldenbach, e-mail correspondence, June 20, 2008.

35. Eric Prisbell and Steve Yanda, "Shoe Company Ties with Maryland, Link to Top Recruit Raise Questions," *The Washington Post,* March 1, 2009, D1.

36. Sean Gregory, "Courting Eighth-Graders," *Time,* October 8, 2007; Tracy Greer, e-mail correspondence, July 8, 2008.

37. Greer, e-mail correspondence, July 8, 2008.

38. Sam Darcy, "Research Looks at Coverage of High School Academics, Athletics," MNDaily.com, October 4, 2006, http://www.mndaily.com/articles/2006/10/04/69236 (accessed May 23, 2007); Hardin and Corrigan, "Media and the Business of High School Sports," 91; Greer, e-mail correspondence, July 8, 2008.

39. Goldenbach, e-mail correspondence, June 20, 2008.

40. Hillary Smith, e-mail correspondence, June 21, 2008.

41. "The Kids Are Alright? Some Critical of High School Coverage," *Sports Business Daily,* September 14, 2006, http://www.sportsbusinessdaily.com/index.cfm?fuseaction=sbd. preview&articleID=105827 (accessed September 14, 2006); Don Shelton, interview, July 8, 2008.

42. Hardin and Corrigan, "Media and the Business of High School Sports," 92; Goldenbach, e-mail correspondence, June 20, 2008

43. Alyssa Quart, "Girls and Boys, Interrupted," *The New York Times,* October 2, 2006,

http://www.nytimes.com/2006/10/02/opinion/02quart.html?n=Top/Reference/Times%20To
pics/Subjects/L/Little%20League (accessed August 29, 2008).

44. Tom Farrey, *Game On: The All-American Race to Make Champions of our Children* (New York: ESPN, 2008), 258.

45. Anne Torpey-Kemph, "Inside Media," *MediaWeek*, no. 44 (1999): 38–39.

46. Mark Alesias, "Showtime's Fine Line," *IndyStar.com*, December 5, 2004, http://www 2.indystar.com/articles/5/239503–7135–114.html (accessed June 14, 2009).

47. Hardin and Corrigan, "Media and the Business of High School Sports," 91.

48. "New ESPN High School Sports Initiative to Launch: ESPN RISE," ESPN news release, May 15, 2008.

49. Joshua Robinson, "Proliferation of High School Polls Spurs Subjective Debate," *The New York Times*, December 5, 2007, http://www.nytimes.com/2007/12/05/sports/05preps. html?_r=1&ref=sports&oref=slogin (accessed April 5, 2008).

50. Charles Rich, "Yahoo! Wants to Get Closer to Teenage Boys," *FanHouse*, April 13, 2007, http://www.fanhouse.com/2007/04/13/yahoo-wants-to-get-closer-to-teenage-boys/ (accessed August 29, 2008).

51. Robinson, "Proliferation of High School Polls."

52. *Ibid.*

53. Alan M. Goldenbach, e-mail correspondence, June 20, 2008.

54. Greer, e-mail correspondence, July 8, 2008; Tracy Greer, "National Ranking Web-sites: The Illinois Youth Soccer Position," *Network News*, Summer 2005, 30–31.

55. Greer, e-mail correspondence, July 8, 2008.

56. William Law, "More Than a Game: The Business and Ethics of Sports Journalism," *Deadlines and Diversity* (Halifax, Nova Scotia: Fernwood, 1996), 187.

57. Phil Mushnick, "ESPN, Schools Invite Trouble," *New York Post*, February 24, 2008.

58. "The Kids Are Alright?" para. 3; Farrey, *Game On*, 258.

59. George Solomon, "Playing Favorites: Viewers Question Game Choices." *ESPN.com*, August 31, 2006 http://sports.espn.go.com/espn/columns/story?columnist=solomon_george &id=2566936 (accessed August 27, 2008).

60. "The Kids Are Alright?" para. 3.

61. Robert Andrew Powell, "Sex Scandals, Stadium Sponsors, and National TV," *Slate.com*, September 14, 2007, http://www.slate.com/id/2173804 (accessed April 14, 2008).

62. Powell, "Sex Scandals," para. 3, 11.

63. *Ibid.*, para. 17.

64. Patterson and Wilkins, *Media Ethics: Issues and Cases*; Coleman, "The Ethical Context."

65. Carey, "Community, Public, and Journalism," 4; Borden, *Journalism as Practice*, 8.

66. Coleman, "The Ethical Context," 42.

67. George Solomon, "In the Digital Age, it's still an American Autumn Ritual," *The Washington Post*, October 5, 2008, http://www.washingtonpost.com/wp-dyn/content/arti cle/2008/10/04/AR2008100401648.html (accessed August 15, 2009).

68. Coleman, "The Ethical Context, 54; Plaisance, "The Mass Media," 306.

69. Plaisance, "The Mass Media," 305.

70. Christians, Ferré, and Fackler, *Good News*, 93.

WORKS CITED

Alesias, Mark. "Showtime's Fine Line." *Indianapolis Star* (5 December 2004). IndyStar.com, <http://www2.indystar.com/articles/5/239503-7135-114.html> (accessed 14 June 2009).

Borden, Sandra L. *Journalism as Practice: MacIntyre, Virtue Ethics and the Press*. Hampshire, UK: Ashgate, 2007.

Carey, James. "Community, Public, and Journalism." In *Mixed News: The Public/Civic/Communitarian Journalism Debate*, edited by Jay Black. Mahwah, NJ: Lawrence Erlbaum, 1997, 1–17.

Christians, Clifford G., John P. Ferré, and Mark P. Fackler. *Good News: Social Ethics and the Press*. New York: Oxford University Press, 1993.

Coakley, Jay. *Sports in Society: Issues and Controversies*, 8th ed. New York: McGraw-Hill, 2004.

Coleman, Renita. "The Ethical Context for Public Journalism: As an Ethical Foundation for Public Journalism, Communitarian Philosophy Provides Principles for Practitioners to Apply for Real-World Problems." *Journal of Communication Inquiry 24*, no. 1 (2000): 41–66.

Darcy, Sam. "Research Looks at Coverage of High School Academics, Athletics." MNDaily. com (4 Oct. 2006). MNDaily.com, <http://www.mndaily.com/articles/2006/10/04/69236> (accessed 23 May 2007).

ESPN news release. "New ESPN High School Sports Initiative to Launch: ESPN RISE." (May 15, 2008).

Farrey, Tom. *Game On: The All-American Race to Make Champions of our Children* New York: ESPN, 2008.

Frank, Anna Marie. *Sports and Education: A Reference Handbook*. Santa Barbara, CA: ABC-CLIO, 2003.

Gerdy, John. *Air Ball*. Jackson: University Press of Mississippi, 2006.

_____. "Pro Sports as Show Business." In *Professional Sports: Examining Pop Culture*. Farmington Hills, MI: Greenhaven, 2003.

Goldenbach, Alan M., e-mail correspondence to coauthor Hardin, 20 June 2008.

Greer, Tracy, e-mail correspondence to coauthor Hardin, 8 July 2008.

_____. "National Ranking Websites: The Illinois Youth Soccer Position." (Summer 2005). *Network News*: 30–31.

Gregory, Sean. "Courting Eighth-Graders." *Time* (27 September 2007). Time.com, <http://www.time.com/time/magazine/article/0,9171,1666283,00.html> (accessed 10 July 2009).

Hardin, Marie, and Thomas F. Corrigan. "Media and the Business of High School Sports." *Journal of Sports Media 3*, no. 2 (2008): 89–94.

Jurkowitz, Mark. "Muckrakers in the Outfield." *The Phoenix*. (5 April 2006). http://the phoenix.com/Boston/News/8312-Muckrakers-in-the-outfield/?rel=inf (accessed 27 April, 2006).

Kelly, Doreen, in discussion with coauthor Hardin. 24 June 2008.

"The Kids Are Alright? Some Critical of High School Coverage." *Sports Business Daily* (14 September 2006). <http://www.sportsbusinessdaily.com/index.cfm?fuseaction=sbd.pre view&articleID=105827> (accessed 14 Sept. 2006).

Law, William. "More Than a Game: The Business and Ethics of Sports Journalism." In *Deadlines and Diversity*, edited by Valerie Alia, Brian Brennan, and Barry Hoffmaster. Halifax, Nova Scotia: Fernwood, 1996.

Merrill, John. "Communitarianism's Rhetorical War Against Enlightened Liberalism." In *Mixed News: The Public/Civic/Communitarian Journalism Debate*, edited by Jay Black. Mahwah, NJ: Lawrence Erlbaum, 1997, 54–69.

Mushnick, Phil. "ESPN, Schools Invite Trouble." *New York Post*. (24 February 2008). <http://www.nypost.com/seven/02242008/sports/espn__schools_invite_trouble_99108.htm> (accessed 10 July 2009).

Oates, Thomas P., and John Pauly. "Sports Journalism as Moral and Ethical Discourse." *Journal of Mass Media Ethics 22*, no. 4 (2007): 332–347.

Patterson, Philip, and Lee Wilkins (2008). *Media Ethics: Issues and Cases*, 6th ed. Boston: McGraw Hill, 2008.

Plaisance, Patrick L. "The Mass Media as Discursive Network: Building on the Implications of Libertarian and Communitarian Claims for News Media Ethics Theory." *Communication Theory 15*, no. 3 (2005): 292–313.

Powell, Robert A. "Sex Scandals, Stadium Sponsors, and National TV." Slate.com (14 September 2007). Available from: <http://www.slate.com/id/2173804> (accessed 14 April 2008).

Prisbell, Eric, and Steve Yanda. "Shoe Company Ties with Maryland, Link to Top Recruit Raise Questions." *The Washington Post* (March 1, 2009): D1.

Quart, Alyssa. "Girls and Boys, Interrupted." *The New York Times* (2 October 2006). <http://www.nytimes.com/2006/10/02/opinion/02quart.html?n=Top/Reference/Times%20Topics/Subjects/L/Little%20League> (accessed August 29, 2008).

Rangel, Enrique. "HS Athletes Pass Steroids Test." *Lubbock Avalanche-Journal* (19 June 2009). <http://www.lubbockonline.com/stories/061908/loc_292671263.shtml> (accessed August 29, 2008).

Rich, Charles. "Yahoo! Wants to Get Closer to Teenage Boys." FanHouse (13 April 2007). <http://www.fanhouse.com/2007/04/13/yahoo-wants-to-get-closer-to-teenage-boys/> (accessed August 29, 2008).

Robinson, Joshua. "Proliferation of High School Polls Spurs Subjective Debate." *The New York Times* (5 December 2007). <http://www.nytimes.com/2007/12/05/sports/05preps.html?_r=1&ref=sports&oref=slogin> (accessed April 5, 2008).

Shelton, Don, in discussion with coauthor Hardin. July 8, 2008.

Smith, Hillary, e-mail correspondence to coauthor Hardin, 21 June 2008.

Solomon, George. "Playing Favorites: Viewers Question Game Choices." ESPN.com (31 Aug. 2006). <http://sports.espn.go.com/espn/columns/story?columnist=solomon_george&id=2566936> (accessed August 27, 2008).

Torpey-Kemph, Anne. "Inside Media." *MediaWeek* no. 44 (1999): 38–39.

Weiner, Jay. "Reporting on the Business of Sports." In *Real Sports Reporting*, edited by Abraham Aamidor. Bloomington: Indiana University Press, 2003, 214–224.

Wilson, Duff. "School That Gave Easy Grades to Athletes Is Closing." *The New York Times* (24 December 2005). <http://www.nytimes.com/2005/12/24/sports/ncaafootball/24schools.html> (accessed August 29, 2008).

CHAPTER 5

The Diaper Demographic: Viewing Very Young Children as an Economically Viable Market

Erin L. Ryan *and* Keisha L. Hoerrner

The data over the past 25 years have shown, and continue to show, that enhancing consumerism in children, tweens, and teens causes harm.[1]

One has only to walk through the various children's sections of a major store to see how popular children's programs become strong franchises for marketing a vast array of products.[2]

Over the past two decades, we've seen corporate America targeting a younger and younger audience. In a country where roughly $2.5 billion is spent annually on advertising to children,[3] popular press articles and academic journals alike report outrage over children being inundated by advertisements for junk food on television, being targeted by online marketers procuring their personal information and generally being turned into little consumers. However, a newer, and potentially more dangerous, corporate trend has arisen, aiming entertainment programming toward infants to gain customer loyalty literally "from cradle to grave." Babies and toddlers under the age of two are being singled out as a key demographic: the diaper demographic. Media companies such as Disney's Baby Einstein quickly learned how to capitalize on this demographic in the mid–1990s, and the trend is steadily growing.

What is perhaps most disturbing to experts is that very young children should not be exposed to media at all — not even "educational" content. The American Academy of Pediatrics has recommended that children under the age of two avoid "screen time" completely. The report states that "although certain television programs may be promoted to this age group, research on early brain development shows that babies and toddlers have a critical need for direct interactions with parents ... for healthy brain growth and the development of appropriate social, emotional, and cognitive skills."[4] Creators of children's television have ignored this recommendation, creating such infant- and toddler-geared programs as *Teletubbies*— even partnering with Burger King to create "Teletubby-shaped" chicken nuggets.[5] Another group of media producers— Baby Einstein, Brainy Baby, Nickelodeon, and even Sesame Workshop — has capitalized on this diaper demographic by creating a highly lucrative infant DVD market. In a 2004 study by Sophia Pierroutsakos and her colleagues, parents reported owning on average more than six infant videos or DVDs.[6] This "baby video" phenomenon has been so successful that it has spawned two 24-hour cable networks devoted exclusively to babies: BabyFirstTV and Baby TV.

The primary goal of this chapter is to investigate the ethics of using entertainment to turn children into "life-long consumers" beginning in infancy. From a purely economic standpoint, this diaper demographic is a key market, full of consumers who can easily recognize brands by preschool.[7] With the help of child psychologists and other childhood experts, media executives and advertisers are trying to become part of the very fabric of children's lives. After presenting some background on very young children and electronic media, this chapter will focus on the ethical implications of targeting these children, even with such seemingly educational media products as Baby Einstein videos and the television series *Dora the Explorer*, via three classical ethical standpoints: Kant's Categorical Imperative, Rawls' Veil of Ignorance, and Mill's Utilitarianism.

Babies, Toddlers, and Electronic Media

Research outlining the sheer number of hours under-twos spend in front of the small screen clearly demonstrates that parents are ignoring the advice of the American Academy of Pediatrics. A study by the Kaiser Family Foundation revealed that very young children are watching more television than they did ten years ago: Infants younger than one now watch an average of 1 hour 8 minutes per day; one-year-olds watch 1 hour 26 minutes; and two-year-olds watch 1 hour 35 minutes.[8] Laura Certain and Robert Kahn's study of infant viewing in the 1990s revealed that, of infants zero to 11 months, 83 percent watched *no television* at all; 52 percent of 12- to 24-month-olds watched no television.[9] In just a few short years, these corresponding "no viewing" numbers dropped to 48 percent of infants under age one, 40 percent of one-year-olds, and 29 percent of two-year olds.[10] In 2007 Frederick

Zimmerman and colleagues found that by age three months, 40 percent of children regularly watch television, and that figure rose to 90 percent by age two.[11] Certain and Kahn also determined that daily TV viewing increases by an average of one hour per year during the first three years of life.

In addition to television viewing, children two and under are exposed to other commercial screen media. Parents in the Kaiser study reported that 70 percent of their under-twos watched videos or DVDs. In a typical day, these parents reported that 68 percent of children under two used screen media: 59 percent watched television programs, and 42 percent watched videos or DVDs. When asked specifically about baby videos, 27 percent of parents reported owning at least one Baby Einstein video developed for children 18 months old and younger. The researchers also determined that a full 30 percent of children ages zero to three had televisions in their bedrooms. Daniel Anderson and Tiffany Pempek speculated that this increase in time spent with television in the last decade may be due to the introduction of baby videos and television series in the 1990s, which substantially increased the amount of "foreground" television available for very young children.[12]

Little research has been done examining why parents are comfortable putting their very young children in front of the TV screen, but there is speculation that the marketing of some entertainment products as "educational" may lead parents to believe that they are aiding their children's cognitive development.[13] Such companies as Baby Einstein and Brainy Baby have been termed the "Baby Genius Edutainment Complex"; their marketing campaigns intimate that they are providing harmless entertainment for infants with the potential to make them smarter.[14] Alissa Quart explained that this "Complex" promises that children who are exposed to such media in infancy will become high-achieving adults. This brand of "extreme parenting"—pressuring children to succeed even in infancy—reflects the faith that "if babies are exposed to enough stimulating multimedia content ... bright children can be invented."[15]

Most parents seem to think there is no harm in exposing infants to these products. Indeed, one popular press article exclaimed, "With primary colors and classical music, Baby Einstein swallowed my guilt as a new parent for feeling the need to plop my son — every once in a while, just for a little while — in front of a TV screen. It was, after all, *educational*. Look at the title!"[16] Recent research also supports this notion; such "guiltless" screen time assuages parental culpability in the area of potential negative media effects.[17]

However, one common thread running throughout most of the media crafted for babies is that these products are *commercially* based. When parents put a child in front of a Baby Einstein video, for example, the baby may see promotions for other Baby Einstein products, Disney products, and opportunities to purchase the toys used in the video itself—in addition to bright colors and child-centered content. An important ethical issue at hand is that these babies (and even most of their older siblings) have no idea they are being targeted with advertising. In fact, it is not until a child is seven or eight years old that she truly begins to understand the nature of advertising and can distinguish between program and non-program content.[18] In essence, these companies are targeting one of the most vulnerable populations with their ads, while at the same time creating a generation of hyper-brand-conscious children.

Children as an Economic Market

Research illustrates how powerful branding can be to the youngest viewer. Take the case of Old Joe Camel of Camel cigarettes fame. In the early 1990s, researchers examined the impact of the Old Joe advertising campaign with surprising results. One study found that children as young as age *three* could make the association between the character of Old Joe and a pack of cigarettes, and elementary school children were as likely to recognize Old Joe Camel as they were to recognize the Disney Channel logo.[19] A second study found that not only did children recognize Old Joe, but they also found the ads appealing.[20]

Though Old Joe is no longer used in marketing materials, Corporate America took note of how effective he was. Brand recognition and loyalty were possible even at a very young age. Chetan Chaudhari and Milind Marathe explained that targeting kids early and often is a stated marketing goal; the corporate aim is to "establish a situation where kids are exposed to their brand in as many different places as possible throughout the course of the day or the week, or almost anywhere they turn in the course of their daily rituals."[21] Indeed, Baby Einstein all but admits to using this strategy on its DVDs, as founder Julie Aigner-Clark explains:

> Along with our growing line of videos, Baby Einstein can be there all day long, with additional new books, toys, and other products—from play time, to bath time, to travel time, to nap time, Baby Einstein can enrich every part of your baby's life. Look for the whole line of videos and DVDs, CDs, books, discovery cards, toys, and puppets at a store near you, or visit our website at Baby Einstein.com.

The fact is that children's programs are blatant and ubiquitous marketing vehicles in and of themselves.[22] "Captain Kangaroo" Bob Keeshan described this phenomenon well: "Today, there's what I call the 'toy shelf' mentality. Shows are built around dolls and games and characters created as toys. They're really glorified sales tools and, I think, exploitive."[23] In fact, many children's programs in the mid–1980s were based on toys and action figures already in the marketplace, such as G.I. Joe and Strawberry Short-cake,[24] and the practice continues today (think Nintendo's *Pokémon* franchise that began as a video game). Action for Children's Television president Peggy Charon explained, "TV is used to educate children to behave as a market segment, to lobby for products they don't need, to consume instead of save."[25] Because of this practice, "it's preposterous to put children under 2 in front of the TV.... You should wait as long as possible, because once they get into it, it's hard to turn off."[26]

Product licensing is a massive money-making enterprise for children's media. In fact, Karen Raugust of *Publishers Weekly* explained that "licensors plan their licensing and promotional strategies a year and a half before a TV show premieres."[27] Thus, the notion that, for example, a thirty-minute episode of *Dora the Explorer* is essentially a thirty-minute advertisement for *Dora the Explorer* merchandise is not far-fetched. Not even "safe" children's programming on commercial-free public television, such as *Teletubbies* (the only television program created specifically for the under-twos), is exempt from this practice. As William Brown noted, "The granting of licenses to product manufacturers to merchandise PBS program characters and content is standard operating procedure for almost all PBS children's television programs."[28] Thus, as Brown succinctly stated, "Being a consumer is at the heart of children's television programming."[29]

Although viewing *babies* as consumers is a relatively new phenomenon, it appears to be just the latest in a series of niche markets created from the broader group that the Federal Communications Commission defines as "children," such as preschoolers, elementary school-aged children, and teens. Following the economic success of firms producing games, toys, and mediated entertainment aimed at the preschool market (think any Playhouse Disney show and its accompanying merchandise), it was only a matter of time before companies began to "discover" the under-two crowd, thus commodifying babyhood.[30] As Clare Dowdy noted:

> The continued commercialization of so many elements of life means that in recent times, branding skills have been extended into hitherto untouched sectors ... [and] whole sectors have been put through the positioning and branding mill in a way that would have been unthinkable ten or 20 years ago.[31]

Patrick Hughes argued that the "baby market" is the "creation of international capital in search of new sites at which to create profits by creating commodities."[32] Hughes explained that this new market has redefined the notion of babyhood, defining babies solely as *learners* whose potential to learn can be harnessed by consuming "educational" electronic media, such as Baby Einstein or Brainy Baby videos.

Although this new baby market is enormously important economically, little has been written about the children themselves. Studies are beginning to show that there may be cause for concern if these young children are exposed to too much media too early,[33] but virtually no work has been done to assess how the commodification of babyhood shapes the children themselves, their outlook on material goods, and their psychological well-being. Branding not only sells products, but also shapes viewpoints, values, and conceptions about the world and how to behave in it.[34] So when entertainment programming becomes a tool for branding campaigns targeted at babies and toddlers—who are too young to even understand the very nature of television itself,[35] let alone the content found on it — there is reason to perform an ethical audit.

Ethical Principles and the Diaper Demographic

If by virtue of classifying babies as a demographic, corporations have found a new method of fostering a generation of materialistic, self-indulgent, and brand-obsessed adults, can it possibly be ethical to continue this practice? According to three classic ethical principles, the answer is decidedly no.

Kant's Categorical Imperative

Immanuel Kant's ethical framework, the Categorical Imperative, offers a stark rebuke to those who view children as a marketing demographic. This is because Kant's ethical theory focuses neither on the possible consequences of the proposed action nor on the context within which the action occurs. Instead, Kant's ethical framework is concerned with the *universal* application of the action.

According to Canadian philosopher James Scott Johnston, the basic explanation of Kant's Categorical Imperative is found in the following statement: "The highest capacity of a rational being, the capacity for self-legislation, was the possibility for all moral law."[36] The expression of this self-legislation is, in Kant's words, "...I ought never to act except in such a way that I could also will that my maxim should become universal law."[37] When faced with an ethical dilemma, one should act only from a rationale that one could comfortably make into a universal moral law. An imperative is a moral law that applies equally to all. Through the development of what Kant called the Formula of Universal Law, he made it clear that autonomy must always be respected: "So act that you use humanity, whether in your own person or in the person of any other always at the same time as an end, never as a means."[38]

Many philosophers use Kant's antagonism toward lying as an example of the Categorical Imperative. Both children and adults in today's society seem to view lying as an action on a continuum. There are what we term "little white lies" at one end and large, destructive fabrications on the other. Many choose whether to lie or tell the truth based on where the statement falls on the continuum. Some lies are not harmful, they say, while others will cause great harm. Kant saw all lying as morally wrong because he said it not only corrupted the one who told the lie, but it also prohibited others from making rational choices, thus harming both their dignity as humans and their autonomy.[39] Kant's suggested solution was to ignore the possible consequences of the lie (i.e., I might hurt her feelings by telling her the truth, so I will lie instead) and focus instead on the universal moral law implied by one's approval of a lie (i.e., Would I approve of everyone else lying in a similar situation?). Humanity will be compromised by lying; therefore, lying should be avoided in all instances. Philosophers who adhere to Kant's deontological framework have faced criticism for its failure to recognize the possibility of conflicting maxims, such as the famous example of whether to lie to a Nazi officer to save the lives of a Jewish family being hidden in the attic. Kantians have argued for the expansion of his framework. When two "grounds of obligation,"[40] as James Johnston put it, are in conflict with one another (such as telling a lie to save someone's life), the stronger one should prevail (making lying morally right in this limited instance).

Kant believed in individual autonomy and moral egalitarianism. As Patricia Kitcher noted, Kant wrote about how those two concepts helped to create a "moral world"—"a world ... [of] rational beings ... [in which] their free choice under moral laws has thoroughgoing systematic unity in itself as well as with the freedom of everyone else."[41] The issues of "free choice" and "freedom" lend themselves to a discussion of very young children being exposed to media messages designed to attract their attention. Do they have free choice in attending to those messages? If they are not capable of cognitively understanding the messages, do they share the same freedoms as older children or adults—those who can change the message, tune out the message, or simply walk away? Are they free to choose which Baby Einstein video or television program they want to watch or whether to watch television at all? These questions must be considered when deciding whether entertainment media should target young children. If the children's autonomy is not being respected, they are simply being used as a means to increase a corporation's consumer base, promote brand recognition, or pad the production company's bottom line. If there is no opportunity for significant choice and no logical reason for children to consent to media exposure (if they could), Kantian ethics would mandate a moral ban on all targeting of the "diaper demographic" through entertainment.

Juli Kramer noted that a group of psychologists petitioned the American Psychological Association (APA) in 1999 to denounce "'use of psychology to exploit and influence children for commercial purposes'" because they felt it was "inherently unethical."[42] The APA did not amend its Code of Ethics to prohibit this action, but the controversy speaks to the relevance of Kantian ethical standards in the debate. Children being "exploited" are children being used merely as a means, denied their autonomy, and deprived of their freedoms. Even when viewing parents as "proxies" making decisions on children's behalf, Kant's Categorical Imperative seems to argue that there is a lack of rational choice. Television programmers and video producers market their products to parents as positive, educational enhancements to their children's development. Given the fact that a majority of parents do not read scholarly journal articles questioning the validity of those claims, the producers and marketers have quite an advantage. They can manipulate parents' desire to do what is best for their children by creating marketing messages that promote the educational benefits of "screen time" for infants despite research indicating that such exposure is actually harmful.[43] Kant's Categorical Imperative cannot accept that form of deceit as a universal maxim.

Kant's ethical framework makes the question of using very young children as a target market for media messages an open-and-shut case. The question, then, is whether other ethical frameworks might lead those embroiled in the debate to a different conclusion.

Rawls' Veil of Ignorance

Political philosopher John Rawls detailed an ethical framework in his 1971 book *A Theory of Justice* that could also be used to determine whether the practice of marketing to very young children is just. Rawls argued that two criteria constitute a just society: (1) basic liberties should be both expansive and equal for all, and (2) any inequality in the distribution of wealth and income must be necessary to benefit the least well off. Much of Rawls' theory is quite hypothetical in nature, because the idea is to start at the ideal "original position" to develop a just society.[44] It is also more of a societal, macro-level framework than either Kant's Categorical Imperative or Mill's utilitarianism. Hilde Bojer explained the original position of the social contract this way:

> Rawls' social contract is the hypothetical one that free and equal human beings would unanimously agree should "regulate the basic institutional arrangements" of society if they were able to overcome the prejudices and self-interest that arise from knowing what is to their own immediate advantage or disadvantage.[45]

Rawls' framework forces those in society to distance themselves from their own perspectives, from looking inward at only what is beneficial to them and those they care about, to a broader perspective of what actually makes a "just society."[46] That is why Rawls proposes going behind a hypothetical "veil of ignorance" that masks the participants' standing in society. When one is thinking behind the veil, one no longer knows his/her race, age, ethnicity, socioeconomic status, profession, standing within the community, or any other self-identifier that might lead people to say, "This is the correct decision" when what they are really saying is, "This is what is most likely to benefit me." As Bojer explained, "From behind this thick veil of ignorance, the contracting parties are to decide upon what the just distribution of goods and burdens should be in a society they themselves would want to live in."[47] Essentially, Rawls' theory ensures that those most vulnerable in a society will be protected because we would want such protection for ourselves should we turn out to be the most vulnerable after emerging from behind the veil of ignorance.

When Rawls' framework is applied to a specific societal issue, such as using infants as a target market for media messages, the same "veil of ignorance" should be employed metaphorically to ensure that those most vulnerable are protected during the decision-making process. From the vantage point of a copywriter, one might rationalize that marketing to young children is not really exploitive. Would going under the veil and looking at the issue from a very different perspective change one's decision? What if the copywriter were one of the children? Would he still hold to the belief that targeting young children was just? There seems to be little doubt that young children are extremely vulnerable to manipulation and even coercion. What if she were one of the parents? Would she then be concerned about the degree to which her child understood what he was watching?

Now let's change the issue. What happens when the concern is whether all children should have the opportunity to benefit from "educational" videos, such as Baby Einstein, or from targeted television, such as *Blue's Clues* or *Thomas the Tank Engine*? Under the veil are the families who can afford the videos (and, probably, the accompanying toys and games) and those who cannot. Also under the veil are the producers/creators, educators, legislators, toy manufacturers, and more. Which group is most vulnerable — all young children or a subset of them? Are those exposed to the media messages more vulnerable (after all, it's not clear that children actually benefit from these products) or those who cannot access the media messages?

Rawls does not help us unpack these ethical dilemmas because he actually spent little time writing about families, women, and children.[48] His determination to promote ethical decision-making from a vantage point of "mutual disinterest" is key, however, to looking at the issue of developing entertainment programs for the youngest members of society and using these media to market consumer products to them. The veil is an effective tool for looking beyond ourselves and thinking about the ramifications of society's institutions and practices for all involved, including the most vulnerable.

Mill's Utilitarianism

The third ethical framework we will explore is utilitarianism, a form of consequentialism that focuses on two major concepts: the consequences of the proposed action (or inaction) and maximizing the good. Seemingly opposite of Kant's deontological ethics, utilitarianism is concerned with context and the impact of one's decisions. It is not concerned with a rigid set of universal maxims.[49]

Andrew Stables summed up the basis of utilitarianism nicely: "Utilitarianism, as developed by Jeremy Bentham in the late 18th century, essentially posits that the rightness of an action is determined by its effect on the overall sum of human happiness."[50] Scholars have consistently noted that Bentham focused on two competing intrinsic values: pleasure and pain. He believed ethical decisions should maximize pleasure while minimizing pain for the greatest number of individuals. Bentham's followers, specifically John Stuart Mill, enhanced utilitarianism by substituting happiness for pleasure as the ultimate good. Thus, the summary explanation of utilitarianism is "the greatest good for the greatest number."[51] There are two primary forms of utilitarianism: rule utilitarianism and act utilitarianism. The former focuses on the development of general rules that, when followed, should lead to the best consequences for the greatest number of individuals involved. The latter treats each ethical decision independently and strives to make ethical decisions that promote the greater good in that specific situation.

When faced with an ethical dilemma, a utilitarian who adheres to act utilitarianism would consider the agents (individuals or groups) involved, the possible actions or inactions available, and the possible results, or consequences, of those actions. Thus, consequences and context (which will affect how consequences are weighed) are the determinants of ethical actions. A rule utilitarian would judge an action right or wrong based upon generally accepted rules within the relevant community. According to philosopher Thomas E. Hill, Jr., "The rules are taken to be public, teachable, socially reinforced rules that should be internalized by all."[52]

How would a utilitarian approach the ethical dilemma of targeting the newborn-to-two group as a consumer market for media entertainment? Either version of the framework reaches a similar conclusion.

Let's use the educational program *Teletubbies* as an example. What benefits are reaped from this TV show and by whom? Arguably, if scientific research revealed that these videos/shows stimulated cognitive development, promoted language skills, enhanced critical thinking, or improved educational performance, the consequences of placing children in front of them would change dramatically. Without that research data, what are the consequences? There's research, however, that notes harm to young children who watch the show. Marina Krcmar, Bernard Grela, and Kirsten Lin's study explored the role of *Teletubbies* in language acquisition, finding that toddlers and preverbal infants learn vocabulary from live adult speakers to a greater degree than they learn from the show.[53] Kimberly Powell and Lori Abels found that *Teletubbies* promoted sex-roles stereotypes to a preschool audience.[54] These are just illustrations of the research questioning the supposed educational and social benefits of these shows. The negative consequences, according to act utilitarianism, clearly outweigh the proposed good of TV producers enjoying the success of a show or parents who need a break. Thus, the utilitarian, while rather distinct in the process he uses to make the determination, reaches the same ethical conclusion as the Kantian ethicist or an adherent to Rawls' theory.

A rule utilitarian would reach the same conclusion. Think of the number of socially reinforced rules regarding children. Think of the number of rules and regulations that have been mandated by Congress and the Federal Communications Commission to protect children, whom they regard as a "vulnerable population," from harm that may result from radio and television programming. Even the media industries themselves seem to agree with the need to protect children from certain programming. The Motion Picture Association of America voluntarily developed the movie rating system to ensure that children were protected from — and parents were informed about — inappropriate content. The television industry voluntarily developed a ratings system in the 1990s to do the same. Therefore, the protection of children from harm caused by entertainment content is one of the rules that a utilitarian would use to judge the "rightness" or "wrongness" of using infants and toddlers as a target market. It would belabor the point to do anything other than conclude that the same research used by an act utilitarian to argue against very young children watching *Teletubbies* would also lead a rule utilitarian to argue against the gamut of programming directed at this audience.

Ethical Conclusions

Marketing aimed at children in their earliest days and months commodifies babyhood in a way never before seen. Infancy is no longer just an innocent time of play, baby talk, and wide-eyed wonder, but also another "market." The marketing strategies of the Baby Genius Edutainment Complex seem to skew ethicists' notion of an infant's inherent worth; she's only a "baby of worth" if she's sporting name brands or learning by leaps and bounds from "educational" videos at three months old. And parents appear to have bought this marketing ploy hook, line, and sinker. They include Baby Einstein videos, for example, as an essential component of a diaper bag and list them as "must haves" on baby shower registries.[55] If the parents are buying into the marketers' message, the babies are not far behind. As Patricia Holland explained, even as babies begin to notice the world around them, "commerce is already working to direct the baby's gaze beyond its parents towards the world of consumer goods."[56] Regardless of the ethical decision-making framework employed, this practice does not seem just. And then what do the parents and society have to look forward to as a result of these trends? Children (and then adults) steeped in a culture of materialism, self-indulgence, and instant gratification. Research revealing that highly materialistic children are unhappy, depressed, and report low self-esteem and symptoms of anxiety — while at the same time reporting less generosity and charity[57] — surely raises a red flag. These long-term results only further the need to protect children from those in the entertainment industry who seek to exploit them.

We are not arguing that newborns to toddlers are capable of resolving their own ethical dilemmas using any of the three approaches we have summarized. Researchers are quite clear regarding children's inability to develop universal maxims, think logically through consequences, or view a situation from multiple perspectives.[58] They are equally clear on cognitive and emotional development required for this level of thinking.[59] Instead, we are obviously focused on the adults who are engaging in the practice of marketing *to* the "diaper demographic." They are capable of using any of the three ethical frameworks — the Categorical Imperative, the Veil of Ignorance, or Utilitarianism — and reaching a consistent conclusion: It is unethical to market to young children who cannot choose which messages they see/hear, are not capable of fully understanding the messages, and cannot remove themselves from the environment if they wish to avoid the messages. The youngest members of our society must be protected by adults — parents, educators, policymakers, and industry representatives — because they are incapable of protecting themselves and because the overall harms of continuing to market entertainment to the "diaper demographic" outweigh the benefits.

NOTES

1. Juli B. Kramer, "Ethical Analysis and Recommended Action in Response to the Dangers Associated with Youth Consumerism," *Ethics and Behavior* 16 (2006): 293.

2. Susan T. Eastman and Douglas A. Ferguson, *Media Programming: Strategies and Practices* (Belmont, CA: Thomson Wadsworth, 2006), 177.

3. Chetan C. Chaudhari and Milind M. Marathe, "Marketing to Children — Issues & Remedies," *Conference proceedings of the International Conference on Marketing and Society*, http://dspace.iimk.ac.in/bitstream/2259/323/1/613–626.pdf (accessed June 21, 2008).

4. American Academy of Pediatrics, "Media Education," *Pediatrics* 104 (1999): 342.

5. Chaudhari and Marathe, "Marketing to Children," 618.

6. Sophia L. Pierroutsakos, Moira M. Hanna, Jennifer A. Self, E. Nicole Lewis, and C. Jamison Brewer, "Baby Einsteins Everywhere: The Amount and Nature of Television and

Video Viewing of Infants Birth to 2 Years" (paper presented at the Biennial International Conference for Infant Studies, Chicago, 2004).

7. Paul M. Fischer, Meyer P. Schwartz, John W. Richards, Adam O. Goldstein, and Tina H. Rojas, "Brand Logo Recognition by Children Aged 3 to 6 Years," *Journal of the American Medical Association* 266 (1991): 3145–3148.

8. Victoria J. Rideout, Elizabeth A. Vandewater, and Ellen A. Wartella, *Zero to Six: Electronic Media in the Lives of Infants, Toddlers, and Preschoolers* (Menlo Park, CA: Kaiser Family Foundation, 2003): 5.

9. Laura K. Certain, and Robert S. Kahn, "Prevalence, Correlates, and Trajectory of Television Viewing Among Infants and Toddlers," *Pediatrics* 109 (2003): 634–642.

10. Rideout, Vandewater and Wartella, *Zero to Six*, 5.

11. Frederick J. Zimmerman, Dimitri A. Christakis, and Andrew N. Meltzoff, "Television and DVD/Video Viewing in Children Younger Than 2 Years," *Archives of Pediatric and Adolescent Medicine* 161 (2007): 473–479.

12. Daniel R. Anderson and Tiffany A. Pempek, "Television and Very Young Children," *American Behavioral Scientist* 48 (2005): 505–522.

13. Erin L. Ryan, *Is Your Baby a* Brainy Baby? *Learning from "Educational" Infant DVD Program Content by 12- to 24-Month-Olds* (Ph.D. dissertation, University of Georgia, 2008), 106.

14. Alissa Quart, "Extreme Parenting: Does the Baby Genius Edutainment Complex Enrich Your Child's Mind — Or Stifle It?" *Atlantic Monthly,* July/August 2006, 110–115.

15. *Ibid.*, 110.

16. Elisa Cramer, "Chew Over This One, Parents," *The Palm Beach Post,* August 10, 2007, http://www.palmbeachpost.com/opinion/content /opinion/epaper/2007/08/10/a10a_elisacol_0810.html. Accessed July 7, 2008.

17. Ryan, *Is Your Baby a* Brainy Baby? 11.

18. Victor C. Strasburger and Barbara J. Wilson, *Children, Adolescents & the Media* (Thousand Oaks, CA: Sage, 2002), 47.

19. Fischer, Schwartz, Richards, Goldstein and Rojas, "Brand Logo Recognition," 3147.

20. Joseph R. DiFranza, John W. Richards, Paul M. Paulman, Nancy Wolf-Gillespie, Christopher Fletcher, Robert D. Jaffe, and David Murray, "RJR Nabisco's Cartoon Camel Promotes Camel Cigarettes to Children," *Journal of the American Medical Association* 266 (1991): 3149–3153.

21. Chaudhari and Marathe, "Marketing to Children," 617.

22. William S. Brown, "Ethics and the Business of Children's Public Television Programming," *Teaching Business Ethics* 6.1 (2002): 74.

23. Cited in Barbara Vancheri, "TV Pioneers Kvetch," *Pittsburgh Post Gazette,* November 30, 1993: C-6.

24. Peggy Charon, "Commercialization of Children's Television" (testimony in hearings before the Committee on Energy and Commerce, U.S. House of Representatives, September 15, 1987), 23–24.

25. Peggy Charon, "What's Missing in Children's TV," *World Monitor,* December 1990, 32.

26. Quoted in David Bauder, "Kid TV Show Maker Disputes Pediatrician's Advice," *New Orleans Times-Picayune,* August 5, 1999, A-9.

27. Karen Raugust, "Licensing for the Ages," *Publishers Weekly,* May 17, 1999, 30–31.

28. Brown, "Ethics and the Business," 77.

29. *Ibid.*, 76.

30. Patrick Hughes, "Baby, It's You: International Capital Discovers the Under Threes," *Contemporary Issues in Early Childhood,* 6 (2005): 30–40.

31. Clare Dowdy, *Beyond Logos: New Definitions of Corporate Identity* (London: RotoVision, 2003), 7.

32. Hughes, "Baby, It's You," 31.

33. See Anderson and Pempek, "Television and Very Young Children." Anderson and

Pempek outlined research linking television viewing with deficits in language, the development and maintenance of attention disorders, and negative impacts on cognitive development, among other negative factors.

34. Chaudhari and Marathe, "Marketing to Children," 616.

35. Anderson and Pempek, "Television and Very Young Children," 511.

36. James S. Johnston, "The Education of the Categorical Imperative," *Studies in Philosophy and Education* 25 (2006): 387.

37. *Ibid.*

38. As quoted in Judith Bessant, "Principles for Developing Youth Policy: Kant's Categorical Imperative and Developmental Ethics," *Policy Studies* 26 (2005): 108.

39. Tim C. Mazur, "Lying," *Issues in Ethics* 6 (1993), http://www.scu.edu/ethics /publications/iie/v6n1/lying.html (accessed July 8, 2008).

40. Johnston, "The Education of the Categorical Imperative,": 388.

41. Patricia Kitcher, "Kant's Argument for the Categorical Imperative," *NOUS* 38 (2004): 580.

42. Kramer, "Ethical Analysis and Recommended Action," 292.

43. See the Federal Trade Commission complaint levied against the Baby Einstein Company, the Brainy Baby Company, and BabyTV by the Campaign for a Commercial Free Childhood at http://www.commercialexploitation.org/babyvideos/ftccomplaint.htm.

44. Stanford Encyclopedia of Philosophy, "Original Position," (2003): http://plato.stanford. edu/entries/original-position/.

45. Hilde Bojer, "Children and Theories of Social Justice," *Feminist Economics* 6 (2000): 31.

46. *Ibid.*

47. *Ibid.*

48. *Ibid.*

49. John Stuart Mill, "Utilitarianism," (1859): http://www.utilitarianism.com/mill1.htm (accessed June 28, 2008).

50. Andrew Stables, "Responsibility Beyond Rationality: The Case for Rhizomatic Consequentialism," *International Journal of Children's Spirituality* 9: 222.

51. Internet Encyclopedia of Philosophy, "Jeremy Bentham," http://www.utm.edu/research/iep/b/bentham.htm. Accessed July 17, 2008.; Lawrence M. Hinman, *Ethics: A Pluralistic Approach to Moral Theory, 3rd ed.* (Belmont, CA: Wadsworth, 2003), 165.

52. Thomas E. Hill, Jr., "Assessing Moral Rules: Utilitarian and Kantian Perspectives," *Philosophical Issues* 15 (2005): 162.

53. Marina Krcmar, Bernard Grela, and Kirsten Lin, "Can Toddlers Learn Vocabulary from Television? An Experimental Approach," *Media Psychology* 10 (2007).

54. Kimberly A. Powell and Lori Abels, "Sex-Role Stereotypes in TV Programs Aimed at the Preschool Audience: An Analysis of *Teletubbies* and *Barney & Friends*," *Women and Language* 25: 14.

55. Ryan, *Is Your Baby a* Brainy Baby? 105.

56. Patricia Holland, *Picturing Childhood: The Myth of the Child in Popular Imagery* (London: I.B. Tauris, 2004), 45.

57. Julie B. Schor, *Born to Buy: The Commercialized Child and the New Consumer Culture* (New York: Scribner, 2004), 167.

58. Stables, "Responsibility Beyond Rationality," 221.

59. See, for example, work on theory of mind in John H. Flavell, "Theory of Mind Development: Retrospect and Prospect," *Merrill-Palmer Quarterly* 50 (2004): 274–290.

WORKS CITED

American Academy of Pediatrics. "Media Education." *Pediatrics* 104 (1999): 342.

Anderson, Daniel R., and Tiffany A. Pempek. "Television and Very Young Children." *American Behavioral Scientist* 48 (2005): 505–522.

Bauder, David. "Kid TV Show Maker Disputes Pediatrician's Advice." *New Orleans Times-Picayune,* August 5, 1999, A-9.

Bessant, Judith. "Principles for Developing Youth Policy: Kant's Categorical Imperative and Developmental Ethics." *Policy Studies* 26 (2005): 108.

Bojer, Hilde. "Children and Theories of Social Justice." *Feminist Economics* 6 (2000): 31.

Brown, William S. "Ethics and the Business of Children's Public Television Programming." *Teaching Business Ethics* 6.1 (2002): 74.

Certain, Laura K., and Robert S. Kahn. "Prevalence, Correlates, and Trajectory of Television Viewing Among Infants and Toddlers." *Pediatrics* 109 (2003): 634–642.

Charon, Peggy. "Commercialization of Children's Television" (testimony in hearings before the Committee on Energy and Commerce, U.S. House of Representatives, September 15, 1987), 23–24.

_____. "What's Missing in Children's TV," *World Monitor,* December 1990, 32.

Chaudhari, Chetan C., and Milind M. Marathe. "Marketing to Children — Issues & Remedies," *Conference proceedings of the International Conference on Marketing and Society,* http://dspace.iimk.ac.in/bitstream/2259/323/1/613-626.pdf.

DiFranza, Joseph R., John W. Richards, Paul M. Paulman, Nancy Wolf-Gillespie, Christopher Fletcher, Robert D. Jaffe, and David Murray. "RJR Nabisco's Cartoon Camel Promotes Camel Cigarettes to Children," *Journal of the American Medical Association* 266 (1991): 3149–3153.

Dowdy, Clare. *Beyond Logos: New Definitions of Corporate Identity.* London: RotoVision, 2003.

Eastman, Susan T., and Douglas A Ferguson. *Media Programming: Strategies and Practices* Belmont, CA: Thomson Wadsworth, 2006.

Fischer, Paul M., Meyer P. Schwartz, John W. Richards, Adam O. Goldstein, and Tina H. Rojas. "Brand Logo Recognition by Children Aged 3 to 6 Years," *Journal of the American Medical Association* 266 (1991): 3145–3148.

Flavell, John H. "Theory of Mind Development: Retrospect and Prospect," *Merrill-Palmer Quarterly* 50 (2004): 274–290.

Hill, Thomas E., Jr., "Assessing Moral Rules: Utilitarian and Kantian Perspectives." *Philosophical Issues* 15 (2005): 162.

Holland, Patricia. *Picturing Childhood: The Myth of the Child in Popular Imagery.* London: I.B. Tauris, 2004.

Hughes, Patrick. "Baby, It's You: International Capital Discovers the Under Threes." *Contemporary Issues in Early Childhood* 6 (2005): 30–40.

Johnston, James S. "The Education of the Categorical Imperative." *Studies in Philosophy and Education* 25 (2006): 387.

Kitcher, Patricia. "Kant's Argument for the Categorical Imperative." *NOUS* 38 (2004): 580.

Kramer, Juli B. "Ethical Analysis and Recommended Action in Response to the Dangers Associated with Youth Consumerism." *Ethics and Behavior* 16 (2006): 293.

Mazur, Tim C. "Lying," *Issues in Ethics* 6 (1993), http://www.scu.edu/ethics/publications/iie/v6n1/lying.html.

Mill, John Stuart. "Utilitarianism" (1859): http://www.utilitarianism.com/mill1.htm.

Pierroutsakos, Sophia L., Moira M. Hanna, Jennifer A. Self, E. Nicole Lewis, and C. Jamison Brewer. "Baby Einsteins Everywhere: The Amount and Nature of Television and Video Viewing of Infants Birth to 2 Years." Paper presented at the Biennial International Conference for Infant Studies, Chicago, 2004.

Powell, Kimberly A., and Lori Abels. "Sex-Role Stereotypes in TV Programs Aimed at the Preschool Audience: An Analysis of *Teletubbies* and *Barney & Friends.*" *Women and Language* 25: 14.

Quart, Alissa. "Extreme Parenting: Does the Baby Genius Edutainment Complex Enrich Your Child's Mind — Or Stifle It?" *Atlantic Monthly,* July/August 2006, 110–115.

Raugust, Karen. "Licensing for the Ages." *Publishers Weekly,* May 17, 1999, 30–31.

Rideout, Victoria J., Elizabeth A. Vandewater, and Ellen A. Wartella. *Zero to Six: Electronic*

Media in the Lives of Infants, Toddlers, and Preschoolers. Menlo Park, CA: Kaiser Family Foundation, 2003, 5.

Ryan, Erin L. *Is Your Baby a* Brainy Baby? *Learning from "Educational" Infant DVD Program Content by 12- to 24-Month-Olds.* Ph.D. dissertation, University of Georgia, 2008, 106.

Schor, Julie B. *Born to Buy: The Commercialized Child and the New Consumer Culture.* New York: Scribner, 2004.

Stables, Andrew. "Responsibility Beyond Rationality: The Case for Rhizomatic Consequentialism." *International Journal of Children's Spirituality* 9: 222.

Stanford Encyclopedia of Philosophy, "Original Position," (2003): http://plato.stanford.edu/entries/original-position/.

Strasburger, Victor C., and Barbara J. Wilson. *Children, Adolescents & the Media.* Thousand Oaks, CA: Sage, 2002.

Vancheri, Barbara. "TV Pioneers Kvetch," *Pittsburgh Post Gazette,* November 30, 1993: C-6.

Zimmerman, Frederick J., Dimitri A. Christakis, and Andrew N. Meltzoff. "Television and DVD/Video Viewing in Children Younger Than 2 Years." *Archives of Pediatric and Adolescent Medicine* 161 (2007): 473–479.

CHAPTER 6

Superbad: A Twisted and Touching Ethical Mess of a Movie

Joseph C. Harry

Released in late summer 2007, the teen comedy movie *Superbad* centers on three middle-class, foul-mouthed, sex-obsessed 17-year-old nerds on a singular mission — to lose their virginity before they graduate from high school and head for college. *Superbad* — which a *Boston Globe* columnist called "spectacularly vulgar"[1] — pushed crass verbal descriptions of sex and other bodily acts to new highs, or lows, for a teen-focused film (though, ironically, not *depictions* — no private parts are ever really seen). Nevertheless, the R-rated movie proved a phenomenal commercial success, raking in more than $120 million in ticket sales within just a few weeks of its release while costing less than $20 million to produce. And it was greeted with near unanimous critical approval. The consensus among movie critics was that the film craftily mixed the most unvarnished gross-out language and sexually based humor with a dramatically compelling, emotionally touching, and even poignant coming-of-age comedy-drama.

This chapter explores how *Superbad* achieves an ethical stance by casting the characters' drunken fun and uncommitted sex within an emergent, ever-wider moral perspective of mutually respectful love, trust, and commitment. That it accomplishes this serious purpose within a burlesque of outrageous X-rated humor bordering on parody poses an ethical contradiction for even the most patient media ethicist. How is it that a film reveling in what even the most sympathetic viewer would likely agree are blatantly disgusting themes and language, whose plot is utterly conventional, whose authority figures are either absent or virtually lacking all authority, can also be seen as having moral weight and ethical justification? Adopting a stance of philosophical pragmatism can take us a long way in unraveling this contradiction. After describing the movie's plot and critics' reactions in more detail, I will explain John Dewey's version of pragmatism. which frames my analytical approach. I will then employ this perspective to explore *Superbad's* underlying ethics.

Superbad Meets Teens and Critics

As the *New York Times* said of *Superbad*: "It works because no matter how unapologetically vulgar their words, no matter how single-mindedly priapic their preoccupations, these men and boys are good and decent and tender and true."[2] The *Times* opined that *Superbad* is a "sweetly absurd high school comedy," offering, via the horn-dog exploits of its two teenage male characters, "anguished lessons" alongside a "limitless storehouse of embarrassments."[3] The *New Yorker* magazine saw *Superbad* as "uproarious and touching," combining "desperately filthy talk with the most tender, even delicate, emotion."[4] The movie is "wise and wacko in equal measures," "vulgar but smart," according to *The Toronto Star,* which concluded: "It's got the insider's view of male adolescent pathology nailed, but it also takes the longer perspective offered by a certain amount of 'adult' distance — in the end, it's about the fading of fleeting, unconditional guy/guy friendships."[5] The *Washington Post* said *Superbad* delivers "outrageously raunchy comedy with a self-conscious wink" and revelations that can actually lead to "wisdom" because the underlying story is "humane."[6]

New York's *Daily News* called *Superbad* a "raunchy comedy" that nevertheless "closely reflects the high school experience of a good many real-life Americans,"[7] and the *National Post* of Toronto quipped that the movie "grossed out audiences" while grossing millions at the box office, a success based on what *Superbad* co-writer Seth Rogen told that newspaper is the movie's "dick-to-heart ratio,"[8] indicating Rogen and co-writer Evan Goldberg consciously plotted an emotional path paved over with sexual crudity. As the *National Post* said, "Its characters may be roughspoken, but they're true to their feelings, and their feelings run deep."

Although most movie reviewers summed up *Superbad* as presenting the unvarnished truth of teenage life, warts and all, there was some dissent. The *Boston Globe* viewed *Superbad* as "thoroughly engrossed in a retrograde adolescence that keeps slipping outside teen comedy into the territory of the horror film."[9] London's *Daily Mail* also saw the movie as a long descent into coarseness with little countervailing charm, not to mention being misogynous and demeaning to women — and *also* to men — thus "one of the most depressing films in more than a decade."[10] Still, the majority view was that *Superbad* somehow achieved a rare thing for what might otherwise be just another in a long list of teen sex-romp comedies: an ethically heightened consciousness about friendship, love, and commitment. And not just love and commitment between adolescent girls and boys, but within the perhaps even more emotionally confusing realm of male friendship, what might traditionally be called brotherly love. This latter theme, in the movie's final scenes, eventually bumps somewhat uneasily into a seriocomic contemplation of the inherent unresolved tension between platonic friendship and homoerotic love.

Superbad's surface storyline is about as *un*contemplative as any movie gets. Two of the three main characters, Evan and Fogell (Fogell's fake driver's license conjuring him as a 25-year-old from Hawaii with a single name — *McLovin*) have been accepted to Ivy League Dartmouth, where they will room together. Their friend, Seth, is destined for a comparatively low-status state university. The inevitable parting of ways, the seething envy Seth feels toward Evan and Fogell for getting into Dartmouth, and, even more, the overt jealously Seth feels about Evan and Fogell rooming together, all steadily cohere as a kind of thematic centerpiece. Nevertheless, Evan, Seth, and Fogell's immediate goal is simply to get drunk and get laid during a party later in the evening, hosted by the smart and sassy Jules, with whom Seth wants to have sex. Jules and the teenage girl Evan likes, Becca, want Seth to buy booze for the party, and Jules gives him $100 to do so.

A successful booze purchase, the boys hope, will be the golden ticket to getting the girls into the sack, but the boys' mission is dependent on someone neither Seth nor Evan really likes or respects — the nerdy and hapless Fogell, who's just obtained his fake driver's license. The surface plot does not thicken; it doesn't really trouble itself with such immediate ethical matters as teenage sex, the underage purchase and consumption of alcohol, or the irrelevance of adult authority figures. Nevertheless, *Superbad* does offer a justifiable ethical stance with respect to the main characters' sensational actions and intensely emotional behaviors.

Because film is a highly visual, intensely character-focused storytelling mode, it is "felt, rather than told," creating an "embodied engagement" between actors and viewers that may come closest to humans' "inter-subjective," "evaluative," emotional, experiential responses in everyday life. Unlike a strictly verbal narrative such as a novel, which is a discontinuous experience usually taking days if not weeks to finish, a movie is a relatively short but continuous narrative experience simultaneously "visual, aural, verbal and metaphorical," therefore "similar to the situations encountered in ethical life where the salient details are rarely, if ever, distinctly separated or succinctly spelt out."[11] This account of film-viewing as *felt* experience relies on a notion of the bundled-together continuity of experience very much like that promoted by John Dewey and his most influential pragmatist mentor, William

James. James's *pure experience* of knowledge acquisition consists of one's having a continuous bundle of experiences, some of which can be disentangled and then connected into higher-level understanding for any meaningful purpose — scientific, literary, common-sensical, ethical, or otherwise. Dewey's similar but more aesthetic notion of *primary experience* was that experience inheres in "things" taken primarily as "objects to be treated, used, acted upon and with, enjoyed and endured, even more than things to be known. They are things *had* before they are things cognized."[12] Neither Dewey nor James ever turned their attention toward films. But their focus on raw experience as primary to a higher-order reflective state is valuable in understanding how movies, as experiential narratives, are at least initially felt or *had*, rather than merely told. Movie-viewing is an immediately emotional, evaluative experience much like everyday life, and consequently a valuable tool for pragmatist ethical analysis.

Pragmatism and the Movies

To borrow from John Dewey, *Superbad's* "immediate good" or immediate value — the movie *as* movie — must be seen as a value or experience in and for itself, thus neither good nor bad. Its existent "qualities" are what the early twentieth-century American pragmatist philosopher called surface "effects." As Dewey noted, "Values are values, things immediately having certain intrinsic qualities. Of them as values there is accordingly nothing to be said; they are what they are."[13] But as a "reflective good," we must place the movie into a larger, more humanistic, social, and, thus, ethical context. In this context, we must consider competing personal and social values that give the film's existent qualities a more socially useful meaning by creatively linking these qualities to ethically meaningful consequences.[14] Here it is possible to view *Superbad's* narrative as possessing a sustained moral weight and enduring ethical values despite its constant dip into the sexual gutter.

Of course, there's no such thing as a unitary meaning inherent in any artistic production because art, by its very nature, as Dewey notes, is often purposely opaque, just as much of everyday experience is. This is why Dewey held that everyday experience has an open-ended aesthetic, immediate quality very much like art. His future-oriented, developmental ethics is methodologically based in gradually transforming a *qualitative immediacy* — an immediately "felt," non-cognitive experience — into what he called a *problematic situation*, a more purposeful, reflective *thinking about* an identifiable problem.[15] Still, Dewey's pragmatism, whether applied to a movie or any other object of problematic interest, provides only a methodological point of entry to a given problem deemed worthy of working out.

The ultimate goal of Dewey's pragmatic ethics is contemplation and intelligent reflection directed at creating an ethical personal character within a given social context via an imaginative reflection surrounding available "means" (causes) and prospective "consequences" (effects) of the problematic situation at hand. This method of reflection aims at continual character formation and *re*-formation, resulting in morally meaningful consequences. Dewey considered all serious reflective thought, regardless of its object, as aesthetic, based on imagination and belief toward valued objects and imagined consequences. Pragmatism, as a regulative method, rejects a more restrictive, openly normative Kantian approach that limits ethical value judgments to strict conformity with preordained moral maxims. A discriminating judgment, for Dewey, becomes an act of pragmatic-philosophical criticism "whenever the subject-matter of discrimination concerns goods and values."[16]

Dewey believed that, to truly understand any phenomenon of more than passing interest (including works of art), one must imaginatively attempt to explore it beyond its own inherent value *as* immediate experience by delving into its "effects" or consequences, its "connections with other things...."[17] He offered an apt metaphor for the overall process when he wrote that the intelligent and imaginative thinker *presses forward* in experience, *glances backward*, and finally *looks outward*. He linked this notion to psychologist and fellow pragmatist William James' description of sustained, reflective, socially meaningful thought as similar to the "flights and perchings of a bird."[18] Transposed to the human environment, flights translate into a consideration of important actions, and, perchings, into reflective rest periods in which the act of flying is placed into a more purposeful context regarding its consequences or destination (though this is never conceived entirely as fixed in place). Dewey believed artistic production is a mode of knowledge every bit as important as any other, perhaps the mode most immediately involved in "flights and perchings," because art is characterized by "repose in stimulation."[19]

Dewey's evolutionary philosophy, much influenced by Darwin's evolutionary science, provides a "growth" metaphor for ethical knowing as continual learning[20] "to achieve an integrative way of acting."[21] This aesthetic mode of ethical character development — and, more broadly, of socially significant knowledge generation and "dramatic" assessment[22] — never evolves to some final destination (no final *perching*). Rather, it progresses to more socially significant and secure stopping points along the way. It is also the basis of his pragmatist morals:

> Morals means growth of conduct in meaning: at least it means that kind of expansion in meaning which is consequent upon observations of the conditions and outcome of conduct. It is all one with growing.... The present is complex, containing within itself a multitude of habits and impulses. It is enduring, a course of action, a process including memory, observation and

foresight, a pressure forward, a glance backward, and a look outward. It is of *moral* moment because it marks a transition in the direction of breadth and clarity of action or in that of triviality and confusion.[23]

Within this scheme, which Thomas M. Alexander sees as "the core of Dewey's theory of ethics,"[24] Dewey defined intelligence as imagination, or as Alexander put it, an ability to "see the actual in light of the possible," to "integrate the possibilities of the present by using the organized experience of the past in reconstructing present action. Character realizes its continuity through the moral imagination. In this process it becomes essential to discover new values, especially as older values come into conflict. Thus, character is our moral imagination in action."[25]

To paraphrase Alexander, the character relations that grow and mature in *Superbad* will lead to the characters' eventual discovery of new values as their older, less mature values "come into conflict." Most of the film's characters press forward, glance backward, and finally look outward toward new ethical understanding. In the rest of the chapter, I draw on these insights to explore how *Superbad* deals ethically with the seriocomic presentation of two interrelated notions, which, for simplicity, I will call sex and suds.

Sex and Suds

Seth and Evan's friendship is founded on platonic — and, in a late scene — latent homoerotic love, the latter humorously depicted as a contradictory moral emotion the boys quietly confront but never clearly resolve. By working within the general notions of male heterosexual friendship and homosexual relations, the filmmakers are able to expand our thinking about love within "guy/guy friendships," to use the *Toronto Star*'s phrase. Lacing this hetero/homosexual contrast within ribald humor also provides a comedic pressure valve for the audience, many of whom would be in their early teens or twenties and might otherwise feel uncomfortable contemplating these notions.

The more immediate surface dilemma is Seth's resentment of Evan's getting into Dartmouth and also, as Seth soon discovers, the fact Evan will be rooming with the nerdy loser, Fogell.[26] Seth takes this as Evan "bailing" or abandoning him, not unlike someone being "dumped" by a girlfriend. Evan's growing interest in Becca, whom Seth claims to "hate," is yet another form of rivalry. This interpersonal dilemma comes into focus early on, when Seth admits to Evan that, as a fourth-grader, he was obsessed with drawing pictures of penises. There follows a hilarious flashback in which tubby fourth-grade Seth secretly plies his trade, producing dozens of elaborately drawn penises, but finally getting found out by his classmate Becca. In this early scene, the filmmakers are already building toward the unveiling of this friendship/sexual-relation theme. Now, with Evan's romantic interest in Becca, Seth has even more reason to resent his friend and hate Becca. He's caught up in his own needs and interests, rather than seeing Evan's growing independence and branching out into new relationships. Seth is stuck in the realm of immediate value, which remains a powerful emotion, but not a meaningfully justifiable ethic, without reflection on its consequences.

The problem of not living up to ("bailing on") vital commitments of trust and caring is the major ethical quandary in the movie's middle and later scenes. After Fogell's attempt at buying alcohol has failed, Seth quickly buys into another plan for getting booze, as he and Evan leave behind Fogell, whom Seth also hates and resents. At an adult party they've subsequently managed to get into in an attempt to steal alcohol, Evan runs out the door to escape getting beaten up by drunken partygoers, leaving Seth alone. "You prick — you bailed on me!" Seth yells when the two finally regroup. "You said you were gonna do something and you didn't do it. That's bailing. You bailed on me this morning when Jesse [a high-school thug] spat on me, and you're bailing on me next year. We were supposed to go to college together."

"You make me feel like I'm a bad guy," Evan replies. "I didn't do anything wrong. I got into a good school.... How fucking selfish are you? You had no problem letting Fogell take the fall back there. You obviously don't want me to go to a good school, so what the fuck do you want? I'm not gonna let you slow me down anymore, Seth." "What are you saying?" Seth responds, shocked at his feeling of being dumped. "I've wasted the last three years of my life sitting around talking bullshit with you," Evan explains, "instead of chasing girls and making friends ... and now I'm going to college a friendless virgin."

Seth wonders why his friend is so fixated on Becca. "I *like* her," Evan says defensively, to which Seth retorts, "Who *gives* a fuck, she's a fucking *girl!*" Seth is acting on his immediate relationship to "girls" as simple objects of pleasure, while Evan's desire for higher meaning is founded on his wanting to connect with someone he actually cares about, and also trying to better himself by going to a "good school." We also see Evan's ethical awareness at the guilt he finally feels for leaving Fogell behind to get busted by cops for underage alcohol consumption. Seth is only pressing forward here — he wants to get to the party and "fuck some fucking girls." Evan's pressing forward by glancing backward at the qualities of past actions and attempting to look outward, toward future consequences.

Sex as a Reflective Good

Sex is really the lens through which everything else in the movie is viewed. It manifests itself in two ways: sex as raw pleasure, or an "immediate good"; and sex as expressive of something deeper, a means of engaging in or at least coming to terms with more reflectively meaningful relations. But a viewer has to weed through a twisted overgrowth of sexual imagery to uncover this consequential meaning. This ironic contradiction keeps us laughing at the gross-out humor even as we delve into the larger philosophical import of what's going on as subtext. Seth and Evan, for example, are active users of Internet pornography. The loud-mouthed, unreflective Seth is addicted to it, while Evan — the quieter, more contemplative one — is getting bored with porn's smutty quality. Evan complains, for example, that the "Vagtastic Voyage" porn site Seth wants to subscribe to is probably full of "amateur stuff" with no artistic "production values." We get a clear sense of how the movie wants us to think of these two best friends, who are in many ways character stand-ins for competing ethical values. Seth is so sex-obsessed he even lusts after Evan's mother's breasts and isn't shy about sharing this with Evan. As characters, Seth and Evan embody, respectively, what Dewey might see as the difference between an immediate good and a reflective good.

Early on, in one of the movie's many tawdry, but often humorous, lines, Seth says he imagines Becca has "good dick-taking abilities." "You think that's a good thing to *say* about someone?" Evan asks. Seth answers that he does indeed think that's a prime quality, as is "dick-giving" ability for a guy. Later, Seth informs Evan that it's OK he didn't get into Dartmouth because at the state school he will attend, "the girls are half as smart but twice as likely to fellate me!" And when contemplating that night's big party, Seth's expressed goal is to use alcohol as a means toward achieving merely *another* means: to "fuck some fucking girls for once." Here Seth remains at the philosophical level of *mere* means, which, from a pragmatist perspective, is in itself neither good nor bad — until we discover, through more reflective ethical contemplation, that this value-as-value attitude is not linked to any higher end. Thus, Seth is stuck in what Dewey would call the "triviality and confusion" of immediate value; he is unable or unwilling to "look outward" toward greater consequences. However, Evan *can* be viewed as successfully meeting the pragmatist mandate of looking outward, as being "in transition in the direction of breadth and clarity of action."[27]

Suds as an Immediate Good

When Evan eventually announces he's not going to "get her [Becca] drunk out of her mind," and that he plans to simply "tell Becca how I feel and maybe she'll get with me," he is still indicating an interest in sex, but within a more meaningful relationship, a more purposeful consequence. A baffled Seth questions this logic: "Then how come you never made a move on her, you pussy?" "Because I *respect* her," Evan replies. "I'm not gonna put

that kind of unfair pressure on her." Still later, once the booze is illegally purchased and that night's party is under way, Evan gets drunk to drum up his
courage to sleep with Becca, who's already drunk. It's obvious he'd rather just
tell her how he feels, but finds that difficult, so he uses suds to sustain his
courage. One of Becca's friends informs Evan that Becca's been looking for
him. Evan asks, "Did she say I'm a good guy?" The friend replies only that
Becca has announced she will "fully blow him tonight." Evan then asks Becca's
friend if having sex with someone who is drunk isn't "unethical." The friend
answers, "No, not if you're drunk, too!"

    This line may have been conceived as a joke. But it doesn't come off as
the least bit funny. One suspects *Superbad's* writers felt an ethical requirement, however contradictory to the otherwise gleeful depiction of getting
drunk and having sex, to account for (though without further examining) a
well-known consequence of drunkenness: rape. This is the only instance in
the movie that deals with any of the serious consequences of reckless alcohol use. Unlike the movie's eventual ethical treatment of sex and relationships, booze is depicted as unproblematic and not worth mention on an
ethical level. It is symbolized as mere means, a convenient pathway to cheap
sex. In *Superbad,* booze begins and ends as immediate value — in ethical
terms, a dead letter.

    It is obvious that Evan is feeling uncomfortable but wants to make a
meaningful connection with Becca and, because she's drunk, sees alcohol as
his only opening. In a toast to Becca, Evan says sheepishly, "To the respecting of women! To people respecting women," to which Becca slurs, "OK."
When the two reach the upstairs bedroom, Evan is reluctant, but Becca's hot
to trot. Evan tells Becca how much he likes her, but she vomits before things
progress too far, putting a stop to any further activity. Here we see Evan
emerge as the one with the moral mission, while Becca, not unlike Seth's
morally slothful character, operates at the lower level of mere means.

    At the same party, a now-hammered Seth is chatting with the party host,
Jules, whom he likes. As they talk, he declares, "I love talking and conversing with you," and asks if Jules wants to go outside to talk more. Once outside, he immediately tries to kiss her. But she indicates she'd rather get to
know him first. He sheds a tear worrying aloud that Jules "wouldn't be with
me if you were sober." She tells him she actually doesn't drink at all, which
he finds hard to believe. He then passes out, face forward, accidentally head-
butting her. But for once even Seth is depicted, however awkwardly, as trying to move out of the lower depths of immediacy and into the higher terrain
of reflection, demonstrating a glimmer of Dewey's view that, "Intelligence
becomes ours in the degree in which we use it and accept responsibility for
consequences."[28] This deceptively simple sentence implies that we must consciously grasp onto and gradually develop "intelligence," a word Dewey used

as a synonym for imaginative, consequential, means-end reflection on ethics, art, politics, and all other modes of knowledge.

In the above scene, we further discover the film's own ethical transposition and development at work: The wise and sensitive Jules (thematically linked with her polar opposite, Seth) is actually an ethical complement of the equally thoughtful Evan (linked with *his* actual opposite in personality, Becca). So the sex-and-booze-focused Becca and Seth are, through most of the movie, actually soul mates in that both function as mere means that do not rise to a higher, more ethically embracing consequence or "end." As Dewey notes on the proper functioning of the means-consequences process:

> Means are always at least causal conditions; but causal conditions are means only when they possess an added qualification; that, namely, of being freely used, because of perceived connection with chosen consequences. To entertain, choose and accomplish anything as an end or consequence is to be committed to a like love and care for whatever events and acts are its means.[29]

Nearing the movie's end, we can see that Evan and Becca represent an attempt to embody a commitment to "love and care" based on *meaningful* means having a "perceived connection with chosen consequences." In other words, *Superbad* eventually makes Dewey's case that one has to contemplate and be committed, through "love and care," to means beyond mere means to achieve an end that's something more than merely value as pure value. But the movie does *not* suggest teenage sex in itself, regardless of whom one has it with and for what reason, is unethical. Nor does it pass judgment on underage drinking. *Superbad* is, therefore, ethically questionable in these respects, open to the charge it's exploiting these themes just to attract its teen and post-teen target audience, most of whom are probably not intellectually engaged enough to get the movie's deeper message about sex as meaningful in its ethically reflective sense.

The fact that *Superbad* does not address the many personal and social problems associated with actual teenage sex and underage drinking at the surface level, where its target audience is likely to comfortably trod, poses an ethical quandary in the film itself. It also highlights a limitation in applying Dewey, or any other interpretive framework, to a movie as culturally contradictory as this one: Those ready to take on the burden of ethical thought (most likely the post–twenty-somethings) can walk away meaningfully illuminated; much of the targeted teen/post-teen audience may walk away with an illuminated interest only in getting drunk and having uncommitted sex.

Toward its end, the movie does nevertheless make clear that Jules and Evan have demonstrated a desire to achieve a more ethically rich and lastingly meaningful state, but Becca and, for the most part, Seth, have not. By contrasting Seth and Evan with their personality opposites (Jules and Becca, respectively), the film gradually leads a thoughtful viewer to an ethically "embodied engagement"[30] about sex as perhaps more than just a transitory value, sex as more than mere means.

Friendship and Love United

If "bailing" has been a ruling metaphor in previous scenes, an important reversal takes place in a concluding scene, bringing the movie to its fullest account of the ethical bonds of relationships. The boys' friendship is reunited, and love, in all its contradictory colors, is displayed with varying amounts of openness.

After the teenage party has been busted up by police, a very drunk Evan awakes in the arms of Seth, who's carrying him out of the party house into safety to escape the cops. Seth shouts out to others who are watching, "He's my best friend!" As Evan comes around he looks up, still cradled in Seth's pudgy arms and asks tenderly, "Are you *carrying* me?" They make it to Evan's house and decide to bunk down for the night. As the drunken teens, rolled up in side-by-side sleeping bags, talk, Seth discloses that he'd already learned Evan and Fogell would be rooming together at Dartmouth because he'd glanced at the housing forms in Evan's room. Evan acknowledges that he should have told his friend about this and that he doesn't really want to live with Fogell. The truth, Evan admits, is that he doesn't "want to live with strangers. I can't *do* it." He continues, "I can't believe you *saved* me! I owe you so much. You *carried* me. I love you. I *love* you, man."

Seth responds, "I love *you*. I *love* you! I'm not even embarrassed to say it — I *love* you!" "Why don't we say that every day, why don't we say it more often?" Evan says. "I love you — I want to go on the rooftop and say I love my best friend, Evan.... I want the world to know. It's the most beautiful thing in the world." Seth and Evan are now face to face. Seth taps Evan gently on the nose and says three times, "Boop, boop, boop." They hug: "I love you. I love you, *too*." The next morning they awake with some obvious embarrassment. Considering the fact that both were drunk, neither is entirely sure what may have happened, much like two lovers who feel a little uncomfortable at the previous night's drunken, half-forgotten exploits. Seth gets up to leave, but Evan asks him if he'd like to go with him later to the mall, because Evan needs "a comforter" for college. Seth agrees and, as he leaves, just to show he still has credentials as a healthy heterosexual, blurts out to Evan, "Your mom's got huge *tits*!"

This last line is humorous without exactly being funny. It quickly undercuts further contemplation about the tension-filled friendship/trust/love/hetero-homosexual theme that would otherwise take center stage. Here, parody and its burlesque sensibility are invoked as a stop-gap, redirecting one's emergent, higher-level thoughts back down to the bawdy horn-dog comedy at hand and away from anything like a studied philosophical stance on the ethical bond of the guy/guy friendship. But, at least to a thoughtful viewer, the mission is accomplished.

By movie's end, the filmmakers have managed to have their cake and eat it, too. Seth and Evan's meeting up with Jules and Becca later at the mall, where all is forgiven, is a pure Hollywood happy ending. But when Seth and Jules go off on their own shopping venture in the mall, and Seth, descending the escalator with Jules, looks back winsomely at Evan, who's now hand-in-hand with Becca, the ethical growth, based on real and respectful love between the two teenage boys, is given formal closure. They've grown up. They've gained mutual respect for one another, learning they must go their own ways without leaving the other behind. They've glanced backward and are looking forward, however nervously.

Conclusion

On the other hand, let's not take all this too seriously. As indicated earlier, there is certainly a ruling ethic at work in *Superbad*, but it's veiled in a thoroughly commercial entertainment ethic, which can't usually afford too much philosophical depth. Very few "serious" movies do $120 million-plus in ticket sales, not to mention garnering many more millions in DVD sales and rentals. For all the pragmatist-consequentialist ethos that we can grab out of *Superbad*, it *is* a matter of persistent grabbing. As every movie critic who liked the movie acknowledged, *Superbad* is indeed a trash-talking comedy that wallows in the cheap, vulgar, and crudely offensive. Its screenwriters want us to have a good laugh. And most of us do. But the screenwriters also seem to be natural pragmatists. They intelligently pose a seriously wrought ethic of responsibility within an afternoon's worth of vaudeville skits. They probably understand (and don't care) that the targeted audience might mostly attend to the value-free vaudevillian aspect. But Dewey *would* probably care about all this. He'd likely want a viewer to use the movie as experiential moving beyond mere *means* toward more-than-immediately-meaningful *ends*. But he'd also recognize that some will, and some won't. Unfortunately, the ethical message in *Superbad* may be available, problematically, as a value-added feature. This contradictory impulse in Hollywood mainstream films is a relatively recent development in commercial entertainment worthy of further analysis.[31]

As Fredric Jameson noted of popular culture products, even the "most degraded type of mass culture" can offer a "transcendent potential," "some genuine shred of content" pointing to the possibility of a "redeemed collective order."[32] This perspective is not all that far from Dewey's own. To place it in his terms, he believed that in *pressing forward* by *glancing backward*, one is able to look outward, to see new values in a brighter light. The flights are then meaningfully integrated with the perchings, so that the continuity discovered during a never-ending flight may be progressively freer and more secure.

If *Superbad* or any other entertainment product affords this kind of perspective, then it has inherent social value. Still, this experiential value will, in Dewey's terms, be only an "immediate good," a mere means, unless moral agents choose to transform entertainment into more *mean*ingful life lessons. This process is what Dewey considered the ethical method behind the evolutionary development of knowledge as learning. However, it requires, additionally, that moral agents go beyond the *merely* individual if moral conduct is to evolve into a social ethics that clears a flight path toward "freer and more secure goods."[33]

NOTES

1. Ellen Goodman, "The Confusing Business of Boyhood," *Boston Globe*, August 31, 2007, A-15.

2. Manohla Dargis, "For Three Virgins, the Path to Sunrise is Paved with Excess," *New York Times*, August 17, 2007, E-1.

3. *Ibid.*

4. David Denby, "Teen Dreams; 'Superbad' and 'Delirious,'" *The New Yorker*, August 20, 2007, 76.

5. Geoff Pevere, "Gimme Some McLovin: A Movie About a Night to Remember for Super-Dweebs on a Mission, Superbad Is Wise and Whacked and Very Funny," *The Toronto Star*, August 17, 2007, E-1.

6. Ann Hornaday, "Superbad: Geeks Gone Wild," *Washington Post*, August 17, 2007, C-1.

7. David Hinckley, "Two Schools of Thought," *New York Daily News*, August 21, 2007, 30.

8. Chris Knight, "Huffing, Puffing and Rolling in the Aisles; Superbad's 'Ratio' of Heart to Smut Makes It a Wolf of a Comedy," *National Post*, December 8, 2007, 26.

9. Wesley Morris, "It's a Nerd, He's in Pain — It's Superbad," *Boston Globe*, August 17, 2007, E-1.

10. Christopher Tookey, "Superbad by Name, Atrocious by Nature," *Daily Mail*, September 14, 2007, 59.

11. Jane Stadler, "Intersubjective, Embodied, Evaluative Perception: A Phenomenological Approach to the Ethics of Film," *Quarterly Review of Film & Video* 19 (2002): 237–248.

12. John Dewey, "Experience and Philosophic Method," in *The Philosophy of John Dewey*, ed., John J. McDermott (Chicago: University of Chicago Press, 1981), 265.

13. McDermott, ed., *The Philosophy of John Dewey*, 328.

14. For recent and more thorough accounts and critiques of Dewey related to contemporary ethics and the value of pragmatism, see John Teehan, "Character, Integrity and Dewey's Virtue Ethics," *Transactions of the Charles S. Peirce Society* (Fall 1995): 842–863; William R. Caspary, "Dewey and Sartre on Ethical Decisions: Dramatic Rehearsal versus Radical Choice," *Transactions of the Charles S. Pierce Society* (Summer 2006): 367–393; and Melvin L. Rogers, "Action and Inquiry in Dewey's Philosophy," *Transactions of the Charles S. Peirce Society* (Winter 2007): 90–115.

15. For a more thorough explanation of this, see Eugene Rochberg-Halton, *Meaning and Modernity: Social Theory in the Pragmatic Attitude* (Chicago: University of Chicago Press, 1986), especially pp. 11–14.

16. McDermott, *Philosophy of John Dewey*, 329.

17. *Ibid.*, 585

18. *Ibid.*, 573.

19. *Ibid.*, 305.

20. Caspary, "Dewey and Sartre on Ethical Decisions," 381–382.

21. Thomas M. Alexander, "John Dewey and the Moral Imagination: Beyond Putnam and Rorty Toward a Postmodern Ethics," *Transactions of the Charles S. Peirce Society* (Summer 1993): 369–400, 385.

22. Caspary, "Dewey and Sartre on Ethical Decisions," 372–375.

23. Quoted in Alexander, "John Dewey and the Moral Imagination," 389.

24. *Ibid.*, 389.

25. *Ibid.*, 386.

26. I do not focus in this chapter on Fogell because his character, while interesting in many ways, is mainly drawn for comic relief.

27. Quoted in Alexander, "John Dewey and the Moral Imagination," 389.

28. McDermott, *The Philosophy of John Dewey,* 713.

29. *Ibid.*, 309.

30. Stadler, "Intersubjective, Embodied, Evaluative Perception," 237–248.

31. For more on this see, Joseph Harry, "*Natural Born Killers* and Media-Born Thrillers: Ethical Contradictions in the Infotainment Age," in *Desperately Seeking Ethics,* ed., Howard Good, 177–194 (Lanham, MD: Scarecrow, 2003).

32. Fredric Jameson, *Signatures of the Visible* (New York: Routledge, 1992), 29.

33. McDermott, *The Philosophy of John Dewey,* 353.

Works Cited

Alexander, T. M. "John Dewey and the Moral Imagination: Beyond Putnam and Rorty Toward a Postmodern Ethics." *Transactions of the Charles S. Peirce Society* (Summer 1993): 369–400.

Caspary, W.R. "Dewey and Sartre on Ethical Decisions: Dramatic Rehearsal versus Radical Choice." *Transactions of the Charles S. Peirce Society* (Summer 2006): 367–393.

Dargis, M. "For Three Virgins, the Path to Sunrise is Paved with Excess," *New York Times,* August 17, 2007, E-1.

Dewey, J. *The Philosophy of John Dewey.* Ed. John J. McDermott. Chicago: University of Chicago Press, 1981.

Goodman, E. "The Confusing Business of Boyhood," *Boston Globe,* August 31, 2007, A-15.

Harry, J.C. "Natural Born Killers and Media-Born Thrillers: Ethical Contradictions in the Infotainment Age." In *Desperately Seeking Ethics.* Ed. Howard Good. Lanham: MD: Scarecrow, 2003, 177–194.

Hinckley, D. "Two Schools of Thought," *New York Daily News,* August 21, 2007, 30.

Hornaday, A. "Superbad: Geeks Gone Wild," *Washington Post,* August 17, 2007, C-1.

Jameson, F. *Signatures of the Visible.* New York: Routledge, 1992.

Knight, C. "Huffing, Puffing, and Rolling in the Aisles: Superbad's Ratio of Heart to Smut Makes it a Wolf of a Comedy," *National Post,* December 8, 2007, 26.

Morris, W. "It's a Nerd, He's in Pain — It's Superbad," *Boston Globe,* August 17, 2007, E-1.

Pevere, G. "Gimme' Some McLovin: A Movie about a Night to Remember for Super-Dweebs on a Mission, Superbad Is Wise and Whacked and Very Funny," *Toronto Star,* August 17, 2007, E-1.

Rochberg-Halton, E. *Meaning and Modernity: Social Theory in the Pragmatic Attitude.* Chicago: University of Chicago Press, 1986.

Rogers, M.L. "Action and Inquiry in Dewey's Philosophy." *Transactions of the Charles S. Peirce Society* (Winter 2007): 90–115.

Stadler, J. "Intersubjective, Embodied, Evaluative Perception: A Phenomenological Approach to the Ethics of Film." *Quarterly Review of Film & Video* (2002) 19: 237–248.

Teehan, J. "Character, Integrity, and Dewey's Virtue Ethics." *Transactions of the Charles S. Peirce Society* (Fall 1995): 842–863.

Tookey, C. "Superbad by Name, Atrocious by Nature," *Daily Mail*, September 14, 2007, 59.

III. Entertainment and Factuality

Chapter 7

Tall Tales: Ethical Storytelling in the Age of Infotainment

Cynthia M. King *and* Deni Elliott[1]

Once upon a time, journalists reported news, companies promoted products, and entertainers produced drama and diversions. Today, news, promotion, and entertainment are blended together in an endless array of offerings, with such labels as infotainment, sportainment, docudrama, advertorials, blogvertising, reality TV, and product placement. The names themselves attest to the hybrid nature of current mass communication forms and providers. People learn about current events from talk radio, magazine shows, and late night comedy. Companies shop their goods through branded entertainment and product placement in documentary-style reality television programs. Meanwhile, in today's "Do-It-Yourself" (DIY) culture, audience members share their self-produced news, promotions, and entertainment in social networks, weblogs, and virtual worlds.

Journalists, advertisers, and entertainers share a common craft of storytelling. Traditionally, however, the stories they told were distinct in terms of style, content, and intended effects. Professionals in each discipline established different codes of ethics and standards. Standards for journalistic and commercial speech have often been guided by a sense of social responsibility to not only report the truth, but also to report it thoughtfully and conscientiously. In addition to these moral obligations, the distinctions traditionally made in news stories and commercial messages were supported by legal and economic sanctions. If journalists or advertisers were caught making false claims, their reputation would suffer and they would lose customers. In some cases, they might even be sued or fined. In novels, films, television programs, and other entertainment fare, however, elaborate fantasies and fabrications are big business. Audiences often seek out entertainment as a means to escape reality. Thus, entertainers traditionally enjoyed greater creative license in their storytelling, while journalists, marketers, and advertisers were expected to make distinctions among fact, fiction, and opinion to varying degrees.

Audience members may come to each traditional category of storytelling with expectations that those delivering the messages will conform to these disciplinary conventions. Contemporary infotainment and related hybrids, however, blur the boundaries between fact and fiction by definition, creating a conflicting mix of values, conventions, and audience expectations. This chapter addresses the challenges of establishing appropriate ethical standards for these blended story types and proposes a voluntary disclosure system to assist storytellers and audiences in distinguishing fantasy from reality in the infotainment age.

Tall Tales

Her name was Bree, a shy home-schooled teenager with a web camera. In the summer of 2006, she started posting video web logs (v-blogs) on YouTube.com under the user name lonelygirl15. Her videos were a hit, attracting thousands of viewers. The problem was none of it was real. In early September, it was revealed that lonelygirl15 was a 19-year-old actress hired to play the part of a 16-year-old.[2]

In 2007 Margaret B. Jones wrote *Love and Consequences*, a critically acclaimed memoir about growing up among gang-bangers in South-Central Los Angeles as a half-white, half-Native American foster child who ran drugs for the Bloods. Within a week of publication, her own sister came forward with the real story of Margaret Seltzer's (aka Ms. Jones') middle-class, suburban childhood in Sherman Oaks, California.[3] Just a week before Seltzer's memoir was exposed as a fake, author Misha Defonseca, whose real name is Monique De Wael, issued a statement admitting that the Holocaust memoir she published 11 years earlier was fiction.[4] De Wael's book, *Surviving with Wolves*, had recently been turned into a film. That same year, James Frey was revealed to have duped readers, his patron Oprah Winfrey among them, with his fictionalized memoir, *A Million Little Pieces*.[5]

In 2008, what appeared to be candid home videos circulated on the Internet seemingly demonstrating that cellular phone radiation was so strong it could pop corn. In less than three weeks, the videos had been viewed more than four million times. Wired.com debunked the video as fake with the help of physicist Louis Bloomfield, speculating that a video-editing program or hidden heating pads caused the popcorn to pop. Bluetooth headset retailer

Cardo Systems confessed that it had commissioned a marketing agency in Paris called Last Fools to make the videos.[6]

Falsehoods and fabrications have a long history in storytelling. In the late eighteenth century, English poet Thomas Chatterton passed his own work off as the verse of medieval "secular priest" Thomas Rowley. The American colonial press ran hoaxes, as did the early penny papers, including an infamous article published in the *New York Sun* in 1835 claiming that astronomer John Herschel had found life on the moon. In 1971 Clifford Irving was found guilty of forging the biography of reclusive millionaire Howard Hughes.

Not all story falsehoods and fabrications raise ethical concerns. Indeed, audiences expect fictional stories in books, television programs, films, and other forms of entertainment. What makes contemporary fabrications of particular concern is their rapid increase in frequency, sophistication, and proliferation. Of even greater interest is the complacency with which storytellers and their audiences are reacting to what would have been called ethical breaches not so long ago. In the following section we will explore the factors that have contributed to this dramatic increase in volume and acceptance of hoaxes, forgeries, and deceptions in entertainment and other media forums.

Technology and the Attention Economy

Economists and futurists have argued that we have moved into a period completely different from the past era of factory-based mass production of material items. During that era, talk of money, prices, returns on investment, laws of supply and demand, and so on made excellent sense, but today's economy is said to be driven more by the production and exchange of information than by the production and exchange of material goods. The statistics documenting the information proliferation in our society are impressive. For example, a typical weekday edition of the *New York Times* contains more information than the average eighteenth-century Englishman encountered in a lifetime. In a mere ten years, 1980 to 1990, the worldwide production of books increased by 45 percent. And it is estimated that a new site emerges on the World Wide Web every minute.[7] Many names for the new era have been invoked: the Information Age, the Third Wave, the move toward cyberspace. Beginning with the advent of television and large mainframe computers, and continuing with personal computers, the Internet, and wireless products, this era is fueled by revolutionary technological advances in electronic data and communication technology.

Some theorists, however, argue that it is not this abundance of information, but the competition for attention that this abundance creates, that drives the economy. Economist Michael Goldhaber uses the term "the attention economy" to describe this evolving era. He explains why he does not see information itself as a driving economic force:

Information ... would be an impossible basis for an economy, for one simple reason:

> economies are governed by what is scarce, and information, especially on the Net, is not only abundant, but overflowing. We are drowning in the stuff, and yet more and more comes at us daily.... What would be the incentive in organizing our lives around spewing out more information if there is already far too much?[8]

It is this overabundance that leads to growing competition for what *is* increasingly scarce — our attention. Consumers today have more choices than ever in everything from television programs to automobiles to breakfast cereals. Nowhere is this more evident than on the Internet. A few keystrokes will direct Net surfers to numerous Web site options for information on countless products, services, and topics. Even though our choices may be plentiful, our time and money are limited. It seems as if everyone wants some of our time and money, but they must first break through the clutter and capture our attention.

Like money, attention has *instrumental* value because it can get you other things that you might want. Persuasion is often described as a process, and attention is always the first step. Thus, many of those who want your attention may really want something else. Advertisers are vying for your attention so they can try to persuade you to buy their products or services. A nonprofit organization may want your attention to persuade you to volunteer or give money. Your friends may want your attention to persuade you to do them a favor. Attention, however, also has what is called *terminal value*, meaning that many people value it for its own sake. Consider what kids will do to get their parents' attention or, worse, what people will do or say to get on tell-all, show-all talk shows. Even the phrase "pay attention" suggests that attention has inherent value. We value both the attention we give and the attention we receive.

The Entertainment Principle

Attention may be valuable, but money can't buy it, at least not directly. Even if you paid people millions of dollars, they could not guarantee you their attention. Most of us can recall books we have tried to read, lectures we have tried to listen to, and programs we have tried to watch. No matter how hard we try, there are times when our minds still begin to wander. And this is where entertainment comes in. If something is boring, we don't pay attention to it. Entertainment captures attention. As a result, an attention economy is also an *entertainment economy*. Whether you are making a film or an advertisement, if you do not hold the interest of your audience — that is, if you do not entertain them — they will stop paying attention.

Ironically, although you may not be able to pay people to get their attention, you may be able to get them to pay you for it. People will pay for entertainment. And as long as you keep people entertained, you will have their attention. Consumers pay for newspapers, magazines, and books to read, movies to watch, and music to listen to. But you had better have something good to offer if you expect them to give you their attention *and* their money. This competition for attention has helped fuel the rise of infotainment. Whether writing a script, news story, or advertisement, your goal is to capture attention. Drama and intrigue offer a better guarantee of engaging audiences than do facts and thoughtful analysis. Thus, today's media face greater pressure to be entertaining than to be honest and accurate.

Traditional economic theory maintained that brands were built for the long term, and that consumer trust was essential for brand loyalty. Accuracy and credibility were viewed as critical for consumer trust in news and other commercial media. Today, however, many companies introduce brands anticipating a limited life expectancy, thereby reducing market incentives to adhere to traditional standards. Furthermore, it may be that audiences have become so bored with predictable products and stories that they are willing to tolerate some falsehood if it makes for a more entertaining experience. As a result, by the turn of the twenty-first century, audiences no longer had clear markers to distinguish one type of communication from another.

Reality Entertainment

Perhaps nowhere is the blurring between fact and fantasy more evident than in the rise of reality television programs. Books and videos presented either implicitly or explicitly as autobiographies, memoirs, and candid home footage can also be viewed as forms of "reality" entertainment. One of the attractions of these entertaining "documentaries" is the supposed "reality" of them — they are supposed to be unscripted, presenting unplanned situations and reactions. However, most reality entertainment isn't nearly as "real" as it pretends to be.

Reality shows have been accused — and, in some cases, found guilty of — manufacturing quotes, constructing crushes and feuds, stitching scenes together out of footage shot days apart, and planning whole episodes in multi-act "storyboards" before taping. Of course, most television programming is fictional. Certainly fabricating events and characters isn't inherently unethical in entertainment. The difference is that in dramatic shows one can expect the audience to understand that what they see on the screen doesn't necessarily reflect the reality of the actors' lives; the same, it is argued, cannot be said for edited and contrived scenes on reality shows.

Reality programs may not have line-for-line scripts (although reality writers have charged that Paris Hilton was fed lines on *The Simple Life*). However, according to Jeff Bartsch, a freelance reality-show editor, there are many ways of using footage to shape a story.[9] Bartsch worked on *Blind Date*, a syndicated dating show that features hookups gone right — and horribly, comically wrong. If a date was dull or lukewarm, the editors would spice up the footage by running scenes out of order or out of context. To make it seem as if a man had been bored, they would cut from his date talking to a shot of him looking around, unresponsive — even though the scene was shot while she was in the restroom and he was alone. "You can really take something black and make it white," Bartsch said.[10]

On the ABC reality show *The Dating Experiment*, one of the female participants disliked one of her suitors, but the producers thought it would make a better story if she liked him. So they sat her down for an interview. Who's your favorite celebrity? they asked. She replied that she really loved Adam Sandler. Later, in the editing room, they spliced out Sandler's name and dropped in audio of her saying the male contestant's name. This trick, said *Dating Experiment* consultant Todd Sharp, is called Frankenbiting.[11] Thus, the most obvious ethical question raised by such blatant fabrications is whether reality entertainment should be labeled "reality" at all.

Producers are quick to emphasize that editorial devices can be used not just to deceive, but also to tell a story more clearly, entertainingly, and quickly. News producers, documentarians, and journalists all selectively edit raw material and get accused of cherry-picking facts and quotes. However, on an entertainment show, the pressure to deliver drama is high, and the standards of acceptable fudging are shadier. Reality producers say they often have to shuffle footage to tell a story concisely or make a babbling interviewee coherent. "We're using things said at different times, put together to imply a statement or observation that may not have been succinctly demonstrated," says J. Ryan Stradal, who was a story editor on *The Bachelorette*. "That's where Frankenbiting may come in."[12] Or producers may withhold information — such as downplaying a budding romance — to create suspense. In this case, the ethical question is whether dramatic editing is wrong if it captures the essence of the moment.

Recently, storytellers have begun to push these limits even further. As we have discussed, seemingly "real" books, such as *Surviving with Wolves*, and videos, such as the lonely girl series and the phone corn-popping hoax, are often completely fabricated.

Consequentialism: Is All Fair in Love and War Stories?

As already acknowledged, not all story falsehoods and fabrications raise ethical concerns. Audiences expect fictional stories in books, television programs, films, and other forms of entertainment. The ethical concern lies in cases where audiences are unable to discern fact from fiction; and, as the examples we have shared illustrate, many contemporary storytellers have knowingly blurred this distinction. Such deception isn't new; it's the spirit in which it is done now — the ease, ubiquity, moral indifference — that seems to have changed. Often the deceivers do not appear to feel that they have done anything wrong.

Monique De Wael continues to defend her fabricated Holocaust memoir. "Ever since I can remember, I felt Jewish," she said in a statement issued by her lawyers. "There are times when I find it difficult to differentiate between reality and my inner world. The story in the book is mine. It is not the actual reality — it was my reality, my way of surviving."[13]

Such fabricators also appear to have little trouble enlisting the support of others. The creators of the lonelygirl15 videos were Ramesh Flinders, a screenwriter and filmmaker from Marin County, California, and Miles Beckett, a doctor turned filmmaker. The project was developed much the same way as more traditional commercial films or television programs are produced, including casting, contracts, and film crew. They enlisted the services of Grant Steinfeld, a software engineer in San Francisco. "We were all under N.D.A.'s," Steinfeld said, referring to non-disclosure agreements the cast — and their friends — were asked to sign to preserve the mystery of lonelygirl15. "They had a lawyer involved."[14] Amanda Solomon Goodfried, an assistant at the Creative Artists Agency, which eventually represented the lonelygirl team, is believed to have helped Flinders and Beckett conceal their identities. Moreover, Goodfried's father-in-law, Kenneth Goodfried, a lawyer in Encino, filed to trademark "lonelygirl1."

Consistent with the artistic mindset traditionally reserved for fictional stories, these content creators appear to feel these hoaxes and lies fall within the purview of fair creative license. If they are guided by any moral sense, it appears to be an ends-justifies-the-means, or consequentialist, philosophy that is almost self-righteous in its dismissal of audience members' interest in knowing the truth from falsity. In her gang memoir, Margaret Seltzer defended her decision to lie, saying the story needed to be told and was based on accounts of real experiences. She said, "I just felt that there was good that I could do and there was no other way that someone would listen to it."[15] Her ends-based argument and dismissal of audience interests should not be accepted as an ethical justification for deception. One cannot simply state prudential interests and get a free pass when it comes to the interests of others, as that simply substitutes one's self-interest for ethics.

In the Netherlands, Patrick Lodiers offered a similar justification for the Dutch reality program he hosted, *The Big Donor Show*. The show was designed as a hoax in which a terminally ill cancer patient pretended to select one of three patients to receive her kidney. Viewers watched testimonials from the three Dutch contestants, ages 18 to 40, and could text message advice to the donor to help her decide who should receive the life-saving operation.

According to one blog account, Lodiers said one aim of the program was to bring about a change in Dutch law surrounding transplants. At present, only family or friends of the recipient can donate organs, a policy that greatly reduces their availability in the Netherlands. "It is reality that is shocking," he said, "because so many people die each year in the Netherlands while waiting for a kidney, and the average waiting time is four years. But we are not giving away a kidney [on the show]. That would be going too far even for us."[16]

Even more interesting is how some industry professionals not only defend, but also praise, these deceptions. According to the news website, News.Scotsman.com, the makers of *The Big Donor Show* were "widely praised when they revealed [the program] was a hoax aimed at raising awareness of the plight of patients waiting for organs."[17] In commenting on the hoax in his blog, marketing communication consultant Sam Smith lauded this ends-justified approach:

> There are two wonderful thing[s] about this little stunt. The first is that you could almost believe it. I mean, given the kinds of things that *do* happen in pursuit of a buck, you could imagine this kind of show happening. The second is that it was conceived as a way to attract attention to a worthwhile cause.... I like the idea here. It's over the top, to be sure, but if you're trying to call attention to a life/death situation, which is worse: this tasteless, offensive display (which, by the way, called the whole damned world's attention to your cause) or a tasteful, conventional, traditional campaign that gets a few hundred signatures on a petition while hundreds continue to die?[18]

In many cases, these hoaxes have been admired simply for their ingenuity and marketing savvy. Arguably, one of the first and most famous Internet hoaxes was the viral promotion of the horror film, *The Blair Witch Project*. The movie, made for $22,000, grossed $248 million at the box office by generating massive pre-opening "buzz" through video clips circulated on the Internet.[19] The rumor was that a camera had been found with real footage taken by three college kids who became lost in the woods while investigating stories about a witch. According to Internet marketing writer Charles Brown, "the hoax took on a life of its own.... By the time the film was released, it had built up fever-level anticipation."[20] In his review, Brown called the hoax "remarkable" and "the stuff of legends." He questioned whether such campaigns must be designed as hoaxes, rather than as fictional stories, to be successful, but did not express any ethical concerns about the strategy. Instead, he appeared more concerned about whether such stories could be used to promote many different products or services. The three men who created *Blair Witch* think they can. They have formed a marketing company called Campfire, which creates viral marketing campaigns for advertising agencies like the one they used to make their movie such a huge success.

On the face of it, audience members are cheated and deceived when they are led by the communicator to expect one thing — an autobiography, a candid home video on YouTube, a reality television show depicting "average" people spontaneously reacting to contrived situations — but are given another — fabricated, product-placed, manipulated, and heavily edited stories that misrepresent the actions and intentions of fantasy characters and low-paid actor-wannabes. Audience members are thereby deprived of opportunity or freedom when they have no way to gauge the intent of a message or when they are given subtle messages without the ability to rationally consider what is contained in the messages.

Yet the possibilities of these harms, inherent in media hybrids, must be balanced against audience members' desire for surprise or suspension of disbelief. Journalistic hoaxes and published rumors, popular in the mid–1800s, were criticized by journalists, not by audience members. According to Fred Fedler:

> When Americans realized that they were fooled, many were embarrassed — but not angry. Most people were frightened for only a moment or two, but some actually enjoyed it, just as millions of Americans continue to enjoy the frightening movies produced by Alfred Hitchcock and the books written by Stephen King. Moreover, readers continued to talk about the hoaxes for years. They also continued to buy copies of them, so the sale of some stories actually increased after they were exposed as hoaxes.[21]

Reactions to contemporary hoaxes, such as the lonelygirl and the cell phone corn-popping videos, have been similar. Although some audiences express outrage about being duped, these hoaxes generate more admiration than criticism for their deception. In their reviews, industry analysts, critics, and news reporters tend to quickly dismiss ethical concerns and focus more on analyzing the entertainment and marketing value of the stories. The Internet and other new media have certainly made it easier to fabricate and disseminate these false tales, and such advances also may also help explain why so many industry professionals, and even audiences, embrace them. New media have also contributed to the rise of another practice that further exacerbates the blurring of fact and fiction in contemporary entertainment: product placements.

The Rise of Product Placements

The entertainment business as we know it today would not exist without the corporations that have supported it, typically through advertising. Some estimates say 40 percent of the revenue stream for the entertainment industry comes from advertisements. Today advertising serves as a primary source of revenue not only for newspapers, magazines, television, and radio stations, but also for Web sites and sporting events. Although audiences will pay for entertainment, entertainment providers still often find it difficult to make a profit only from the sales of that content.

Newspapers and magazines, for example, rarely make money from publication sales. Their profits usually come from advertising revenues—from advertisers who pay to take advantage of the attention that the publication captures. In fact, the content that actually captures your attention is often provided for free. Broadcast television and radio have always been "free" for their audiences. That free entertainment is provided in an effort to capture audience attention for advertisers. Traditionally, however, the distinction between entertainment and the corporate advertising content that supported it was more distinct. As audiences become more adept at filtering out traditional advertising, efforts to infuse corporate messages more directly into entertainment and other media content are becoming increasingly important, both as a platform for advertisers and as a revenue stream for entertainment media.

Global paid product placement spending in TV, film, and other media surged to $2.21 billion in 2005. Infusing organizational messaging more directly into editorial and entertainment programming content not only lends credibility, but also may provide companies greater assurance that their messages are not filtered out. According to Jeff Greenfield, vice president of 1st Approach, a strategic media marketing company, "Since the explosion of the Internet and new technology like TiVO, viewers are demanding fewer interruptions."[22] With more than half a million households using the TiVO-style personal video recorders, users skip commercials 72.3 percent of the time — a much higher rate than those watching live TV or those using videotape recorders.[23] As a result, cutting-edge companies eschew traditional advertising in favor of media relations and other non-traditional entertainment-infused strategies, such as celebrity endorsements and product placements in films, television programs, and at celebrity events and photo shoots.

Following the analogy of using a spoonful of sugar to help the medicine go down, embedding products in entertainment can be simultaneously more captivating and more subtle than traditional advertising, thus making it easier to "swallow." Marketers hope that audiences will not only pay more attention to placed products, but also be less guarded and more open to influence than they are when exposed to direct commercial messaging. As audiences become increasingly savvy and sensitive to these placements, however, such ploys become less effective, and marketers must search for even more creative ways to promote their products. One way they are doing this is through entertaining, but deceptive, YouTube and viral videos, such as those for *Blair Witch*, the lonely girl series, and the phone-popping-corn hoax. In some cases, this deception is simply used to gain an audience for the stories themselves; in others, it is designed to draw attention to consumer goods, such as the Bluetooth headsets marketed by the creators of the popcorn hoax.

Infotainment and News Media

Companies are not the only ones having difficulty getting their messages seen and heard. Concerned over declining audiences for news programs and publications, many news organizations have turned to "infotainment" strategies. Today's editorial decisions are often based as much on a story's ability to entertain audiences as to inform them. A 2001 report by Thomas Patterson found that soft news has dramatically increased in the twenty-first century. News stories lacking public policy content jumped from less than 35 percent of all stories in 1980 to roughly 50 percent by 2001. Stories with a moderate to high level of sensationalism rose from about 25 percent of news stories in the early 1980s to a more recent tally of 40 percent. The regular features of network news magazines *Dateline* NBC, ABC *Primetime Live*, CBS *48 Hours*, and the made-for-soft-news spinoff ABC *20/20 Downtown*, are notorious for their soft news formats.[24]

Perhaps even more disturbing is the emergence of paid product placement in news publications and broadcasts. In July 2008, the Fox affiliate in Las Vegas, KVVU, agreed to a six-month promotion for McDonald's in which news anchors sat with cups of McDonald's iced coffee on their desks during the news-and-lifestyle portion of their morning show. Executives at the station said the promotion was meant to shore up advertising revenue and, as they told the news staff, would not influence content. However, *The New York Times* reported that the ad agency that arranged the promotion said the cups would most likely be whisked away if KVVU chose to report a negative story about McDonald's.[25] "If there were a story going up, let's say, God forbid, about a McDonald's food illness outbreak or something negative about McDonald's, I would expect that the station would absolutely give us the opportunity to pull our product off set," said Brent Williams, account supervisor at Karsh/Hagan, the advertising agency that arranged the deal.[26]

Confounding Audience Expectations

In sum, we are seeing a convergence of forces that make it increasingly difficult for both content creators and their audiences to distinguish among news, entertainment, and commercial speech — in other words, to know when messaging is objective and truthful, promotional, or possibly fabricated or fictional. Such practices inadvertently — and, arguably, often even intentionally — create confusion for audience members. According to Philip Patterson and Lee Wilkins, "By blending information and entertainment into an internally coherent package, the possibility for abuse of an unsuspecting audience exists."[27] To understand how this can happen, we must look to the mass-communication theory of "uses and gratifications." People bring something to the message, and what they bring affects what they take away.

For example, seeking news and information is a common use of media, with an expected gratification of getting information necessary for citizenship. Entertainment has its own expected gratifications — escape, fantasy, mood management — but it can also often serve an informative function regarding popular culture and behavior. The problem arises when entertainment provides fundamentally flawed information about important political figures or about important institutions in U.S. culture, such as the court system or medical practice.[28]

The potential for individuals to glean misinformation from fictional storytelling has always existed. Much media research has focused on studying what audiences may inadvertently learn and imitate from fictional stories. What makes contemporary infotainment more alarming is that the *intentional* blurring of fact and fiction almost guarantees that audiences will be misled. Indeed, in many cases deception is the storytellers' intent, as with fabricated biographies and viral hoax videos. As discussed earlier, reality programs have been similarly accused of deception and fabrication. Even product placement is contrived to suggest to audiences that characters, and the actors who play them, endorse the products featured in fictional stories.

As the lines between entertainment, journalism, and commercial speech blur, so have the ethical principles that guide them. This confusion is exacerbated by user-generated content contributed by individuals with no grounding in or allegiance to ethical conventions in any of the traditional media disciplines. The next section reviews some of the traditional standards and ethical philosophers and then explores how they might be applied to storytelling in the infotainment age.

Traditional Communication Boundaries and Standards

More than a thousand years before the ability to speak to the masses was technologically enhanced, Plato observed, "The orator has the ability to speak against everyone on every subject, so as in gatherings to be more persuasive, in short, about anything he likes, but the fact that he has the ability to rob doctors or other craftsmen of their reputations doesn't give him any more of a reason to do it. He should use oratory justly."[29] Plato was so concerned about the power that politicians, orators, and teachers had over citizens less schooled or savvy that he argued throughout *The Republic* that stories and poetry, be they fact or fiction, should be accessible by citizens only if those tales promoted the good of the community and proper respect for the gods. Plato concluded:

> So this is what the skilled and good orator will look to when he applies to people's souls whatever speeches he makes.... He will always give his attention to how justice may come to exist in the souls of his fellow citizens and injustice be gotten rid of, how self-control may come to exist there and lack of discipline be gotten rid of, and how the rest of excellence may come into being there and evil may depart.[30]

Arguments for ethical standards in mass communication have a long and prestigious history in Western democracies that have been shaped largely by the theories of libertarianism and social responsibility theory. Together, these theories have been used to shape traditional standards, along with accompanying codes of ethics for news, public relations, advertising, and entertainment. While some argue for a return to traditional standards, that seems unlikely and undesired by audience members as well as practitioners. With the blurring of media boundaries, Plato's philosophy speaks to the matter more directly than the traditionally separate ideas of ethical message formation and delivery.

Mass Communication Ethics for a New Era

Mass communicators are in a position to influence audience members. There must be some guiding principle to define which uses of this power are ethical and which are not. We have identified that essential guiding principle as disclosure.

Our conclusion that disclosure provides the essential ethical component to addressing blurred story types and distinctions is based on the historical fact of humans as storytellers. As storytellers, we have shared ethical expectations long before the conventions of the more recently invented specific categories, such as news, opinion, and entertainment. We are, above all, "storytelling animals."[31] For thousands of years, storytellers have successfully communicated to audience members what they can reasonably expect. Based on the writings of Walter Fisher, the narrative paradigm is composed of narrative probability — what constitutes a story coherent within itself — and narrative fidelity, how well the story being told corresponds with other beliefs held by the audience to be true.[32] "Convention ... aids in establishing narrative probability. Audiences or readers have certain expectations about what they are about to receive."[33]

Deception and Disclosure

The harm principle provides a basis for making that determination. At an ethical minimum, it is wrong to cause unjustified harm. Harms that are caused audiences in the blurring of message boundaries include deception and cheating.[34]

Audience members are deceived and cheated when they have been led to falsely expect that they will be given a story that is accurate (to the best of the storyteller's ability). Deception is a prima facie wrong because it deprives audience members of their right to establish the offered narrative in the context of their other beliefs. If they believe that the story is true to the storyteller's best ability, they will make fidelity assumptions of one sort; if they believe that the story is fiction or possibly not true, they contextualize it differently. Deception is also parasitic on the social interaction in community. Unless given good reason to think otherwise, we operate on the assumption of truth-telling.

But requiring full disclosure at the beginning of a narrative begs the question of suspense and intrigue that often accompanies stories designed to entertain. Sometimes, in an entertainment context, people want to be deceived. The important element is that audience members should always be in control of whether they "know the truth" or not. They should have a way to discern a storyteller's intent and values.

Proposed Framework for Voluntary Disclosure

One model that might be consulted for how such disclosure could be facilitated is a voluntary licensing arrangement that was created to address similar confusion regarding copyrighted materials. Any creative work is automatically copyrighted when it is produced. You do not have to file any paperwork or make any claim to receive a copyright. A copyright means all rights reserved. No one can legally use or adapt the work without gaining explicit permission from the copyright holder. New media, however, have facilitated not only a blurring of fact and fiction, but also a blending of old and new creative works. For example, it has become increasingly common for entertainment artists to digitally sample, alter, or parody older work in creating new music, videos, art, and images. If these artists did not get permission to use the original works, they may be guilty of copyright violations. The courts have ruled that, in some cases, a work that adapts or transforms an original creation falls within acceptable limits of parody or fair use and, therefore, is not a copyright violation, but there are no clear standards for when this might apply. As a result, it can be difficult to know when permission is legally necessary. In addition, with proliferation of content on the Internet, it can be difficult to track down who created a work and ask them for permission.

These concerns inspired a group of legal experts and industry executives to develop a system that would enable individuals to protect their rights to their creative work, as well as their rights to allow others to legally share and build upon that work, if they so wished. They formed a non-profit organization called Creative Commons (CC) and released several copyright licenses known as Creative Commons licenses.[35] These licenses, depending on the one chosen, restrict only certain rights (or none). The Creative Commons licenses enable copyright holders to grant some or all of their rights to the public, while retaining others through a variety of licensing and contract schemes, including dedication to the public domain or open content licensing terms. The intention is to avoid the problems current copyright laws create for the sharing of information.

Creative Commons defines the spectrum of possibilities between full copyright ©, meaning *all rights reserved,* creative commons licenses (cc), meaning *some rights reserved,* and the public domain (pd), meaning *no rights reserved.* When you see the (cc) symbol, you can look up the license type to find out what uses and restrictions the creator has placed on the work. A growing percentage of the entertainment that found on the Internet, such as music on MySpace.com and videos on YouTube.com, is covered by these licenses. Although such licensing does not completely resolve the debate about intellectual property rights versus creative freedom, it does appear to offer some relief.

It might be possible to develop a similar ethical system for voluntary disclosure in "storytelling." Borrowing standards from existing ethical codes for journalism and commercial speech, a system of symbols could be developed for disclosing which standards an author/artist applied in the creation of a work. For example, a symbol could be created for a journalistic code of ethics, a public relations code of ethics, and so on. Symbols might even be created for the specific intent or nature of a piece, such as a symbol signaling that a work is promotional in nature (i.e., advertisement), contains some promotional elements, or was promotionally funded. Likewise, a symbol might warn audiences when "creative license" (i.e., exaggeration or even outright fabrication) may have been taken in the development of a piece. As with Creative Commons licenses, content creators could label different work with the appropriate symbols. When audiences saw the symbols, they could look them up for details on what standards had been followed. Although choosing to label one's work with these symbols would be voluntary, repeated use could result in conventional expectations, just as repeated behaviors of mass communicators created the conventional expectations of a century past.

A more sophisticated approach might even encourage authors to create their own personal statements about their work, which could be archived in a disclosure database available online. One symbol might be created to alert audiences that details on a given work were available at the disclosure site. This might be an option for those who want to maintain a certain amount of mystery or have fun with a hoax, but still provide people with the ability to ultimately obtain the "truth" or an explanation of a given work.

Of course, like the Creative Commons licenses, such a system would not be perfect. There are so many different intents, uses, and types of creative works that it would be impossible to create an exhaustive list of symbols. The system would need to be kept reasonably simple, and thereby might provide only limited, rather than full, disclosure. But even the most transparent mass communication that adheres to traditional standards provides only limited disclosure. A news story may include information about why a source is being presented without identification, but audience members will never know the persuasive techniques used by the journalist to develop that anonymous source.

Such challenges are inherent to the development and adoption of any set of ethical standards or practices. The increasing use of Creative Commons licenses suggests that content creators are open to the idea of voluntary systems that may help them and their audiences better negotiate the new media world. Ethical codes always fall short of our ideals in providing clear, impeccable standards that are uniformly adopted by an entire community. Nonetheless, they can serve as valuable guidelines that often do become widely embraced. Intentionally or not, mass communicators are in the process of shaping conventional behaviors and audience expectations for the future. That shaping ought to account for the power that storytellers have to influence public discourse and, ultimately, to serve the public interest.

NOTES

1. With thanks to University of South Florida, St. Petersburg, student Amanda Smith for her research assistance for this chapter.

2. Virginia Heffernan and Tom Zeller, Jr., "The Lonely Girl That Really Wasn't," *New York Times*, September 13, 2006, http://www.nytimes.com/2006/09/13/technology/13lonely.html?_r=1&ref=business&oref=slogin (accessed August 22, 2008).

3. Rich Motoko "Gang Memoir, Turning Page, Is Pure Fiction," *New York Times*, March 4, 2008, http://www.nytimes.com/2008/03/04/books/04fake.html?_r=1&pagewanted=1&oref=slogin (accessed August 22, 2008).

4. Lawrence Van Gelder, "Holocaust Memoir Turns Out to Be Fiction" *New York Times*, March 3, 2008, http://www.nytimes.com/2008/03/03/books/03arts-HOLOCAUSTMEM_BRF.html?ref=arts (accessed August 22, 2008).

5. "Gang Memoir the Latest Among Literary Fakes," Findingdulcinea.com, March/April 2008, http://www.findingdulcinea.com/news/entertainment/March-April-08/Gang-Memoir-the-Latest-Among-Literary-Fakes.html (accessed August 22, 2008).

6. Jenna Wortham, "Company Fesses Up to Corn Popping Cellphone Clips," Blog. wired.com, June 2008, http://blog.wired.com/underwire/2008/06/bluetooth-compa.html (accessed August 22, 2008).

7. Eli Noam, "Visions of the Media Age: Taming the Information Monster," paper presented to the Third Annual Colloquium Alfred Herrhausen Society of International Dialogue (Frankfurt, Germany, 1995).

8. Michael H. Goldhaber, "The Attention Economy and the Net," *First Monday* 2 no. 4, April 7, 1997, para. 10, www.firstmonday.dk/issues/issue2_4/goldhaber/index.html. accessed October 12, 2006).

9. James Poniewozik, "How Reality TV Fakes It," Time.Com, January 29, 2006, http://www.time.com/time/magazine/article/0,9171,1154194-1,00.html (accessed September 16, 2008).

10. Cited in Poniewozik, "How Reality TV Fakes It," para. 6.

11. Cited in Poniewozik, "How Reality TV Fakes It," para. 2.

12. Cited in Poniewozik, "How Reality TV Fakes It," para. 10.

13. Quoted in Bruno Waterfield, "Wolf-woman Invents Holocaust Survival Tale ('Surviving with Wolves' author admits fabrication)," *The Telegraph (U.K),* February 29, 2008, para. 4, http://www.freerepublic.com/focus/f-news/1978327/posts (accessed August 22, 2008).

14. Quoted in Heffernan and Zeller, "The Lonely Girl That Really Wasn't," para. 8.

15. Quoted in Motoko, "Gang Memoir," para. 6.

16. Quoted in Richard Elias, "World Media Duped by Hoax Organ Donor Show," Scotlandonsunday.scotsman.com, June 3, 2007, para. 15, http://scotlandonsunday.scotsman.com/realitytv/World-media-duped-by-hoax.3291612.jp (accessed May 20, 2009).

17. Quoted in Ethan McNern, "Dutch Organ Donor Numbers Soar After 'Win a Kidney' Show Hoax," News.scotman.com., July 17, 2007, para. 10, http://news.scotsman.com/latestnews/Dutch-organ-donor-numbers-soar.3304820.jp (accessed August 22, 2008).

18. Sam Smith, "Reality-TV Hoax Raises Interesting Marketing Question," Blackdog Strategic.com., (June 3, 2007), para. 9, http://blackdogstrategic.com/2007/06/03/reality-tv-hoax-raises-interesting-marketing-question/ (accessed June 8, 2008).

19. Charles Brown, "Blair Witch Marketing," 2006, Ezinearticles.com, http://ezinearticles.com/?Blair-Witch-Marketing&id=333148 (accessed June 30, 2008).

20. Brown, "Blair Witch Marketing," para 3.

21. Fred Fedler. *Media Hoaxes* (Ames: Iowa State University Press, 1989), xiv–xv.

22. "Product Placement with a Twist," Bnet.com, August, 2002, para. 4, http://findarticles.com/p/articles/mi_pwwi/is_200208/ai_mark03045742 (accessed August 22, 2008).

23. Study cited in "Product Placement with a Twist."

24. Thomas Patterson, "Doing Well and Doing Good: How Soft News and Critical Journalism Are Shrinking the News Audience and Weakening Democracy — And What News Outlets Can Do About It," research paper published by the Joan Shorenstein Center for Press, Politics, & Public Policy (Harvard University, 2001).

25. Stephanie Clifford, "A Product's Place is on the Set," *New York Times*, July 22, 2008, http://www.nytimes.com/2008/07/22/business/media/22adco.html?_r=2&scp=1&sq=a%20product's%20place%20is%20on%20the%20set&st=cse&oref=slogin&oref=slogin (accessed August 14, 2008).

26. Clifford, "A Product's Place is on the Set," para. 7.

27. Philip Patterson and Lee Wilkins, *Media Ethics*, 6th ed., (Columbus, OH: McGraw Hill, 2007), 273.

28. Philip Patterson and Lee Wilkins, *Media Ethics*, 317.

29. Plato, *Gorgias*, trans. Donald J. Zeyl (Indianapolis: Hackett, 1986), 15.

30. *Ibid.*, 84.

31. Kathleen Glenister Roberts, "Texturing the Narrative Paradigm: Folklore and Communication," *Communication Quarterly*, 52, no. 2 (2004): 129–42, 130.

32. Walter Fisher, "Narration as a Human Communication Paradigm: The Case of Public Moral Argument," *Communication Monographs*, 51 (March, 1984): 1–18.

33. Alan J. and Victoria Davies Bush, "The Narrative Paradigm as a Perspective for Improving Ethical Evaluations of Advertisements," *Journal of Advertising*, 23, no. 3 (September, 1994): 38.

34. For a complete explanation of justification of harms and what counts as harm, see Bernard Gert, *Common Morality: Deciding What to Do* (New York: Oxford University Press, 2004).

35. See http://creativecommons.org/.

WORKS CITED

Brown, Charles. "Blair Witch Marketing," 2006, http://ezinearticles.com/?Blair-Witch-Marketing&id=333148 (accessed June 30, 2008).

Bush, Alan J., and Victoria Davies. "The Narrative Paradigm as a Perspective for Improving Ethical Evaluations of Advertisements." *Journal of Advertising* Vol. 23, No. 3 (September 1994): 38.

Clifford, Stephanie. "A Product's Place Is on the Set," *New York Times*, July 22, 2008, http://www.nytimes.com/2008/07/22/business/media/22adco.html?_r=2&scp=1&sq=a%20product's%20place%20is%20on%20the%20set&st=cse&oref=slogin&oref=slogin (accessed August 14, 2008).

Fedler, Fred. *Media Hoaxes.* Ames: Iowa State University Press, 1989.

Fisher, Walter. "Narration as a Human Communication Paradigm: The Case of Public Moral Argument," *Communication Monographs* 51 (March 1984): 1–18.

"Gang Memoir the Latest Among Literary Fakes," Findingdulcinea.com, March/April 2008, http://www.findingdulcinea.com/news/entertainment/March-April-08/Gang-Memoir-the-Latest-Among-Literary-Fakes.html (accessed August 22, 2008).

Gert, B. *Common Morality: Deciding What to Do* (New York: Oxford University Press, 2004.

Goldhaber Michael H. "The Attention Economy and the Net," *First Monday* 2 (4), April 7, 1997, www.firstmonday.dk/issues/issue2_4/goldhaber/index.html.

Heffernan, Virginia and Zeller, Tom, Jr. "The Lonely Girl That Really Wasn't," *New York Times*, September 13, 2006), http://www.nytimes.com/2006/09/13/technology/13lonely.html?_r=1&ref=business&oref=slogin (accessed August 22, 2008).

McNern, Ethan. "Dutch Organ Donor Numbers Soar After 'Win a Kidney' Show Hoax," News.scotman.com. http://news.scotsman.com/latestnews/Dutch-organ-donor-numbers-soar.3304820.jp (accessed August 22, 2008).

Motoko, Rich. "Gang Memoir, Turning Page, Is Pure Fiction," *New York Times*, March 4, 2008, http://www.nytimes.com/2008/03/04/books/04fake.html?_r=1&pagewanted=1&oref=slogin (accessed August 22, 2008).

Noam, Eli. "Visions of the Media Age: Taming the Information Monster," paper presented to the Third Annual Colloquium Alfred Herrhausen Society of International Dialogue, Frankfurt, Germany, 1995.

Patterson, Philip, and Lee Wilkins. *Media Ethics*, 6th Ed., Columbus, OH: McGraw Hill, 2007.

Patterson, Thomas. "Doing Well and Doing Good: How Soft News and Critical Journalism Are Shrinking the News Audience and Weakening Democracy — And What News Outlets Can Do About It," 2001, research paper published by the Joan Shorenstein Center for Press, Politics, & Public Policy at Harvard University.

Plato, *Gorgias*. (D. J. Zeyl, trans.) Indianapolis: Hackett, 1987.

Poniewozik, James. How Reality TV Fakes It. Time.Com, January 29, 2006, http://www.time.com/time/magazine/article/0,9171,1154194-1,00.html (accessed September 16, 2008).

"Product Placement with a Twist." Bnet.com, August 2002, http://findarticles.com/p/articles/mi_pwwi/is_200208/ai_mark03045742 (accessed August 22, 2008).

Roberts, Kathleen Glenister. Texturing the Narrative Paradigm: Folklore and Communication, *Communication Quarterly*, Vol. 52, No. 2 (2004): 129–142, 130.

Smith, Sam. "Reality-TV Hoax Raises Interesting Marketing Question." BlackdogStrategic. com, June 3, 2007, http://blackdogstrategic.com/2007/06/03/reality-tv-hoax-raises-inter esting-marketing-question/(accessed June 8, 2008).
Van Gelder, Lawrence. "Holocaust Memoir Turns Out to Be Fiction" *New York Times,* March 3, 2008, http://www.nytimes.com/2008/03/03/books/03arts-HOLOCAUSTMEM_BRF. html?ref=arts (accessed August 22, 2008).
Waterfield Bruno. "Wolf-Woman Invents Holocaust Survival Tale ('Surviving with Wolves' Author Admits Fabrication)," *The Telegraph (U.K),* February 29, 2008, http://www.free republic.com/focus/f-news/1978327/posts (accessed August 22, 2008).
Wortham, Jenna. "Company Fesses Up to Corn Popping Cellphone Clips," Blog.wired.com. June 2008, http://blog.wired.com/underwire/2008/06/bluetooth-compa.html (accessed August 22, 2008).

CHAPTER 8

This Time It's Personal:
The Ethics of 9/11 Docudrama

Steve Lipkin

Part of the evil brilliance of the events of 9/11 is that they were conceived as spectacle. The terrorism of 9/11 endures as it recurs in images seared indelibly into our memories and cultural imagination.

The impact of important historical events, magnified further by the power and ubiquity of their spectacular images, guarantees the interest of Hollywood. Equally inevitable will be the ethical implications of treating these events through feature films. This essay focuses on Paul Greengrass's film *United 93* (2006) to examine how its re-creation of the hijacking of one of the 9/11 aircraft responds to the question of the morality of its storytelling. As a 9/11 docudrama *United 93* is both similar to and different from Oliver Stone's *World Trade Center* (2006) in viewing world-altering events on the scale of personal space rather than political dynamics. *United 93* argues that comprehending the terror of 9/11 terrorism must begin with confronting the fear of what we can only imagine about the horror of that day. The challenge morally for any 9/11 docudrama is to tell the stories of true people and events without distortion or emotional exploitation.

As feature films and movies of the week based on true stories, docudramas generally raise two interrelated ethical concerns. The first tends to focus on questions of fidelity. How valid — how proper — is the work's contribution to history? What does it contribute (and how) to our understanding of the past? A concern for "fidelity" considers the accuracy of record, but at the same time recognizes the limits of what "accuracy" entails. Any record will be circumscribed by the time, place, and means of its creation, as well as the terms of its reception. How does a work claim to correspond with what it represents? How true to the "true story" is what we're seeing on the screen?

Did these events really occur "this way"? Is this really the history it purports to be? In previous work discussing the ethics of docudrama, I focused on the problem of fidelity in terms of the "proximity" of a work to the sources upon which it is based.[1] For a work to be "based on" a true story suggests that it faces a moral obligation to maintain a close basis to the variety of historical materials that allow its story to be told.

The second concern is related to form. Is a feature film or a movie of the week an appropriate means of presentation? Should the material of history, people who lived and acted and events that occurred, appear before us through the codes and conventions of classic Hollywood storytelling and melodrama that are characteristic of docudrama?[2] Is it ethical to represent sober actuality through a medium that purports to entertain? Is it proper to render the complexity of an individual's life through the conventions—the rules and expectations—of characterization that govern feature film storytelling? Can the structure of a two-hour story that develops and resolves major and minor dramatic conflicts serve properly the multifaceted, often contradictory, views of events historical records represent?

The ethical questions and concerns that docudramas raise become more acute in proportion to the importance and the notoriety of the subject matter the works re-create. One need look no further than responses to the "outlaw history" of the Kennedy assassination Oliver Stone proposes in *JFK* (1991), or critics' concerns over the "sentimental" treatment of the Holocaust Steven Spielberg offers us in *Schindler's List* (1993).[3]

Feature films and movies of the week based on "true stories" of September 11 will be subject to the same kind of scrutiny. The events of 9/11 remain lived history for the audiences of works that examine the impact of that day. The enormity of those events only heightens the importance of the historical fidelity and structural appropriateness of works purporting to depict them.

In the summer of 2006, the first two major Hollywood productions to re-create the terrorism of 9/11 appeared in theaters, *United 93* and *World Trade Center*. Although the films both tell stories about individuals caught up in the events of that day, the conventionality of *World Trade Center* puts it on different ground, ethically, from the more documentary visual style and collective development of character groups in *United 93*. *United 93* focuses on the hijacking of the one airliner that did not reach its designated target. *World Trade Center* re-creates the fate of two firefighters trapped beneath the rubble of the collapsed World Trade Center (WTC) buildings and makes traditional use of melodrama as a narrative framework, centering on victims and their families as a means to moralize about the fates of its characters. The restricted focus of both films favors a personal, rather than a larger, political view of 9/11 terrorism. The films argue that our understanding of the impact of 9/11 begins with this restricted focus on the experiences of individuals, and, by extension, our own reactions to those stories.

As it takes this focus, these films, and 9/11 docudrama generally, will raise the following questions: Is a more personal approach to storytelling a useful and appropriate means of creating an understanding of these events and these people? Do these films have a responsibility to explore further the larger contexts that frame their stories? Should they risk alienating either the Republican or Democratic half of a potential American audience, for example, by addressing the political implications of the failure of leadership 9/11 revealed? Is it sufficient to confine the United 93 story to the actions we see, as a way of understanding why these people, as opposed to those on three other aircraft, were able to resist? Is *United 93's* categorical view of those involved, its withholding of names and the conventions of individualized characterization, an asset to the larger purposes of its storytelling? Is it appropriate — not just aesthetically, but also morally — to confine our understanding of these victims to these portrayals? Has the speculative humanizing of the United 93 hijackers allowed the film to venture onto morally questionable ground? Does a restricted scope of representation enhance or limit remembrance? Does the sense of access to events through Hollywood storytelling adequately serve their magnitude? Is this kind of representation the best way to remember, allowing an appropriate memorial to victims and survivors?

Re-creating the fates of 9/11 victims in Hollywood feature films heightens even further the ethical challenges to docudrama, because these are commercial works made to be sold to as many viewers as possible.

The fact that they are produced, distributed, marketed, and exhibited as feature films underlines an important consideration to keep in mind about docudramas: They do not purport to be documentaries. Docudramas assert that they are "based on" true stories, indicating no claim to be a literal record of actuality. In attempting to re-create known figures and events, docudramas instead propose a version of history. Further, just as docudramas tend to signpost their status as hybrid narratives (melodramas incorporating "true," documentary materials), they also foreground their work as performance. In re-creating true stories docudramas perform their subjects. This is "performance" in the broadest sense of representation, of selecting, arranging, and framing the space and time of known people, actions, and events. It is also the more specifically theatrical performance *World Trade Center* foregrounds by casting a star, Nicolas Cage, as John McLaughlin, the New York City firefighter who endured the events that film depicts.

The ethical questions of 9/11 docudrama arise as these stories perform the momentous events of 9/11 in re-creating the actions of individuals. The emphasis on the personal space of key figures allows performance to provide both a means of access to history as well as the opportunity to confront the fears that history elicits. Docudramatic performance in these works must account for both the fundamental ethical concerns of fidelity and appropriateness. We are offered performances that are modeled on the known, bringing the result in close proximity to the historical record. As performance in personal space reenacts and reclaims the time and space of the real, it affords the opportunity to frame the terror that, at bottom, is the goal of terrorism.

Fidelity: Addressing What We Know

Both *United 93* and *World Trade Center* presume their viewers have shared the 9/11 "experience" as members of a media audience. As different as they are in scope and style, both films address the surrealism of our encounter with 9/11 as a media creation. That experience is probably typified by the almost inestimable repetition of several traumatic images. These include images of the penetration and eruption of the towers and their nightmarish, slow-motion collapses. Broadcast repetition of these images remains our initial and perhaps one of our more definitive means of access to the actual. Each repetition asserts "this actually happened" but does so, ironically, in this dream-like way. Repetition must be the reference point for "experiencing" what happened, whether on one of the planes, at Ground Zero, in one of the control towers, or in the WTC itself. Michael Moore in *Fahrenheit 911* (2004) appears to have decided that we can all relive that mediated trauma without having to show it exactly that way again, and that it's only necessary to refer to it to re-evoke it. Moore does so, however, with black screens, shocked, upturned faces, and repeated images of sheets of paper, cascading like confetti in the air around the towers.

With that cultural vision as a given reference point, *United 93* and *World Trade Center* share a common persuasive strategy — that the reality of the 9/11 experience is accessible by claiming personal space as public. Both argue for the "truth" of their stories through fear appeals that characterize the physical space occupied by the main characters as claustrophobic. Both films render the space of their settings as constricted and oppositional. The plane cabin on United 93 offers minimal terrain, with its seats and aisles, shut doors, and slim opportunities, not to mention the confined drama danced out on the monitor screens and through the windows in various control rooms. The rubble in *World Trade Center* kills, with its masses of concrete, twisted pipe, sparking wires, and the impossibly small gaps left for human remains. In emphasizing the claustrophobic, both films convert America's experience of terrorists and terrorism to the specific and personal. *United 93* and *World Trade Center* strive to persuade us that when we view the enormity of 9/11's public events through constricted, claustrophobic, visceral images, what we see has a meaning for us that is direct, immediate, and personal, rather than abstract, ideological, and mythic.

Persuasion begins in docudrama with the convention of performing actual people and events. "Performance" in docudramas about real events appears as modeled action within contested space. Drama arises not only from the conflict of the desires and actions of the performers, but also inheres within the contestation the space itself creates, whether it is the natural environment (*Erin Brockovich* [2000]; *A Civil Action* [1998]; *The Perfect Storm* [2000]), or a social one (the streets of Derry in Greengrass's *Bloody Sunday* [2002]; the cabin of United 93). Docudramas strive to balance the attention given to characters' actions and the settings in which those actions occur. Watching events re-created in contested space offers something like a trip to an arena or coliseum, where staging reflects the roles and functions of those involved. Contested space associates physical and ideological conflict. Action based on contestation makes visible the meanings at issue.

Greengrass approaches the contested space of his docudramas, *Bloody Sunday* and *United 93*, as one would a chessboard, in which the space of action puts the rules of engagement into play, and the principals are comparable to all the pieces from kings to pawns. *Bloody Sunday* concentrates on several groups of characters whose functions in the actual events depicted arise from their desires to move within and control the streets of Derry. These groups include: the protest leaders debating whether or not to march for their civil rights and their supporters; the youth of Derry who join the march and are the particular target of the British troops there to control the city; the soldiers themselves, who are characterized as preoccupied first with how violent they should be, and then with how to cover up the consequences of their violence; and the officers in command of the troops who constantly compare wall-mounted street maps tracing the march and the placement of troops against radio-relayed information about the unfolding conflict. Re-creating these events extends outward from what characters desire to the environment in which the consequences of their decisions are enacted. We see the wall map, then the streets filled with combatants, then hear the information from observers both above and within those same streets. The film's emphasis on space and how it is structured continually underlines the modeling of events and argues for the authenticity — the fidelity — of its depiction.

The "Truth" of Terror

United 93 similarly addresses the 9/11 experience of its audience by focusing not on the terrorism that precipitated the events of that day, but by re-creating the places of terror of both victims and perpetrators. Although terrorism's impact on events and lives provides the premise of the story, we are not offered any kind of socio-political analysis of terrorism. Both *United 93* and *World Trade Center* argue for the fidelity of their representations by working emphatically with the settings of 9/11 terrorism. The buildings, workplaces, and modes of transportation — the visible surface of what is normally innocent and everyday — are turned by that day's terrorism into tools of destruction.

United 93's settings become claustrophobic as it examines the three interrelated experiences of terror that develop this particular chapter of 9/11. We see the story of the doomed flight from the perspectives of the hijackers, the passengers, and the flight controllers. From the microcosmic experiences of these three groups, we are to view the destructive, ideological commitment of the perpetrators, the heroic resistance of their victims, and the inadequate preparation of the professionals in charge of airline security.

United 93 operates in somewhat the same way as a snuff film. The film's purpose is to deliver a known outcome, building interest by developing the horror of the moments before death. We know the fate of the people on the flight before the film even begins. A snuff film, however, would exploit the prurient appeal of the moment that an actual life is extinguished (see, for example, the popularity of online videos of the Daniel Pearl beheading, or the hanging of Saddam Hussein.[4]) *United 93* re-creates this particular chapter of 9/11 in order to make the moment of impending doom accessible. Staging the last hours of the doomed crew and passengers imagines the unimaginable for an audience that may now relive vicariously what "it" must have been like — what it must have been like to prepare and execute the attack, what it must have been like for passengers and attendants to have this violence erupt out of the mundane routine of a cross-country flight, and what it must have been like to have the strict procedures of domestic air traffic go bad so quickly.

The film depends upon two basic strategies to create and sustain the atmosphere of doom it explores. First, *United 93* unfolds in approximately the same amount of elapsed time as the events it re-creates. Consequently, the opening image showing Jarrah, the hijacker who will pilot the plane, at morning prayers in his hotel room, is tantamount to lighting the fuse of a two-hour time bomb. We know what will happen and approximately when. The film's real-time chronology indicates the lengths to which Greengrass's production went in maintaining the closest possible proximity to what was known about the events it re-creates. Interviews with Greengrass and reviews of the film make much of the production's work with its source material, drawing not only on the chronology graphed out in the 9/11 Commission Report, but also upon the cockpit recordings, the transcripts of the calls passengers made, and the extensive interviews with the recipients of those calls, other family members, and the professionals involved in the events depicted.[5]

The second strategy the film develops is to show doomed passengers through images that are relentlessly claustrophobic. The tight limits of the visual world of the film echo appropriately the closed fate of its principals. This imagery grows in part out of *United 93*'s reliance upon elements of documentary style. In addition to casting unknown or relatively low-profile actors as passengers and hijackers, many of those in the roles of professionals are doing in the film what they do in life, including the air traffic controllers, some of whom play themselves in the film.[6] Here, and in his earlier work in *Bloody Sunday*, Greengrass has shown his roots in the British drama-documentary tradition.[7] The images showing how these people respond to the situation rapidly changing around them are in the vein of direct cinema, shot with hand-held cameras, shifting quickly with the flow of information, and maintaining a tight, conversational proximity to the actors.[8] As viewers we are wedged visually into the same situations as the people we see on screen.

The film shifts between two kinds of worlds. We see the work areas of various civil and military air traffic control rooms in Virginia, upstate New York, Boston, Newark, Cleveland, and Indianapolis. These alternate with the surroundings of those boarding the plane. Once the control rooms are established, the story becomes confined to events graphically rendered on arrays of monitors and the reactions of those trying to make sense of and cope with what they see there. The many shots of the passengers on the plane emphasize the mundane, universal nature of the experience of flying, confining action to the areas in and around seats, and the aisle of the plane. The passengers read, work, eat, and converse. The flight attendants engage in their routines within and around their work stations. In all cases the film constricts its story to personal space bound by the physical limits of the setting. As events develop, all of these normally innocent elements take on new meaning as they become oppositional, and the space of events constricts into the space of confrontation.

The Propriety of Storytelling Form: The Melodrama of Fear

By contrast, *World Trade Center* establishes and then shifts away from necessarily tight shots of its trapped characters, to allow them (and us) the opportunity to escape into the space of memory. Through the film's flashback structure we see the two main characters, Jimeno and McLaughlin, in bed with their wives or playing with their children. The flashbacks suggest that memory provides both relief from the crushing reality of the physical space that constrains them and motivation to live by reinforcing what is most meaningful to the men.

World Trade Center develops its story through a traditional melodramatic structure, building on the configurations possible because of vulnerable, self-sacrificing characters victimized by destructive physical and social settings. The return to the unrestricted space of normal life at the conclusion of the story suggests not only resolution of the conflict we have seen unfold, but also an affirmation of the moral system the film's story serves. The virtuous triumph through their survival. The film's closure has a sense of ethical incongruity; it is a 9/11 story with a happy ending.

Alternatively, the three groups of characters in United 93 replace the conventional, individual characters that provide the customary comforts of a dramatic, classical Hollywood narrative film. Greengrass has remained emphatic about how the film's "collective" approach to its characters was both fundamental to the project's creative process and necessary for understanding how the passengers came to take the action they did as a group.[9] Individuals become reference points for us within these groups. However, who they are as people — this is not a film that uses or reinforces names, for example — remains secondary to how we see them respond to the building confrontation. Their similar, yet differing, responses create the film's identification strategies.

Since it is a story in which death is certain, United 93 foregrounds its killers. The four terrorists provide one of the most consistent, unifying elements of the dramatic structure of the film. Unlike the controllers or passengers, the terrorists are present in every stage of United 93's narrative development. Taken together, as four members of a group, the hijackers contribute an arc of character development following what classical Hollywood narrative conventions require to establish, build, and resolve conflict. They develop from a preparatory stage (morning prayers, followed by the passage through airport security) that marks both what they desire and what might oppose it, continuing through the wait that leads up to the attack, and climaxing with the attack on the plane itself and its resolution. Even though we are never offered the opportunity to learn anything about the hijackers as individuals, actions that signal their different kinds of apprehension serve to individualize them.[10] The pilot prays. The co-pilot reads. The third hijacker appears the most agitated, nervously leaving his seat to demand from the hijacker pilot that the time has come. The bomber hunches into his zipped jacket and clutches his flight bag.

United 93's consistent return to and emphasis on the emotions of the hijackers strives to humanize rather than demonize them. The stress of their pending suicides illustrates their relatable fears of both failure and success. This forms one of the film's dramatic cornerstones.

Against this line of development, *United 93* compiles what one might expect to be the film's preferred area of identification, a growing familiarity with the plane's passengers and flight attendants. This group remains less individualized, however. As the story returns to a few of them, they become reference points. One of the attendants[11] calls United and reports the hijacking. Subsequently, she is allowed to tend briefly to a mortally stabbed passenger and move up the cabin and back to relay information. One of the male passengers, a younger man in a baseball cap,[12] reacts first by attempting to flee, and then helps lead the fight. One of the businessmen[13] speaks for most of the others and helps provoke their resistance. Their story also develops in a group arc. They grow from everyday innocence to progressive awareness, not only of their immediate situation, but also of the larger events of 9/11 and their place in it. Knowledge culminates in an understanding that they will need to fight back in order to have a chance to survive.

United 93's development of the air traffic controllers as a third character group focuses, ironically, on their spiraling loss of control. The arc of their development is their transformation from informed "insiders," the group that should be and strives to be in control, to increasingly helpless witnesses. The controllers are not even present in the last stage of the story. Consequently, the film renders the controllers' experience of that 9/11 morning in a way that visually approximates our own, underlining their status as bystanders, viewers of events in which they should have greater agency.

As with the hijackers and plane occupants, several individuals within the group of controllers function as reference points. Most notably, Ben Sliney, playing himself, becomes the face of institutional frustration as he tries to patrol the point position in the Federal Aviation Administration's national center in Herndon, Virginia. Sliney is one of the only characters in *United 93* given a name; however, his function in the story is limited to what he is supposed to do and what he can't do in his job. Sliney maintains his professionalism, embodying the need to adhere to procedure even when procedure deteriorates under a barrage of information and misinformation. We see Sliney's counterparts in the military equally frustrated when flights vary from their routes and radio patterns and begin to crash into targets on the Eastern seaboard.

The film repeatedly emphasizes the controllers' 9/11 experience as one of viewing. Shots alternate briskly between the aircraft icons on air traffic screens and the controllers watching and commenting on what they see there. The film also renders through screens how the controllers, like us, must watch 9/11's climactic moments. The airport control tower window at Newark has a view of the burning WTC towers that resembles a large-screen TV. Sliney's group is watching CNN monitors when the second plane strikes the South Tower. So are the military responsible for the air space over Manhattan and

Washington, D.C. Everyone in these rooms gasps in horror, their reaction mirroring the responses of everyone else watching the events on television at that moment. To show the experience of the air traffic controllers as helpless, distanced viewers emphasizes the helplessness we all felt as we watched.

In *World Trade Center* it is the families waiting for news that provide viewpoint and consequently the film's key identification opportunities. The film's concentration on waiting families, summed up by the image(s) of the "missing" posted on the bulletin board in the hospital cafeteria where relatives have been told to wait, visualizes the impact of events in the domestic terms of melodrama. The film repeatedly turns to view the aftermath of the collapsed towers from the perspectives of anxious, extended families. The Jimenos disagree on what the name of the new baby will be. The McLaughlins' younger son castigates his mother for not getting down to the site and searching the rubble. In sum, the attack on the WTC, in the view of the film, is best understood as an attack on families.

A Moral Argument for Heroism

As *United 93* integrates documentary material and the narrative strategies of melodrama, the film's three basic character configurations provide the structure for moral argument. The moral implications of victims striving to take heroic action develop within a narrative built on cornerstones of suicidal commitment, belated but necessary resistance, and frustrated professionalism. Melodrama in film tends to focus on victims of repressive circumstances in order to clarify the moral ramifications of the interactions between individual and context, desire and setting. *United 93* situates its known, documentary material within these parameters. Both news reports at the time[14] and the 9/11 Commission Report defined the primary victims, the crew and passengers as heroes for succeeding in preventing the plane from reaching its intended target (the Capitol building in Washington, D.C., as the photo the pilot clips to the control console would suggest). The film shows that as their realization of larger events grows, the passengers act primarily out of self-preservation. They know planes have crashed into the WTC, but have no idea of what the intended target of their flight might be. What is heroic is their willingness to fight back in the face of evident obstacles. The film's argument is visual. It equates ethical action with the loss of physical space. Courage increases as space constricts to the narrow door to the cockpit, the last and most impenetrable obstacle to self-preservation.

The controllers are secondary victims, but suffer from the ineffectiveness of the procedures and protocols of their profession. They are victimized both by their commitment to their professional training and the tools they have to live up to its obligations. The visual concentration on the overwhelming flow of information from monitors and phone calls, and the exchanges of this information between control centers, underlines how the circumstances were, in the terms of the 9/11 Commission Report, "unprecedented," suggesting the system's inadequate preparation for such events.[15] The repeated images of the hijackers in prayer before and after they launch their attack suggests that this group of characters has been victimized by the destructiveness of its ideological commitment. We see this strictly as an aspect of character. Why this extreme religious belief would compel these (and the other) 9/11 hijackers to this most extreme kind of action is clearly not within the scope of the film's exploration of the event.

United 93 rigorously concentrates its view of the repressive circumstances that create victims on the immediate, visually constrained surroundings of the plane and the control centers, emphasizing how the principal players performed within those spaces of constricted possibilities. The energy of the film's narrative is focused not so much on what larger causes doomed the victims, but on what the experience of that doom must have been like.

Evoking Memory Ethically

What kind of understanding results, then, from the docudramatic performance of United 93's history? The answer Greengrass's film proposes is this: Before 9/11, for most Americans, the experience of terrorism was largely an abstraction, events reported in other parts of the world that happened to other people. Living 9/11 indirectly, through reported, mediated events, brought the experience of terrorism closer both geographically and personally with the incessant repetition of the traumatic images that form the iconography of 9/11: the striking of the towers, towers enflamed, bodies falling from great heights, and perhaps the most relatable images of all, the hopelessness of passengers on doomed airliners. As we re-inflict this with each re-imagining of what the claustrophobic finality of United 93 must have been like, we relive the very terror the perpetrators desired us to suffer.

Several reviewers of the film have faulted this approach, shown from the perspective of groups, rather than conventionally individualized protagonists, for failing to allow the possibility of a cathartic experience.[16] This critical position rests upon two assumptions, that the film's re-creation aims at catharsis, and that a cathartic effect must result from our identification with the desires of individual characters.

The first assumption addresses the event as tragedy. Certainly the story of those tragically doomed to death on United 93 creates the opportunity to purge pity and fear. However, there is a difference when the story re-creates the fates of real-life individuals rather than literary characters. The grounding of the United 93 story in actuality makes the process of imagining the unimaginable closer to a secondary memory than to the identification strategies of literary characterization.[17] None of us might have been on United 93, but in reliving the terror of the experience as if we were, we create for ourselves a posttraumatic, secondary memory of what it "must" have been like. Given that what we see is grounded in the actuality that creates the sense of terror for us, the first function of *United 93*'s storytelling will be to confront the event as a source of fear.

The second assumption also grows out of the conventions of character development in feature film. We identify customarily with individual characters. In this case is it appropriate to do so? Characterization in *United 93* suggests an alternative and arguably ethical choice in avoiding the potential emotional exploitation that could result from portraying actual individuals as characters we should identify with. It is the very unconventionality of *United 93*'s group characters, coupled with its shifting, hand-held, direct cinema shooting style, that allows the style of storytelling to evoke the experience of posttraumatic memory.

Film has the capacity to evoke traumatic experience when representation finds alternatives to the conventions of realism. Janet Walker defines "trauma cinema" as "films that deal with a world-shattering event or events, whether public or personal ... in a nonrealist mode characterized by a disturbance and fragmentation of the films' narrative and stylistic regimes."[18] It is necessary to do so, Walker suggests, to model effectively the memory of traumatic experience "by drawing on innovative strategies for representing reality obliquely, by looking to mental processes for inspiration, and by incorporating self-reflexive devices to call attention to the friability of the scaffolding for audiovisual historiography"[19] *United 93*'s performance of collective experiences, shot in a documentary style, foreground the film's processes of re-creating traumatic events.

Strictly conventional means of representation imply that traumatic experience can, and perhaps should, be contained by the sense of control and closure of classic Hollywood narrative form. The "happy ending" of *World Trade Center* argues for this kind of containment through the release of its main characters, their return to their families, and the epilogue's suggestion that their lives now go on. In order to confront traumatic experience, rather than repress its disturbing effect, the films that "invite a posttraumatic historical consciousness" blend the strategies of conventional realism and the formal provocations of modernism.[20] Such films belong to a "discourse of trauma," texts that arise after a traumatizing historical event and attempt to represent its often unrepresentable nature.

The ethical aim of film in this instance is

... to overcome defensive numbing. Documentary images must be submitted to a narrative discourse the purpose of which is, if not to literally traumatize the spectator, at least to invoke a posttraumatic historical consciousness—a kind of textual compromise between the senselessness of the initial traumatic encounter and the sense-making apparatus of a fully integrated historical narrative.[21]

Joshua Hirsch suggests that "posttraumatic cinema" evokes the traumatic experience but in a context that strives to "make sense" of it.[22] In Hirsch's view, conventional historical narrative contains trauma too neatly, conveying the erroneous impression that it has been controlled in the telling. Making sense of trauma in a constructive way, in a way that will frame it without defusing it, requires a self-conscious narrative — that is, a narrative that can accommodate calling attention to its own processes:

> Posttraumatic memory may not be self-conscious *per se*. But insofar as posttraumatic memory is a kind of failure of memory, its therapeutic treatment requires a degree of self-consciousness that is uncharacteristic of narrative memory.[23]

By adhering to unconventional strategies of characterization in performing the experiences of the groups whose story we see, and by foregrounding both dramatic and cinematic performance as a model of the process of memory, *United 93* aims for confrontation with the unthinkable and unrepresentable, rather than with the conventions of cathartic realism.

United 93's performance of people and events is both modeled on and directly linked to the actuality it represents. Consequently, it allows the access to the real that Hirsch and Walker suggest can be one of the main goals of the process of dealing with traumatic history. By identifying and confronting the source of fear, it becomes possible to short-circuit the compulsive reliving of the experience of terror.

United 93 does not address directly the larger social, political, economic, and cultural forces at work in the events of 9/11. If it limits its re-creation to one flight's passengers, hijackers, and flight controllers, its docudramatic framework provides the first and most personally relevant kind of understanding of its subject for any of us, an understanding that is an essential prerequisite for a further reckoning with the larger issues of the sources of terrorism. As we relive the finality of United 93, the film's performance of the real shows us that these were people like us and that confronting the terror that terrorism creates must begin with the personal.

NOTES

1. See Steven N. Lipkin, *Real Emotional Logic: Film and Television Docudrama as Persuasive Practice* (Carbondale: Southern Illinois University Press, 2002), 47–54.

2. For discussion of the defining characteristics of docudrama as a hybrid mode of representation see Lipkin, *Real Emotional Logic*, 1–11.

3. Many are referenced in my discussion of *JFK* (Lipkin, *Real Emotional Logic*, 47–50). For a sampling of the discourse surrounding *Schindler's List*, see Yosefa Loshitzky, ed., *Spielberg's Holocaust: Critical Perspectives on Schindler's List* (Bloomington: Indiana University Press, 1997).

4. According to the NBC *Evening News*, January 2, 2007, YouTube reported more than 1 million hits on its link to the Hussein video.

5. See discussions of the film's production in Missy Schwartz, "Ready or Not," *Entertainment Weekly* 874/875, April 28, 2006-May 5, 2006, 13–14, as well as articles by Richard Corliss, "Let's Roll," *Time* 16, April 17, 2006, 70–72; Heather Timmons, "Four Years On, A Cabin's Eye View of 9/11" *New York Times*, January 1, 2006, AR 7; 22; and Kenneth Turan, "*United 93*" *Los Angeles Times*, April 28, 2006, http://www.calendarlive.com/movies/turan/cl-et-united28apr28,0,7956334.story.

6. Roger Ebert, "*United 93*," *Chicago Sun Times*, April 28, 2006, http://rogerebert.suntimes.com/apps/pbcs.dll/article?AID=/20060427/REVIEWS/60419006/1023; Turan, "United 93."

7. See Turan, "United 93," for example, for some comparison of Greengrass's approach here to the work of Humphrey Jennings. See Pavlus for comparison to the methods of Ken Loach (in John Pavlus, "A Doomed Flight and a Broken Romance." *American Cinematographer* June 2006, 26–30).

8. Greg Marcks, "A Credible Witness," *Film Quarterly* 60 no. 1 (Fall 2006): 3.

9. Gavin Smith, "Mission Statement," *Film Comment* 42 no. 3 (May/June 2006): 25.

10. The hijackers' names, as I identify them here through their functions, are: pilot Ziad Jarrah; copilot Ahmad Al Nami; instigator Saeed al Ghamdi; bomber Ahmad al Haznami. See *The 9/11 Commission Report*, New York: W. W. Norton, 2004, p. 4.

11. Sandra Bradshaw, played by Trish Gates, a United Air Lines flight attendant.

12. Mark Bingham, played by Cheyenne Jackson.

13. Thomas Burnett, played by Christian Clemenson.

14. See Longman (Jere Longman, "Paul Greengrass's Filming of Flight 93's Story, Trying to Define Heroics." *New York Times*, April 24, 2006, http://www.nytimes.com/2006/04/24/movies/24unit.html?_r=1&scp=10&sq=united%2093&st=cse) for some discussion of the film's approach to the problem of the political discourse of the time exploiting passenger heroics.

15. *The 9/11 Commission Report*, p. 31; Peter Bradshaw, "United 93," *Guardian Unlimited*, June 2, 2006, http://www.guardian.co.uk/culture/2006/jun/02/1.

16. Manohla Dargis, "Defiance Under Fire: Paul Greengrass's Harrowing 'United 93,'" *New York Times*, April 28, 2006, http://movies.nytimes.com/2006/04/28/movies/28unit.html?scp=1&sq=dargis,%20united%2093&st=cse); Turan, "United 93"; Stephanie Zacharek. "United 93." *Salon.com*, April 28, 2006, http://www.salon.com/ent/moview/review/2006/04/26/united_93.

17. Allison Landsberg has termed this kind of mediated, secondary memory as "prosthetic memory." See Allison Landsberg, *Prosthetic Memory: The Transformation of American Remembrance in the Age of Mass Culture* (New York: Columbia University Press, 2004): 4.

18. Janet Walker, *Trauma Cinema: Documenting Incest and the Holocaust* (Berkeley: University of California Press, 2005), 19.

19. *Ibid.*, 19.

20. Joshua Hirsh, "Posttraumatic Cinema and the Holocaust Documentary," *Film & History* 32 no. 1 (2002): 9–20.

21. *Ibid.*, 11.

22. Hirsch, "Posttraumatic Cinema" writes: "Documentary images must be submitted to a narrative discourse the purpose of which is, if not to literally traumatize the spectator, at least to invoke a posttraumatic historical consciousness—a kind of textual compromise between the senselessness of the initial traumatic encounter and the sense-making appara-

tus of a fully integrated historical narrative..." (11) This is necessary because: "As trauma is less a particular experiential content than a *form* of experience, also the discourse of trauma in this second phase is defined less by a particular image content than by the attempt to discover a form for presenting the content that mimics some aspects of PTSD itself—the attempt to formally reproduce for the spectator an experience of once again suddenly seeing the unthinkable. And insofar as what is historically thinkable is partly constituted by the conventions of the historical film genre, the instigation of a cinematic discourse of trauma becomes a question of upsetting the spectator's expectations not only of history in general, but also of the historical film in particular." (11–12)

   23. *Ibid.*, 12.

WORKS CITED

Bradshaw, Peter. "United 93." *Guardian Unlimited*, June 2, 2006.

"Brave and the Bold." *Entertainment Weekly*, 874/875, April 28-May 5, 2006, 13–14.

Corliss, Richard. "Let's Roll." *Time* 16, April 17, 2006, 70–72.

Dargis, Manohla. "Defiance Under Fire: Paul Greengrass's Harrowing 'United 93.' *New York Times*, April 28, 2006, http://movies.nytimes.com/2006/04/28/movies/28unit.html?scp =1&sq=dargis,%20united%2093&st=cse.

Doherty, Thomas. "*United 93.*" *Cineaste* 31:4 (Fall 2006): 73–75.

Ebert, Roger. "*United 93.*" *Chicago Sun Times,* April 28, 2006, http://rogerebert.suntimes.com/ apps/pbcs.dll/article?AID=/20060427/REVIEWS/60419006/1023.

Hirsch, Joshua. "Posttraumatic Cinema and the Holocaust Documentary." *Film & History* 32:1, 2002, 9–20.

Landsberg, Allison. *Prosthetic Memory: The Transformation of American Remembrance in the Age of Mass Culture.* New York: Columbia University Press, 2004.

LaSalle, Mick. "Agony, Heroism of 'United 93' Shown with Nearly Unbearable Realism." *San Francisco Chronicle,* April 28, 2006, http://www.sfgate.com/cgi-bin/article.cgi?f=/c/a/ 2006/04/28/DDG6SIEM6H14.DTL&hw=united+93&sn=022&sc=433.

Longman, Jere. "Paul Greengrass's Filming of Flight 93's Story, Trying to Define Heroics." *New York Times,* April 24, 2006, http://www.nytimes.com/2006/04/24/movies/24unit. html?_r=1&scp=10&sq=united%2093&st=cse.

Marcks, Greg. "A Credible Witness." *Film Quarterly* 60:1 (Fall 2006): 3.

The 9/11 Commission Report. New York: W. W. Norton, 2004.

Pavlus, John. "A Doomed Flight and a Broken Romance." *American Cinematographer* (June 2006) 26–30.

"Ready or Not." *Entertainment Weekly* 874/875, April 28, 2006-May 5, 2006, 13–14.

Smith, Gavin. "Mission Statement." *Film Comment* 42:3 (May/June 2006): 24–26.

Timmons, Heather. "Four Years On, A Cabin's Eye View of 9/11." *New York Times*, January 1, 2006, AR 7; 22.

Turan, Kenneth. "*United 93.*" *Los Angeles Times*, April 28, 2006, http://www.calendarlive. com/movies/turan/cl-et-united28apr28,0,7956334.story.

Walker, Janet. *Trauma Cinema: Documenting Incest and the Holocaust.* Berkeley: University of California Press, 2005.

CHAPTER 9

Bread and Circuits: Politics in an Entertainment Culture

Mike Dillon

"Is it real? Or is it Memorex?"

That 1970s tagline for an audiotape ad poses an existential riddle when applied to our mediated politics.

There's Barack Obama poised to launch a football before a 2008 Democratic presidential primary event. Is it a candid glimpse of a lighthearted interlude during a grueling campaign? Or is it a performance, an entertainment, whose purpose is to convey the impression that in the midst of a grueling campaign the candidate exudes Kennedy-esque vigor and lightheartedness?[1]

There's Hillary Clinton, spent and teary-eyed during a campaign visit to New Hampshire.[2] Is it a rare unguarded peek at the raw emotions of a passionate candidate? Or does her tear fall on cue in a script aimed at showing that the candidate, often perceived as cold and conniving, possesses human emotions?

There's GOP candidate John McCain striding commandingly through a Baghdad marketplace at the onset of the troop "surge" he supports.[3] Is he in Baghdad because he is concerned about the condition of U.S. troops and Iraqi citizens? Or is he in Baghdad, trailed by a phalanx of photojournalists, to demonstrate symbolic concern? Is he seeing the same Baghdad a visitor not surrounded by a forbidding security detail would see?

Performance has ever been part of politics. For better and worse, history remembers the charismatic leaders who captivated multitudes. But in a virtual age, have politics *become* performance? And if they have, what are the ethical ramifications for politicians, the media, and the public? What are the consequences for democracy? What is the truth standard of political entertainment? What truth standard can be applied to a candidate crying or throwing a football?

135

According to media critic Neil Postman, there isn't one: "If politics is like show business, then the idea is not to pursue excellence, clarity or honesty, but to *appear* as if you are, which is another matter altogether."[4] Of course, since politics *is* dramatic, since political careers and campaigns *do* follow familiar story arcs, it would be unusual if the techniques and conventions of mass entertainment did not shape the political sphere.

The issue, then, is one of proportion. The near-complete transformation of politics and political issues into "politainment" transforms the public, an active body, into an audience, a passive one. A century ago, when radio was in its infancy, film was still silent, and television had yet to appear, Walter Lippmann observed that politics had become so complex and opaque that the "private citizen today, has come to feel rather like the deaf spectator in the back row, who ought to keep his mind on the mystery off there, but cannot quite manage to keep awake."[5]

The purpose of modern "politainment," however, is to keep the citizen awake and watching — but as an amused spectator rather than an informed citizen with a sense of control over his or her political fate. The result, according to Gary Woodward, is that "Political life is often seen as a *performance for the public* by agents who in reality serve a different and privileged group of 'special interests.'"[6]

The subtler methods and motivations of the political message-makers and commercial news outlets that work symbiotically to project images of politics and politicians are often hidden backstage. Peering behind the curtain allows us to assess the consequences of packaging politics as just another form of entertainment.

Catapulting the Propaganda

Throughout history, the ruling classes of totalitarian, theocratic, and republican societies have produced pageants and entertainments to communicate authority and construct civic ideals for citizens or subjects. From the Roman Circus to the public beheadings of the French Revolution to the elaborate American political conventions of the nineteenth and twentieth centuries, those who would seize or maintain power used entertainment to persuade and instruct.

As satirist Juvenal observed of Rome as it sunk into decadence in the second century A.D.: "Two things only the people anxiously desire — bread and circuses!" Roman poet Fronto saw the matter from the rulers' point of view: "Spectacles are necessary for the contentment of the masses." Across cultures and political systems, spectacles and rituals serve to reinforce the terms of the social contract and provide answers to such questions as: What do we stand for? What is the proper order of things? What is the good life?

As America struggled to establish independence and then a national identity, native politicians and their advocates cultivated anecdotes from childhood and the battlefield to illustrate distinctly democratic ideals such as opportunity and merit.

Outsized political fables became enduring myths thanks to Parson Mason Locke Weems' hagiography of George Washington and the *McGuffey Reader*, two widely used schoolbooks that projected Calvinist values into the lives of great Americans. By the 1800s, American politicians added to the circulation of salutary anecdotes actual performances (popularly known as "publicity stunts") that symbolized their embodiment of desirable characteristics.

In 1960 historian Daniel Boorstin called attention to what he labeled "pseudo-events"— seemingly spontaneous happenings that are actually carefully staged to promote a political or corporate agenda. The director of a pseudo-event places a politician in a facsimile of the public sphere (a farmer's field, a soup kitchen) where he or she can interact with extras who play the role of the public. The rituals of democracy are expertly reenacted with no actual democracy taking place.

The timing of Boorstin's observation was not coincidental: 1960 marked the near complete penetration of television into American households, as well as the first presidential campaign to unfold primarily on television. From then on, political messages could be, and were, tightly scripted, rehearsed, and, if necessary, restaged or re-edited to appeal to multiple audiences.

Rapidly evolving new forms of electronic communication have multiplied the platforms through which pseudo-events can be promoted, performed, and disseminated. No matter the medium, political performance is designed to:

- Allow candidates to project characteristics that demonstrate they are worthy heirs of pioneer archetypes (from Teddy Roosevelt's strenuous wilderness outings to the recent presidential mania for "clearing brush").
- Allow candidates to show symbolic support for popular policies (such as Michael Dukakis' ill-fated 1988 helmeted joyride in a tank, designed to symbolize his commitment to a strong military).
- Show solidarity with a particular voting bloc, such as farmers (the Iowa caucuses) or union laborers (assembly line photo ops in Detroit). In 1992, Bill Clinton courted the MTV generation by donning sunglasses and blowing a saxophone solo on *The Arsenio Hall Show*.
- Demonstrate that, while the candidate aspires to the most exalted office in the world, he or she is a regular American (successful: Ronald Reagan quaffing a beer in a Boston pub during his 1984 campaign;[7] unsuccessful: George Bush's visit to a supermarket, during which he reportedly expressed wonder at register scanners, which had been in use for years).[8]

Neal Gabler points out that while politicians had always borrowed from the theater, television added significantly to the power of pseudo-events: "...However much the theater might have affected politicians, no entertainment could theatricalize politics more powerfully than television."[9] In politics, as in all things, television demands formula, repetition, action, and personality.

Or, as President George W. Bush put it in a 2006 interview: "See, in my line of work you got to keep repeating things over and over and over again for the truth to sink in, to kind of catapult the propaganda."[10] That politics hinges on symbolic behavior and the construction of theatrical personas should surprise no one. Soon after the nation's founding, George Washington compared America to "a most conspicuous Theater ... designed by Providence for the display of human greatness of felicity."[11] Two centuries later, Richard Nixon and his advisors turned that idea on its head by demonstrating that a staged performance of greatness set against the backdrop of a carefully crafted symbolic representation of the nation could be substituted for the reality of both.

In *The Selling of the President*, his extraordinary fly-on-the-wall chronicle of the 1968 campaign of the "New Nixon," journalist Joe McGinnis documented the process by which a tired old ideological brand was slickly repackaged. Nixon's 1968 campaign marked the tipping point when a new breed of advisors, far less interested in the mundane substance of policy than in creating emotional illusions through performance, came to the fore of American politics. As an advisor explained to Nixon: "Voters are basically lazy, basically uninterested in making an *effort* to understand what we're talking about.... Reason requires a higher degree of discipline, of concentration; impression is easier. Reason pushes the viewer back, it assaults him, it demands that he agree or disagree; impression can envelop him, invite him in, without making an intellectual demand."[12]

The power of vague but emotionally resonant messages has deep roots in psychology. The "Elaboration Likelihood Model" posits that there are two ways to persuade: via a "central route" that involves analysis, reasoning, and reflection, or via a "peripheral route" that relies upon relatively unreflective impression and emotional response.[13] In a fast-paced, image-driven culture, peripheral routes to emotional persuasion are the ones most traveled, according to Postman. When news and politics came to us primarily through written media, individuals could analyze, review, and compare messages using rules of logic and even the basic rules of grammar. "We have recognized, reputable ways of judging the relative truth or falsity of [spoken or written] statements," Postman explained in a 1990 documentary. But images are different. "Is an image true or false?" he asked. "The words don't seem to apply. It just is. There's no way to assess that the way we do statements, linguistic utterances. Basically we're out of the realm of logic and perhaps into the realm of aesthetics. You either like Ronald Reagan, or you don't. You either like McDonald's, or you don't. But you can't talk about their truth or falsity. So we now need a different kind of defense against 'the seductions of eloquence.'"[14]

A defense against seductive, but irrational, political eloquence can be constructed from the following materials:

- A reinvigoration of the press' watchdog function.
- The restraint of political message-makers.
- Accountability on the part of media companies that employ emotive partisan ranters and produce sensational, profit-oriented entertainment masquerading as news.
- An emphasis on media literacy in public education.
- A commitment by individual citizens to recognize their responsibility to be *informed participants* in politics rather than sideshow gawkers.

In the electronic age, a candidate's handlers fashion a comprehensive "life script" that is projected with endless variety or emphases depending on the day's "talking points." When they cannot control the stage upon which they perform, politicians reach the public through the largely uncritical channels of entertainment, bypassing forums in which knowledgeable journalists might ask difficult questions. Arnold Schwarzenegger, for example, announced his bid for the governorship of California on *The Tonight Show*. Political figures also appear frequently on lightweight morning shows whose hosts are neither informed enough nor expected to conduct penetrating interviews. Instead, they offer a congenial, chatty environment where a politician might appear between a cooking segment (or even in one) and the weather. A television "personality," such as Matt Lauer or Al Roker, not only doesn't ask difficult questions, he constructs a venue in which politicians can peddle what they have really come to sell: likeability.

As entertainment has subsumed serious journalism, it has also stolen its conventions. The set and production values of *Entertainment Tonight* are virtually indistinguishable from those of CNN (which increasingly features regular segments modeled on shows like *Entertainment Tonight*). Ironically, the hosts of satirical, pseudo-news programs, such as *The Daily Show* and *The Colbert Report*, frequently ask tougher, more insightful questions than supposedly hardcore journalists. However, when a political guest misspeaks or makes embarrassing revelations, it usually makes barely a ripple in the national political conversation because their words are framed within the comic context of the shows.[15]

Much has been made of the fact that young people get more news from comedy shows than from traditional news sources, but satire has a much longer journalistic lineage than modern conventions of "hard news." And despite the absurdist nature of these shows—or because of it—politicians are often more candid talking to Stewart or Stephen Colbert than they are to NBC anchorman Brian Williams or CBS anchorwoman Katie Couric. Candidates risk appearing foolish, but the risk is outweighed by the opportunity to gain exposure and demonstrate wit and spontaneity. The political purpose of appearing in an entertainment venue is to enhance "approval," which has supplanted accomplishment as the measure of political efficacy. Alas, just as Nielsen ratings are no predictor of programming excellence, approval ratings have little correlation to effective governance.

The Players and Their Parts

A clear understanding of the roles of the main players in the creation and propagation of "politainment" can help us sort out how the process works and who is accountable for its consequences. Even though each set of players in the world of mediated politics has distinct objectives, they all operate within recognizable normative frameworks.

The TARES inventory was created to "establish ethical boundaries that should guide persuasive practices, and serves as a set of action-guiding principles directed toward a moral consequence in professional persuasion."[16] It asks the following questions: 1) Is the message Truthful? 2) Are the claims in the message Authentic? 3) Does the message take a Respectful stance towards the receiver? 4) Does the message contain Equity? 5) Is the message Socially responsible? By making some adaptations, we can use the TARES inventory to analyze the roles and obligations of the various actors in the process of politainment: candidates, journalists, the punditariat, the public, and gatekeepers. Each player in the political process is ideally suited to assume *primary* responsibility for a component of the TARES inventory vis-à-vis the uses of entertainment in political discourse, but should strive to honor *all* the components of ethical persuasion within their influence.

The Candidate (Truth): Candidates are primarily responsible for the truth of their claims but often evade accountability by blaming misstatements or even outright lies on overzealous operatives. Ultimately, though, candidates *do* approve every message that represents them — whether it's a gauzy patriotic tableau, an attack ad by an interest group tacitly connected to the campaign, a photo-op with a fringe character with a valuable following, or a symbolic appearance (such as union-buster Ronald Reagan drinking beer with blue-collar Massachusetts voters in 1983) that belies their true intentions.

Only the candidates can know the truth value of their motives, statements, and symbolic actions. Ethically, their public performances should reflect their true intentions. So, as candidates review their schedule of photo-ops and symbolic appearances, they have a moral obligation to ask: Is this a true representation of my beliefs or a dog-and-pony show to impress voters with whom I have no common cause?

Reporters (Authentication/Verification): The symbiotic relationship between the campaign and the press determines what the public sees or hears—or doesn't—about a candidate or campaign. Presidential "debates" focus on issues the moderator chooses to ask about. Condensed and scripted, they are hardly contests in the Lincoln-Douglas mold. They enact the rituals of debate, but lack substance. Postman observed that during the 1988 presidential debates that candidates "were less concerned with arguments than with 'giving off' impressions, which is what television does best. Post-debate commentary largely avoided any evaluation of the candidates' ideas, since there were none to evaluate." Covering this performance ritual is more in the line of a theater critic than a political correspondent (and indeed, one of the country's leading political columnists, Frank Rich of the *New York Times*, is a former theater critic).

Since news coverage thrives on human interest, conflict, and suspense, stories that focus on horse-race information or who is polling better or who made an inane slip of the tongue take on disproportionate significance and crowd discussion of substantive issues out of the frame. A report by the Project for Excellence in Journalism and Shorenstein Center for Press, Politics and Public Policy found that, as the 2008 primary season unfolded, fully 63 percent of the press coverage focused on campaign tactics, while less than 20 percent focused on candidates' policy proposals. Just 1 percent focused on the candidates' records—seemingly an excellent predictor of what policies they might actually pursue if elected.[17] The same survey found that citizens were in diametric disagreement with reporters about what should be covered; citizens wanted substance on issues and policies and cared not a whit about campaign tactics.[18]

To better serve citizens, journalists should swear off trivia and fulfill their role as watchdogs over civic affairs. They should aggressively verify or debunk politicians' claims of achievements or experiences. In other words, they should *authenticate* the assertions of candidates and their operatives.

A prime example of the press' failure to do so arose during the 2008 campaign when Hillary Clinton repeatedly described her 1996 arrival at the airport in Kosovo in Hollywood action-movie terms, claiming she landed "under sniper fire," but bravely fulfilled her mission. When Clinton first made this claim in Cleveland in January 2008, it was quickly debunked by a local newspaper reporter, who used archived news stories to authenticate. National reporters following (or dropping in on) her campaign did not bother to authenticate her fictional tale until months later.[19]

Journalism is not a science. The front page of even the most reputable newspaper represents merely the best version of the facts attainable by deadline, not a guarantee that every statement is 100 percent true down to the last decimal point. Nonetheless, despite the complexity and fragmented nature of news gathering and the tyranny of deadlines, it *is* possible for reporters to conduct "due diligence," to authenticate purported statements of fact.

Photo-ops present other problems, and news photographers are too often complicit in the creation of this visual propaganda. When President George W. Bush gave a 2002 speech at Mount Rushmore, White House media handlers positioned photographers so that Bush's profile would be in symmetry with the presidential icons sculpted out of the mountain. What did the president *say* at Mount Rushmore? According to White House communications director Dan Bartlett, it scarcely matters: "We pay particular attention to not only what the president says but what the American people see. Americans are leading busy lives, and sometimes they don't have the opportunity to read a story or listen to an entire broadcast. But if they can have an instant understanding of what the president is talking about by seeing 60 seconds of television, you accomplish your goals as communicators. So we take it seriously."[20]

Bush topped that act of stagecraft by landing in a fighter jet (which he allegedly co-piloted) on the aircraft carrier Abraham Lincoln to declare "mission accomplished" a few months after the start of the Iraq war (at this writing entering its seventh year). Alas, this *Top Gun* homage was about as subtle as the bulging codpiece under the president's flight suit and was widely ridiculed.

The Punditariat (Social Responsibility): Robust debate, even — and perhaps especially — conducted at high volume, is reflexively understood to be good for democracy. But when punditry serves a hidden agenda, when the punditariat selectively quotes facts, distorts them, or ignores inconvenient perspectives, it is hard to see how democracy is served.

Asking cable pundits to have ethics may be akin to asking cats to have manners, but all communicators, not just reporters, have ethical obligations. If commentators insist on being called journalists— and most do— they are obligated to operate within professional standards, such as the Society of Professional Journalists (SPJ) Code of Ethics, which exhorts journalists to "Seek the Truth and Report It," "Minimize Harm," "Act Independently," and "Be Accountable."

Unfortunately, ethical standards are rarely evident. The pundits' seeming role is to provide lowbrow entertainment predicated on cartoonish conflict and high-volume verbal combat. Particularly raucous political talk shows are nearly indistinguishable from similar non-ideological programming like *Jerry Springer*. The medium is indeed the message.

If the goal of opinion is to clarify issues, pundits should operate within parameters of intellectual honesty and base their views, no matter how ideologically tinged, on a fair review of the facts, not simply cherry-pick bits of data to buttress ideological loyalties. They should conceive of minimizing harm in the broadest possible terms, taking into consideration the toxic effects of sensationalism, outlandish personal attacks, and fear-mongering, such as a June 2008 instance when commentator E.D. Hall, the host of Fox News' *America's Pulse,* suggested that Obama's fist bump with his wife might be a "terrorist" gesture.[21]

Commentators should also value independence and transparency by avoiding, or at least disclosing, connections to political advocacy groups. They rarely do. A recent *New York Times* investigation revealed that dozens of military and political "experts" who appeared on news programs to opine on the progress of the war in Iraq were either in the direct employ of the Pentagon or had agreed with military and White House officials to mouth inaccurate administration "talking points" during press appearances.[22]

Pundits must be accountable when they misreport or misinterpret facts or when they cross lines of fair play and good taste. A tacit assertion that a pundit operates within a particular ideological worldview and that, therefore, deceptions, distortions, and omissions are acceptable does not pass ethical muster. The standard must be higher.

The Public (Respect and Equity): Who is the public? Does public opinion drive politics, or is manipulation of it merely the vehicle by which ambitious people gain power? Modern political campaigns depict the public as something to be led or served, but don't citizens—the individual members of the public—have some obligation to do some research or critical thinking to fulfill their roles in the democratic process?

Messages and pseudo-events that mislead or irrationally promote fear or bigotry demonstrate a profound lack of respect for citizens. Policy makers and propagandists will always have more facts, "experts," and media access than ordinary citizens. But our current lack of equity is not foreordained. Individual citizens, singly or in collaboration with others, can significantly narrow the knowledge gap between themselves and the political spin artists. But first they must work to attain the tools needed to function in a political culture rife with sophistry, contorted statistics, and ambiguous symbolism.

Not all voters can be as well-informed as *New York Times* columnist Thomas L. Friedman, but nearly all can read and acquire the habits of critical thinking. Promoting media literacy skills would surely be easier if American schools ceased bartering away the attention of their captive student audience and began to reject subsidies from marketing firms like Channel One—a corporation that supplies "free" video equipment and news programming to schools, along with a generous helping of commercial messages aimed at children who need a hall pass to escape them.

As National Council for Social Studies President Denee Mattioli put it: "Our Founding Fathers understood that a democratic republic could not survive without an informed participatory citizenry. It is essential in our citizenship role to view critically, analyze, ask powerful questions and draw our own conclusions. Media literacy then is essential to the citizenship role."[23]

Gatekeepers (Equity and Social Responsibility): Pundits and other media figures do not simply appear, genie-like, on the airwaves. Someone hires and pays them. Media owners and executives who make policy at major news outlets share responsibility when pundits promote hidden interests, lie, or generally drag political discourse into the sewer.

Media executives should allocate resources to ensure that substantive news is adequately covered and that reporters in the field have the tools they need to authenticate political claims. A troubling new trend, however, is for networks to hire partisan political operatives and rechristen them "journalists" or "commentators." After his failed presidential campaign, failed GOP presidential candidate Mike Huckabee was invited by Fox News to host a political talk show. The deal represents a cynical exchange: Huckabee attracts his demographically desirable supporters to Fox, and Fox provides Huckabee with a platform to launch his next campaign.

More troubling than the hosts are the guests, who are often chosen for ratings-driven shock value and are allowed to hold forth without rebuttal even when they are demonstrably inaccurate in their representation of "facts" or irrational and extreme in their political prescriptions. Conservative gadfly Ann Coulter, for instance, casts acidic, but vague, charges that those not of her political stripe are not only "godless," but also guilty of "slander" or even "treason." Whatever else they are, pundits like Al Franken, Rush Limbaugh, Bill O'Reilly, and Coulter are skilled and entertaining communicators.[24] But when ratings-driven entertainment is disguised and promoted as "fair and balanced" political discourse, the audience is deceived, democracy is cheapened, and media owners and executives fail as citizens and as stewards of the public forum.

Is it possible that programming that accomplishes the dual purpose of entertaining and enlightening the public could be successfully developed? We'll never know as long as the noisy political dreck that fills the airwaves continues to reap ratings and profits.

Enlightenment, Camera, Action

Aristotle defined rhetoric as "the available means of persuasion." In a media- and entertainment-drenched world, it would be naïve to suggest we can or should somehow reproduce an august political forum outside of the modern conventions of rhetoric and persuasion. The key is for all the parties that constitute the political-entertainment complex to make a commitment to using the powerful tools they wield responsibly. The technologies through which politainment is produced, delivered, and consumed are new. The basic tenets of ethical communication are old. But that doesn't mean they are outdated. The task for politicians, mediators, educators, and the public is to re-imagine and adapt time-tested ethical standards to new media realities. They might start by brushing up on ethical codes like those of SPJ, the American Association of News Editors, and the Public Relations Society of America.

Adapting to new media technologies, and the ethical and interpretive challenges they pose, has confronted nearly every generation of Americans. Each major shift in media focus, grammars, conventions, technologies, and genres (such as the appearance of the penny press in the 1830s or its descendant, the tabloid television of our age) has created ethical crises that seemed to threaten the promise of the First Amendment and even democracy itself. Yet each generation has adapted with more or less success, and journalism, the public, and democracy more or less persist. For every ambitious sensationalist such as William Randolph Hearst, there has been a public-spirited critic like Walter Lippmann. For every rapacious network CEO, there has been an Edward R. Murrow. And far below the upper strata of media moguls and their nemeses, there have been (and are) anonymous small-town newspaper editors who ran a tight ship and tended to the facts—and community members who watched them closely, just in case, challenging their work in community forums and letters to the editor.

Traditional media outlets are imperiled and possibly on their way to extinction, along with the ethical standards the best ones strove for. Into this breach, however, has stepped the blogger, that oft-maligned civic loudmouth at whom editors and critics scoff. Given that real journalism takes resources and expertise, it is unlikely that bloggers can replace journalists. The cyber territory they inhabit is virtually lawless, and bloggers both anonymous and notorious are at the root of great reservoirs of misinformation. But bloggers and other online gadflies have also *exposed* deceptions staged by politicians and transmitted by the mainstream media. Bloggers may not be the answer to the future of journalism, but perhaps the debunkers among them are the canaries in the coal mine, reminding politicians and the media that you can't fool all of the people all of the time. Eventually they catch on. Just as media are evolving into we-know-not-what, so might online debunkers be in the vanguard of a critical mass of media-savvy citizens unwilling to succumb to the wiles of politainers.

Murrow debunked political chicanery that was aimed at a mass audience through the broad, popular mediums of his time — the big TV and radio networks. Those mediums are still with us, but do not dominate the public sphere the way they once did. As a result, today's political stage-managers are crafting increasingly elaborate entertainments for media fewer people are attending to. Today's debunkers, meanwhile, are naturally as diffused as the media that reach a hyper-fragmented audience. Politicians and big media still play the big arenas, but their audience — especially the young — has migrated to smaller, more specialized venues.

So how do things change? Politicians are beholden to ossified party structures and often rigidly ideological constituencies. Journalists answer to corporate bosses. Even the most powerful pundits answer to a corporate boss— and a fickle audience.

Of all the players in the adapted TARES inventory described earlier, only two groups have the loose allegiances that allow for rapid adjustment to changing conditions: the public, which follows cultural trends until it suddenly doesn't, and media executives, who are quick to scrap products that serve ideological goals at the expense of the bottom line. In one sense, the public follows the political parade organized by media companies, but media companies plan the parade route for thoroughfares where the public is likely to be gathered.

Gary C. Woodward argues that "if members of a society feel that they are not getting accurate information, their faith in the democratic process cannot but be eroded."[25] That may be true, but the erosion of democracy is unlikely to move political handlers to swear off the tricks of stagecraft that get their charges elected, nor the media owners who transmit these fictions. It's also possible, however, that if citizens tune out or even debunk politainment, a new wave of media owners might (out of necessity, if not virtue) create higher standards for the political discourse they transmit. The online audience knows how to talk back, as countless Web services (such as Facebook) have learned when they have proposed policies repugnant to their constituents.

With its increasing emphasis on entertainment and its complicity in politainment, traditional media companies seem to be betting that the public is less interested in thoughtful, ethical, proportionate discourse than in being amused. But what if the opposite is true? What if traditional news media are in decline in part *because* of their emphasis on entertainment and sensation? Perhaps today's rejection of traditional media institutions and products is *not* a rejection of the professional and ethical standards whose decline editors and critics fret about. Perhaps it is a rejection of news and political programming in which those values have declined.

Perhaps it is a rejection of politainment itself. The popularity of Jon Stewart and Stephen Colbert indicates the public not only understands the cynical nature of politainment but sees it as deserving of ridicule. Stewart and Colbert don't produce "news" but instead act as gadflies who debunk individual instances of politainment and deconstruct the facetious structure of politainment in general.

New media technologies that can seamlessly commingle the authenticate and the fake increase the potential for deceptive and unethical politainment. But unlike in times past, the tools of deception are not exclusively in the hands of political operatives or media organizations. The technologies that abet deception are cheap and ubiquitous, which means that deceptions can be created — but also deconstructed and exposed — by nearly anyone with technological savvy and the inclination to do so. Paradoxically, it is becoming easier to create political deceptions, but harder to convince the public of their reality.

The task for media workers is to use the new tools available to them to help illuminate the political environment rather than to collaborate in the creation of a pseudo-environment that advances the agenda of one vested interest or another. A commitment to carrying sound ethical practices into this new media landscape, along with the awareness that a significant portion of the public is capable of seeing through and debunking political deceptions, may bring a refreshing sense of realism to the realm of politainment.

NOTES

1. Obama merely took a drop-back pose; challenged to toss the ball by press photographers, he declined, admitting he was not very good at football. Mackenzie Carpenter, "Obama's Latest Persona: The King of Cool," *Pittsburgh Post-Gazette*, February 29, 2008, E-1.

2. Patrick Healy, "Clinton Tears Up; Talks About Campaign Strains," *New York Times*, January 7, 2008, 1.

3. Kirk Semple, "McCain Wrong on Iraq Security, Merchants Say," *New York Times*, April 3, 2007, www.nytimes.com (accessed February 1, 2008).

4. Neil Postman, *Amusing Ourselves to Death* (New York: Penguin, 1986), 126.

5. Walter Lippmann, *The Phantom Public* (New York: Harcourt, Brace, 1925) 3.

6. Gary C. Woodward, *Center Stage: Media and the Performance of American Politics* (Lanham, MD.: Rowan and Littlefield, 2007), 1.

7. Mission accomplished. In a *Boston Globe* story commemorating the president's visit, a regular who was there that night confessed he did not support Republican policies, but that Reagan's visit to the Dorchester Eire Pub made him feel that Reagan "seemed to have a grasp of the common person, the worker." Adam D. Krauss, "At Dorchester Pub, a President Made the Rounds," *Boston Globe*, June 6, 2004, http://www.boston.com/news/nation/articles/2004/06/06/at_dorchester_pub_a_president_made_the_rounds/ (accessed February 1, 2008).

8. It was later revealed that Bush had not been "amazed" by the scanner during his 1988 campaign visit and had, according to his press spokesman, visited stores that used them before. Bush did say he was "amazed" by the technological systems that helped companies manage stores. It just proves the adage: A lie can make it twice around the world before an indifferent teenager can scan your cantaloupes.

9. Neal Gabler, *Life The Movie: How Entertainment Conquered Reality* (New York: Vintage, 1998), 99.

10. Roger Cohen, "The 'Decider' Has Rules, All of Them Are Big, 'Yo,'" *New York Times*,

July 22, 2006, http://select.nytimes.com/iht/2006/07/22/world/IHT-22globalist.html?scp
=1&sq=catapult+the+propaganda&st=nyt (accessed 06/04/08).

11. Joseph Ellis, *American Creation: Triumphs and Tragedies at the Founding of the Republic* (New York: Alfred A. Knopf, 2008), 5.

12. Joe McGinnis, *The Selling of the President 1968* (New York: Trident, 1969), 36.

13. Richard E. Petty, John T. Cacioppo, Constantine Sedikides, and Alan J. Strathman. "Affect and Persuasion: A Contemporary Perspective," *The American Behavioral Scientist* 31, no. 3 (1988) 355.

14. *The Public Mind with Bill Moyers: Consuming Images* [Television Program]. New York: Public Affairs Television, 1990.

15. That may be changing, however. In the wake of the recent economic collapse, Stewart took CNBC financial "reporter" Jim Kramer to task in a blistering interview that called to mind Edward R. Murrow rather than Chevy Chase. Stewart pointed out that CNBC uncritically passed along dubious financial information provided by banks and corporations and pointed out that the mainstream media often shy away from critical coverage because their subjects are often also financial benefactors, i.e., advertisers. Alessandra Stanley, "High Noon on the Set: Cramer vs. Stewart," *New York Times,* March 13, 2009, 1.

16. Sherry Baker and David L. Martinson, "The TARES Test: Five Principles of Ethical Persuasion," *Journal of Mass Media Ethics* 16, nos. 2–3 (2001) 148–175.

17. The Project for Excellence in Journalism and the Joan Shorenstein Center on the Press, Politics and Public Policy, *The Invisible Primary — Invisible No Longer: A First Look at Coverage of the 2008 Presidential Campaign,* October 29, 2007, http://www.journalism.org/node/8187 (accessed April 1, 2008).

18. *Ibid.*

19. *CBS News,* "1996 Clinton Bosnia Trip" [Video], http://www.cbsnews.com/video/watch/?id=3962000n%3fsource=search_video (accessed March 1, 2009).

20. Elisabeth Bumiller, "Keepers of the Bush Image Lift Stagecraft to New Heights," *New York Times,* March 16, 2003, http://query.nytimes.com/gst/fullpage.html?res=9803EFDC173EF935A25756C0A9659C8B63&scp=8&sq=president+bush+and+mount+rushmore&st=nyt (accessed June 4 2008).

21. Alex Spillius, "Fox News Presenter Taken Off Air After Barack Obama 'Terrorist Fist Jab' Remark," Telegraph.com.uk, June 8, 2008. Hill quickly apologized for the remark, but her show was canceled anyway; she was later dropped by Fox altogether. http://www.telegraph.co.uk/news/newstopics/uselection2008/2118953/Fox-News-presenter-taken-off-air-after-Barack-Obama-%27terrorist-fist-jab%27-remark.html (accessed November 2, 2008).

22. David Barstow, "Behind TV Analysts, Pentagon's Hidden Hand," *New York Times,* April 20, 2008, 1.

23. Quoted in D. M. Considine, "Linking the Literacies: Teaching and Learning in a Media Landscape," *Wisconsin State Reading Association Journal* 44 (5) (2004): 49–53.

24. Politicians rarely repudiate, and often actively seek the approval of incendiary commentators. A rare exception to this practice occurred after Limbaugh, a powerful force in the GOP, declared his hope that newly elected President Obama would fail and criticized GOP leadership for their not attacking the president more fiercely. Party Chairman Ronald Steele was forced to denounce Limbaugh as incendiary and admitted that he's just an "entertainer." http://www.politico.com/news/stories/0309/19498.html (accessed March 10, 2009).

25. Woodward, *Center Stage*, xiii.

WORKS CITED

Baker, Sherry, and David L. Martinson. "The TARES Test: Five Principles of Ethical Persuasion." *Journal of Mass Media Ethics* 16, nos. 2–3 (2001): 148–175.

Barstow, David. "Behind TV Analysts, Pentagon's Hidden Hand," *New York Times,* April 20, 2008, 1.

Bumiller, Elisabeth. "Keepers of the Bush Image Lift Stagecraft to New Heights," *New York Times*, March 16, 2003, http://query.nytimes.com/gst/fullpage.html?res=9803EFDC173 EF935A25756C0A9659C8B63&scp=8&sq=president+bush+and+mount+rushmore &st=nyt (accessed June 4, 2008).
Carpenter, Mackenzie. "Obama's Latest Persona: The King of Cool," *Pittsburgh Post-Gazette*, February 29, 2008, E-1.
Cohen, Roger. "The 'Decider' Has Rules, All of Them Are Big, 'Yo,'" *New York Times*, July 22, 2006, http://select.nytimes.com/iht/2006/07/22/world/IHT-22globalist.html?scp= 1&sq=catapult+the+propaganda&st=nyt (accessed June 4, 2008).
Considine, D. M. "Linking the Literacies: Teaching and Learning in a Media Landscape." *Wisconsin State Reading Association Journal* 44:5 (2004): 49–53.
Ellis, Joseph. *American Creation: Triumphs and Tragedies at the Founding of the Republic.* New York: Alfred A. Knopf, 2008.
Gabler, Neal. *Life the Movie: How Entertainment Conquered Reality.* New York, Vintage, 1998.
Healy, Patrick. "Clinton Tears Up; Talks About Campaign Strains," *New York Times*, January 7, 2008, 1.
Lippmann, Walter. *The Phantom Public.* New York: Harcourt, Brace, 1925.
McGinnis, Joe. *The Selling of the President 1968.* New York: Trident, 1969.
Petty, Richard E., et al. "Affect and Persuasion: A Contemporary Perspective." *The American Behavioral Scientist* 31, no. 3 (1988): 355–371.
Postman, Neil. *Amusing Ourselves to Death.* New York: Penguin, 1986.
The Public Mind with Bill Moyers: Consuming Images. DVD. New York: Public Affairs Television, 1990
Stanley, Alessandra. "High Noon on the Set: Cramer vs. Stewart," *New York Times*, March 13, 2009, 1.
Woodward, Gary C. *Center Stage: Media and the Performance of American Politics.* Lanham, MD: Rowan and Littlefield, 2007.

CHAPTER 10

The *Common Morality* of Interviewers: Evaluating Moral Guidelines of Non-Journalists

David Charlton

When Jon Stewart appeared on CNN's *Crossfire* on October 15, 2004, and lambasted the hosts for "hurting America" with their "partisan hackery," conservative host Tucker Carlson responded in kind. Referring to Stewart's recent interview with Democratic presidential nominee Sen. John Kerry, Carlson said, "Kerry won't come on this show. He will come on your show.... Didn't you feel like — you got the chance to interview the guy. Why not ask him a real question, instead of just suck up to him?" Minutes later, Stewart responded to another of Carlson's criticisms by saying, "It's interesting to hear you talk about my responsibility.... I didn't know that — and maybe this explains quite a bit — is that the news organizations look to Comedy Central for their cues on integrity." Later Carlson asked, "But you can ask him a real question, don't you think...?" To which Stewart replied, "I don't think I have to."[1]

"I don't think I have to." Is this an appropriate response? Is it an adequate response? On the one hand, it seems rather unsatisfying, given the tremendous opportunity Stewart has through his program to conduct probing interviews with some of the most influential and powerful people in the country. On the other hand, perhaps Stewart has a valid point: He is a comedian, not a journalist, so why should viewers expect anything of substance to come from his interviews? Some might even argue that there should be a presumption *against* Stewart and other non-journalists acting as journalists (conducting "real" interviews and the like). They might argue that a non-journalist should leave these tasks to real journalists because of specific harms that may befall the non-journalist's audience and guests.

Using the deontological moral framework of Bernard Gert's *Common Morality*, in which he lists and defends 10 moral rules, I explore these and similar questions regarding the roles and duties of Stewart and other non-journalists as they conduct interviews, especially interviews with highly influential political figures, such as presidential candidates. I am interested in whether we should accept Stewart's response as morally justifiable or if we should expect him to conduct solid interviews with the political guests of his show — and hold him morally accountable if he does not.

I first examine the responsibilities generally assumed by journalists, including the obligation they have to their audiences and the public at large. Then, arguing from the standpoint that Stewart and other entertainers are not journalists, I examine whether it is appropriate in the first place for them to conduct interviews. I argue that it is ethically permissible for them to do so and that they are not bound by the same moral expectations as *bona fide* journalists, though there are restrictions on the kinds of interviews they should conduct. Specifically, non-journalists should avoid deception by keeping their interview styles consistent, so that guests and viewers may have reasonably accurate expectations of what they can expect from interviews.

In addition, I argue that non-journalists are morally permitted to conduct both "serious" and "entertaining" types of interviews, but are not allowed to switch between these two styles in a way that will harm their guest or audience.[2] I will further show that non-journalists, because of their access to politicians and influential people, actually *do* have a duty to act as a journalist would (in terms of interview styles) in situations in which there is a reasonable expectation that this interview will provide the public's only access to the subject. This is a special case, but I believe this duty arises when the non-journalist is the only medium that exists between the public and the interviewee. However, because of the present American media environment — and specifically, the 24-hour coverage provided by cable news channels — Stewart, David Letterman, and the hosts of *The View* (as examples) are not often in this exclusive position and thus have quite a bit of freedom in how they conduct their interviews with American politicians.[3]

It will be helpful to illustrate a few examples of interviews conducted by Stewart. In particular, I have chosen two that I believe Tucker Carlson or another of Stewart's critics might point to as problematic. They illustrate two "typical" types of interviews that Stewart conducts. The first is the interview with John Kerry that lies at the heart of Carlson's above criticisms; the second is an August 2004 interview with then-Texas-congressman Henry Bonilla, who had recently participated in the Republican "Rapid Response Team" during the Democratic National Convention.

Kerry's August 24, 2004, appearance on *The Daily Show* was the focus of much of Carlson's ire. He accused Stewart of going too soft on the presidential candidate, asking such questions as: "How are you holding up?"; "Is it hard not to take the attacks personally?" and "Have you ever flip-flopped?" The overall feel of the interview was congenial, as evidenced by Stewart's playfully pretending at one point to ask a serious question, mocking the current cable-news discourse: "Sir, I'm sorry — were you or were you not in Cambodia on Christmas Eve?"[4] Kerry was at ease throughout the exchange, and at the end of the interview, Stewart thanked him for "taking time out to come to the program and to have just a *normal conversation* with us."[5] The segment was not directed at challenging Kerry — Stewart generally let his guest reiterate his usual talking points as answers to the questions he posed, which is precisely the issue Carlson had with the exchange. He was disappointed that Kerry would not appear on *Crossfire*, where he *would* have pressed those talking points. He felt Stewart missed an excellent opportunity to do so himself.

We might contrast this interview with one Stewart conducted a few weeks prior, on August 2, with Republican congressman Henry Bonilla. The differences between the two interviews are striking. Where Stewart's attitude during the Kerry interview was disarming and distinctly non-confrontational, his treatment of Bonilla was a spectrum apart. Stewart asked Bonilla direct questions about the oft-quoted statistics that Kerry was "the first most liberal senator" and that his running mate in the election, Sen. John Edwards, was the fourth most liberal, then challenged him on his indirect and vague answers. He asked Bonilla to clarify exactly whom he and other Republicans were citing when they called Kerry and Edwards the first and fourth most liberal senators, and when Bonilla's answers were continually not to Stewart's liking, he kept pressing the point, asking ever more bluntly for specifics. Stewart asserted that he had no political agenda, but was tired of all of the "spin" and wanted honest conversation, both from politicians and the media. He lamented the "rapid response team" of which Bonilla was a member and other groups and pundits who report facts and figures out of context.[6]

It is clear that Stewart intended both interviews to be humorous and entertaining. Significantly, though, he intended the first to be entertaining for his audience and guest alike; the humor of the second was for the *benefit* of his audience and *at the expense of* his guest.

Gert's Common Morality

The moral framework I will utilize for my analysis is from Bernard Gert's system of moral rules.[7] Gert lists 10 moral rules that he argues are rational to follow. The rules are:

1. Do not kill
2. Do not cause pain

  3. Do not disable
  4. Do not deprive of freedom
  5. Do not deprive of pleasure
  6. Do not deceive
  7. Keep your promises
  8. Do not cheat
  9. Obey the law
 10. Do your duty

As Michael Pritchard notes, "None of these rules is 'absolute,' in the sense of having no exceptions; there are occasions when they conflict with one another" or with other elements of Gert's system.[8] Gert views his system as one built on common sense. Certainly some rules need more explanation than others, but these are the sort of rules each of us would like others to abide by when interacting with us or those we care about. I do not want others to deprive me of pleasure, for instance, and likewise I do not want others to deprive my friends and family members of pleasure (or disable them, cheat them, etc.). It is thus rational for each of us to ask others to follow these rules. In addition, since morality demands proper impartiality on the part of moral agents, Gert argues that our decisions for action should come while we are wearing the metaphorical "blindfold of justice," which limits our beliefs to only those that all rational agents hold.[9] We accordingly cannot privilege ourselves or our loved ones, our religion or nationality, or perpetuate any other similar biases when making moral decisions. If we limit ourselves thus, Gert argues that our actions will always conform to those of rational, moral agents. We will always follow the rules set out by the "common morality" or will have good overriding reasons not to (for instance, we may be justified violating the rule against killing if our victim is himself a murderer about to kill innocents).

I will utilize this framework to show that the actions of non-journalists, even if they do not fall under the moral obligations of journalists, at least can be guided by Gert's rules, specifically rules 6 ("Do not deceive") and sometimes 10 ("Do your duty").

Are Entertainers to Be Considered Journalists?

Our initial question is whether the accepted standards of journalism — including its moral commitments— apply to people who engage in activities normally performed by journalists, but who may not be *bona fide* journalists themselves. Do such entertainers as Stewart and Letterman qualify as journalists? After all, they do conduct interviews, an activity that falls within the purview of journalism. If they are not journalists, then should we still expect the same moral commitments from them that we expect from journalists?

Sandra Borden and Chad Tew argue that we should not accept these individuals as journalists precisely *because* they are not held to the same ethical standards as *bona fide* journalists, either by the public or themselves.[10] The authors deal explicitly with Stewart as an example, but any arguments they give to show that he is not a journalist may likewise be used for Letterman and the hosts of *The View* (at least those not named Barbara Walters, a former *ABC World News* co-anchor). Borden and Tew "argue that performing the functions of journal*ism* is not sufficient, morally speaking, to fully inhabit the role of journal*ist*— that is, to 'live it' or 'be it,' rather than just to 'act it' or 'imitate it.'"[11] They contend that a person is not a journalist unless she has a vested interest in the profession of journalism, including adhering to all of the moral commitments that go along with it in "the self-conscious pursuit of excellence *as* a journalist."[12] She may *act* as a journalist — that is, she may report news, conduct interviews, or snap pictures— but unless she accepts the moral standards of the profession and allows her actions to be evaluated in accordance with these standards, she remains an imitator. Stewart, they argue, does not accept these standards and thus is not a journalist. He is instead a media critic and serves a useful function to journalism, but should not be regarded as a *bona fide* journalist.

Among the entertainment shows that feature interviews, though, Stewart's is the one most often compared with those that do real journalism. This may be an unfair assessment of the program by the public, as it may be based entirely on the show's having a "news flavor," rather than the standard late-night talk show feel. Yet Stewart and, to a lesser degree, Letterman and the hosts of *The View,* all *act* like journalists, at least minimally, when they conduct interviews. If they are not to be held to the moral standards of journalists, what other sorts of moral standards, if any, might they be subject to? Before looking into what is required or permitted of non-journalists, perhaps I should explore some of the functions of *bona fide* journalists and the expectations they have for themselves and their profession.

The Interview and Other Journalistic Practices

The press is often charged with being a "surrogate" or "watchdog" for the public's interests. As Bill Kovach and Tom Rosenstiel write, "The primary purpose of journalism is to provide citizens with the information they need to be free and self-governing."[13] Citizens demand that journalists keep them informed about the news that matters, and in return, they support the interests and profession of the journalists by buying newspapers, tuning in to the evening news, and affording the press the freedom it needs to do its job. Even absent the explicit demands or monetary support of the citizenry, though, journalists still recognize that their duty is primarily to the public and its well being. Without proper access to proper news, journalists believe, the public will be disadvantaged and democracy, threatened. Journalism's purpose is to prevent this from happening.

These do not seem to be the standards that entertainers are held to—in a moral sense or any other. Entertainers who conduct interviews with politicians may be serving some sort of public good, but their job is not defined by such a public service. Instead, their primary function is to entertain, and any social benefit they provide in the course of entertaining is seemingly incidental.

Nevertheless, non-journalists *do* conduct interviews of politicians and other important and influential public figures. This raises two important questions: First, whether such interviews are ethically permissible; and second, whether non-journalists have the option of conducting *either* a serious or a trivial interview. That is, precisely because they *are* sometimes mistaken for journalists, is it even morally *permissible*, let alone required, for non-journalists to conduct "serious" interviews? One might argue that to do so would be to violate Gert's rule against deception, since an audience member might take the interview as conforming to the professional standards of journalism, when, in fact, it does not. I believe that the answer to the first question is that non-journalists are permitted to conduct interviews with politicians and other such individuals. To the second question, I also answer in the affirmative, provided the non-journalist is candid and not deceptive about her intentions and methods of interviewing.

Moral Obligations and Moral Constraints for Non-Journalists

Here a hypothetical will be illustrative. Suppose I have the opportunity for a private five- to seven-minute conversation with a presidential nominee from a major political party. Given this once-in-a-lifetime chance to personally interact with the potential leader of the nation and the myriad of things I might learn from him, one might say that I have squandered this opportunity if I simply ask this candidate about his family life and other trivial interests. Alternatively, if I use this opportunity to bicker with the candidate about our disagreements, then many will say I should have instead tried to hold a civil, informative conversation about these disagreements. I may be chastised in either case for having squandered this golden opportunity, but it doesn't appear that either of these approaches is inherently unethical, at least according to Gert. His theory prohibits us from bringing about unjustified harms, but merely encourages us to bring about benefits.[14] Since no one is harmed by my choice to either steer the conversation toward the trivial or to contentiously engage the candidate's positions without actually learning anything from the interaction, it seems that either of these options is ethically permissible. I might greatly benefit from having an honest and educational discussion with such an influential and powerful politician, but my rejection of this potential benefit is not enough by itself to render my actions unethical.

It is significant that others may never be aware of the contents of this private conversation. As I am the only one with anything to gain by conversing with the candidate, likewise I am the only one who could be subject to harm, if any harms came from my squandering this opportunity.[15] It is plain that if I were to tell others of this private conversation, I should be honest about the questions I asked, the responses I received, and so on. I should not, for example, intentionally mislead this audience about the context and content of the discussion, as deception is explicitly prohibited by the sixth of Gert's moral rules (again, "Do not deceive").

Let us take the presence of an audience a step further, though, and suppose others know beforehand that I am going to have this conversation with the candidate and that they are going to expect a report on it. This seems akin to the model of interviewing on television and in other forms of media. Keeping in mind Gert's tenth moral rule ("Do your duty"), even though I am not a journalist, one might question whether I have a duty to act as a journalist would, given that others will view or otherwise come to know the content of my conversation. Should this expectation guide my approach to the questions I ask and how I steer the conversation? The answer may be, "It depends." Gert writes: "The rule requiring a person to do his duty requires doing those actions that are a person's duty because of a special role, such as being a doctor, lawyer, parent, or teacher. It also requires doing those duties that arise from circumstances, such as helping someone in great need when one is in a unique or close-to-unique position to provide that help and can do so at little cost."[16] Not being a journalist, I certainly do not have such a duty to ask journalistic-style questions because of a special role, but the second consideration, that of uniqueness of position, may be applicable.

For example, if my conversation (or interview) with this politician is the only way for my audience to learn about this person, then it seems as if I might be bound by duty to help inform the audience. However, given that this is generally not the case — and is actually not the case in the present American media landscape — it is not clear that even this second criterion for duty is applicable. Knowing that members of my audience have, in fact, many news options available to them, and not understanding myself to be a "legitimate" or "traditional" outlet for news, it becomes less clear that I have any sort of duty to the public discourse.

This, it seems is the situation in which Stewart finds himself. He recognizes that others are actually trained in and responsible for informing the public about the qualifications and positions of presidential candidates, and this leaves him quite a bit of wiggle room to goof around when he chooses to do so. He wants his viewers to get their news from traditional sources and not from his show. Moreover, according to Gert's framework, this is not a moral failing on his part — precisely because these other sources are available.[17]

It thus appears that non-journalists are ethically permitted to interview politicians and other individuals of public significance. So long as the interviewer avoids violating Gert's rules unjustifiably, the act of interviewing — by journalists and non-journalists alike — is *prima facie* acceptable. The presence of an audience, though, and audience expectations for the interview, introduce certain obligations even for the non-journalist. Among these is the duty to serve a public need — by gathering vital information about our politicians — if there is a reasonable expectation that the interviewer is in a "unique or close-to-unique position" to achieve this good.

Another worry is whether it is just as permissible for a non-journalist to conduct a "serious" interview as an "entertaining" one. Some might object that a television program's guests and audience members might not know what to expect from any given interview, since one day the host might be jovial and concerned only with finding out what kinds of restaurants the politician has been visiting on the campaign trail, while the next day she might ask hard-hitting questions about foreign relations.

To reduce this worry, I propose that non-journalists borrow some of the basic conventions of journalists when deciding how to prevent or minimize harms to their audience and guests. In particular, I believe standards of transparency and honesty are crucial here. Such standards are widely supported within journalism as well as demanded by Gert's rule against deception.[18] He writes of his sixth rule, "['Do not deceive'] is preferable to the more familiar formulation 'Do not lie' because intending to deceive by making a false statement, which is what lying is, is only one way of intentionally deceiving. Intentionally deceiving someone in a nonverbal way is as much a violation of this rule as lying."[19]

Interviewees of journalists and non-journalists alike should expect similar treatment from their interviewers. An interviewer would harm his guest if he brings her to the show under the pretenses of one style of interview and then turns the tables and conducts an entirely different type of interview. Likewise, the interviewer might harm his guest or his audience by constantly switching between one interview style and another, or by adopting a mixture of the two within any given interview, because this might cause confusion in the guest or the viewers (or both) about the intended nature of the interview. Because this is the case, we might say that Stewart and others should develop some basic principles by which they conduct their interviews and that they should generally follow these principles.

For example, it is well known among the viewers of both Stewart's and Letterman's shows that they adapt their interview styles to the type of guest they bring on. Letterman tends to be harder on people who have somehow "wronged" him (for an example we might look to Sen. John McCain's "makeup" appearance on his show during the 2008 presidential campaign season[20]), while Stewart has a history of being more confrontational with conservative politicians than with liberals. This is acceptable, though, because of the general standard the two hosts have set through their years on the air and the hundreds of interviews they have conducted. Of course, this raises questions for interviewers without the established histories of Stewart and Letterman. If another entertainer begins hosting a program that includes an interview segment, what sorts of expectations should his guests and audience have? Would he be obliged to conduct interviews of a particular sort? Like Stewart or Letterman, he should be consistent in his interviewing techniques, and he should avoid deceptions, such as bringing guests on the program under false pretenses. In time, viewers and potential guests will have a body of work to use in understanding the basic interview guidelines employed by the show.

Entertainers need not actually draft and distribute ground rules that will govern their interviews. Instead, they should consider when their actions might bring harm to their guests and viewers and should avoid causing such harms when possible. One way to avoid harms of deception is to have general, if unwritten, guidelines that govern the interviews that take place on the program. As for the viewers and guests, anyone familiar with and having reasonably thought about the program should have a sense of the *sorts* of interviews that can be expected.

This is not to say Stewart or Letterman cannot deviate from their established and recognized interview styles. Rather, if they decide to deviate significantly for a particular interview, or if they choose to adopt entirely new and different interview techniques as their standards, they should make this fact known, at least to the guests who will be affected, before the interview takes place. In an effort not to deceive his guest, either of these hosts might consider letting her know that she should expect an interview style different from that generally seen on the program — and far enough in advance to allow the guest to prepare for this deviation and perhaps opt out from the appearance altogether.

The View

An actual example of such a shift in technique recently took place on the set of the ABC morning talk show *The View.* During the 2008 presidential campaign, the hosts and producers of that program decided to alter their show's scope and seek out political discourse from its guests. This was evident during the September 12 broadcast, which featured McCain, the Republican presidential nominee.[21] Hosted by women and aimed at a predominantly female audience, *The View* has traditionally discussed important political and social matters in a roundtable format. Typically, though, any serious contention expressed on the show has arisen among the program's hosts and not between the hosts and the guests. McCain's appearance was different, with the hosts asking him serious questions about his choice of Gov. Sarah Palin of Alaska as his running mate, his stance on *Roe v. Wade*, his view of the separation of church and state, and the attack ads his campaign was running against Democratic presidential candidate Barack Obama.[22]

The change in style of questioning on *The View* is a good test for my suggested standard. I believe that the line of questioning posed to McCain was morally justified if he was made aware ahead of time that the hosts would be asking him more rigorous questions than normal. If this was the case, then the hosts were transparent and honest in allowing the guest to prepare for the interview and should be commended. If, however, they sprung this style of interview on McCain without any warning and only afterwards realized, "Hey, that went pretty well — let's adopt that as our new standard," then their actions are not morally acceptable. In that case, the program's hosts acted wrongly by withholding information in a way that deceived and potentially harmed their guest.

Recent news articles suggest that *The View* did, in fact, act in a way that deserves our disapprobation. Walters has said she ran into McCain at a recent Washington event and expressed her hope that he would come on the program again. His response: "Not anytime soon."[23] This leads me to suspect that McCain did *not* expect the more rigorous line of questioning he was subject to, and for this reason, I believe *The View*'s actions fail my standard of non-deception.

Conclusion

Viewed from the perspective of Gert's *Common Morality*, Stewart and other non-journalists do, in fact, have moral obligations when conducting interviews, but these moral obligations are minimal. They do not include, for example, commitments to the journalistic notion of objectivity, public service, or other professional standards to which *bona fide* journalists are held. Instead, they have at least the basic ethical obligations that, according to Gert, govern everyone, including prohibitions against deception. A further commitment to duty appears in certain media environments, such as where no other source of information on a politician is present.

While this chapter has focused on non-journalists, I believe it raises ethical questions for *bona fide* journalists as well. For instance, non-journalists are generally free to conduct interviews in a style of their choosing. Are established journalists free to do likewise, or are their duties to the public such that they should always be in "watchdog mode" so as to avoid becoming (or even seeming) overly chummy with their subjects? Could, or should, softball or "humanizing" types of interviews reduce the professional credibility of *bona fide* journalists? Even if not, should we say that since there is always something "serious" for the journalist to report or uncover, she should be digging for this story, which would ostensibly serve the public good more than an interview with a politician focused primarily on trivial matters?

I do not propose to answer these questions, but I believe their future exploration would prove useful to the field of media ethics, as would further discussion of the increasing role non-journalists are taking in the reporting and interpreting of news events. What moral constraints and obligations, for instance, should govern the activities of private bloggers and citizen journalists? At first glance, it appears that these individuals should at least follow the same common morality that governs the rest of us and thus should refrain from deception and the like. According to Gert's rules, they may also be obligated to report on newsworthy topics when the professional journalists are unable or unwilling to do so.

NOTES

1. Quotations pulled from this appearance have been culled either from "YouTube — Jon Stewart on Crossfire" <http://www.youtube.com/watch?v=aFQFB5YpDZE> or "Media Matters— Jon Stewart on Crossfire: 'Stop, stop, stop, stop hurting America'" <http://media-matters.org/items/200410160003> (accessed October 23, 2008).

2. There is another group that may potentially be harmed by the non-journalist's actions— the greater public. For instance, we might easily think of a scenario in which the program's frequent viewers and guests are all "in" on a program's publicity stunt, whereas most of the populace — specifically, those members unfamiliar with the program's antics— doesn't understand the stunt and is somehow harmed by it (whether by deception, disgust at the event, etc.). However, while avoiding harm to the public should be a concern for the journalist and non-journalist alike, my primary focus here will be on the potential harms that might befall the audience of the program — including the viewers at home — and the program's guests.

3. Here I am concerned primarily with interviews of individuals with political significance. Many of my arguments may be transferable to interviews of, say, entertainers, but interviews with politicians, I think, are especially interesting because it may be forcefully argued that they are important to the general public.

4. *The Daily Show* (August 24, 2004) <http://www.thedailyshow.com/video/index.jhtml?videoId=108481&title=John-Kerry---Part-1> (accessed October 25, 2008).

5. *Ibid.* Emphasis mine.

6. *The Daily Show* (August 2, 2004) <http://www.thedailyshow.com/video/index.jhtml?videoId=129451&title=Henry-Bonilla> (accessed October 25, 2008).

7. Bernard Gert, *Common Morality: Deciding What to Do* (New York: Oxford University Press, 2004, 20.

8. Michael Pritchard, "Comments on *Common Morality*," *Teaching Ethics*, 7.1 (2006): 89.

9. Gert, *Common Morality*, 83.

10. Sandra L. Borden and Chad Tew, "The Role of Journalist and the Performance of Journalism: Ethical Lessons from 'Fake' News (Seriously)," *Journal of Mass Media Ethics* 22 (2007): 300–314.

11. *Ibid.*, 301.

12. *Ibid.*, 302.

13. Bill Kovach and Tom Rosenstiel, *The Elements of Journalism: What Newspeople Should Know and the Public Should Expect* (New York: Three Rivers, 2007), 12.

14. Gert, *Common Morality*, 24.

15. According to Gert, it is irrational for me to bring harms upon myself, so I should not squander this opportunity if doing so would harm me, but I do not believe that it would.

16. Gert, *Common Morality*, 50.

17. Stewart routinely deflects the label of journalist and denies that *The Daily Show* is a news show of any kind. In fact, at the beginning of the program featuring the interview with Kerry, Stewart offers this disclaimer: "We are not a news show, obviously. Uh, some people confuse us with a news show; they say, 'Are you a news show?' uh, and that either says something terrible about the state of news in this country, or something terrible about the state of comedy on our program. I like to think both." Elsewhere, in various interviews he makes similar claims regarding where people should get their news—and it isn't from him.

18. We might also, of course, concern ourselves with the potential for deception on the part of the guests. Politicians are practiced in the art of "spin" and will often demonstrate their prowess when asked questions they are not prepared for or would prefer not to answer. Certainly some have and will grant interviews under the guise of full disclosure and then fall short of this promise. We should hold them blameworthy for this and assert their obligation to honesty and transparency as well. My focus here, though, is with the moral obligations and restrictions of the interviewer and not the interviewee.

19. Gert, *Common Morality*, 40

20. McCain was scheduled to appear on *The Late Show with David Letterman* on September 24, 2008, but decided to cancel the appearance, noting that he had to get back to Washington to work on the proposed bailout of U.S. financial institutions. When McCain finally did appear on the program on October 16, he and his actions were the butt of many of Letterman's jokes. Probably most of these were in good humor, but one still senses Letterman's displeasure in the way the events transpired.

21. Jacques Steinberg, "'The View' Has Its Eye on Politics This Year," *The New York Times*, September 23, 2008, late edition—final.

22. Video of the appearance can be found (in three parts) at the following web addresses: <http://www.youtube.com/watch?v=xyQpmN-nH64> (part 1/3); <http://www.youtube.com/watch?v=BoQ_G6eMJAQ&feature=related> (part 2/3); and <http://www.youtube.com/watch?v=VvEDfwAgIng&feature=related> (part 3/3)

23. "McCain Blacklists The View?" *CNN Political Ticker*, February 19, 2009, <http://politicalticker.blogs.cnn.com/2009/02/17/mccain-blacklists-the-view/> (accessed February 17, 2009).

WORKS CITED

Borden, Sandra L. "Gotcha! Deciding When Sources Are Fair Game." *Journal of Mass Media Ethics* 10 (1995): 223–235.

_____, and Chad Tew. "The Role of Journalist and the Performance of Journalism: Ethical Lessons from 'Fake' News (Seriously)." *Journal of Mass Media Ethics* 22 (2007): 300–314.

Gert, Bernard. *Common Morality: Deciding What to Do.* New York: Oxford University Press, 2004.

Kovach, Bill, and Tom Rosenstiel. *The Elements of Journalism: What Newspeople Should Know and the Public Should Expect.* New York: Three Rivers, 2007.

Pritchard, Michael. "Comments on *Common Morality.*" *Teaching Ethics* 7(1) (2006): 85–92.

Steinberg, Jacques. "'The View' Has Its Eye on Politics This Year." *New York Times,* September 23, 2008, late edition —final.

Chapter 11

Cops and Reality TV: Public Service or Public Menace?

Jack Breslin

On a sultry Manhattan summer night, a disheveled and deranged cop killer is shoved into the back of a police car as a horde of TV cameras record the breaking news.

Amid the commotion, a high-ranking police officer angrily confronts the host of a tabloid TV show, which has just exclusively broadcast a graphic video of the cop killing. Only minutes before, the fugitive had surrendered to the host after being paid $1 million for the uncut video footage.

"And you!" the officer shouts, pointing his finger into the host's face. "You ought to be ashamed of yourself!"

"Bullshit, Leon!" the host fires back. "Ashamed of what? I got him off the streets. Because of me, the son of a bitch...."

"Bravo, Mr. Hawkins!" the officer interrupts, clapping his hands in sarcastic applause. "You are sick!"

The confrontation then becomes physical and a public information officer attempts to intervene.[1]

This climactic scene from the fictional feature film *15 Minutes* is not that far from the realm of reality television. Fugitives have surrendered to print and TV journalists either for their moment of fame or to protect themselves from possible police brutality. In exchange, the TV news got the exclusive footage of the surrender.

But would a prime-time television show, even the most ratings-starved, pay a fugitive for a video tape of his murdering a police officer, then broadcast the unedited footage to a stunned, but riveted national audience? It depends—on the ethics of those making that decision.

As the killer warns the host over the phone, "If you don't want my film, I'll call another show. And they will show it."[2]

Police and crime have long been featured in fictional movies and TV shows, some created or written by former law enforcement officers to give an extra element of credibility. Even before the term "reality television" was coined in the late 1980s, real police, real criminals, real crimes and real victims had moved from TV newscasts and magazine shows into prime-time entertainment television.

Both law enforcement and TV benefit from reality crime shows. TV gets powerful stories ready-made for prime time. These low-budget productions result in consistently good ratings and programming profits. In return, law enforcement officials get good public relations. And the audience gets to see police officers in action, ordinary people caught in bizarre and embarrassing behavior, and criminals committing all sort of crimes. Sometimes they even get to help catch the bad guys.

But what happens when this genre of reality TV entertainment reverses the roles of the respective partners? What happens when TV becomes the police by creating sting operations to lure suspects into criminal acts, negotiating with wanted fugitives or stalking them in another country? And what happens when law enforcement become entertainers by compromising police procedures to provide "good TV," giving vital information exclusively to entertainment shows while ignoring the news media, "hamming it up" for the ever-present cameras, or seeking the limelight of celebrity and its financial rewards?

Using a theoretical framework of ethical values to analyze the partnership between TV and police in reality crime programming, this chapter will examine three shows: Fox's *America's Most Wanted*, Fox's *COPS* and "To Catch a Predator," a regular segment on NBC's *Dateline*. Although some might argue that these shows also contain news elements and are produced by journalists, especially *Dateline*, they can also be considered entertainment. For example, does a viewer of "To Catch a Predator" remember the investigative reporting of the segment or the entertaining nature of the suspects ("Did you see the one where the guy was wearing his underwear?")?

In the interest of full disclosure, I was the original Fox publicist on both *America's Most Wanted* (*AMW*) and *COPS* and worked from 1981 to 1985 in the NBC Press Department. During my career at NBC in New York and Burbank, I publicized daytime dramas, movies of the week and miniseries. Among those projects was the TV movie *Adam*, the story of Reve and John Walsh, now the host of *AMW*.

As part of the publicity team that launched Fox in 1987, my work with *AMW* began with publicizing its national debut in April 1988, until leaving Fox in February 1993. I also wrote a 1990 paperback book, *America's Most Wanted: How TV Catches Crooks*, published by HarperCollins, which like Fox Broadcasting, is owned by Rupert Murdoch's News Corporation. For *COPS*,

I publicized the show from its national debut in March 1989 until June 1990, when I moved to Washington, D.C., to work exclusively on *AMW*.

This chapter combines my behind-the-scenes knowledge of the entertainment industry with ethical analysis. As I tell my students, rather than focus on third-person case studies from a textbook, my adventures with Fox and NBC provide real-life ethical examples from the entertainment TV industry.

How the Partnership Flourished

America's Most Wanted and *COPS* both debuted on the new Fox network within a year of each other. After being tried out on the seven Fox owned-and-operated stations in major markets, they went national on the "fledging" network of some 90 affiliates, which did not even cover the entire American TV viewing audience and had only two nights of programming.

America's Most Wanted was not an original concept. Fox executive Stephen Chao got the idea from another News Corporation executive, Jim Platt, who had read about successful crime-fighting shows in Great Britain, Australia and Germany that profiled fugitives and solicited viewer tips to help police apprehend them.[3] In this country there had been two unsuccessful attempts at crime-fighting shows, *Counterattack: Crime in America* on ABC in 1982 and *Wanted* on CBS in 1955–56.[4] Crime Stoppers programs had appeared on local television stations since 1976.[5] Following the success of *America's Most Wanted*, NBC's *Unsolved Mysteries* (later broadcast on CBS and Lifetime) started including fugitive profiles.[6]

Chao hired veteran TV journalist Michael Linder to produce the first thirty-minute show, profiling FBI Top Ten fugitive David James Roberts on February 7, 1988. Within four days, Roberts was apprehended in Staten Island, making national news.[7] Based on that success, *America's Most Wanted* went national April 10, 1988,[8] and expanded to a full hour in the fall of 1990, shortly after the current executive producer, Lance Heflin, took over.

The first law enforcement agency *America's Most Wanted* contacted was the FBI, whose director endorsed the show. Other federal agencies, such as the U.S. Marshals Service, soon followed, as did several local and state law enforcement agencies, which realized the value of such a partnership, namely catching fugitives through national television exposure.

Now in its twenty-second season and Fox's longest-running series, the show has helped apprehend more than 1,000 fugitives and recover more than 60 missing children and persons.[9] The show was briefly cancelled by Fox in 1996, but resumed its run six weeks later after strong opposition from viewers, law enforcement and government officials. A short-lived spin-off, *Amer-*

ica's Most Wanted: Final Justice, featured updates of captured fugitives in the criminal justice system.

In the late 1980s, John Langley and Malcolm Barbour produced a series of live syndicated law enforcement specials, *American Vice: The Doping of a Nation* with Geraldo Rivera, featuring live drug busts with real police officers and suspects. After unsuccessfully proposing a similar half-hour weekly show called *COPS* to the three major networks, they pitched the concept to Chao at Fox.

On *COPS,* the viewers would ride along with the police in their squad cars and the camera would tell the story in a "video vérité" style. There would be sparse editing, no script, no stars, just real-life stories of cops, criminals and victims, all on a low production budget. Each show would feature two or three self-contained segments with officers pursuing and sometimes arresting suspects for a variety of crimes, including sale and possession of drugs, prostitution, fleeing arrest and outstanding warrants. If the suspect signed a consent form, his or her face would be shown; if not, it would be blurred to prevent recognition. Amazingly, most signed the form.

At first some police departments were reluctant to allow the *COPS* crews to accompany their officers without having any editorial control over the broadcast. While good cops would promote a positive image of law enforcement, rogue officers would damage an already tarnished public image. Police officials soon realized the producers would allow them to select the featured officers and thus ensure a positive image. The partnership flourished as *COPS* began traveling around the country and overseas.

COPS premiered January 7, 1989, on the seven Fox owned-and-operated stations, then went national on March 11. Beginning with Broward County, Florida, where Barbour and Langley had shot parts of *American Vice,* *COPS* crews have followed law enforcement officers in some 140 American cities, as well as in Great Britain, Hong Kong and Russia. Nominated for four Emmys and a Peabody Award, *COPS* is now in its twenty-first season as Fox's second longest-running series. Fox currently broadcasts two back-to-back half-hour *COPS* episodes, followed by original, on-location, hour-long *America's Most Wanted* episodes on Saturday nights.[10]

After a decade of failed attempts to compete with successful newsmagazines on ABC and CBS, NBC News launched *Dateline* in 1992. Now broadcast on multiple nights in the NBC schedule, the award-winning prime-time newsmagazine features a mix of investigative reports, news updates, health features and celebrity interviews. Based on increasing reports of sexual predators luring unsuspecting teens through online chat rooms, *Dateline* began an on-going series "To Catch a Predator" with correspondent Chris Hansen on November 11, 2004.[11]

Since the first segment — an investigative piece titled "Dangerous Web" reported from Bethpage, New York—*Dateline* has featured twelve "hidden camera investigations" that have netted more than 250 individuals, who have been charged, convicted, released, or plead guilty to crimes relating to attempted sexual contact with minors. Working with Perverted Justice, a volunteer online watchdog group, Hansen and his production team spend up to four days in pre-production to set up an undercover house with hidden cameras, microphones and security. Perverted Justice lures suspected sexual predators to the house by posing as teenagers in online chat rooms.[12]

Once in-person dates with multiple suspects have been arranged at the house by the watchdog group, a female decoy, seemingly under age 18, greets the arriving suspect, then disappears. Without identifying himself as a journalist or revealing that cameras are videotaping, Hansen confronts the individual. In his lengthy interview of the suspect, Hansen reads from transcripts of the online chats, often featuring explicit and disturbing sexual language. Eventually Hansen reveals his true identity, and the camera crew emerges from another room. After being invited to make a final statement for the camera, the suspect is asked to leave, then is immediately arrested by local police waiting outside. The camera crew videotapes the arrest and the interrogation of the suspect by a police officer.

In a *Dateline* segment "Where Are They Now?" Hansen boasted that of the 200 suspects caught by the show to that point, "not one has been let off."[13] Perhaps that was true when Hansen made that statement, but problems have arisen since. In June 2008, NBC settled a lawsuit brought by the sister of William Conradt, Jr., an assistant district attorney in Rockland County, Texas, who shot himself when the local police, accompanied by a *Dateline* crew, surrounded his house to arrest him in November, 2006. Conradt did not show up at the undercover house, so police decided to arrest him at home. He later died from his gunshot wound.[14]

ABC News *20/20* reported that two former detectives of the Murphy, Texas, police department stated the decision to go to Conradt's house was made on the suggestion of Hansen and Perverted Justice, which NBC denied.[15] Collin County District Attorney John Roach refused to prosecute the 23 men arrested by Murphy police in the sting set up by *Dateline* and Perverted Justice.[16]

What Is an Ethical Value?

When media ethics professors tell someone what they teach, they sometimes hear the reply, "Media ethics? Isn't that a contradiction in terms?" The same might be true with a book about ethics in the entertainment industry. There are no ethics in the entertainment industry. Or at least there don't seem to be any to those looking in from the outside.

During my decade in various areas of the entertainment industry, I never once heard the words "ethics" or "morals." Nor did I ever encounter a discussion about the ethical implications of an entertainment company's programming or publicity plans. I worked with people I would consider ethical individuals. But their personal ethics sometimes conflicted with demands of their jobs.

For example, at *America's Most Wanted*, I sometimes questioned the excessive display of violence in on-air promo spots and show re-enactments, which a producer insisted was "action." I based this concern on my personal ethical values of decency, dignity and compassion for crime victims. Or in writing my *America's Most Wanted* book, a Harper attorney cautioned against my use of a rape victim's name even though she had given her consent to disclose her identity.

An ethical value is a good that is "esteemed, prized, [or] regarded highly"[17] for use in ethical reasoning. Ethical values can also be used to build attitudes and behavior[18] and can serve as "desirable goals" in formulating ethical principles or guidelines.[19]

Certain "well-founded" ethical values (honesty, loyalty, compassion) can support ethical decisions and resulting action. However, ethical values can sometimes come into conflict with each other or other kinds of values. For example, a public relations practitioner may be told by a corporate executive to deceive the media about an embarrassing scandal. In such an instance, the ethical value of truth-telling collides against the non-ethical values of advancing and keeping one's job. Both ethical and non-ethical values may be shared within an organization's culture or by the various persons who belong to that culture. Furthermore, different occupations—such as journalism and law enforcement—may be guided by different values, or they may rank shared values differently. So individuals and groups must determine a "hierarchy of values" to develop a system of ethics[20] that can help them clarify and prioritize competing values when confronting moral dilemmas.[21]

Value Conflicts in Cop Reality Television

Entertainment Versus Journalism

The primary value for entertainment television is a business one: making a profit. There are several production values necessary for a profitable television show, such as story, casting, direction and budgets. A successful reality TV show provides dramatic entertainment through diversion, information, interpretation and emotional and intellectual stimulation. Those shows also create bonds among audience members and transmit certain social values, e.g., police can be both good and bad.

Reality television incorporates those values, as well as others that are not usually considered wholesome, such as violence or voyeurism. As one TV critic stated on *Nightline, America's Most Wanted* promoted a "pornography of violence."[22] A spokesperson for the American Civil Liberties Union also criticized the show's graphic violence.[23]

All three shows examined in this chapter, whether entertainment or news, share traditional journalistic values, such as truth, accuracy and fairness. While *Dateline* is primarily a news program, are *COPS* and *America's Most Wanted* news shows or entertainment programs? Entertainment shows prioritize one set of values (drama, emotional impact, poetic license) that will conflict with traditional journalistic values (truth, accuracy, fairness) prioritized in news programs. In trying to entertain, truth-telling might be sacrificed to give the audience a more compelling story despite the facts of the case.

Law enforcement understands the entertainment values involved in reality television, such as providing drama through fast action, suspenseful stories and compelling players. For the *COPS* ride-alongs, police officials carefully select officers who are attractive, articulate and law-abiding. There are no rogue cops on *COPS*, so the audience only sees "good" police officers. Those "highly proactive type police officers" have disappeared from law enforcement since the Rodney King incident, John Langley, the show's executive producer and co-creator, insisted.[24] But showing acts of police brutality could create liability for the show, as well as make other jurisdictions less likely to invite the show into their communities. But this raises the question whether the audience sees what really happens or what the producers show to avoid liability and create a positive image of law enforcement so other agencies will cooperate.

For *COPS*, as Langley explained, "Our hallmark is shooting 'video vérité,' shoot as it happens. You demonstrate; you discover the truth as it happens."[25] Each thirty-minute episode features two or more segments of police doing their jobs on the streets. These segments have been edited from hours of videotape to focus on the dramatic action (pursuits, stings, arrests) rather than showing the audience routine patrols where "nothing happens." The audience sees the action "as it happens," but it doesn't see the officer's entire eight-hour shift.

This question of entertainment versus news caused considerable debate in the early years of *America's Most Wanted*. Fox executives maintained that the show was entertainment with news elements. Coming from journalism backgrounds, the producers insisted that the show was a news program. In emphasizing the news elements of the show, they incorporated such journalistic elements as correspondents, informational segments and an "anchor desk." Yet the show's dramatic re-enactments sometimes take poetic license to enhance the entertainment elements.

Even though the primary entertainment staple of the show has been re-enactments of crimes based on news stories, police reports and victim interviews, the show's executive producer stated that *America's Most Wanted* maintains journalistic truth-telling values. The show also includes magazine-style feature segments about law enforcement, victims and the criminal justice system. But do audience members tune in to be informed or entertained?

When asked if the show was news or entertainment, *America's Most Wanted* executive producer Lance Heflin replied, "It's just a damn fine show. The problem is we've always sort of been neither fish nor fowl. That's one of the reasons that the Emmy people don't know how to classify us as news or entertainment. We follow news guidelines, news reporting, journalistic guidelines in our work. Most of the people here are trained journalists, but I think it's entertaining as well."

In explaining the show's emphasis on journalistic accuracy, Heflin noted that the show has turned down cases where a case file lacks consistency or truth: "There are occasional times that we've looked at cases and said, 'You know, this just doesn't smell right, we're just not going to go forward with it.' Or it looks like a malicious prosecution, we're not going to help this out."[26]

Most cases are selected during story meetings when reporter-researchers "pitch" cases from a variety of sources. During meetings that I attended, stories were sometimes rejected because they lacked a compelling story or the dramatic elements necessary for an entertaining re-enactment.

Heflin explained that *America's Most Wanted* has an advantage over news organizations in "getting access to all sides," but some critics, such as the ACLU and defense attorneys, would argue that the show does not interview the fugitives being profiled. But after helping catch Wisconsin fugitive Laurie "Bambi" Bembeneck, a former Milwaukee police officer and subject of two made-for-television movies, the show assisted her attempt to get her second-degree murder conviction reversed.

However, if there were enough inconsistencies in her case to cause a reversal, why didn't those factors make *America's Most Wanted* hesitate in profiling her after she escaped from prison? Or did the entertainment elements of her boyfriend aiding in her escape and her previous occupation as a *Playboy* bunny override those concerns?

Produced by *Dateline*'s award-winning team of journalists, "To Catch a Predator" incorporates the values of investigative journalism, such as access, advocacy, accuracy and fairness. Although the video vérité taping by hidden cameras shows the suspects in an embarrassing fashion, they have voluntarily come to the decoy house lured by on-line chat with Perverted Justice. But Hansen does not immediately reveal his identity as a reporter doing a story or the hidden cameras, which raises ethical questions, given that truth figures so highly in journalism's hierarchy of values.

In contrast to the truth value of journalism, *Dateline* practices deception in luring suspects and taping them with hidden cameras. Proponents of hidden camera techniques insist with an "end justifies the means" principle that truth can sometimes be overridden by other values, such as justice and public health. For example, the practice has exposed dangerous food practices, corruption in small business regulation, and abuse of patients in homes for the mentally challenged.

Some reality-show practices conflict with the journalistic value of independence. In May 1990, *America's Most Wanted* assisted in the recovery of a Massachusetts girl abducted by her babysitter. In exchange for exclusive access, *America's Most Wanted* flew her parents to Florida and back home in a private jet, escorted by a production crew and publicist (me). Just as an FBI agent was about to bring the girl into a Tallahassee hotel room to greet her parents, another FBI agent attempted to stop our taping the reunion, but relented when we cited our agreement with the family. Yet as the competing news media in Florida and Massachusetts pursued the family (and me) for the next 24 hours, had *America's Most Wanted* exploited or helped them in controlling access?[27] In paying the family's expenses in return for exclusive access, the show engaged in the unethical practice of "checkbook journalism," which is considered unethical by journalists because it conflicts with the core journalistic value of independence. As spokesperson for the show, I would have justified the deal to protect the family's privacy from prying journalists knocking on their hotel door at midnight.

Dateline has also been criticized for a lack of taste since Hansen reads verbatim transcripts of on-line conversations between the suspect and Perverted Justice decoys. These often contain graphic descriptions of sexual acts, which raise the same concerns as *America's Most Wanted*'s use of violence, in the potential effect on children during prime-time family viewing hours. Here *Dateline*'s journalism values of truth and accuracy conflict with family values of decency and sensitivity to the innocent, particularly children.

Journalism Versus Law Enforcement

Police and these reality shows share some universal values. Their primary shared value would be seeking justice — one to maintain order and fight crime, the other to create entertainment and make profits. In advocating for justice, security, and order, they also promote social causes, such as compassion for crime victims and their rights. By setting up its sting operations, "To Catch a Predator" provides public service both in helping to apprehend criminals and educating the public about the dangers of on-line predators.

In helping their camera crew friends, however, would police officers prolong an arrest to provide enough footage for a segment or become overzealous in taking down a suspect for guaranteed action? Knowing they are being videotaped for national television may bring such temptations.

This raises the problem of conflicting values between law enforcement and reality TV. Reality television production requires unlimited access to law enforcement operations, which is allowed as long as it does not create danger to police, suspects, or civilians. But that unlimited access can create some compromising situations, as critics point out in *Dateline*'s access to the attempted arrest of William Conradt, Jr., who fatally shot himself.

Although one might argue that convicted criminals surrender any right to privacy, some of those featured on "To Catch a Predator" have complained about being harassed in public due to their sudden national celebrity.[28] After serving their jail time or paying a fine, they should be allowed to rehabilitate themselves into law-abiding community members, not forced into moving somewhere else to anonymously start over.

Such value conflicts cloud the respective roles of the police and reality television. Does law enforcement become the entertainers? Does reality television become the police? Do the journalists become entertainers without the audience realizing that the line has been blurred? How can the news media be watchdogs over law enforcement if they take the role of police? In one *America's Most Wanted* episode, Walsh traveled to France to confront a fugitive murderer living openly after being convicted *in absentia*. Was he acting as a journalist, a reality TV host, or a pursuing cop? The resulting dramatic footage between crime fighter and fugitive is entertaining. The staged event is not necessarily newsworthy, however, and borders on created news to attract publicity.

In his "Predator" conversations with the suspects lured to the decoy house, Hansen's role often seems confused. Is he preaching, interviewing or interrogating? Is he a journalist probing the mind and motives of a suspected predator or a detective gathering evidence for an arrest and prosecution?

By not identifying himself immediately as a journalist, Hansen interrogates the suspect, often asking personal and embarrassing questions. In this "holier than thou" attitude, Hansen is looking for a probing interview with little regard for the suspect's right to remain silent. The confused individual does not know if Hansen is a cop, a counselor, a clergyman, or a reporter. Having not been advised of the right to counsel or to refuse to answer Hansen's questions—which are being videotaped without the suspect's knowledge—the suspect could make incriminating statements later used against him in court.

Hansen is not obligated under law to advise the suspect of his rights, but when he plays interrogator, his deception contradicts the journalistic value of truth-telling. In staging these stings to help expose the problem of sexual predators on the Internet, *Dateline* crosses the line from reporting to creating news. There is no story or show unless the producers set up these stings.

Although *Dateline* would insist "To Catch a Predator" incorporated the traditional journalistic values of investigative reporting, critics charge the segments have corrupted those values, especially by its deception and staging. Is the show reporting or creating news? Douglas McCollam wrote in *Columbia Journalism Review* that the series is "enterprise journalism ... suited to the Internet age." By clouding "the distinction between enterprise and entertainment," *Dateline* no longer covers a story, but creates one, and damages "the barrier" between police and news media necessary for journalism, he stated.

"If humiliating perverts and needlessly terrifying parents is the best use that newsmagazines can make of hours of primetime television, then perhaps they should be allowed to die and the time given over to the blood sport of reality programming," McCollam wrote. "At least no one would dare to call it news."[29]

While *Dateline* might eventually discontinue "To Catch a Predator," *COPS* and *AMW* will probably remain as the Saturday Fox crime lineup for years. In examining shared and conflicting values, the producers of reality television and law enforcement can better understand their common and contrasting goals. Perhaps ethical dialogue could preserve the necessary barrier between their missions, distinguishing the line between news and entertainment, and between news and law enforcement, while giving audiences and networks the programming that gratifies needs and makes money.

In my media ethics classes I caution students that their own personal values might conflict with those of a supervisor, particularly in an ethics-deprived business as the entertainment industry. Do you sacrifice those well-founded personal values to satisfy professional goals or stick to your ethical identity?

Fortunately, only one boss challenged my values by ordering me to deceive the media about an embarrassing incident involving a show's star. I refused, and the supervisor convinced another staff member to perform this unethical action. This resulted in a bigger embarrassment for the show. While that ethical stand cost me points with the boss, I have no regrets about following an ethical "higher road." A few years later, a potential employer asked a newspaper TV columnist who reported that incident about my reputation as a publicist. He gave me a solid recommendation, even mentioning the word "ethical."

Notes

1. *15 Minutes.* Produced, written and directed by John Herzeld. 2 hr. New Line Productions, 2001. Videocassette.

2. *15 Minutes.*

3. Jack Breslin, *America's Most Wanted: How Television Catches Crooks* (New York: Harper, 1990), 1–3.

4. Tim Brooks and Earle Marsh, *The Complete Directory to Prime Time Network TV Shows, 1946–Present*, 5th ed. (New York: Ballantine, 1992), 189, 958.

5. Breslin, *America's Most Wanted*, 358–60.

6. *Ibid.*, 360–1.

7. *Ibid.*, 143.

8. *Ibid.*, 180.

9. *America's Most Wanted*, "About AMW," <http;//www.amw.com> (accessed September 2, 2008).

10. *COPS*, "About Us," <http://www.cops.com/about.html> (accessed September 2, 2008).

11. Chris Hansen. "Dangers Children Face Online," *Dateline NBC*, <http://www.msnbc.msn.com/id/6083442/> (accessed August 31, 2008).

12. Hansen, "Dangers Children Face."

13. Chris Hansen, "Reflections on 'To Catch a Predator," *Dateline NBC*, <http://www.msnbc.msn.com/id/17601568/> (accessed August 30, 2008). An NBC publicist for *Dateline* "passed" on my request to interview Chris Hansen and a "Predator" producer.

14. Vic Walter and Maddy Sauer, "NBC News Settles 'To Catch a Predator' Lawsuit," June 23, 2008, *ABC News*, <http://abcnews.com/5238922> (accessed August 30, 2008).

15. Brian Ross and Vic Walter, "'To Catch a Predator': A Sting Gone Bad," *ABC News*. September 7, 2007, <http://blogs.abcnews.com/theblotter/2007/09/to-catch-a-pred.html> (accessed August 30, 2008).

16. Grant Slater, "Sex Sting Backfires in Texas Town, Turns into Fiasco," Associated Press, *Pittsburgh Post-Gazette*, July 1, 2007, A5. http://proquest.umi.com/pqdweb?index+36&sid=3&srchmode=1&vinst=PROD&fmt=3&st... (accessed September 1, 2008).

17. Peter A. Angeles, *Dictionary of Philosophy* (New York: Barnes and Noble, 1981), 17.

18. Albert A. Harrison. *Individuals and Groups: Understanding Social Behavior* (Pacific Grove, CA, 1976), 192.

19. Shalom Schwartz and Sipke Huismans, "Value Priorities and Religiosity in Four Western Religions," *Social Psychology Quarterly* 58 (1995): 89.

20. Elaine E. Englehardt and Ralph D. Barney, *Media Ethics: Principles for Moral Decisions* (Belmont, CA: Wadsworth Learning, 2002), 47, 50.

21. Louis Alvin Day, *Ethics in Media Communications: Cases and Controversies*, 5th ed. (Belmont, CA: Thomson Wadsworth, 2006), 25.

22. Ron Powers. Interview by Ted Koppel. *Nightline*. ABC, November 11, 1988.

23. Breslin, *America's Most Wanted*, 299–300.

24. Interview with John Langley by author, August 18, 2008.

25. Langley interview.

26. Interview with Lance Heflin by author, August 21, 2008.

27. Laura Meade. "When Nicole Was Found, 'Most Wanted' Took Control, *The Providence Sunday Journal*, 13 May 1990, A1. As the reporter noted, AMW's access to the reunion was not totally exclusive, since we allowed the *Boston Herald*, also a Murdoch media property, to cover and photograph the scene.

28. Vanessa Grigoriadis, "The New American Witch Hunt," *Rolling Stone*, August 9, 2007, 65.

29. Douglas McCollam, "The Shame Game." *Columbia Journalism Review*, January/February 2007, 28–33.

Works Cited

Angeles, Peter A. *Dictionary of Philosophy*. New York: Barnes and Noble, 1981.

Breslin, Jack. *America's Most Wanted: How TV Catches Crooks*. New York: Harper, 1990.

Brooks, Tim, and Earle Marsh. *The Complete Directory to Prime Time Network TV Shows, 1946–Present.* 5th ed. New York: Ballantine, 1992.

Day, Louis Alvin. *Ethics in Media Communication: Cases and Controversies.* 5th ed. Belmont, CA: Thomson Wadsworth, 2006.

Englehardt, Elaine, and Ralph Barney. *Media Ethics: Principles for Moral Decisions.* Belmont, CA: Wadsworth Learning, 2002.

Grigoriadis, Vanessa. "The New American Witch Hunt." *Rolling Stone,* August 9, 2007, 65.

Harrison, Albert A. *Individuals and Groups: Understanding Social Behavior.* Pacific Grove, CA: Brooks/Cole, 1976.

Heflin, Lance. Interview by Jack Breslin. 21 August 2008.

Langley, John. Interview by Jack Breslin. 18 August 2008.

McCollam, Douglas. "The Shame Game," *Columbia Journalism Review,* January/February 2007, 28–33.

Meade, Laura. "When Nicole Was Found, 'Most Wanted' Took Over." *Providence Sunday Journal,* 13 May 1990, A1

Schwartz, Shalom, and Sipke Huismans. "Value Priorities and Religiosity in Four Western Religions." *Social Psychology Quarterly* 58 (1995): 89.

IV. ENTERTAINMENT AND AUTHORSHIP

CHAPTER 12

Documentary Tradition and the Ethics of Michael Moore's *SiCKO*

Sandra L. Borden

May I take a minute to ask a question that's been on my mind: Who are we? Is this what we've become: A nation that dumps its own citizens like so much garbage on the curb 'cause they can't pay their hospital bill?
—Michael Moore's voiceover in *SiCKO*

Michael Moore's distinctive brand of filmmaking provokes questions about what's ethical in documentary film by destabilizing our expectations of the genre. His work is usually received warmly by film critics, the Academy of Motion Pictures, and liberals, who see him as a subversive humorist breathing new life into documentaries and progressive politics. However, criticism of Moore's work has been just as passionate. Journalists criticize the accuracy of his facts as well as the fairness of his arguments. Moore's 2007 film, *SiCKO*, provoked ABC reporter John Stossel to write a dismissive op-ed piece in the *Wall Street Journal*, and CNN medical correspondent Dr. Sanjay Gupta had it out on television with the filmmaker over the film's truthfulness. Conservatives, as well as the folks on the receiving end of Moore's biting wit, also have had their say. A number of books, films, and websites directly rebut Moore's work. Examples include the book *Michael Moore Is a Big Fat Stupid White Man* (criticizing Moore's 2001 tome *Stupid White Men*) and *FAHRENHYPE 911* (criticizing the 2005 film *Fahrenheit 9/11*). There are websites and blogs that exist solely to denounce him, including Moorewatch.com ("Watching Michael Moore's Every Move"). Peter Barry Chowka, in a column written about *SiCKO* for the *American Thinker*, captures the animosity with which the political right greets every new film by Michael Moore:

"Almost shockingly devoid of fact and content, it's instead based on highly selective, emotionally-driven, and deeply flawed anecdotes, strung together by writer-director-producer Moore's trademark folksy, soft-spoken, whimsical personal narrative. SiCKO is ... a naked propaganda exercise on behalf of full-bore socialism. A better title for it would be Pinko."[1]

I will tackle the ethics of Moore's documentaries using virtue theory, which calls attention to the way that traditions inspire us to perform our various roles with moral integrity.[2] Using his 2007 documentary, *SiCKO*, by way of illustration, I will argue that, on the one hand, Moore's performance as a documentary filmmaker generally exhibits coherence, continuity, and creativity within the documentary tradition. On the other hand, his performance is not entirely consistent with the moral commitments of documentary filmmakers.

The Moral Authority of Traditions

Like any role, that of documentary filmmaker involves commitments to certain shared goods, such as knowledge and justice. To achieve these goods, documentary filmmakers must cultivate and exercise certain moral and intellectual virtues, such as fairness, justice, and intellectual honesty. These virtues have special significance in the context of their work, but also inform their individual lives and the larger tradition to which they belong. To be properly described as a virtue, in fact, a quality must promote the achievement of what is good in all three contexts: one's social roles, one's entire life, and the traditions that weave our life together with those of others.[3]

The documentary film tradition provides Moore and other documentary filmmakers with a common purpose and bonds them to a certain way of living a good life — a life lived *as* documentary filmmakers. It sensitizes them to the multiple ways in which they can perform their role with integrity; that is, in ways that match performance to motivation. It helps us to understand how the various parts of their moral selves — rational, emotional, aesthetic — are unified in their role performances.[4] Just as the narrative of a single human life provides the context needed to make intelligible that person's intentions, the narrative of a tradition provides the context needed to make intelligible the motivations animating performances of a social role. Without knowledge of intentions, according to virtue theory, we are not in a position to evaluate moral conduct. In short, the documentary tradition functions as a source of moral authority for documentary filmmakers and gives the rest of us a coherent basis for understanding what Moore is (supposed to be) up to, morally speaking. It provides a framework for moral accountability.

The documentary tradition has been passed down by previous generations of documentary filmmakers. As virtue theorist Alasdair MacIntyre explains traditions: "What I am, therefore, is in key part what I inherit, a specific past that is present to some degree in my present. I find myself part of a history and that is generally to say, whether I like it or not, whether I recognize it or not, one of the bearers of a tradition."[5] Traditions get passed down in various "sites of storytelling activity." These sites would include the lives of current and former documentary filmmakers, as well as models of morality from other traditions that have intersected historically with documentary. Other possible sites are published film reviews and scholarship, blogs, oral and written histories, and documentaries themselves. All together, these elements provide "mimetic options and value choices" that Moore could use to "script" his own virtuous performance.[6]

Yet far from being a static relic from the past — or worse, excuses for unthinking conformity — traditions are arguments-in-progress. After all, a narrative suggests "the ongoing communication and connection of ideas and events over time."[7] A tradition must provide a coherent narrative that makes its elements intelligible, but it also must be accountable for the way in which it intersects with the narratives of other traditions and the way in which it integrates the goods of various roles and human lives. Traditions, then, must be constantly interpreted in light of their history and current challenges to ascertain which performances "fit" and which don't.[8] Performances must be adjusted if, upon reflection, the tradition has moral limitations that hinder the objective conditions for human flourishing.[9]

MacIntyre mentions a specific virtue needed to ensure that a tradition itself will flourish: "the virtue of having an adequate sense of the traditions to which one belongs or which confront one."[10] In my discussion of *SiCKO*, I will focus particularly on how Moore's performance invokes elements from various strands in the journalistic tradition, including muckraking, New Journalism, and investigative journalism. This virtue of appreciating one's legacy also involves understanding how one's tradition opens up possible paths for transformation, given where its adherents have been and where they are going. In other words, a tradition "can be a resource for invention, not just continuity."[11] For documentary filmmakers, this could mean adapting documentary conventions to new modes of story telling or adopting anthropological protocols for protecting the rights of the people they interview.

For the analysis that follows, I have adapted four of the "formal processive norms" that James A. Donahue has suggested as a framework for ethical decision making based on virtue theory.[12] These norms can help clarify the degree to which Moore expressed the virtue of appreciating his tradition in *SiCKO*.[13] Specifically, I will use:

- *Coherence* — regard for how events are connected to each other throughout the tradition's history and how different aspects of the tradition relate to each other (*How does this fit within the framework of my tradition's narrative?*)
- *Consistency* — embodying the moral commitments passed down by the tradition (*Is this appropriate, given the distinctive expectations of my tradition that others have come to count on? What kind of precedent am I setting?*)
- *Continuity* — correspondence between one's performance and some legitimizing element from the tradition (*How does this follow from my tradition? How can I best further my tradition?*)
- *Creativity* — giving sufficient weight to novel approaches compatible with one's tradition (*Have I been open to new ways of achieving my tradition's goals?*)

SiCKO as Documentary

Moore has developed a recognizable "storytelling strategy" that includes heavily publicized antics, seriocomic contrasts, and Moore himself as the film's comic investigator.[14] Nevertheless, the way he plays around with the documentary genre's conventions can leave some critics and audiences genuinely puzzled. *SiCKO* was no different: "People argue over whether to call it a documentary, an essay, a polemic, a piece of agitprop, or a work of performance art, because each name asserts something different about the film's relationship to truth."[15] No matter. Moore has a huge following, whatever his films are supposed to be. The films have enjoyed significant box-office success, especially his 2004 anti-war film *Fahrenheit 9/11*, which, propelled by controversy and critical acclaim, exceeded all previous documentary records in theaters.[16] Moore's earlier work, beginning with his 1989 film *Roger & Me*, also cast him as the ingénue ironist who guides audiences through an onscreen landmine of laughs and malfeasance at the highest levels of power. Moore has taken aim at GM's CEO in *Roger & Me*, the National Rifle Association in *Bowling for Columbine*, and the U.S. president in *Fahrenheit 9/11*. He set his sights on the health-insurance industry in *SiCKO*.

Released in 2007, just as the 2008 presidential race was starting to take shape, *SiCKO* aimed to put health-care reform on the national agenda, with a particular emphasis on the shortcomings of employer-provided health insurance managed through HMOs. Although he acknowledges the plight of the 45 million uninsured, Moore explicitly focuses his argument on those lucky enough to have health-care coverage. He rejects incremental approaches that do not fundamentally change a system that he sees as corrupt. He ultimately concludes that the social democracies of Great Britain, France, and Canada have gotten it right with tax-funded health care or health insurance provided to all comers. He ridicules the socialist label applied to such systems, most provocatively by comparing the U.S. system unfavorably to the one in Cuba.

When *SiCKO* was released widely in theaters in the summer of 2007, health care was the top domestic issue among registered voters for the 2008 presidential election, trailing only behind the Iraq war. Anxiety about health care has increased because fewer employers are providing coverage. More businesses are hiring part-time workers who do not qualify for health coverage or refuse to provide health coverage altogether. Those that do provide it have reduced benefits and charge their employees more for their share of insurance premiums. This situation creates special hardships for low-income workers, who either do not qualify for coverage or cannot afford the coverage offered.[17] Nevertheless, Moore did not focus on them in *SiCKO* either. Instead, he chose to summon the righteous indignation of those who drive election results: the middle class. In this approach, he took a page from the storied history of muckrakers in the journalistic tradition. Like Ida Tarbell, Upton Sinclair, and the other muckrakers who wrote sensationalistic exposés of political and business corruption at the turn of the nineteenth century, Moore has also been accused of being a socialist for his anti-establishment views. How are we to judge the performance that resulted from Moore's decision to embody the muckraker's sensibility for social justice?

Coherence of Documentary Voice

Perhaps more than other genres, documentary films express the convictions of their makers. Whereas mainstream journalistic pieces efface the voice of their authors to appear "objective," and Hollywood fiction blows off questions about intentions by claiming to be "just entertainment," documentaries imply a seriousness of purpose that invites us to scrutinize the filmmaker's intentions, as virtue ethics would have us do.[18] Film historians Jack C. Ellis and Betsy A. McLane name as the "traditional documentary impulse" the desire "to educate and broaden the public's horizons."[19] Similarly, film scholar Bill Nichols suggests that all documentaries aim to make arguments about the historical world.[20] It makes no sense, therefore, to accuse a documentary film of "lying" just because it portrays a point of view. We might say a documentary gets it wrong as far as the "point" or the "moral" of the film is concerned.[21] However, detachment as such is not required for responsible filmmaking in documentary and, in fact, may actually thwart its ends.[22]

The totality of stylistic choices that a filmmaker chooses to achieve these ends is known as documentary voice. As explained by Nichols in *Film Quarterly*:

> It is a voice that issues from the entirety of each film's body as an audiovisual presence: we hear it speak to us from the selection of shots, the framing of subjects, the juxtaposition of scenes, the mixing of sounds, the use of titles and intertitles—from all those stylistic means by which a filmmaker conveys a distinct perspective on a given subject and seeks to persuade the viewer to adopt this perspective as his or her own.[23]

As Nichols notes, documentary voice is largely a matter of style, and style fluctuates depending on the ideological, generic, and historical demands of the moment. Nichols traced four major documentary styles:

- *Commentary*— the conventional documentary with its didactic purpose and omniscient, authoritative narration.
- *Vérité*— the observational documentary with its recording purpose and unmarked gazing.
- *Interview*— the witness-participant documentary that relies on fragmented recollections and perceptions of interview subjects, as well as of the narrator.
- *Self-reflexive*— the transparent documentary that uses elements of the vérité and interview styles while making obvious that the "film-maker was always a participant-witness, a producer of cinematic discourse rather than a neutral or all-knowing reporter of the way things truly are."[24]

In view of documentary history, and how the various documentary modes have interacted with each other and have evolved over time, Moore's performance in *SiCKO* demonstrates coherence with his tradition. In fact, he uses all of these styles at various points. Moore uses objective forms of documentary evidence, particularly visual and aural documents that convey historicity. For example, he traces the genesis of HMOs to the Nixon administration by playing an Oval Office recording of Chief of Staff H.R. Haldeman (shown with the president in an archival photograph) pitching the idea in 1971 as a private, for-profit plan in which "all the incentives are toward less medical care." Moore follows this recording with a sound bite of Nixon delivering a speech the very next day proposing "the finest health care in the world and access for everyone." At other junctures, Moore seems to simply follow the stories of his subjects unobtrusively in vérité style, as when his camera crew records the move of Larry and Donna Smith to their new home in their daughter's basement. We see their humiliation at having to impose on their daughter after being pushed to financial ruin by medical bills.

Moore makes extensive use of interviews with current and former health-insurance industry employees, expatriates, and foreign nationals living in countries with universal public health care, and, of course, with people who have war stories to tell. His documentary voice also is self-reflexive in a number of ways: We see how the anecdotes he selected resulted from an online call for health-care "horror stories." We see how a Michigan woman has to quickly leave a Canadian clinic on the other side of the U.S. border when Moore's camera crew arouses suspicion. We see Moore renting boats to take 9/11 rescue workers to Guantanamo Bay for medical treatment, and he tells us that he personally asked the staff at a Cuban hospital to provide the same care to 9/11 rescue workers that they would offer to any Cuban citizen.

Nichols later suggested a newer style called the *performative* documentary mode. In this mode, the filmmaker effectively becomes the film's onscreen protagonist.[25] Although Moore does not appear in *SiCKO* as much as he does in some of his earlier works, his voice in this film can be classified as performative. Sometimes he is off-screen asking interview questions or providing the voiceover. But at other times, he's front and center, globe-trotting to personally investigate the differences between the U.S. health-care system and other national systems, egging on the Coast Guard as he defiantly leads a quixotic flotilla to Cuba, and finally dropping off his laundry at the White House (hey, if France's health-care system will do laundry for new moms, why not here?).

Moore's decision to invoke the fullness of his tradition in *SiCKO* disrupts the film's unity at one level. But, at another level, it invites us to experience the struggle around documentary voice that has been taking place for decades. It also prods us to encounter the health-care problem from a variety of vantage points, shedding light on its complexity. By being mindful of how the different parts relate to the whole, Moore expresses the virtue of appreciating his tradition by demonstrating coherence within the narrative context tradition provides.

Consistency with Documentary Truth

Film scholar Garnet C. Butchart notes that documentaries, like journalism, struggle with the popular belief that there is an essential truth that can be captured in an unbiased way.[26] To distort, fake, or conceal this truth is considered unethical. However, we have increasingly come to accept that things are not that simple: that everyone in a given situation will perceive a "reality" about those circumstances that is widely shared, but, at the same time, is variously experienced by individuals in that situation. Nichols prefers "the story teller's open resort to artifice" to the pretense of objectivity.[27] How, then, to evaluate truth in documentary? Butchart points out that the constant in documentary filmmaking is "the role of visual perception in the construction of documentary images." Voice may vary, but this "vision" remains the same. This, he says, is "*the truth of the documentary enterprise.*" What matters ethically, he suggests, is whether the filmmaker is upfront about how she intentionally uses this mode to structure perception and thereby produce knowledge. Too often, he claims, the truth of documentary is not visible onscreen.[28]

To be a truthful documentary filmmaker in this sense, Butchart suggests three major strategies: "unconcealing the camera" by drawing attention to it onscreen and allowing subjects to "actively collaborate with or contribute to the filmmaking process rather than simply allowing the documentation of events they create"; calling attention to the filmmaking process itself, including editing choices that clarify the filmmaker's perspective and the filmmaker's own appearance onscreen; and "maintaining consistency to the idea of reflexive filmmaking" — that is, remaining open to the possibilities of new forms and new questions in documentary. Thus defined, truth in documentary is not about what gets put in or what gets left out, but whether filmmakers are transparent about their intentions — in virtue theory terms, whether they provide enough of the "back story" to meet the test of narrative accountability.[29] What we're left to judge in this framework are the filmmakers' intentions and how well they revealed them to us in their films.

By this measure, Moore's performance in *SiCKO* is not only consistent with the tradition's moral commitments, but practically exemplary. Although the documentary tradition includes objective narration, it is simply inadequate to use literal accuracy as the only measure of Moore's truthfulness in *SiCKO*. Not only does objective narration represent just one mode of documentary filmmaking, it is not even the only legitimate mode in journalism's tradition either. For example, New Journalists like Norman Mailer and Truman Capote openly embraced such literary techniques as composite characters and imagined conversations in the 1960s to convey a larger "truth." The "Gonzo" journalism associated with Hunter S. Thompson in the following decade pushed the envelope further with the conscious use of sarcasm and exaggeration by the reporter who also was part of the story. We can see some clear connections between this strand in journalism's tradition and Moore's work in *SiCKO*. Indeed, by making obvious how he has put together this documentary, Moore is arguably more truthful about what he's up to than your average news anchor. Nevertheless, to reject a naïve positivistic view of the world is not the same as to reject all truth claims. Reality, as we experience it, matters even with visual perception:

> In theory, my perception of a baseball flying at my head may be no more than an imaginary construct — a fiction, if you will. Nevertheless, if it does not cause me to duck, I am liable to get quite a lump. Documentary has some of the same practical implications.[30]

It is no small matter, film scholar Dirk Eitzen reminds us, how viewers "take" documentaries. They do not understand documentaries to be merely inviting us to consider a particular reality that might be *similar* to the real world (the "fictive" stance). Rather, viewers assume that the state of affairs documentaries present *is* real (the "assertive" stance). That is not to say that viewers focus primarily on the truth claims documentaries present. They may, in fact, pay more attention to humor and sentiment — to the meaning of the film rather than to its logic — not because they think truth does not matter but because they take it for granted. They may experience documentary as melodrama or comedy, but they always assume that documentaries, underneath it all, are "telling the truth." Conventional documentaries with an objective stance are no less problematic. As Nichols points out, interview-style documentaries implicitly claim that "Interviewees never lie." And, yet, of course, sometimes they do. What separates fiction from nonfiction, Eitzen concludes, is whether we can sensibly ask, "Might it be lying?"[31]

So there are still questions we can ask about Moore's truthfulness in *SiCKO*: Did the events depicted really happen? Were the people who appeared really who they said they were? Did they tell what they believed to be the truth? Moore's foray into Cuba was clearly a stunt he devised for the movie. However, audiences expect that the people he took really were 9/11 rescue workers, that they really did suffer from respiratory illnesses caused by environmental conditions at Ground Zero, that the hospital scenes really were taped in Cuba (as opposed to a Hollywood back lot), and so forth. Moore clearly intends for the audience to hold him accountable for such truth claims (as demonstrated in his online defenses against accusations of fudging the facts). If we found out that any of these claims were false, he would rightly stand accused of lying and, therefore, of being inconsistent with a core moral commitment of his tradition.

Continuity with Documentary Argument

Another question we can ask is whether Moore presents a fair argument in the film. For example, does he use non-representative anecdotes or other kinds of faulty evidence? Does his construction of villains lend his own viewpoint a credibility it doesn't deserve? Does the film leave out certain events, people, and interpretations that are essential to the argument? Is his "plain folks" approach just a ploy? In other words, is *SiCKO* just a piece of manipulative propaganda, or does it demonstrate continuity with argumentative techniques that have legitimacy within the documentary tradition?

Moore has been accused of presenting only the most favorable information for his side and ignoring or downplaying the positives on the other side.

However, Su Hi Choi suggested that objective documentaries can be just as guilty of what the Institute for Propaganda Analysis called "card stacking."[32] In her textual analysis of PBS' 2001 documentary, *Battle for Korea*, she showed how a documentary can make certain events and personalities more prominent than others without seeming to do so. Likewise, the stories and images of health-care "victims" are highly visible in *SiCKO*, compared with alternative perspectives. There are no anecdotes of people who have had positive experiences with their health-insurance coverage. There is no acknowledgment of people who have tried to defraud a health insurance company. We see no testimonies of people who have had negative experiences with health care in Cuba or Canada. Another way in which Moore downplays the "other side" is by objectifying them: Health-insurance executives and hospital administrators are faceless, anonymous villains whose voices are heard secondhand or not at all. Politicians are mocked as sexist cartoon characters with a price tag. Meanwhile, people working in the health-care industry and people who have experienced national health systems in other countries are selectively presented. We see only former medical reviewers who think HMOs are corrupt; we see only people who give raves to the systems in Canada, Britain, and France.

Moore has responded that *SiCKO* was about the horror stories in health care, not about the happy endings. Focusing on social problems that need solutions is a classic subject matter of documentary (as well as news), and Moore can reasonably argue that he had to limit the scope of his argument (in fact, Robert Brent Toplin suggests Moore could have argued more responsibly had he tried to cover even less ground). To his credit, Moore does not simply throw up a bunch of disconnected images and statements without any context, as some documentary filmmakers have done. His voiceover unifies all the pieces of the puzzle by laying out his line of argument over the course of the film. Even more impressively, he does not ignore the larger context in which the U.S. health-care system persists: "the chokehold of medical bills, college loans, day care and everything else that makes us afraid to step out of line."[33]

That being said, Moore is at least occasionally guilty of what Choi calls reductive narration — replacing complex explanation with abstractions, terms, images, or sounds that oversimplify things, making us less apt to question Moore's point of view and press for more evidence. The segment in *SiCKO* dealing with Hillary Rodham Clinton is illustrative. Moore introduces her as Bill Clinton's "little lady" after a quick boyhood snapshot of the former president on a pony. This is followed by a montage of still photographs depicting a glamorous, vibrant Hillary to the tune of The Staple Singers' 1972 hit, "I'll Take You There." Moore's voiceover purrs, "Sassy. Smart. Sexy. Some men couldn't handle it." By making Clinton's gender an issue, Moore suggests that resistance to her health-care plan was rooted in sexism — at the very same time that he trivializes her by dwelling on her femininity rather than on the substance of her plan.

Next, we see a news shot of Bill Clinton announcing his wife's health-care task force. The voiceover says, "She drove Washington insane." This is followed by a montage of sound bites featuring Republicans bashing her plan as a bureaucratic, socialist experiment. Moore points out the manipulative nature of this criticism by juxtaposing these sound bites with archival footage of public service announcements against communism from the 1950s, followed by grainy footage of Chinese soldiers marching in lockstep at the height of the Cold War. The voiceover teases, "Ooooh. Socialized medicine. Nothing put more fear in us than the thought of *that*." He unloads on the American Medical Association next (with its unlikely spokesman, then-actor Ronald Reagan) for opposing free universal health care, then ties together all these disparate images and sound with his conclusion: "The times had changed, but the tactics had not." Ultimately, Clinton is vanquished. Moore illustrates her last seven years as First Lady with a news story of Clinton leading the White House Easter egg roll. On the one hand, this juxtaposition accurately depicts Clinton's diminished public role for the remainder of her husband's administration. On the other hand, it falsely implies that she did nothing more than participate in ceremonial functions with no substance from that point on.

Although film critic Stuart Klawans gives Moore credit for mounting a logical argument in *SiCKO*, he questions some of the evidence: "He's like a man who opens the neatly alphabetized drawers of a filing cabinet and pulls out a pair of pajamas, a children's storybook, half a roast beef sandwich, and a live hen."[34] Whether he is guilty of card stacking — intentional or not — Moore gets moral credit for protecting audiences from the effects of this potentially misleading technique. True to his everyman persona, he seeks perspective the way most of us would: by asking relatives or friends. When he wants to know what health care is like in Canada, for example, he interviews his aunt and uncle who live across the Michigan border. They confide in him that they wouldn't dream of going to the United States without taking out a health-insurance policy, in case something happened to them on foreign soil and they got stuck with thousands in medical bills. Their obvious suspicion of the "American way" is unexpected and, therefore, humorous. But it is also troubling.

Moore also uses an objective technique for balancing truth claims in documentary: He entertains counterarguments. Like a good reporter, he asks the sorts of questions that a skeptic might. Across the border, he asks an elderly golfer why he expects fellow Canadians who don't have his problem to pay for a problem that he has. The man answers matter-of-factly, "Because we would do the same for them." Acting perplexed, Moore asks him whether he's a member of the Socialist or the Green parties. The golfer says he's a member of the Conservative Party. Then comes Moore's conclusion: "What's *wrong* on this issue with us?" Similarly, he tests out pharmaceutical transactions in Great Britain and visits with a government-paid doctor to see whether his standard of living is any good (it is). So, despite his tendency to demonstrate animosity toward the villains in *SiCKO*, Moore does seek to address the most important objections made by those who oppose government-run universal health care. In the end, Moore's use of documentary argument is a mixed ethical bag when considering the norm of continuity. He presents a unifying line of reasoning and entertains serious counterarguments, as we would expect from a performance corresponding to the highest standards of the practice. However, he uses selective evidence and reductive narration — argumentative techniques of questionable legitimacy within the documentary tradition.

Creativity with Humor and Irony

Unlike Jon Stewart of *The Daily Show*, who can use humor in certain ways because he's just pretending to be a journalist, Moore confounds expectations by using humor in his role *as* a documentary filmmaker.[35] Certainly, there are moments in *SiCKO* that use a tragic frame.[36] At other times, Moore is almost melodramatically preachy, as in the quote appearing at the beginning of this essay. But, at other times, he frames the film humorously, a strategic choice that turns out to be anything but trivializing. As Aloys Fleishmann notes, Moore's humor helps to dissipate the anger that audiences might feel because of the filmmaker's "unbalanced" approach. "Comedy clears a safety zone, a testing ground." Humor helps us to let down our guard, to encourage us to accept inferences we might otherwise scrutinize, but also to open our minds to ideas that we might otherwise reject. In a comparison that illustrates how indebted Moore is to the tradition of political satire, Fleischmann compares Moore to Charlie Chaplin in the way he juxtaposes "injustice and tragedy with absurdity and laughter."[37] Likewise, Moore's performance is reminiscent of an important character in both the journalistic and literary traditions: Mark Twain. Like Twain's, Moore's creativity issues from the nexus of several overlapping traditions, resulting in a performance that is grounded in fact, motivated by frustrated idealism, and stylistically marked by exaggeration.

Moore rhetorically manages his overlapping roles by adopting a tragicomic frame synthesized by irony.[38] Juxtaposition, in fact, is fundamental to conveying the two levels at which irony works: the way things seem to be and the way they really are. The incongruity between the anecdotes of health-care victims and the cheerful music and images Moore culls from vintage ads, movies, and newsreels makes us laugh and cringe at the same time. Juxtaposition also is essential to the way in which Moore constructs the villains in his film. One of his techniques is to contrast what his villains say in public with what they do behind closed doors—between what they promise and what they actually deliver. Like *Fahrenheit 9/11, SiCKO* "highlights the struggle between political commitment and the postideological cynicism embodied by the governing elites: it is they, not *the people*, who laugh cynically."[39] Moore uses irony to make an argument about right and wrong, adopting, in effect, a stance that is not only *assertive*, but also *normative*. From this point of view, it makes sense that he should focus on the plight of the insured in America: They presumably are "covered," yet when they need their coverage, they cannot rely on it.

Media ethicists James Ettema and Theodore Glasser note in their analysis of irony in investigative reporting that irony can "elevate the illegal, the unethical, and even the merely improper to the outrageous." For journalists, the challenge is to suffuse "facts" with meaning while remaining within the confines of objectivity. For Moore, the challenge is to present a viewpoint that many consider to be "radical" while appealing to a mainstream audience.[40] Irony allows him to come off at once serious and funny, dangerous and harmless. Irony turns out to be the essential stylistic choice in Moore's documentary voice, demonstrating creativity in the way that he challenges documentary conventions and incorporates insights and techniques from traditions outside his own.

As the ironist, Moore can pretend to be an innocent wading through the complexities of the U.S. health-care system and learning about health care in other countries. He's amazed that any prescription you could ask for at a London pharmacy costs the equivalent of $10—and for children, retirees, and the unemployed, it's free. What? He laughs in awe at the French government's largesse in paying someone to do laundry for the mother of a newborn. Are you kidding? Of course, there are victims of irony in *SiCKO* as well: those who think they will be taken care of when a fateful diagnosis comes or when they've risked their health for their country. The look of utter incomprehension on a Canadian man's face when Moore tells him about the guy who had to choose which finger to reattach because he couldn't afford to repair both is priceless. Like Voltaire's Candide, Moore is the ingénue ironist[41] who goes from one outrageous experience to the next, winking at the audience as he reassures them that the U.S. health-care system must be the "best of all possible worlds." When he discovers that the cashier window in a British hospital gives money to patients (not vice versa), he feigns suspicion: "Clearly, I was just the butt of a joke here." The protagonists in Moore's "horror stories" themselves have stumbled innocently into the quagmire and have run into situations so absurd, they are funny — almost. "The laughter is generated not only to ridicule but also to produce catharsis. We can laugh at the characters, but then the difficult feelings of uneasiness and shame come.... If it is really this way, it is not funny."[42]

In fact, one way to read *SiCKO* is as a *parody* of propaganda. Moore is arguably drawing an analogy between the hooey he thinks we've been getting on health care and other kinds of hooey we've gotten over the years. He focuses in particular on the myths of prosperity and national unity in the 1950s. The basic message is: "You're living in a fantasy, just like the ones we bought in the 1950s about the nuclear family, consumerism, and communism. Wake up!" If he is pulling a Voltaire — parodying our misplaced optimism about having the "best health care in the world" — Moore may be implicitly encouraging us to guard against propagandistic techniques. In effect, he may be fighting the narrative of health care put forth in official pronouncements and industry lobbying with an alternative narrative — a symbolic tit for tat.[43]

Moore's Legacy as a Character in Documentary Tradition

Any tradition features *characters*, or moral representatives, that "embody moral beliefs, doctrines and theories." Moore may be more Hollywood than History Channel, but he has joined the likes of Errol Morris and Ken Burns as a bone fide *character* in the documentary tradition, encouraging the kind of creativity that helps traditions to thrive and the kind of debates that can act as "catalysts of moral change."[44] The question is, Does Moore provide a role model to imitate or a cautionary profile to avoid?

Anna Misiak argues that Moore's decision to make stories interesting is a legitimate rhetorical choice for adapting to his target audience. Moore's choice to "adapt facts to the narrative demands of a nonfiction feature film" has clear antecedents in the documentary tradition.[45] Indeed, some of the inferential shortcomings I have identified are inherent to the narrative structure of documentaries and, if anything, are magnified by the omniscient voice of objectivity in more conventional films. Moore's techniques actually dissipate these tendencies somewhat by drawing attention to the way in which he has constructed his argument.

That being said, the ironic jokes in *SiCKO* do encourage slippery inferences and hostility without the investigative reporter's assurances of accountability or the political humorist's disavowal of serious intent. As Ettema and Glasser note, the danger of irony is that it will degenerate into "the language of cynicism with its vocabulary of derision, reversal, and parody."[46] In other words, a language that encourages viewers to react with cool disdain rather than with indignant action — not at all what Moore probably intended. Subversive humor like Moore's "tends to be spurned, rejected, or just ignored,"[47] which may be why Moore includes a plea right before he closes with one more joke. He notes that, in other countries, people think of themselves as being in the same boat:

> They live in a world of "we," not "me." We'll never fix anything until we get that *one* basic thing right, and powerful forces hope we never do and that we remain the only country in the Western world without free, universal health care.

In that moment, Moore's cultural authority inheres in his stance as a political activist, rather than his comic abilities or his investigative chops. This is what makes documentary uniquely suited for Moore's performance: The tradition is one in which the filmmaker is expected to have a perspective on a serious subject that he educates others about and hopes to persuade them is "true." This is the key moral commitment of documentary filmmakers. Just as there are various morally appropriate performances within journalism,[48] the documentary tradition authorizes various morally appropriate performances along the dimensions of documentary voice, argument, and truth.

Moore ultimately achieves coherence among the various parts of his moral (and rhetorical self) in *SiCKO* by adopting the tragicomic stance. However, his performance is unconventional enough to risk straying from the legitimate moral expectations associated with the role of documentary filmmaker. The criticism aimed at his films illustrates the extremely partisan context in which Moore is working, to be sure, but also the seriousness with which audiences take the tradition's assurances about truth claims and fair argument. Then again, the success of Moore's films suggests a willingness by audiences to adjust their expectations if the moral demands of the situation warrant it. Nichols, for example, suggests that Moore and other independent filmmakers are reacting justifiably to "today's official story of war, social injustice, and human rights" by offering alternative viewpoints that are not available in established media.[49] In this respect, Moore demonstrates the kind of transformational creativity that the tradition needs to remain vibrant and relevant.

An earlier version of this chapter was presented in August 2008 at the annual convention of the Association for Education in Journalism and Mass Communication in Chicago.

NOTES

1. Peter Barry Chowka, "Prepare to be Sickened by SiCKO," *American Thinker* (June 22, 2007). Available: *http://www.americanthinker.com/2007/06/prepare_to_be_sickened_by_sick.html* (accessed August 4, 2008), para. 1.

2. Sandra L. Borden and Chad Tew, "The Role of Journalist and the Performance of Journalism: Ethical Lessons from 'Fake' News (Seriously)," *Journal of Mass Media Ethics* 22.4 (2007): 301–302.

3. Alasdair MacIntyre, *After Virtue*, 3rd ed. (South Bend, IN: University of Notre Dame Press, 2007), 275.

4. James A. Donahue, "The Use of Virtue and Character in Applied Ethics," *Horizons* 17.2 (1990): 232–233.

5. MacIntyre, *After Virtue*, 221.

6. Richard Bondi, "The Elements of Character," *The Journal of Religious Ethics* 12 (1984): 213); Edmund B. Lambeth and James Aucoin, "Journalism, Narrative and Community: Implications for Ethics, Practice and Media Criticism," *Professional Ethics* 2.1/2 (1993): 71. Detailing the elements and ancestry of the documentary tradition is beyond the scope of this chapter. However, important moral commitments and historical developments of the tradition will be discussed in the context of *SiCKO*.

7. Donahue, "Use of Virtue," 233.

8. Borden and Tew, "Role of Journalist," 311–313.

9. Sandra L. Borden, *Journalism as Practice: MacIntyre, Virtue Ethics and the Press* (Hampshire, England: Ashgate, 2007), 76–77.

10. MacIntyre, *After Virtue*, 223.

11. Borden, *Journalism as Practice*, 76.

12. Donahue, "Use of Virtue," 235.

13. These norms can also be applied to Moore's character within the context of his individual life narrative. For example, the norm of coherence suggests the following questions: Do the different aspects of my performance demonstrate unity, or are they self-contradictory? How does this performance fit in with the body of my work?

14. Robert Brent Toplin, *Michael Moore's Fahrenheit 9/11: How One Film Divided a Nation* (Lawrence: University Press of Kansas, 2006), 39.

15. Stuart Klawans, "Fever Pitch: Michael Moore's *SiCKO* Swears to Tell the Whole Truth and Nothing But the Truth. But Does It?" *Film Comment* 43.4 (2007), 27).

16. See pp. 52–70 in Toplin, *Michael Moore's Fahrenheit 9/11*, for a summary of the criticisms lodged against the film.

17. Kaiser Family Foundation. "Kaiser Health Tracking Poll: Election 2008," *http://www.kff.org/kaiserpolls/h08_pomr030708pkg.cfm*.

18. Borden and Tew, "Role of Journalist," 302–303.

19. Jack C. Ellis and Betsy A. McLane, *A New History of Documentary Film* (New York: Continuum, 2005), 334.

20. Bill Nichols, *Representing Reality: Issues and Concepts in Documentary* (Bloomington: Indiana University Press, 1991), 111.

21. Dirk Eitzen, "When Is a Documentary?: Documentary as a Mode of Reception," *Cinema Journal* 35.1 (1995): 97.

22. Strict impartiality, if anything, may discourage people from trusting us because it denies difference and obscures our intentions. Being honest about our perspective on a subject can serve as evidence of our good motives, as can transparency about our methods for arriving at and representing that viewpoint (Borden, 2007).

23. Bill Nichols, "The Time of the Orator," *Film Quarterly* 59.2 (2005/06): 3.

24. Bill Nichols, "The Voice of Documentary," *Film Quarterly* 36.3 (1983): 18.

25. Bill Nichols, *Blurred Boundaries: Questions of Meaning in Contemporary Culture* (Bloomington: Indiana University Press, 1994), 92–106.

26. Garnet C. Butchart, "On Ethics and Documentary: A Real and Actual Truth," *Communication Theory* 16 (2006): 428–431.

27. Nichols, "Voice of Documentary," 18.

28. Butchart, "Ethics and Documentary," 427, 437.

29. Lambeth and Aucoin, "Journalism, Narrative and Community," 74.

30. Eitzen, "When Is a Documentary?" 82.

31. Eitzen, "When Is a Documentary?" 85–89; Nichols, "Voice of Documentary," 24.

32. Su Hi Choi, *"History, Collective Memory, and TV Documentary: Analysis of* Battle for Korea *(PBS, 2001).* Paper presented in May 2005 at the annual meeting of the International Communication Association in New York City, http://www.allacademic.com/meta/p13047_index.html, 13–16; Klawans, "Fever Pitch," 28; Garth S. Jowett and Victoria O'Donnell, *Propaganda and Persuasion,* 2nd ed. (Newbury Park, CA: Sage, 1992), 182.

33. Klawans, "Fever Pitch," 28; Toplin, *Michael Moore and Fahrenheit 9/11,* 142.

34. Klawans, "Fever Pitch," 27–28.

35. Borden and Tew, "Role of Journalist," 309–311.

36. Examples include segments in which Moore is silent and instead lets poignant music do the talking. These include the surveillance video of an indigent woman dumped by a hospital on Los Angeles' Skid Row and the montage of 9/11 rescue workers receiving free treatment in Cuba after years of battling U.S. health-insurance companies in vain.

37. Aloys Fleischmann, "The Rhetorical Function of Comedy in Michael Moore's *Fahrenheit 9/11,"* *Mosaic* 40.4 (2007): 73, 76.

38. Susan Schultz Huxman, "The Tragic-Comic Rhetorical 'Dance' of Marginalized Groups: The Case of Mennonites in the Great War," *Southern Communication Journal* 62.4 (1997): 305–318.

39. Fleischmann, "Rhetorical Function of Comedy," 83.

40. James S. Ettema and Theodore L. Glasser, "The Irony in — and of — Journalism: A Case Study in the Moral Language of Liberal Democracy," *Journal of Communication* 44.2 (1994):7. In this respect, he is unlike the typical propagandist who exploits the audience's "common sense," according to Jowett and O'Donnell (*Propaganda and Persuasion,* 221–222).

41. Ettema and Glasser, "Irony in Journalism," 19.

42. Anna Misiak, "Not a Stupid White Man: The Democratic Context of Michael Moore's Documentaries," *Journal of Popular Film and Television* 33.3 (2005), paragraph 28. Retrieved from First Search database.

43. Fleischmann, "Rhetorical Function of Comedy," 81–82.

44. Lorraine Code, *Epistemic Responsibility* (Hanover, IN: Brown University Press, 1987), 30; MacIntyre, *After Virtue,* 28.

45. Misiak, "Stupid White Man," paragraph 35.

46. Ettema and Glasser, "Irony of Journalism," 26.

47. David L. Paletz, "Political Humor and Authority: From Support to Subversion," *International Political Science Review* 11.4 (1990): 486.

48. Borden and Tew, "Role of Journalist," 309–313.

49. Nichols, "Time of the Orator," 3.

WORKS CITED

Bondi, Richard. "The Elements of Character." *The Journal of Religious Ethics* 12 (1984): 201–218.

Borden, Sandra L. *Journalism as Practice: MacIntyre, Virtue Ethics and the Press.* Hampshire, England: Ashgate, 2007.

_____, and Chad Tew. "The Role of Journalist and the Performance of Journalism: Ethical Lessons from 'Fake' News (Seriously)." *Journal of Mass Media Ethics* 22 no. 4 (2007): 300–314.

Butchart, Garnet C. "On Ethics and Documentary: A Real and Actual Truth." *Communication Theory* 16 (2006): 427–452.

Choi, Su Hi. "History, Collective Memory, and TV Documentary: Analysis of *Battle for Korea* (PBS, 2001)." Paper presented to the annual meeting of the International Communication Association, New York City, May 2005.

Chowka, Peter Barry. "Prepare to be Sickened by SiCKO." *American Thinker* (June 22, 2007), http://www.americanthinker.com/2007/06/prepare_to_be_sickened_by_sick.html.

194 PART IV : ENTERTAINMENT AND AUTHORSHIP

Code, Lorraine. *Epistemic Responsibility*. Hanover, NH: Brown University Press, 1987.

Donahue, James A. "The Use of Virtue and Character in Applied Ethics." *Horizons* 17 no. 2 (1990): 228–243.

Eitzen, Dirk. "When Is a Documentary? Documentary as a Mode of Reception." *Cinema Journal* 35 no. 1 (1995): 81–102.

Ellis, Jack C., and Betsy A. McLane. *A New History of Documentary Film*. New York: Continuum, 2005.

Ettema, James S., and Theodore L. Glasser. "The Irony in — and of — Journalism: A Case Study in the Moral Language of Liberal Democracy." *Journal of Communication* 44 no. 2 (1994): 5–28.

Fleischmann, Aloys. "The Rhetorical Function of Comedy in Michael Moore's *Fahrenheit 9/11*." *Mosaic* 40 no. 4 (2007): 69–85.

Huxman, Susan Schultz. "The Tragic-Comic Rhetorica 'Dance' of Marginalized Groups: The Case of Mennonites in the Great War." *Southern Communication Journal* 62 no. 4 (1997): 305–318.

Jowett, Garth S., and Victoria O'Donnell. *Propaganda and Persuasion*, 2nd ed. Newbury Park, CA: Sage, 1992.

Kaiser Family Foundation. "Kaiser Health Tracking Poll: Election 2008," http://www.kff.org/kaiserpolls/h08_pomr030708pkg.cfm.

Klawans, Stuart. "Fever Pitch: Michael Moore's *SiCKO* Swears to Tell the Whole Truth and Nothing But the Truth. But Does It?" *Film Comment* 43 no. 4 (2007): 26–28.

Lambeth, Edmund B., and James Aucoin. "Journalism, Narrative and Community: Implications for Ethics, Practice and Media Criticism." *Professional Ethics* 2 no. 1/2 (1993): 67–88.

MacIntyre, Alasdair. *After Virtue*, 3rd ed. South Bend, IN: University of Notre Dame Press, 2007.

Misiak, Anna. "Not a Stupid White Man: The Democratic Context of Michael Moore's Documentaries." *Journal of Popular Film and Television* 33 no. 3 (2005): 160-168.

Nichols, Bill. *Blurred Boundaries: Questions of Meaning in Contemporary Culture*. Bloomington: Indiana University Press, 1994.

_____. *Representing Reality: Issues and Concepts in Documentary*. Bloomington: Indiana University Press, 1991.

_____. "The Time of the Orator." *Film Quarterly* 59 no. 2 (2005/06): 3.

_____. "The Voice of Documentary." *Film Quarterly* 36 no. 3 (1983): 17–30.

Paletz, David L. "Political Humor and Authority: From Support to Subversion. *International Political Science Review* 11 no. 4 (1990): 483–493.

Toplin, Robert Brent. *Michael Moore's Fahrenheit 9/11: How One Film Divided a Nation*. Lawrence: University Press of Kansas, 2006.

CHAPTER 13

"Just a Cartoonist": The Virtuous Journalism of Joe Sacco

Howard Good

The Platonic ideal of the cartoon may seem to omit much of the ambiguity and complex characterization which are the hallmarks of modern literature, leaving them only suitable for children. But simple elements can combine in complex ways, as atoms become molecules and molecules become life. And like the atom, great power is locked in these few simple lines, releasable only by the reader's mind.[1]
— Scott McCloud, *Understanding Comics*

Although largely forgotten today, Michael J. Kirkhorn's "The Virtuous Journalist: An Exploratory Essay" made quite an impression when published in the February 1982 issue of *The Quill*, official magazine of the Society of Professional Journalists (SPJ). Unfortunately, it wasn't a unanimously favorable one. The essay caused considerable head-scratching, especially among the older set, who vented their bewilderment in sarcastic letters to the editor. "I was amazed to see fifteen pages of the February issue devoted to publication of what amounts to a doctoral thesis," Robert A. Willier wrote from Green Valley, Arizona. "If the piece is so inspirational to some readers, may I request that they, or you, summarize it in three or four paragraphs in the next issue as a courtesy to all your fifty-year-old-and-over members." Carlos T. Parsons of Jacksonville, Florida, also admitted that he "foundered" against the essay, adding that he recently attended a local SPJ gathering where he met only one person who had read it — or, rather, "tried to read it." From Sylvania, Ohio, Kathy Lewton complained that the essay "literally gave me a headache."[2]

But not everyone found the essay such a huge turnoff. At least a few readers found it genuinely insightful. Just out of journalism school, Sherri

Gilman-Tompkins of Chicago called it "one of the most important pieces of information on the subject of journalism to be published in a long time." Rich Finlinson of Intermountain Network, Inc., in Salt Lake City responded to it as if it were a blessing or a prayer. "Amen, Amen, and Amen to Michael J. Kirkhorn's essay...," he said.[3]

So which is it? Was the essay merely a pretentious piece of academic claptrap or a work of quirky brilliance? Kirkhorn was perhaps capable of writing either. Previously a feature writer for the *Milwaukee Journal* and *Chicago Tribune*, he had taught at several universities, including the University of Kentucky and New York University, and been the recipient of a Nieman Fellowship in journalism from Harvard University in 1971. He had earned his Ph.D. in 1978 from Union Institute & University in Cincinnati.

This chapter exists for two reasons, and one of them is to rescue Kirkhorn's concept of journalistic virtue from undeserved neglect. Kirkhorn worked for many years on a long manuscript about the journalist as moral arbiter. He hoped it might turn out to be an acceptable book, but died in 2001 at the age of 64 with that hope unrealized.[4] "The Virtuous Journalist" is thus likely to remain the most complete and coherent expression of his ideas available.

The other reason for this chapter is to demonstrate that virtuous journalism can show up almost anywhere, including the comic books of Joe Sacco. Not that virtuous journalism is more than just a fraction of the enormous output of American journalism. "Much if not most journalism is frivolous," Kirkhorn says in his essay, "and it can be seen in all its frivolousness, as a sort of *fussing*—fussing about the weather, about some pitcher's losing streak, about the presence or absence of Presidential statements on foreign policy ... or as impersonation, a subdued kind of clowning, a sterile theater in which the solemn faces (or silly faces) of the broadcast reporters and anchors conceal everything but the chosen facts...." Virtuous journalism, in contrast, requires "the *possession* of the subject, arrived at through research, conversation, observation, hanging around, sympathetic understanding." It requires "a sense of mission."[5]

In Kirkhorn's view, journalism, as typically practiced, stifles this sense. He argues that few newsrooms are "organized to release the best energies of reporters and editors." "American journalism provides great opportunities for the technically proficient," he writes, "and for those who willingly accept the limitations on inquiry and understanding implied by the code of brevity, clarity, and directness of expression which most journalists are expected to follow." But, he adds, such "journalistic reflexes" impose on public discourse restrictions as severe as any resulting from censorship. What is needed are journalists who exercise imagination — not philosopher Blaise Pascal's "delusive faculty," the deceiving vision, but poet Wallace Steven's "clue to reality."

Journalistic imagination, which Kirkhorn defines as "the grasp of things in their wholeness, the constant search for connections," produces "the kind of comprehension of society, the larger disclosures," essential to democracy.[6]

Kirkhorn identifies George Orwell, Heywood Broun, Edward R. Murrow, Margaret Bourke-White, W. Eugene Smith, Frederick Wiseman, Don Marquis, Jacob Riis, Ida Tarbell, Lillian Ross, Ernie Pyle, Hannah Arendt, and Hunter S. Thompson, among others, as virtuous journalists. They are a diverse group assembled from different countries, decades, and genres. But, for all their differences, they do have at least one important thing in common. "These are journalists who contribute to our education and fortify our convictions...," Kirkhorn points out. "They reveal to us something which seems truthful, and quite often the act of revealing requires that ... they must sweep aside a clutter of inferior and obscuring journalism, and resist the journalistic stereotyping which compounds falsification."[7]

It's discouraging that news organizations generally pursue the most convenient and profitable course and leave it to exceptional figures like those mentioned above to salvage journalistic virtue. Then again, it's encouraging that such figures exist despite widespread indifference to questions of integrity. For example, Sacco, who calls himself "just a cartoonist ... doing journalism in comics form," has demonstrated in book-length comics on the Palestinian-Israeli conflict and the Bosnian war most of the virtues that Kirkhorn ascribes to the virtuous journalist.[8]

Sounds far-fetched, doesn't it? After all, it wasn't so long ago that comic books were near the very bottom of the cultural ladder. "Newspaper comic strips were always recognized as something read by everyone," comic-book historian Stephen Weiner notes, but from the beginning, "comic books were perceived as a format for children."[9] And, he might have added, immigrants, laborers, and uneducated dimwits, of which there were apparently many. Comic books sold in such numbers following World War II — 60 million a month in 1947 — that the custodians of traditional culture took fright. Among them was Dr. Frederic Wertham, senior psychiatrist of New York City's Department of Hospitals, who, in 1954, published *Seduction of the Innocent*. At a time when juvenile delinquency was spiking, Wertham warned that comic books, "the marijuana of the nursery," would lead children into a life of degradation and crime. He urged parents to shield their kids from Superman (a symbol of "violent race superiority"), Batman and Robin ("a wish dream of two homosexuals living together"), and comic art itself (a "corruption of the art of drawing"). His criticisms instigated congressional committee hearings and a comic-book burning rally in Chicago, as well as a petition to President Eisenhower to impose a ban.[10] The comic-book industry fended off official regulation only by adopting a production code that publicly confirmed its commitment to wholesome Americanism.

Decades would pass before the grip of the code on comic-book artists would be broken. The underground comics of the sixties, with their raunchy portrayal of sex and drugs, began the process, but commentators agree that the real turning point came in 1986, with the publication of Art Spiegelman's *Maus: A Survivor's Tale*. Spiegelman used comic-book conventions in recalling the ordeal of his father in the Holocaust, rendering Jews as mice and Nazis as cats. The critical and commercial success of *Maus* — a second volume won a special Pulitzer Prize in 1992 — served to "ratify comic art as a literary form" and "repositioned [comics] within our culture."[11] Throughout the rest of the nineties, there was increasing recognition that comics had "outgrown their superhero underpants."[12] Sober journals of politics and culture reviewed them, libraries put them on the shelves, and universities offered courses on them. Some weren't even called comics anymore, but "graphic novels."[13]

It's a term Sacco personally rejects. "What I do I don't see as a novel," he has said.[14] He prefers the older term "comics" and has been explicit in interviews about the advantages of the comics form in doing journalism. "The main benefit is that you can make your subject very accessible," he told Duncan Campbell of the *Guardian*. "You open the book and suddenly you're in the place. Maybe there's also a guilty pleasure as people think back to their childhood days reading comics and they think, 'This might be fun, it might be an easy way to learn something about this.'"[15] Surprisingly, Sacco seems unaware of, or at least untroubled by, the possibility that comics might trivialize the suffering in Palestine or Bosnia, turn it into voyeurism and entertainment, but, then, seriousness of tone isn't necessarily commensurate with seriousness of purpose. As Kirkhorn says of virtuous journalists, "Their characteristic gravity of tone need not imply gravity is required, or even words," and cites the case of newspaper humorist Don Marquis, who created the profoundly human tales of Archy the cockroach and Mehitabel the alley cat.[16]

By now it should be apparent that Kirkhorn's concept of journalistic virtue requires journalists to assume responsibilities not normally associated with journalism. He describes virtuous journalism using many of the same terms used in the SPJ Code of Ethics—fairness, independence, vigilance, courage, truth, integrity — but gives them a startlingly different meaning. As he puts it, "There are codes of ethics, there is professional responsibility, there is integrity, and they are not always identical or even ... compatible."[17]

The codes say, for example, that journalists aren't supposed to be involved in the stories they cover; in the name of fairness or independence or objectivity (or all three!), a journalist should get no closer to a story than is necessary to scrap away a few pertinent facts.[18] But Kirkhorn condemns this kind of detachment as premature distancing and a "violation of the journalist's responsibility." "Journalists must move close, and closer," he urges. "The only detachment which has the least value is the detachment which comes through the effort, moral, intellectual, physical, of extricating oneself from a story closely observed and deeply understood." To underline his point, he recalls that Robert Capa advised young war photographers that if their pictures weren't good, it was probably because they were too far from the action.[19]

One of the key themes of Kirkhorn's essay is that journalists like Capa, who stand out not only for their technical skill, but also for their feelings and moral outlook, ought to be at the center of journalistic activity rather than at its margins. But even in the early 1980s, a decade or more before newspapers became roadkill on the Information Highway, the likelihood that a massive shift to virtuous journalism would occur was, at best, remote. Kirkhorn himself recognizes that the wealthy and powerful corporations that own the news media can't — or won't — readily assimilate innovative approaches. "Caution and calculation," he writes, "are atmospheric factors in most if not all large journalistic organizations, and corporate expectations touch lightly but significantly the decisions of editors, news directors, and reporters. The editor of any newspaper owned by a chain or group will say with absolute assurance that overt corporate restraint rarely if ever reaches the newsroom — but, then, that editor's intuitive understanding of what is permissible is so keen that overt restraint will never be required."[20]

In recent years, virtuous journalism has only grown more, not less, marginalized. To maintain profitability, newspapers, particularly the big, urban dailies that were once the pride and glory of American journalism, have resorted to layoffs and buyouts. Since 2000 the newspaper industry has lost 3,500 to 3,800 newsroom jobs, or roughly 7 percent of the total. The long-running battle at the top of media corporations between idealists and accountants is finally over, and the accountants have won. "If you argue about public trust today," one editor told the Project for Excellence in Journalism, "you will be dismissed as an obstructionist and a romantic."[21]

With print and broadcast journalism struggling to adapt to the booming popularity of the Internet, and with the idea of social responsibility coming to seem passé, the boundaries separating news from entertainment, advertising, and propaganda are fast disappearing. Gannett Co., Inc., has already banished the term "newsroom" from its corporate vocabulary. At the 90 Gannett-owned papers around country, newsrooms are now called "Information Centers."[22]

Virtuous journalism requires, in Kirkhorn's words, "determined attempts to cross boundaries"— between journalist and society, journalist and subject, journalist and journalist, journalist and ideas, journalist and feelings— a kind of convergence.[23] But "convergence" in today's newsrooms merely refers to journalists working across different media. A reporter acquaintance complained recently about his increased workload now that he is considered a digital as well as a print journalist. "You know those beer helmets?" he asked.

He was referring to the hard hats that have a cup holder on both sides and a plastic drinking tube snaking down from the top, allowing their soused wearers to keep their hands free to commit various kinds of mayhem. "We'll probably be issued some soon," he said, "with a video camera on one side and a computer on the other — make us more efficient." Then he laughed as if he actually wanted to cry.

Who could blame him? Mark Dueze of Indiana University warns that convergence isn't "an attempt to innovate and further invest in the quality of the news product," but part of "a strategy to cut costs, facilitate flexible productivity across media channels, achieve economies of scale, offer multimedia packages and thus more inclusive audience reach to advertisers, and use digital technologies to streamline the creative process of news work."[24] That is, it isn't about journalistic virtue; it's about money.

And so virtuous journalism remains what it's always been, the extraordinary accomplishment of unorthodox individuals who feel "restricted neither by tradition nor by habit, nor by fashion, technology, or pompous professionalism."[25] Individuals like Sacco. "I don't really believe the idea of objective journalism...," he has said. "I find a lot of the journalism that's written as if you're a fly on the wall is really sort of phony.... It has this pretense of being very fair-minded and removed, and that's not true at all. I mean, an American reporter has all the framework of an American person inside him or her. And it shows in the work whether they think they're being objective or not. I'd rather just get rid of that completely and say: It's me, these are my prejudices, these are my doubts, and I'm writing about this, and you're seeing it through my eyes."[26]

Sacco's words echo the credo of the great photojournalist W. Eugene Smith, which Kirkhorn quotes not once, but twice, in his essay: "My only editor would be my conscience and my conscience would be of my responsibilities — in constant disciplined rejudgement [sic] of my failures and my fulfillments...."[27] For Sacco, who often depicts "history's losers," whether the Palestinians in the Occupied Territories or the Bosnian Muslims in the former Yugoslavia, these responsibilities include trying to raise the American public's awareness of global politics.[28] "I think the American population should be sent to The Hague to be judged," he told an interviewer. "This is a country that has an enormous impact around the world. What is decided in Washington, D.C., when George Bush lifts his little finger — someone around the world is going to feel it. To me it seems almost criminal that the people who live here, who elect someone like that — if they really knew how other people's lives are affected by American policies, maybe they would pay more attention."[29] In his desire to truly inform the public, rather than just entertain or pacify them, Sacco meets Kirkhorn's description of the virtuous journalist. "The reporting and interpreting offered by such journalists," Kirkhorn writes, "is unsparing — neither we nor they are spared; their understanding is hard-won — won *from* the facts and not confined to them, and clarified by rigorous and sometimes painful and discouraging reflection."[30]

Born in Malta in 1960, Sacco spent his childhood in Australia and his teenage years in the United States. He grew up listening in horrified fascination to his parents' accounts of the air raids they endured on Malta during World War II. Later he realized that their stories prepared him to be intensely curious about war zones.[31] And yet he doesn't think of himself as a war reporter. "To me a war reporter is really anxious to get onto the war, and I'm not quite that way," he has said. "I'm more interested in the effects. There doesn't have to be shooting around for me to get my story."[32]

Sacco's literary influences include New Journalists Michael Herr and Hunter S. Thompson and British author George Orwell, whom he has proclaimed his "ultimate hero."[33] Although best known for the political novels *Animal Farm* and *Nineteen Eighty-Four,* Orwell also courageously examined the orthodoxies and despotisms of his day in journalistic essays like "A Hanging," "Shooting an Elephant," and "Marrakech." One of his biographers observed that Orwell "would appear never to have diluted his opinions in the hope of seeing his byline disseminated to the paying customers...."[34] What Sacco seems to admire about Orwell's journalism is what is perhaps most admirable about his own — absence of cant, independence of mind, and sympathetic attention to the humanizing details of suffering.

Critic Rocco Versaci nonetheless finds Sacco's prose more reminiscent of Herr's hip, imagistic riffs on the Vietnam War in *Dispatches* and quotes a passage from "Christmas with Karadzic" (1997) to prove it: "Admittedly, the picture of Bosnia's rebel Serbs didn't look too good in those days ... it looked like fucking hell, if you want to know the truth, like that thing locked away in Dorian Gray's attic, degenerating through successive layers of ugliness with each new outrage ... but, anyway, we hadn't come to help Dragan pull off an 11th-hour makeover." Versaci adds that comics journalism in general, and Sacco's comics in particular, have reinvigorated the salient features of the New Journalism of the late 1960s and early 1970s, such as "the foregrounding of the individual perspective" of the author and "a pointed anti-'official' and anticorporate attitude." It's his contention that unlike New Journalism, which has since been redubbed "creative" or "literary" nonfiction and absorbed into the commercial mainstream, comics journalism retains a powerful outsider status, and with it, a willingness to challenge authority.[35]

As celebrated as Sacco has become among the comic-book cognoscenti, he had years of false starts and dead ends. He wanted to be a foreign correspondent, but after graduating from the University of Oregon in 1981 with a bachelor's degree in journalism, did something far less elevating. He took a series of "half-assed reporting jobs" at small newsletters and trade magazines, including the journal of the National Notary Association.[36] The work, he has said, was "exceedingly, exceedingly boring," though it would provide him with material for his early autobiographical comics *Tales of the Office* and *White Collar Incursion.*[37]

Sacco never formally studied art. In fact, he never took any art classes after junior high school. But he has been cartooning ever since he was a kid. He produced his first comic book when he was six or seven years old, drawing crude characters based on popular comic-book heroes of the day. It wasn't until he hit his twenties, though, that he accepted that "cartooning was in [his] blood" and considered giving up a "regular" job to try to make it as a comic-book artist.[38]

In the winter of 1991-92, Sacco traveled to Israel, Gaza, and the West Bank because he was curious about the conditions in the Occupied Territories and the treatment of Palestinian refugees and felt that he wasn't getting the full story from the U.S. news media. During his visit, he talked with hundreds of Palestinians, as well as with Israeli soldiers and American tourists. He hung out, wandered, recorded conversations, wrote down what he saw — followed the kind of gentle, unsystematic, open-ended approach to reporting that Kirkhorn cites in his essay as one of the essential differences between virtuous journalism and mainstream journalism, with its official press conferences and hit-and-run interviews, all conducted under deadline pressure.[39] "I think a journalist always connects better with the people around her or him than with a general or a politician," Sacco has explained. "Those people are built to spin.... I'd much rather hang out in a café. That's where things are really happening."[40]

Sacco wasn't sure that anyone would even print a comic about the Mideast conflict, especially one that sympathized with the Palestinian perspective. "I thought it was almost commercial suicide," he recalled in an interview.[41] But, in 1993, the first of nine comics, all titled *Palestine*, appeared. They were later collected in book form, with an introduction by the noted Palestinian-born literary critic Edward W. Said. "With the exception of one or two novelists and poets," Said wrote, "no one has ever rendered this terrible state of affairs better than Joe Sacco ... as he moves and tarries ... attentive, unaggressive, caring, ironic."[42] Others must have agreed. In 1996 *Palestine* received a special American Book Award.

About the time he was halfway through the *Palestine* series, Sacco found himself drawn to the complexities and horrors of the war in the former Yugoslavia, where an estimated 100,000 to 300,000 people would be killed between 1992 and 1995. "I started getting books about it and trying to figure out what was going on," he has said. "Then ... it became clear to me that there was this ethnic cleansing, and what that meant, what the implications of that were.... The sorts of things that were going on there just seemed like very big and important issues."[43] In 1995 Sacco headed to Bosnia to learn firsthand about the situation. He lived on and off for several months with a Muslim family in a UN–designated "safe area" known as Gorazde. But calling the area "safe" was quite an exaggeration. Two other UN–designated safe areas, Srebrencia and Zepa, had recently been overrun by the Serbs. Gorazde was surrounded by Serb forces and virtually cut off from the rest of the world.[44]

Sacco turned his experiences in the besieged enclave into *Safe Area Gorazde: The War in Eastern Bosnia*, published in 2000. David Rieff, who covered the war and wrote his own book about it, *Slaughterhouse: Bosnia and the Failure of the West*, describes *Safe Area Gorazde* as "the best dramatic evocation of the Bosnian catastrophe."[45] On page after page, Sacco presents, often in the form of flashbacks, women being gang-raped, villages being massacred, the dead being mutilated, the whole nightmarish catalog of man's inhumanity to man. The harrowing images recall Francisco Goya's *Los desastres de la guerra* (*The Disasters of War*), more than 60 etchings depicting the murderous French occupation of Spain from 1808 to 1814 and "the true ancestors of all great visual war reporting." "What the common people of Europe discovered in the 20th century, that atrocious epoch of failed dreams and triumphant death, a time of ideology-driven suffering beyond the previous imagination of mankind, Goya foreshadowed in the *Disasters*...," art historian Robert Hughes says.[46] Like Goya, Sacco didn't see everything he portrays, but only heard about some of it from others. Also like Goya, he shows in stomach-churning detail why there is nothing the least noble about war.

Despite frequently praising the artistic latitude the comics form affords— "I can make the crane that allows me to hover above a city ... and I can take the reader into someone's past"[47]— Sacco doesn't consider himself "a particularly good artist."[48] It can take up to three days for him to complete a page, and this only after he has gone through dozens of notebooks filled with observations, interviews, and anecdotes.[49] He works exclusively in black and white, which tends to disguise the visual subtlety of his drawings. "In black and white," Scott McCloud, the foremost theorist of comics, explains, "the ideas behind the art are communicated more directly. Meaning transcends form; art approaches language."[50]

Throughout both *Palestine* and *Safe Area Gorazde*, Sacco offers heartbreaking panoramas, now of the bombed-out Bosnian capital of Sarajevo, now of a Palestinian refugee camp in the Occupied Territories, cold wastelands of mud and rubble, where the sky is always stormy, and the human figure is isolated or entirely absent, and the trees, if there even are any, are charred skeletons. But, more typically, he works on a personal rather than on an epic scale. "All I want to do is be a medium of other people's stories," he has said. "Just present them in a way the audience can digest."[51] This is the same motive Kirkhorn attributes to virtuous journalism —"a feeling of obligation not only to readers but to the unheard sources whose daily lives are filtered" out by standard reporting practices.[52]

Sacco tells other people's stories according to a visual pattern he established in *Palestine* and has continued through *Safe Area Gorazde* into his later books, *The Fixer* (2000) and *War's End* (2005). We see a source — a Palestinian detainee, for example, or a Bosnian survivor of "ethnic cleansing" — in extreme closeup, a device Sacco adapted from the Spaghetti Westerns he enjoyed as a kid.[53] Although the source is ostensibly addressing Sacco, the closeup creates the impression that he or she is giving eyewitness testimony directly to us, the readers. As the source relates his or her experience in his or her own words, the accompanying images don't show Sacco listening, but flash back to the time and place the source is describing. Thus, in *Palestine*, when Ghassan, sitting around his house with Sacco, recounts his arrest by the Israeli Defense Forces, the images depict him with a hood over his head and chained to a pipe in an isolation cell. To better convey the hopelessness of Ghassan's situation, the panels in the sequence shrink a little further with each day of his imprisonment.[54]

Photojournalist W. Eugene Smith, asked once about his most consistent personal philosophical concern, answered, "Humanity. I try to take what voice I have and give it to people who don't have one at all."[55] Many of the stories to which Sacco gives voice make you feel ashamed to even belong to the human race. In *Safe Area Gorazde*, these include grisly firsthand accounts of atrocities committed by Serb soldiers and paramilitaries against the Bosnian Muslims.[56] Gorazde had been cut off from cameras that might have captured the suffering of the town — random shelling, dead children, shrieking parents. Instead the suffering was solely the property of those who endured it. That is, until Sacco arrived and put pen to sketchbook. Now there is a record, and though it doesn't compensate the victims for everything they lost, it does at least prevent the addition of forgetfulness to the list of war crimes.

Kirkhorn remarks that the virtuous journalist needs "a superior understanding not just for factual reconstruction, but for the actual, discernible history of events."[57] Sacco displays this kind of understanding as he untangles for readers the dense, complicated roots of the conflicts in Palestine and the former Yugoslavia. He inserts maps, highlights key historical moments — the signing of the Balfour Declaration, the death of Tito[58] — and does whatever else he can through a clever mixture of words and images to provide the context that is generally lacking in daily news coverage. "For me," he has said, "one advantage of comic journalism is that I can depict the past, which is hard to do if you're a photographer or filmmaker. History can make you realize that the present is just one layer of a story. What seems to be the immediate vital story now will one day be another layer in this geology of bummers."[59]

Even so, there are tensions in Sacco's work that undercut, or, at the very least, problematize, its truthfulness. Consider how he visually represents himself. He is "a hilarious, self-mocking character" in his comics, "a balding, slouching little man with his hands in his pockets, bumbling and innocently lecherous, full of self-doubt and feelings of guilty privilege."[60] Yet interviewers who have met Sacco in person get quite a different impression. He "doesn't seem like he could come from even the same side of the family as the guy in his books," one says, and another notes, "The real Joe Sacco is slim and wiry and very fit. His eyes communicate ... intelligence and intensity."[61] What is going on here?

Well, what is going on is what always goes on in comics. "Its chief tools are distortion and symbolic abstraction...," Douglas Wolk writes in *Reading Comics: How Graphic Novels Work and What They Mean.* "Cartoonists can draw characters who look only vaguely like actual people do, and backgrounds with only the faintest hint of real-world complexity, and get away with it — often, that's the idea."[62] Sacco's drawing may rely on careful observations of weather and houses and rubble-strewn streets, but being a cartoonist as much as a journalist, he just can't resist mixing in elements of caricature.

Nor perhaps should he. It's practically axiomatic in autobiographical comics that "the outward guise reflects inward attitudes."[63] The cartoon self-image offers a way for the cartoonist to externalize his or her subjectivity. In Sacco's case, his dorky appearance is linked to his ambivalence about his role as a journalist at scenes of desolation and suffering. A sequence in *War's End* depicts Kasey, a stringer for NBC Radio, driving through the shattered Bosnian landscape on a frantic search for a saleable story. "Come on!" he rages in the car. "Shoot! Fuckers! Will someone open up with a machine gun out the window!! This is bullshit!"[64] Along for the ride, Sacco is morally implicated in the bloodthirsty parasitism of the U.S. news media. See him there in his puffy vest? He looks like a camera-toting tourist on a holiday in hell, and, worse, he knows it. His round shoulders, middle-age paunch, sausage lips, and Coke-bottle glasses are all symbols, the objectification of his anguished conscience.

Ironically, the more Sacco exposes his own personal and professional defects, the more the reader is intended to trust him. "In comics journalism, more so perhaps than in any other medium," critic Kristian Williams says, "the reporter's role is consistently emphasized. He is often present, not merely as a voice or a talking head," a neutral conduit for news and information, but as "a person like ourselves — a fallible human being, vulnerable to bias and ignorance and error. By acknowledging his own humanity," Williams adds, "the writer can encourage the reader to think critically about what he or she reads."[65] Or, as Sacco sums up, "I think it's more honest to show that your involvement affects people."[66]

From the very beginning of *Palestine,* Sacco pours out his sympathy for the Palestinians living under Israeli rule and his frustration that the U.S. news media don't adequately cover their plight. He has no desire to be fair or objective in his book. If the news media haven't been, why should he? But there is a difference between his bias and theirs. It's the difference between what literary scholar Merle Browne called the *fictive* and the *fictitious*. A story may be "fictive yet truthful" insofar as it "implies as part of itself the art of its making." In contrast, a story, journalistic or otherwise, that doesn't acknowledge its own making is merely fictitious.[67] Sacco acknowledges everything that goes into the making of his story; he strives for transparency. Conventional journalism, despite its plain-speaking, hard-nosed, facts-are-facts tone, doesn't.

Sacco even includes a scene in which two young Israeli women question his reporting methods. After he explains to them that he has been talking almost exclusively with Palestinians, one of the women asks, "Shouldn't you be seeing *our* side of the story, too?" His reply—"I've heard nothing but the Israeli side most of my life"—not only reveals his particular prejudices, but because of its disarming honesty, also tends to increase our trust in his moral viewpoint. So does the fact that no matter how often he criticizes the brutality of the Israeli occupation, and he criticizes it relentlessly, he doesn't excuse fanaticism or hatred on the part of the Palestinians either. He gives those who preach the destruction of Israel and the murder of Jews the faces of monsters.[68]

Comics, with their ability to alternate between the realistic and the symbolic, their hybrid, visual-verbal nature, are hardly "true" in any straightforward sense. The "truth" in comics like Sacco's is "not so much a matter of verifiability, but of trustworthiness, not so much a constant quality as the result of a continual renegotiation between the cartoonist, his materials, and his audience."[69] Traditional journalists do their best to downplay or ignore all the many ways in which their perspective might be limited. They want the audience to take for granted the truth of what they report. Not Sacco. "I have my prejudices, and I have my preconceived notions," he has said. "Like anyone does, like any reporter does, but I'm just sort of 'fessing up to it."[70] The paradox is that by flaunting his subjectivity, Sacco doesn't forfeit the trust of readers—he virtuously earns it.

Epilogue

> If alternative cartoonists acknowledge any sort of heroism, it consists
> in a collective effort to assert the versatility of comics as a means of
> expression.... Part of this project is the promotion of comics that refuse
> fiction altogether, favoring history, reportage, the essay, and the memoir.
> Thus "nonfiction" comics have come into their own.[71]
>   —Charles Hatfield, Alternative Comics

"As an occupation, journalism is an enormous vibrating hodge-podge," Kirkhorn says in his essay, referring to the fact that journalists come in all sorts of flavors, from bland political reporter and tart fashion columnist to delectable TV news anchor.[72] What was true of journalism back in Kirkhorn's day may be even truer now, especially with bloggers and so-called "citizen journalists" having recently joined the fun.

If you think that amid this much variety, there ought to be room for at least a few comics journalists, you would be right. "More editors seem to be aware of how comics can be melded with journalism and are interested in experimenting with the form," Sacco has said.[73] In *The Edmonton Journal*, David Staples and Jill Stanton used the comics form to tell the story of North America's first paraplegic long-distance trucker. The *Oregonian* publishes a regular comics column, "CulturePulp," in which M. E. Russell has depicted, among other things, his experiences running a marathon and watching a risqué lounge act. *The New Yorker* had Art Spiegelman cover the 2004 Republican national convention, while *Details* featured Sacco's coverage of the Bosnian war crimes trial.[74]

But, overall, newspapers and magazines continue to shy away from comics journalism. The inherent subjectivity of the comics form contrasts sharply — and, to the orthodox minds of most editors, disturbingly — with the golden rule of journalistic objectivity. These are the same people, remember, who convinced themselves that the Internet was largely science fiction, who woke up to its incontrovertible reality only after their audiences began defecting to it en masse. Buried in the conservative culture of the newsroom, they are no more eager or able to embrace comics journalism, even if the comics form does offer the kind of personal vision that readers seem to be seeking and have turned increasingly to blogs and e-zines to find.

In many newsrooms, journalistic virtue is understood to mean doing what is expected of you, doing what you have been told, doing what everyone else around you is doing. It's behaving like a member of the Light Brigade and refusing to reason why.[75] Things haven't changed greatly from thirty years ago when you could read want ads in *Editor & Publisher* warning, "No newsroom philosophers need apply." To newsroom managers, journalistic virtue has less to do with being a good journalist — independent, curious, attentive — than with being a good employee — cheap, quiet, amenable.

And professional codes of ethics don't clarify the situation. John Kultgen, in his monumental *Ethics and Professionalism*, describes professions as "organized interest groups" striving for "a privileged place in the socioeconomic order." He notes that professions formulate codes of ethics to gain the public recognition and trust necessary to control a particular service. But the codes are often so vaguely worded, as well as so poorly enforced, that they are ineffective in shaping professional practices. Not that this vagueness doesn't have its advantages. "The net effect of vagueness," Kultgen writes, "is to convey to the casual reader that the profession is dedicated to high ethical standards without imposing stern and arduous duties on practitioners."[76]

The SPJ Code of Ethics is typical. After a preamble full of fine-sounding phrases—"Professional integrity is the cornerstone of a journalist's credibility," etc.—the code is divided into four sections. At the head of each section is a fundamental journalistic principle, stated in the stark, indisputable form of a commandment: "Seek Truth and Report It"; "Minimize Harm"; "Act Independently"; and "Be Accountable." There is just one problem: The principles contradict each other. How, for example, do journalists manage to "Act Independently" and at the same time "Be Accountable"? Or "Seek Truth and Report Truth" and at the same time "Minimize Harm"? They can't. The SPJ code provides mainly a public relations function, not practical guidance for the ethically perplexed. It can facilitate the impression that journalists are professionals, and thus deserving of prestige and power, but it can't help them actually become deserving.

Only journalists themselves can do that. This is the major lesson of both Kirkhorn's essay and Sacco's work. Virtuous journalism isn't about doing what codes of ethics dictate or the culture of the newsroom allows. It's about demonstrating certain qualities of heart and mind, qualities Kirkhorn identifies as "inquiry, observation, and understanding" or, alternately, as "sympathy, attention, imagination."[77] Sacco proves with his two acknowledged masterpieces, *Palestine* and *Safe Area Gorazde*, that these qualities can emerge in anyone anywhere at anytime. You don't need to work for a big news organization. You don't need to have all your journalistic credentials in order. You just need to be crazy enough to love the world and all the sad and broken people in it.

Notes

1. Scott McCloud, *Understanding Comics: The Invisible Art* (Northampton, MA: Kitchen Sink, 1993), 45.

2. "Letters," *The Quill*, April 1982, 3.

3. *Ibid.*

4. "Nieman Notes," *Nieman Reports*, Fall 2002, 87.

5. Michael J. Kirkhorn, "The Virtuous Journalist: An Exploratory Essay," *The Quill*, February 1982, 11, 17, 21, 23.

6. *Ibid.*, 11, 13, 19.

7. *Ibid.*, 9.

8. Quoted in Rebecca Tuhus-Dubrow, "Joe Sacco," *January Magazine*, http://january-magazine.com/profiles/jsacco.html (accessed September 21, 2007).

9. Stephen Weiner, *Faster Than a Speeding Bullet: The Rise of the Graphic Novel* (New York: Nantier Beall Minoustchine, 2003), 3.

10. David Michaelis, *Schulz and Peanuts* (New York: HarperCollins, 2007), 291–92.

11. Charles Hatfield, *Alternative Comics: An Emerging Literature* (Jackson: University Press of Mississippi, 2005), xi; see also Weiner, *Faster Than a Speeding Bullet*, 38, and Kris-

tian Williams, "The Case for Comics Journalism," *Columbia Journalism Review*, March/April 2005 (accessed October 24, 2007).

12. Tuhus-Dubrow, "Joe Sacco."
13. Weiner, *Faster Than a Speeding Bullet*, 55–56, 58.
14. Quoted in Campbell, "I Do Comics." See also Marshall, *Joe Sacco*, 92.
15. Quoted in ibid.
16. Kirkhorn, "Virtuous Journalist," 9.
17. *Ibid.*, 15.
18. Society of Professional Journalists Code of Ethics, http://www.spj.org/ethicscode.asp (accessed 18 January 2008).
19. Kirkhorn, "Virtuous Journalist, 13.
20. *Ibid.*,11.
21. The statistics and quote are drawn from Project for Excellence in Journalism, "Executive Summary," *2006 Annual Report on the State of the News Media*, 4, 8, 16, http://www.state ofthenewsmedia.org/2006/.
22. Kathleen Norton, "Welcome to the 'Information Center,'" *Poughkeepsie* (NY) *Journal*, November 12, 2006, np.
23. Kirkhorn, "Virtuous Journalist," 13.
24. Mark Deuze, "Books," *Journalism & Mass Communication Educator* (Autumn 2006): 331.
25. Kirkhorn, "Virtuous Journalist," 9.
26. Tuhus-Dubrow, "Joe Sacco."
27. Quoted in Kirkhorn, "Virtuous Journalist," 15.
28. Edward W. Said, "Homage to Joe Sacco," *Palestine* (Seattle, WA: Fantagraphics, 2001), v.
29. Christopher Farah, "Safe Are America," Salon.com, http://dir.salon.com/story/ books/int/2003/12/05/sacco/index.html (accessed September 21, 2007).
30. Kirkhorn, "Virtuous Journalist," 9.
31. Monica Marshall, *Joe Sacco* (New York: Rosen, 2005), 8.
32. Quoted in Tuhus-Dubrow, "Joe Sacco."
33. *Ibid.*
34. Christopher Hitchens, *Why Orwell Matters* (New York: Basic, 2002), 5. See also Judith Shulevitz, "What Would Orwell Do?," *New York Times Book Review*, September 8, 2002, 31.
35. Rocco Versaci, *This Book Contains Graphic Language: Comics as Literature* (New York: Continuum, 2007), 110–11, 137.
36. Sacco quoted in Dave Gilson, "The Art of War," *Mother Jones*, July/August 2005 (accessed 21 September 2007).
37. Marshall, *Joe Sacco*, 35; Duncan Campbell, "I Do Comics, Not Graphic Novels," *Guardian*, 23 October 2003, http://www.guardian.co.uk/print/0,,4780394-103680,00.html (accessed September 9, 2007).
38. Marshall, *Joe Sacco*, 12, 15, 22; Campbell, "I Do Comics"; Howard Price, "CBR News: Joe Sacco Interview," *Comic Book Resources*, http://www.comicbooks.org/news/newsitem. cgi?id+618 (accessed September 21, 2007).
39. Kirkhorn, "Virtuous Journalist," 11, 21.
40. Gilson. "Art of War."
41. Quoted in Campbell, "I Do Comics."
42. Said, "Homage," iii.
43. Quoted in Gary Groth. "Joe Sacco, Frontline Journalist," *The Comics Journal*, http://www.tcj.com/aa02ws/i_sacco.html.
44. Marshall, *Joe Sacco*, 75.
45. Quoted in Campbell, "I Do Comics."
46. Robert Hughes, *Goya* (New York: Alfred A. Knopf, 2003), 265, 319.
47. Quoted in Kristine McKenna, "Brueghel in Bosnia," *LA Weekly*, January 1, 2004,

http://www.laweekly.com/news/fratures/brueghal-in-bosnia/2120/ (accessed 21 September 2007).

48. Quoted in Campbell, "I Do Comics."
49. Marshall, *Joe Sacco*, 70.
50. McCloud, *Understanding Comics*, 192.
51. Quoted in Tuhus-Dubrow, "Joe Sacco."
52. Kirkhorn, "Virtuous Journalist," 11.
53. Marshall, *Joe Sacco*, 21.
54. Sacco, *Palestine*, 102–11.
55. Quoted in Kirkhorn "Virtuous Journalist," 19.
56. Joe Sacco, *Safe Area Gorazde: The War in Eastern Bosnia, 1992–95* (Seattle, WA: Fantagraphics, 2000), 78–93, 109–19, 120–21.
57. Kirkhorn, "Virtuous Journalist," 17.
58. Sacco, *Palestine*, 12–13; Sacco, *Safe Area Gorazde*. 20.
59. Gilson, "Art of War."
60. Tuhus-Dubrow, "Joe Sacco."
61. *Ibid.*; Price, "Joe Sacco Interview."
62. Douglas Wolk, *Reading Comics: How Graphic Novels Work and What They Mean* (New York: Da Capo, 2007), 120.
63. Hatfield, *Alternative Comics*, 116.
64. Joe Sacco, *War's End: Profiles from Bosnia 1995–96* (Montreal: Drawn & Quarterly, 2005), 55.
65. Williams, "Case for Comics Journalism."
66. Quoted in ibid.
67. Browne's theory is neatly summarized in Hatfield, *Alternative Comics*, 124.
68. Sacco, *Palestine*, 126, 130, 165, 256.
69. Hatfield, *Alternative Comics*, 150–51.
70. Quoted in Tuhus-Dubrow, "Joe Sacco."
71. Hatfield, *Alternative Comics*, 111.
72. Kirkhorn, "Virtuous Journalist," 11.
73. Quoted in Gilson, "Art of War."
74. The examples are cited in Williams, "Case for Comics Journalism."
75. This is a paraphrase of Heywood Broun's quote in Kirkhorn, "Virtuous Journalism," 9. Broun himself was alluding to Alfred Lord Tennyson's poem "The Charge of the Light Brigade."
76. John Kultgen, *Ethics and Professionalism* (Philadelphia: University of Pennsylvania Press, 1988), 99, 106, 210–12, 226.
77. Kirkhorn, "Virtuous Journalist," 9, 19.

Works Cited

Campbell, Duncan. "I Do Comics, Not Graphic Novels," *Guardian*, October 23, 2003.
Farah, Christopher. "Safe Are America," Salon.com, http://dir.salon.com/story/books/int/2003/12/05/sacco/index.html.
Gilson, David. "The Art of War," *Mother Jones*, July/August 2005.
Groth, Gary. "Joe Sacco, Frontline Journalist," *The Comics Journal*, http://www.tcj.com/aa02ws/i_sacco.html.
Hatfield, Charles. *Alternative Comics: An Emerging Literature*. Jackson: University Press of Mississippi, 2005.
Hitchens, Christopher. *Why Orwell Matters*. New York: Basic, 2002.
Hughes, Robert. *Goya*. New York: Alfred A. Knopf, 2003.
Kirkhorn, Michael J. "The Virtuous Journalist: An Exploratory Essay," *The Quill*, February 1982, 9–23.

Kultgen, John. *Ethics and Professionalism*. Philadelphia: University of Pennsylvania Press, 1988.

Marshall, Monica. *Joe Sacco*. New York: Rosen, 2005

McCloud, Scott. *Understanding Comics: The Invisible Art*. Northampton, MA: Kitchen Sink, 1993.

McKenna, Kristine. "Brueghel in Bosnia," *LA Weekly*, January 1, 2004.

Michaelis, David. *Schulz and Peanuts*. New York: HarperCollins, 2007.

Sacco, Joe. *Palestine*. Seattle, WA: Fantagraphics, 2001.

_____. *Safe Area Gorazde: The War in Eastern Bosnia, 1992–95*. Seattle, WA: Fantagraphics, 2000.

_____. *War's End: Profiles from Bosnia, 1995–96*. Montreal: Drawn & Quarterly, 2005.

Shulevitz, Judith. "What Would Orwell Do?" *New York Times Book Review*, September 8, 2002, 31.

Tuhus-Dubrow, Rebecca. "Joe Sacco," *January Magazine*, http://januarymagazine.com/profiles/jsacco.html.

Versaci, Rocco. *This Book Contains Graphic Language: Comics as Literature*. New York: Continuum, 2007.

Weiner, Stephen. *Faster Than a Speeding Bullet: The Rise of the Graphic Novel*. New York: Nantier Beall Minoustchine, 2003.

Williams, Kristian. "The Case for Comics Journalism," *Columbia Journalism Review*, March/April 2005.

Wolk, Douglas. *Reading Comics: How Graphic Novels Work and What They Mean*. New York: Da Capo, 2007.

CHAPTER 14

Whose Tube Is It Anyway?

John Chapin

The Public Relations Society of America (PRSA) Code of Ethics provides a number of guidelines for members:

1. We serve the public interest by serving as responsible advocates for those we represent.
2. We provide a voice in the marketplace of ideas, facts, and viewpoints to aid informed public debate.
3. Protecting and advancing the free flow of accurate and truthful information is essential to serving the public interest and contributing to informed decision making in a democratic society.

The code is based on the "marketplace of ideas" concept grounded in the First Amendment and freedom of expression. Commercial speech enjoys less First Amendment protection than political speech, but is viewed as a valuable contributor to the marketplace of ideas as long as the input is not false, deceptive, or misleading. In *Ethics in Public Relations: Ethical Advocacy*, Kathy Fitzpatrick argues that four fundamental principles to the marketplace of ideas establish an ethical baseline for responsible advocacy in public relations: access, process, truth, and disclosure.[1]

Access refers to citizens' rights to receive information needed for decision-making. While politicians often refer to the public interest, there are in fact multiple publics with varying interests. This makes the process of deciding policy as important as or more important than the emerging policies themselves. The final two principles are interrelated: Failure to disclose is a lie of omission. Truth can be defined as what is verifiable, replicable, and universal. This chapter uses these four fundamental principles to examine ethical dilemmas brought forth by YouTube and related social networking sites. The introduction of new technologies often brings unforeseen social and ethical issues. YouTube provides an ideal environment for this discussion.

The Birth of YouTube

The origins of YouTube have already reached the status of Internet lore. Three ex-employees of PayPal — Chad Hurley, Steve Chen, and Jawed Karim — wanted to share some video with friends. The files were too large to e-mail, so they worked in a garage to create a video-friendly website. YouTube was launched with footage of Chen's cat. A year later, Hurley and Chen's love child was showing 30 million videos a day from their corporate headquarters over a California Pizza shop.[2] The throngs of loyal users soon caught the attention of Google, which spent $1.65 billion to acquire YouTube after its first year in business.

Typing "cat" in YouTube's search engine yields nearly a half-million hits. There's "a hungry cat resorts to increasingly desperate measures to gain its owner's attention" (over 3 million views), "an engineer's guide to cats" (over 2 million views), "cats playing piano" (over 9 million views), and even "scuba cat." With 500,000 views, this plucky California cat dons full scuba gear and plunges into the deep for one minute and 21 seconds of viewing pleasure. Combine "stupid pet tricks," would-be Jedi-Knights wielding golf clubs as light sabers, video diaries shot with web cams, and countless amateurs lip-synching or dancing to their favorite tunes, and you have the public face of YouTube. Indeed, more than 55 million views of a short video of a laughing baby lands "Hahaha" in the top 10 most-viewed videos in YouTube's brief history. These are all examples of viral video. Viral video is video clip content that gains widespread popularity through the process of Internet sharing, typically through e-mail, IM messages, blogs, and other media-sharing websites. Viral video is often humorous in nature and includes televised comedy sketches, such as *Saturday Night Live's* "Lazy Sunday"; unintentionally released amateur video clips, such as the "Numa Numa" song; and web-only productions, such as "I Got a Crush on Obama."

Despite the promise that YouTube allows users to broadcast themselves, user-created content is only part of the story. Six of the top 10 most-viewed videos were not shot with camera phones or web cams. They are professionally produced and copyright-protected music videos. Music videos are a form of advertising in their own right. The short clips advertise current singles, album releases, and the artists themselves. On the top of the list in 2008 (more than 93 million views), Avril Lavigne chirps, "Hey, hey, you, you, I wanna be your girlfriend" to legions of fans. Like most of the major studios, RCA Records provided the clip in exchange for shared advertising revenue. YouTube longs to provide every music video ever produced. It's starting to look like a possibility, but not everyone is on board. Universal Music executives claim that copyright infringement is costing the industry tens of millions of dollars as users illegally upload and freely share videos and bootleg concert footage.[3] From an audience perspective, viral video increases access to content they may have missed on television and provides access to user-created content of which they would otherwise be unaware. From a provider perspective, unauthorized access to broadcast content is a copyright violation.

1. Star Wars Kid (900 million views)
2. Numa Numa (700m)
3. One Night in Paris (400m)
4. Kylie Minogue: Agent Provocateur (360m)
5. Exploding Whale (350m)
6. John West Salmon Bear Fight (300m)
7. Trojan Games (300m)
8. Kolla2001 (200m)
9. AfroNinja (80m)
10. The Shining Redux (50m)

Music Videos, Mash-Ups and Access

To cultivate a rich marketplace of ideas, speakers must have the right to free expression and listeners must have the right to receive information needed for decision-making. Both of these rights represent flip sides of the access issue. On its face, YouTube equalizes access. By "broadcasting themselves," users are able to cast their own voices among politicians, opinion makers, advertisers, and public relations specialists. Given that the most popular videos on YouTube are commercially sponsored music videos, it appears that YouTube gives amateur singer-songwriters access equal to that of Avril Lavigne. Any aspiring teenage stars can post their videos alongside their idols' and compete equally for fame and fortune.

Tale of Two Videos

Familiar to more than 1 million people who viewed, downloaded, or purchased it, *Bubbly* launched the career of 21-year-old Colbie Calliat. Her story plays like a digital-age fairy tale: Perky blonde singer-songwriter writes a bunch of songs and puts them on MySpace, hoping for a modern-day miracle. Nothing much happened for a few months, according to Calliat's official website, "Then I wrote this song called Bubbly and put it up there and it got this huge reaction. I mean thousands and thousands of hits every day."

The lyrics were paired with a montage of scenes from the beach, a small cottage nestled in the woods, and young people in love. Calliat's look, reminiscent of the girl next door crossed with Jennifer Anniston, blended perfectly with faded jeans and an acoustic guitar.

The results were a Cinderella story shared by thousands of young hopefuls uploading their music, acting, or comedy. Racking up an impressive 10 million views, Calliat became the No. 1 unsigned artist on MySpace for four successive months. Universal Republic, taking notice of the growing fan base, signed her to a recording contract and released her debut CD, *CoCo* in 2007, featuring *Bubbly* as the lead single. By the year's end, *CoCo* sold more than 1 million copies and a bona fide star was born. Despite ties to the record industry (her father, Ken Calliat, co-produced Fleetwood Mac's *Rumours* and *Tusk* albums), Calliat credits MySpace with her rise to fame. "The great thing about MySpace," she says, "is that you can build up an army of fans and then when you go to a record company; there's no point in them trying to change what you do because it's already been tried and tested."

Meanwhile, back on YouTube, another acoustic songbird was taking flight. Familiar to millions of Rihanna fans, an acoustic version of the R&B hit "Umbrella" made a household name of Marie Digby (pronounced Mar-ee-yah) among YouTube fans, who played the video more than 2 million times. It seems the Internet had produced another Cinderella story for yet another California native. According to a 2007 press release by the Walt Disney Company, Hollywood Records discovered Digby online. As in the case of Calliat, the established fan base on YouTube and MySpace was cause enough to sign the new artist. "I NEVER in a million years thought that doing my little video of Umbrella in my living room would lead to this," Digby shared with fans on MySpace, "TV shows, I-tunes, etc!!!" Unfortunately, a 2007 *Wall Street Journal* story revealed all was not as it seemed.[4] Digby, it turns out, was already signed to Hollywood Records two years before appearing on YouTube. After the article, the "label" portion of Digby's MySpace page changed from "none" to "major."

By allowing users to upload their videos alongside the videos of established performers, YouTube equalizes access. The ethical dilemma is on the part of the users and the record labels that represent them. In both these cases, the performers were not what they seemed, violating the principles of truth and disclosure. Calliat was part of an established musical dynasty prior to her exposure via social networking sites. Digby failed to disclose that she was already signed to a major record label. Posting on MySpace that she had no record label was clearly deceptive. The deception was corrected following the news reports. Although the record company denied planning the deception, its press release declaring Digby to be the first recording artist discovered online was also untrue and a clear violation of the PRSA ethical code.

Digby's case poses another ethical issue. Like many amateurs, Digby posted acoustic versions of other artists' songs. This is a clear copyright violation. Calculating the copyright infringement happening daily on YouTube is virtually impossible, as it might include every homemade lip-synching video, dance routine video, and mash-up posted by users. YouTube does its part by swiftly removing (within 24 hours) any copyrighted material flagged by a user or requested by a copyright holder. Its response conforms to the legal guidelines established in 2006 by the Digital Millennium Copyright Act (DMCA). Monitoring these sites for protected materials is a daunting task. Each day, individual users upload videos. The users provide tags that will be used by the search engines. A web cam or camera phone rendition of a teen in her bedroom lip-synching to a Madonna song is more likely to be tagged "Me being goofy" than "Warning Sire Records: Copyright infringement!" Copyright holders are left to scour the site for infringements and issue takedown requests. From a user perspective, uploading copyrighted materials increases access to the materials and also increases potential access for amateurs to record producers. From the copyright holders' perspective, it's a simple matter of theft. YouTube's policy of removing the infringements adheres to legal guidelines, but fails to educate users about the legal and ethical implications of the behavior.

Perhaps the most difficult kind of amateur content to navigate ethically is the mash-up. Mash-ups consist of copyrighted materials edited (or remixed in the case of music) by users. Mash-ups can be tributes, parodies, or scathing condemnations. Anyone who watches television is familiar with the popular Mac commercials featuring two men representing computer platforms ("I'm Mac.... I'm a PC"). Dozens of parodies litter YouTube. Some use footage from the commercials; some use live actors; others are animated. Most are irreverent; many contain harsh criticisms of MAC computers. Once the mash-ups are identified, copyright holders may be within their rights to insist that YouTube remove any videos containing copyrighted materials. However, doing so risks offending potential consumers, and in all likelihood the videos have already been forwarded via e-mail and uploaded to other websites. Mash-ups are frequently viewed as threats by advertisers because they lose control over trademarks and copyrighted materials and may yield public postings of negative feedback about their product by unhappy consumers. But in 2007, 20th Century–Fox found a way to use the mash-up as a stealthy means of product placement. Like many unknown bands, New York–based rock band Guyz Nite counted on such sites as YouTube and MySpace to get exposure. For their song, *Die Hard*, a tribute to the popular movie trilogy featuring Bruce Willis, the band opted for a mash-up of scenes from the films. Without copyright clearance (and payment), MTV would not air the clip. It was, however, viewed more than 100,000 times on YouTube before Fox asked for its removal. Then Fox had second thoughts. With a fourth installment of the franchise, *Live Free or Die Hard*, about to be released, it relinquished control of its copyright and paid the band to release a new version of the video, complete with a new verse to promote the theatrical release. The new version also yielded nearly 100,000 views before opening weekend. "We aggressively protect our intellectual property, but look for, welcome and support creative voices on the Internet, and in this case we really liked what they had done and we supported it," a spokesperson for Fox said.[5]

Political Videos and Process

A true marketplace of ideas necessitates an open forum for public discourse and debate. Again, YouTube seems to be ideally suited to allow a broader range of people unfettered access to a multitude of positions. On its surface, YouTube resembles *Candid Camera* or *America's Funniest Home Videos* or a repository for music videos and movie trailers. Moving from the "most-viewed" list to the "most-discussed" list shifts the reality. Avril Lavigne and "Chocolate Rain" still make the list, but the clear majority of the clips (60 percent) are political. The current champ, "Macedonia is Greece" (more than 2 million views and more than 400,000 comments), provides a thoughtful review of the geopolitical lines of Greece. The comments, in multiple languages, show that not just the United States is utilizing YouTube and that people are using the site for more than just mindless entertainment. The most heated clash of cultures emerges among the more than 200,000 comments in response to "Tibet WAS, IS, and ALWAYS WILL BE a part of China." The clip, produced in English in response to a video posted in Chinese, is both educational (Did you know that China is more diverse than Canada, made up of 65 distinct ethnic groups, including Han, Mongols, Koreans, Muslims and Tibetans?) and politically charged.

Nationalism and geographic boundaries account for the largest single chunk of the "most-discussed" list. Titles like "I am a Muslim," "Atheist," and the second top-rated "10 Questions that Every Christian Must Answer" (more than 2 million views and nearly 300,000 comments) show that religious tension is alive and well on the Internet. "10 Questions," posted by Whywontgodhealamputees.com, takes a logical approach to debunking belief in God. User comments are a virtual potpourri of enthusiastic support and counterarguments. In 2007, GodTube.com offered the faithful a safe haven to post and share Gospel-inspired viral video. Unlike YouTube, all content is scanned and approved by Christian editors before posting. Sex jokes, anti–Semitism, racism, blasphemy, and general rudeness don't make the cut, but parody persists. One popular clip parodies the popular Geico insurance ads: "Creation: So easy a caveman can get it."[6]

If literally millions of people are willing to watch and participate in the discussion of Greece's claim on Macedonia, sites like YouTube are obvious fertile grounds for political debates. Computer specialist and political enthusiast Bob Adams made his political voice heard in 2006 by producing and posting around 50 anti–Joe Lieberman clips to YouTube. "This is another option for people who want to see what's really going on," Adams told *The Guardian*. "And it's a very democratic thing: anyone with a video camera and a computer can get the same shots CNN can get. If you want people to hear your voice, you put up a video, and you're out there."[7] Adams added that civic-minded citizens have an advantage over journalists, because they cannot be pressured by political figures for continued access to campaigns. Lieberman lost the nomination of his party and was forced to defend his seat as an independent. In this case, the ethical principles of access and process are enhanced for the average citizen. Users are able to participate in the political process in a similar fashion as journalists.

Barack Obama found a niche in the 2008 presidential campaign by refusing corporate contributions and doing most of his fund-raising online (nearly $200 million during the primaries alone).[8] A look at www.barackobama.com illustrates the candidate's savvy use of social networks. One of the most popular YouTube elements to the campaign was produced not by the Obama campaign, but by BarelyPolitical.com. "I Got a Crush on Obama" was created as part of a public relations campaign to start political discussion on YouTube and drive traffic to BarelyPolitical.com.[9] The video featuring the attractive "Obama Girl" was viewed more than 9 million times during the campaign, garnering mainstream media attention and dozens of response videos. Among the most popular: "Obama Girl and McCain Girl Go to Battle" and "I Got a Crush on Hillary." While allowing access to the political process is a good thing, the "YouTube election" isn't entirely positive. A quick search of "Obama and Osama" yields about 1,500 videos. Some are news clips, in which commentators apparently slip up by saying Osama when they meant to say Obama. Others are direct attacks, attempting to color the candidate as a radical Muslim. Some of the videos are morally legitimate contributions of users; others are violations of the ethical principles of truth and disclosure.

A YouTube user identified as Toutsmith (29-year-old male from Beverly Hills, according to his MySpace profile), uploaded "Al Gore's Penguin Army" following the acclaim generated by Gore's film, *An Inconvenient Truth*, and the subsequent award of the Nobel Peace Prize. The clip (more than 500,000 views) showed Al Gore dressed as the Penguin from the classic *Batman* TV series, boring a bunch of animated penguins with a Power-Point presentation and blaming everything from the Middle East crisis to Lindsay Lohan's skinniness on global warming. A 2008 *Wall Street Journal* article linked "Toutsmith" to a computer registered to a Republican public relations firm, whose client list includes Exxon.[10]

YouTube and similar social networking sites increase access to political discourse beyond public figures and political parties. Public relations professionals may interfere with the marketplace process by promoting the ideals of clients and/or stifling a multitude of alternate voices. Part of an ethical process is ensuring that the information presented is truthful and transparent.

Commercial Sponsorship, Truth and Disclosure

The final two principles, truth and disclosure, are presented together because, as said earlier, they are invariably related.[11] Some public relations professionals take the position that their role is to present only information that supports their client's best interest; counterbalancing their advocacy is left to others. Examples of truth and disclosure dilemmas are easy to find on YouTube.

The first case to gain national attention involved crudely shot web-diaries from a teenager. In 2006 *The Los Angeles Times* broke the story of "Bree," aka "lonelygirl15," a 16-year-old girl podcasting from her bedroom. The clips actually originated from Beverly Hills-based talent agency Creative Artists.[12] lonelygirl15's clips were regularly featured in the "most-viewed" portion of YouTube, each averaging more than 200,000 views. Creative Artists told the *Times* the series was the beginning of a new art form, though commercially sponsored web serials weren't anything new. Established stars, such as Paris Hilton and Tom Hanks, had appeared in such episodes on YouTube and MySpace, but were not a hit. Users preferred to "broadcast themselves," as the YouTube slogan promises. lonelygirl15 was appealing specifically because she was one of the crowd. As a user-generated creation, the videos provided a glimpse into the everyday exploits of an ordinary girl; as a scripted web-based vehicle featuring an unknown actress, they just weren't that interesting. More important, the videos were an early violation of trust. Users were realizing for the first time that they were being deceived.

lonelygirl15 wasn't the only one deceiving YouTube users by failing to disclose. Gary Brolsma (aka Numa Numa) lip-synched to a Romanian pop song ("Dragostea din tei" by O-Zone). His grainy web cam video has been seen more than 700 million times and launched him to international fame. Brolsma cashed in on his new-found fame by appearing on multiple television shows and securing a contract from Apple to appear as himself in advertisements for iPod headphones. Once an amateur provider such as Brolsma reaches a level of notoriety, YouTube offers profit sharing or pay-per-view arrangements to produce more materials for the site. These profit-sharing schemes are not made explicit to YouTube users, thus adding another layer to the disclosure issue. Users are faced with blatant commercial messages (music videos, advertisements), advertisements masquerading as amateur videos (stealth marketing), and amateur videos sponsored by YouTube to drive additional traffic to the site. Users can differentiate the blatant ads from other content by looking at the source of the upload. Stealth marketing messages and YouTube-sponsored content are not identified as such.

Stealth Marketing

Music videos aren't the only commercials on YouTube. Among the top 10 most-viewed viral videos (ranked by *Totally Viral*), four are amateur videos, and three are advertisements. The most-viewed ad is for Agent Provocateur D. Pop sensation Kylie Minogue promises to prove that Agent Provocateur is the "most erotic lingerie in the world" by stripping to her undies and riding a red velvet mechanical bull. Minogue concludes the spot by asking all the men to "stand up" while an old woman goads any apparently flaccid viewers. The advertisement would never have passed muster for broadcast television, especially in the United States. As a viral video, it was seen nearly as frequently as clips from Paris Hilton's infamous home-porn. Trojan garnered 300 million views with a similar not-ready-for-TV approach. The "Trojan Warrior" spot features a sumo-type wrestler preparing for a battle. His opponent is a female, and the result is both crass and painful to watch. The effectiveness of the ads is questionable. No doubt millions of "free" consumer views raised awareness for Agent Provocateur, but the user feedback is pretty consistent: Kylie is hot; the underwear, not so much. As with the Trojan ad, viewers respond mostly to the humor of the John West Salmon spot, in which a fisherman gets the tastiest salmon away from a bear by means of kung fu and a well-timed kick to the bear's groin. Most of the popular viral advertisements push the limits of broadcast standards, but they are still clearly advertisements.

Viral marketing refers to techniques that use existing social networks to produce increases in brand awareness or to achieve increased product sales or other marketing objectives. In 2002, Sony Ericsson Mobil launched a viral marketing campaign to promote its T68i mobile phone and digital camera. The "Fake Tourist" initiative placed 60 attractive actors at popular tourist attractions. They simply asked passers-by to take their photos, thus demonstrating the camera phone's ease of use and handy features. The actors never identified themselves as sales representatives. The example also illustrates the importance of truth and disclosure in ethical public relations. The tourists may have been more skeptical of the camera if they were aware that they were experiencing a sales pitch rather than helping a stranger. More recently, Proctor and Gamble launched a new marketing division called Tremor. Tremor offered free products to 250,000 teens to promote Proctor and Gamble products to their peers.[13] Both campaigns were included in a 2006 complaint to the Federal Trade Commission (FTC). The FTC guidelines are clear: If you're being paid, you should disclose that. Proctor and Gamble argues that, because the teens are actually volunteers, they are not required to disclose their relationship. A spokesperson told the *New York Times* that some participants receive product samples so they can better offer their honest opinions to interested peers.[14]

Blatant ethical issues emerge when public relations professionals representing corporate interests pose as anonymous Internet users. Participants at the 2007 Association for Education in Journalism and Mass Communication (AEJMC) Convention were wowed by Miguel Monteverde, executive director of AOL Video Programming, as he shared example after example of "viral video" clips professionally produced for clients like Axe body spray, Nokia phones, and HP laptops. Advertisers, according to Monteverde, want to embed their promotional videos alongside the amateur videos uploaded by users. The HP video is a perfect example. In "A skunk walks into a coffeehouse," a skunk's untimely entrance into a busy establishment gets captured by a webcam of one of many young patrons. In the chaos, the laptop falls to the floor, coincidentally perfectly framing the stinky invader; the webcam is still running (That's a mighty sturdy laptop!). HP is never identified as the sponsor, but some users spot the plant:

(Reply)
i think that is video is very fake. i have owned two skunks before, and if the people made that big of a deal that skunk would be running everywhere. my skunks got scared when i would just walk by. and theyre domestic. ha, and skunks have terrible eye sight, and mine once ran into a bed post. it was hilarious and sad at the same time.

(Reply)
LOL XD! I remember when a Skunk got into my house at night. The door was opened, and he passed by us like there was nothing ... of course we panicked!

(Reply)
In response to who ever said you can tell it's a kid in a costume: Thats a real skunk, and it's not to fat to be wild, I almost hit one that size last night as a drove home. As for it's calm behavior, skunks are just like that, they don't get particularly agitated, even when they spray. I say this video is real.

One of the more memorable viral campaigns was SONY's "All I Want for Christmas is a PSP" campaign. The videos combined amateur-looking footage and personal blogs. Backlash from consumers after it was revealed that SONY and its agency Zipatoni masterminded the campaign was swift, resulting in a formal apology from SONY.[15] Long-term effects on the brand loyalty of duped consumers are less clear. The underlying ethical issue is disclosure. Had SONY disclosed the clip was an advertisement, users still may have enjoyed the video and forwarded it to others. In absence of the disclosure, users felt lied to and betrayed.

The bedrock of the PRSA ethical code is a requirement that members identify corporate sponsors of promotional messages. Whether promoting a performer or a product, these examples illustrate blatant violations. The Word of Mouth Marketing Association, aimed at viral marketers, endorses the Federal Trade Commission stance on identifying sponsored messages. The Chicago-based association attempts to hold its 300 members accountable for ethical violations. Among the recent reviews is the Edelman Group, which reportedly gave positive comments to bloggers who posted PR materials for client Wal-Mart without mentioning the source and later admitted that some of the blogs were written by employees.[16] Young people are drawn to viral video sites because everyone can be the star. YouTube's slogan is "broadcast yourself." Despite this expectation, users are exposed to just another channel for corporate interests.

Because it is relatively easy to duplicate others' work and appear anonymous online, the Internet functions on trust. Stealth marketing violates this trust, resulting in consequences to consumers and corporations. When faced with a sales or persuasion scenario, consumers rely on product knowledge, persuasion knowledge, and agent knowledge to inform their reaction.[17] The dominant reaction is skepticism. By undermining two of the three types of knowledge, stealth marketing deprives consumers of healthy skepticism as a defense mechanism.[18] Once stealth marketing has been identified, news spreads quickly over the same electronic channels used to distribute the original message. The result: loss of trust in the organization. Organizational trust can be defined as the extent to which a company is thought to be honest, dependable, and sensitive to consumer needs. Once organizational trust is violated, it may be impossible to rebuild.

So, Whose Tube Is It?

YouTube was launched in 2005, with the gentle meow of its founder's cat. Now more like the MGM lion's roar, the site has emerged as a forum for diverse opinions where users can literally "broadcast themselves." It has also emerged as a challenge to mainstream media, since users turn to the site to watch music videos and see what they missed on television (sans those pesky commercials).

The chapter began by defining the four fundamental principles that establish an ethical baseline for responsible advocacy in public relations: access, process, truth, and disclosure.

YouTube increases user access to entertainment and political content. This access allows citizens to participate in the political process at unprecedented levels. User access to entertainment content also poses legal and ethical issues. The copyright issues facing YouTube could cost Google over $1 billion. These only begin to scratch the surface, as individual users continue to upload not only copyrighted media clips, but also use copyrighted materials in their more creative endeavors. Indeed, the mash-up has become an art form for the new millennium.

The final two ethical principles, truth and disclosure, present the biggest challenges on YouTube. As corporate sponsors and political campaigns shroud their identities with poor production quality, the public is left to personally discern which messages are legitimate amateur contributions to the marketplace of ideas and which are manipulative propaganda produced by subversive hacks. Regulation has yet to keep pace with technology, and the ethical grey zone expands exponentially into cyberspace. Media regulation has always lagged behind technological development. For a number of years, television was governed by radio regulation, cable by broadcast standards, and the Internet by a combination of print and broadcast standards. This phenomenon continues as digital technology quickly evolves, leaving much of the content under the purview of ethics. Popular sites like Twitter and Facebook allow users to instantaneously share thoughts, images, and video with millions of subscribers via high-speed Internet and cell phones. On the positive side, individuals have unprecedented access to large audiences. This amplifies political commentary and freedom of expression, but equally amplifies defamation, hate speech, and copyright infringement. Wherever the audience goes, advertisers will follow. Stealth marketing is likely to increase. As the technology evolves, viral marketing will also evolve, occupying an expanding ethical grey zone. "The Internet functions on trust," corporate communications specialist Joel Postman said. "As more and more people do business in the digital world, more consumers than ever need to know who they can rely on to tell the truth."[19]

NOTES

1. Kathy Fitzpatrick, "Baseline for Ethical Advocacy in the 'Marketplace of Ideas'" in *Ethics in Public Relations: Responsible Advocacy,* Eds. Kathy Fitzpatrick and Carolyn Bronstein (London: Sage, 2006), 1–17.

2. John Harris, "Focus," *The Guardian,* October 11, 2006, 6.

3. Jim Carroll, "They Say Yes, They Say No, We Say OK Go," *The Irish Times,* September 22, 2006, 14.

4. Ethan Smith and Peter Lattman, "Download This: YouTube Phenom Has a Big Secret," *Wall Street Journal,* September 6, 2007, A1.

5. Maria Aspan, "A Spurned Parody of 'Die Hard' Returns to YouTube, Approved," *The New York Times,* June 25, 2007, 7.
6. Cathy Lynn Grossman, "GodTube.com Jazzes Up the Word with Video," *USA TODAY,* December 18, 2007, 6D.
7. Harris, "Focus," 6.
8. "6 Lessons We Can Learn from Barack Obama's On-line Marketing Strategy," WebProfits.com, July 23, 2008.
9. Danielle Lipp, "BarelyPolitical Touts Viral Video," *PR Week,* October 22, 2007, 27.
10. Barb Palser, "Artful Disguises: Sultans of Spin Masquerade as Amateurs on Citizen Media Web Sites," *American Journalism Review,* 2008, 90.
11. Philip Patterson and Lee Wilkins, *Media Ethics: Issues and cases,* 5th ed. (New York: McGraw-Hill, 2005).
12. Pete Cashmore, "YouTube's Lonelygirl15 a Fake," *Social Networking News,* September 8, 2006.
13. Annys Shin, "FTC Moves to Unmask Word-of-Mouth Marketing," *Washington Post,* December 12, 2006, D01.
14. *Ibid.*
15. Emma Hall, "U.K. Cracks Down on Word-of-Mouth with Tough Restrictions," *Advertising Age,* April 28, 2008, 132.
16. Shin, "TC Moves to Unmask Word-of-Mouth Marketing," D01.
17. Carl Obermiller and Eric Spangenberg, "Development of a Scale to Measure Consumer Skepticism Toward Advertising," *Journal of Consumer Psychology,* 7 no. 2, (1998): 159–86.
18. Kelly Martin and Craig Smith, "Commercializing Social Interaction: The Ethics of Stealth Marketing," *Journal of Public Policy and Marketing,* 27 no. 1 (2008): 45–56.
19. Gloria Goodale, "Who's That Selling at Your (Online) Door?" *Christian Science Monitor,* March 17, 2008, 13.

WORKS CITED

Aspan, Maria. "A Spurned Parody of 'Die Hard' Returns to YouTube, Approved," *New York Times,* June 25, 2007, 7.
Carroll, Jim. "They Say Yes, They Say No, We Say OK Go," *The Irish Times,* September 22, 2006, 14.
Fitzpatrick, Kathy. "Baseline for Ethical Advocacy in the 'Marketplace of Ideas'" in *Ethics in Public Relations: Responsible Advocacy,* Eds. Kathy Fitzpatrick and Carolyn Bronstein. London: Sage, 2006, 1–17.
Goodale, Gloria. "Who's That Selling at Your (Online) Door?" *Christian Science Monitor,* March 17, 2008, 7.
Grossman, Cathy Lynn. "GodTube.com Jazzes Up the Word with Video," *USA TODAY,* December 18, 2007, 6D.
Hall, Emma. "U.K. Cracks Down on Word-of-Mouth with Tough Restrictions," *Advertising Age,* April 28, 2008, 132.
Harris, John. "Focus," *The Guardian,* October 11, 2006, 6.
Lipp, Danielle. "BarelyPolitical Touts Viral Video," *PR Week,* October, 22, 2007, 27.
Martin, Kelly, and Craig Smith. "Commercializing Social Interaction: The Ethics of Stealth Marketing." *Journal of Public Policy and Marketing* 27 no. 1 (2008): 45–56.
Obermiller, Carl, and Eric Spangenberg. "Development of a Scale to Measure Consumer Skepticism toward Advertising." *Journal of Consumer Psychology,* 7 no. 2, (1998): 159–86.
Palser, Barb. "Artful Disguises: Sultans of Spin Masquerade as Amateurs on Citizen Media Web Sites." *American Journalism Review,* 2008, 90.
Patterson, Philip, and Lee Wilkins. *Media Ethics: Issues and Cases,* 5th ed. New York: McGraw-Hill, 2005.

Shin, Annys. "FTC Moves to Unmask Word-of-Mouth Marketing," *Washington Post,* December 12, 2006, D01.
"6 Lessons We Can Learn from Barack Obama's On-line Marketing Strategy." WebProfits.com, July 23, 2008.
Smith, Ethan, and Peter Lattman. "Download This: YouTube Phenom Has a Big Secret," *Wall Street Journal,* September 6, 2007, A1.

CHAPTER 15

Enlightenment Ethics in DIY Culture

Bill Reader

This essay considers the moral framework of those media generally categorized as "alternative" or "indie" (slang for "independent") or, in the more modern parlance, "DIY" (short for "do it yourself"). In *The Alternative Media Handbook*,[1] authors Tony Dowmunt and Kate Coyer define such enterprises as "media forms that are on a smaller scale, more accessible and participatory, and less constrained by bureaucracy or commercial interests than the mainstream media and often in some way in explicit opposition to them."[2] Cultural critic Amy Spencer, in her book *DIY: The Rise of Lo-Fi Culture*, makes a similar argument: "The DIY movement is about using anything you can get your hands on to shape your own cultural identity; your own version of whatever you think is missing in mainstream culture."[3]

Those aspects of DIY culture set it apart from the mainstream on a philosophical basis rather than simply a material basis. DIY is not just an effort by amateurs to mimic the mainstream — it is a reaction to the limitations and influences of the mainstream, a reaction guided largely by anti-establishment sentiments, revolutionary attitudes, and an emphasis on the rights and needs of individuals over the hegemonic forces of mass culture. We've seen those attitudes before: They are among the general characteristics of that eighteenth-century movement in the West referred to as the Age of Enlightenment. This essay argues that the moral relativism that flourished during the Enlightenment continues today as the dominant moral framework within the growing DIY media movement.[4]

Assigning moral categories to either "the mainstream" or "the underground" is risky business. People often take their artistic preferences personally and are easily offended at the suggestion that one paradigm is morally superior to the other. At the outset, then, I want to be absolutely clear on this point: To suggest that there are different moral frameworks between mainstream and DIY media is not to suggest that one is better than the other. Those frameworks are simply *different*, and it is those differences that are worth exploring. That is accomplished in this essay by considering the opinions of a variety of artists working in the DIY media, such as fan-fiction writers, "indie" musicians, and independent filmmakers. What emerges is a collage of opinions regarding media ethics that defies generalization, but that also positions moral relativism as something much more refined than "anything goes." In fact, what these artists construct is a collective ethical framework in which "the mainstream" is viewed with distrust and in which the concept of "selling out" has more to do with maintaining artistic autonomy (i.e., not having to make concessions to the "money people") than it does with eschewing financial success (indeed, some of the artists who participated in this project have been able to make a living from their work).

As cultural scholar Stuart Hall suggests, popular culture is always at odds with itself, "a sort of constant battlefield"[5] in which the struggle is for popular culture "constantly to disorganize and reorganize popular culture."[6] What Hall claims is that the struggle is not necessarily between the mainstream and the "alternative" cultures, but rather an internal struggle within popular culture between dominant and subordinate/resistant forms.[7] For example, punk rock emerged in the 1970s as a youthful opposition to mainstream popular culture; when punk rock became more widely popular a few years later, the "punk" aesthetic was assimilated into mainstream culture, essentially "killing" the punk movement (three decades later, punk anthems are so mainstream that they are used as background music in TV commercials, major-studio films, and television shows).[8] Meanwhile, other DIY media movements evolved to pick up the counter-cultural mission of punk and other anti-establishment art movements, many to be in turn assimilated into the mainstream and replaced by newer counter-culture movements.

The moral frameworks under which such movements operate are culturally relative — that is, there are no universal ethical standards embraced by artists working within specific media forms. For example, independent filmmaker Alex Cox suggests that in trying to appeal to huge audiences, mainstream film studios that produce high-grossing action movies should also bear moral culpability for creating media that "brutalize young people, and lead to racism, sexism and mistaken life choices such as joining the military and dropping cluster bombs on Afghans, Iraqis and Serbs."[9] Yet some independent films are, arguably, much more gruesome than anything the mainstream studios would dare put into general release. Consider the 2002 French independent film *Irréversible* by director Gaspar Noé, which film critic Roger Ebert described as "a movie so violent and cruel that most people will find it unwatchable."[10] The film also garnered several nominations for awards from various respected film festivals and even had two wins.[11] The most controversial part of the film is a long, single-shot scene depicting the brutal rape of a young woman in a pedestrian tunnel under a busy Paris street; another horrific scene includes the brutal, bloody revenge murder of a man wrongly accused of the rape.

If, as Clifford Christians and other media ethicists suggest, there must be universal ethical norms, such as not harming innocents, telling the truth, and embracing beneficence, then where does a film such as *Irréversible* fall in the ethical spectrum? The film's explicit depiction of rape and murder is both truthful and harmful, both disturbing and informative. It addresses very real issues in a realistic manner, so much so that it is doubtful any mainstream movie studio would stand behind such disturbing footage. It is not a film that any reasonable person would necessarily "like" or "enjoy" in the common sense; not surprisingly, the violent scenes drove many viewers from the theaters in disgust and discomfort.[12] Does the disturbing nature of those scenes make it a "bad" film? Or, more to the point, does that mean the filmmaker was "wrong" to make it? Such questions, when applied to mass-market media may be easier to tackle, as one can bring to the discussion the norms of the dominant culture that the mainstream media both reflect and influence. If *Irréversible* had been a major-studio release mass-marketed to society at large via expansive marketing campaigns, it probably would have drawn even more derision than it did. However, as an indie film intentionally targeted to small audiences (essentially, devotees of independent film festivals), the movie was able to fly under the radar of dominant culture and, as a result, enjoy a certain liberation from the norms of that culture. Whether the work is right or wrong, in an ethical sense, may largely be determined by what the artist in question hopes to accomplish and whether that artist is trying to embrace dominant culture, operate begrudgingly within that culture, or operate in direct opposition to it.[13] Because indie/DIY media operate largely from an oppositional position to mainstream culture, it should be no surprise that the products of DIY artists often challenge and break with the ethical norms of dominant society. Such opposition isn't necessarily absent from mainstream culture, or from the artists working within mainstream media, but it is far less common. Mainstream media always must keep in mind the culture in which they circulate; DIY artists, on the other hand, can create their own culture, and their own cultural norms.

Reflections of Western Enlightenment Ethics

That sense of moral autonomy—what is morally right for one artist is not necessarily morally right for another—reflects the ethics of the Western

Enlightenment movement that flourished in Europe and colonial America in the 1700s. The Enlightenment was primarily concerned with the supremacy of reason over dogma, or as one scholar put it, Enlightenment thinkers "are perhaps best described as skeptics who collectively framed fundamentally liberal objections to what they took to be the universalist bigotry of sacred truth."[14] Reflecting a diverse range of interpretations of classical Greek philosophy, and built upon the concurrent advancement of the first truly "mass" medium — the press— the Enlightenment ushered into the West many of the personal freedoms and ethical norms we now take for granted, including the advancement of ethical inquiry itself, but also the freedom of artistic expression.

The overarching ethical framework of the Enlightenment is complex and nuanced, but a few basic commonalities of Enlightenment moral thinking are generally accepted:

1. Enabling and protecting personal freedoms is a moral obligation of civil society (the concept we now call "basic human rights").
2. It is immoral for centralized power structures— such as governments and organized religions— to not be responsive to, and protective of, those basic human rights (the modern concept of liberal democracy).
3. If those power structures do not cede power to the masses, then the masses have a moral obligation to overthrow those power structures (the concept of popular revolution).

For artists of that time, the Enlightenment presented a moral framework that allowed for greater creative freedoms, particularly in regard to challenging the power structures that suppressed anti-establishment themes and controversial expressions.

The Enlightenment philosophers were largely working against theological dogma and authoritarian governments. In the entertainment industry today, the power structure is clearly centralized in what is deemed the "mainstream"— the large media corporations that dominate the markets for literature, video games, movies, and music recordings.

In terms of revenue alone, the mainstream corporate media far outstrip independent media. Just 10 major film studios (most of them subsidiaries of global media conglomerates) "control in excess of 90 percent of the worldwide and domestic film grosses," according to one scholarly assessment.[15] The same is true of the music industry, in which "90 percent of worldwide gross music sales accrued to six multinational corporations."[16] The book-publishing industry is similarly consolidated, such that "only five conglomerates publish 80 percent of U.S. trade books."[17] And in the home video game industry, the dominance in sales rests with the three companies that make the most popular video game consoles, SONY (via its Playstation hardware), Nintendo, and Microsoft (via its XBox hardware), which in 2007 accounted for $8.6 billion of the industry's total sales of $9.5 billion in game-software sales alone.[18]

Operating in the shadow of those media behemoths are the little-known, but much more numerous, denizens of the media underground: the uncountable artists producing their own media for small groups of fans.[19] In discussing media ethics with producers of such underground media as fan fiction, indie computer games, avant-garde films, and lo-fi psychedelic music, I found that today's DIY movement is complex and multifaceted, but does have as hallmarks the same ethical principles that unified Enlightenment-era thinkers: a fierce regard for personal freedoms, strong anti-establishment attitudes, a penchant for rebellion, and a privileging of their artistic goals over fame and/or fortune.

Art for the Artist's Sake: Individualism and Fan Fiction

A clear example of the modern implementation of individualism is the DIY authorship of fan fiction, a phenomenon by which fans of popular culture create their own subcultures around the objects of their affection.[20] One of the most recognized forms of that phenomenon is the *Star Trek* fan culture built upon that science-fiction franchise. It has resulted in all manner of fan-produced objects, from custom-made costumes to unlicensed (and unsanctioned) fan-written stories about homosexual romance between Captain Kirk and Mister Spock. Such examples of fan fiction now can be found for many popular television shows and other media franchises, such as J.R.R. Tolkien's "Middle Earth" or daytime television's *Days of Our Lives*. The original amateur stories, commonly called "fics," have been the subject of considerable study.[21]

For this essay, I interviewed two prolific "fic" writers from England who publish their work on www.fanfiction.net, a Web site that carries fan-written storylines for thousands of television shows and other media. Jane Tavener, who publishes under the pseudonym "Jane0904," has at this writing produced more than 220 fics based on the short-lived *Firefly* television show. The other, Jayne Leigh, has at this writing posted 65 fics to www.fanfiction.net based on three television programs: *Friends*, *Studio 60 on the Sunset Strip*, and the celebrated political drama, *The West Wing*.

Both said they have aspirations to become professional writers, but their impetus to write and publish fan fiction begins not with their career goals but with their love for the shows they write about. Leigh said she started as a teenager: "It was just a bit of fun with some friends that I had made online. I just like being able to write about characters from shows that I love to watch."[22] For Tavener, the inspiration came from her frustration when *Firefly* was cancelled halfway through its first season. It was a quirky, genre-crossing show (a sci-fi Western mixing action, comedy, drama, and mystery themes) created and directed by Joss Whedon, creator of the *Buffy the Vampire Slayer* series. Notes Tavener: "I felt cheated that [*Firefly*] didn't have the chance to grow and evolve, as it surely would have done, over the seven seasons Joss Whedon planned. And there were stories I could see in my mind's eye that were never going to get made, so I decided to write them down. I didn't want to lose any of them, so fan fiction seemed the way to go. Not that I initially uploaded them anywhere, just kept them to myself. It wasn't until I entered an online writing competition for *Firefly* back in 2006 (which I won, by the way) that I decided to see what others thought of my scribblings."[23]

What elevates such work from private hobby to DIY entertainment is that both authors publish their work online, where they have small followings of fans, many of whom post anonymous feedback. Both noted that the publishing and resultant feedback informs their art. "I feel, as a writer (and I do class myself as such), that I am learning all the time, and can use this platform to try out different styles, different techniques," Tavener said.[24] Leigh said this about the feedback she receives: "I've actually been quite lucky in the sense that if I do receive negative reviews, then it's been constructive at the same time. Where I struggle with updating a series is if I'm not getting any feedback.... I don't need 100 percent positive reviews to continue writing, but I do need to be excited about writing it. Good reviews are just an added bonus."[25]

There is also a diminished sense of risk in writing fan fiction, which is something both writers said they would miss if they were to ever gain success as mainstream authors. "The one thing I enjoy about writing fanfics and would miss would be it's a bit of harmless fun," Leigh wrote. "Whereas I'm quite protective, I would probably take it too much to heart if someone overly criticized something I've created from scratch.... If someone doesn't like my fics, then, yeah, it's disappointing, but it's just something I do to relax and to kind of keep alive a show I love that has ended."[26] Leigh said one appeal of becoming a mainstream writer would be making a living doing something she enjoys, but the primary goal is to have her work reach more people: "Simply I just like to write and the main pro of being a published author with an established publisher ... would mean, hopefully, more people would read. I like that people enjoy my writing."[27] Tavener said that even if she were to become a published author under her own name, "Jane0904" would probably "continue to pen my little tales and no-one would be any the wiser." Why? "It gives me the opportunity to try out new things, which might be difficult in a newly published author role. So unless it were strictly forbidden, I would continue to do so. Besides, the anonymity means you can make a total fool of yourself and no one knows it's you!"[28]

That last point reflects a key aspect of Enlightenment-era thinking — that one's ideas should be considered independent of the identity of the author, that anonymity can promote more robust discourse and bolder expressions. For example, Søren Kierkegaard, who wrote many of his most important works under pseudonyms, explained in "The Point of View of My Work as an Author"[29] that his use of pseudonyms was to encourage readers to consider the arguments in his works on their own merits, rather than with any attitudes toward Kierkegaard himself — an early example of a celebrity recognizing that his fame could overshadow his work. In today's society, in which fame and celebrity seem to be synonymous with "success," the relative obscurity of DIY artists may seem to be a marker of "low value" when actually, in true Enlightenment fashion, that obscurity gives DIY artists the autonomy they need to produce works that satisfy their individual standards of artistic integrity.

Independence as "Integrity": Shareware Computer Games

The rhetoric of "integrity" comes up quite a bit in the DIY paradigm, but how that term is defined is, again, relative to the individual. In the case of indie computer game developer Jeff Vogel, "integrity" is a blend of artistic independence and duty to the fans of his games (who also happen to be paying customers).

On the Web site for Vogel's Spiderweb Software, a small, three-person computer-game company based in Seattle, Washington, there is an entire page devoted to the philosophy behind "shareware" computer games. Shareware is not a type of computer software, but rather a marketing strategy. Shareware developers allow potential customers to download and play the games for a period of time, and if they like the software, they can buy a license, usually at a low price compared to major-label video games. "The brilliant thing about shareware," Vogel wrote, "is that it's a way for a lone person to create great software, sitting in his or her basement, with nothing but a computer, hard work, some potato chips, and some Mountain Dew.... Creating great software is both art and business, and there can be no success in either arena without pain."[30]

In an e-mail interview, Vogel said he created his first game in 1994 while in graduate school and, like the fan-fiction writers mentioned earlier, entirely for fun. "It was purely a hobbyist thing," he wrote. "I didn't intend to make it my business or anything. I released it as shareware because it was simply the easiest way to get it out there." Now having developed more than a dozen games of the popular role-playing variety (akin to the *Dungeons & Dragons* role-playing games, or "RPGs"), Vogel says Spiderweb Software provides his family with a nice income and a comfortable lifestyle.

Vogel offers the public free demo versions of his game that critics have described as "huge" (meaning that players get several hours of free, unrestricted playing time).[31] Like some indie game developers, Vogel also offers "scenario editors" for two of his games, which allow players to create and share playable modules for Spiderweb's games, a relatively rare surrender of creative control in the computer game industry.

Giving away so much content and control to game players is just one way that the indie-game movement stands apart from the mainstream game industry. With little in the way of marketing and promotion, such games rely heavily on word-of-mouth and favorable reviews from customers in online discussion boards. In articulating the moral concept of "integrity," Vogel suggested that artistic autonomy is as important as being responsible to paying customers: "You get to work alone, be your own boss, make your own decisions, and avoid focus groups, endless meetings, and all the soul-killing productivity-sucking features of the corporate world."[32]

Vogel is not necessarily opposed to crossing over to work in the mainstream game industry, but he would not do so at the expense of his current lifestyle, suggesting that his definition of "integrity" transcends his work to include his personal life, the two becoming intertwined. "If someone offered me money comparable to what I make now (which is a very respectable amount) and let me stay in Seattle, I would consider it very, very strongly," he said. "I love Seattle so much that it would be really hard to make me move."[33]

Like many who work in indie/DIY entertainment, Vogel has given some thought to the pros and cons of working in the underground, but also sees the pros and cons of being in the mainstream. He did indicate that one company he would not consider working for is the software giant Microsoft, which is generally reviled by indie software makers.

The concept of "selling out" is perhaps the antithesis of "integrity" in the DIY media milieu, and just like the concept of "integrity," "selling out" is a relative term, with no clear, fixed definition among various DIY artists as to what constitutes "selling out." It is largely a matter of personal limits and what the marketplace will support. To the fan-fiction writer Jayne Leigh, it is that point where profit motive supersedes artistic goals: "Once you start thinking of the money or fame side of things, then you're not as passionate as you could be if you're simply writing for the love of it."[34] To Vogel, the term is negative, but unwieldy: "It's an insult just about anyone can apply in just about any situation. I'm honestly not sure what I would have to do to 'sell out.'"[35] Indie musician Clint Takeda, of the Philadelphia-based band Bardo Pond, said, "'Selling out,' to me, is just going against your love: Following a hunch about other people's wants and going there with intentions of 'making it.'"[36] And to independent filmmaker Alex Cox, "selling out" means an artist is giving in too much to the pressures of the "money people."

Dealing with Devils: The High Costs of Indie Film

The "money problem" of DIY media is perhaps most pronounced in the wildly expensive art of filmmaking. Even a very small film project can cost hundreds of thousands of dollars, consumed by set creation, equipment and studio rentals, film stock and processing, and payment to the dozens or sometimes hundreds of actors, technicians, and support crews.[37] Alex Cox, who has been making movies on the fringes of the mainstream for more than three decades, sees fundraising as the necessary evil of the indie film industry, with emphasis on "evil." "Fidel Castro and Che Guevara in the early days of the Cuban revolution felt money was an evil thing and wanted to abolish it. I agree with them," Cox wrote in an e-mail. "Where it comes from is less important than the fact that money in our society is already treated like a nasty little god; hence the weird way people act around it."[38] He continued:

> And yet one needs money to make films and must treat the ethical angle on a case-by-case basis. Is it worse to take money from Sir Richard Branson, who made millions wrecking the British rail system, or from Rupert Murdoch, who made billions wrecking everything else? Is it better to work for GE, or Gazprom? Everyone must decide for themselves, and lucky, too![39]

Cox is best known for writing and directing the cult classic *Repo Man* and the critically acclaimed punk biopic *Sid & Nancy*, both of which were released more than 20 years ago. The seven films Cox has made since then barely register in the public consciousness, although some starred celebrities (Joe Strummer, Ed Harris, Peter Boyle, and Christopher Eccleston, among them) and many have garnered critical acclaim (such as 1991's *El Patrullero* and Cox's most recent film at this writing, the limited-release buddy/road movie *Searchers 2.0*). His films are typically about "unsympathetic characters"[40] who have few redeeming qualities; "unsympathetic characters" is a term that Cox says "has been the response of money people to almost all of my scripts"—that is, a reason to turn down the film.[41] One of those characters, and the one who perhaps made Cox's career one of financial difficulty, was the title role in 1987's *Walker*.

Cox describes *Walker* as "my best, my most expensive, and my least-seen film." A fictionalized biopic of William Walker, the American mercenary who in the mid–1850s seized control of and became president of Nicaragua (and was executed in Honduras soon thereafter), the film was a victim of Cox's impeccable sense of cultural timing. Cox was in Nicaragua in 1984 the week national elections were won by the left-wing Sandinistas. The Reagan administration would soon begin to secretly funnel funds to anti–Sandinista rebels.[42] Cox recalled that he was invited to make a film in Nicaragua to bring American dollars to the impoverished country, and he thought the tale of William Walker, an American meddling in the internal affairs of Nicaragua more than a century earlier, was perfect for such a film. Cox said he and his partners "wanted to make a radical film. We wanted to make it in collaboration with the Sandinistas, and to spend dollars in Nicaragua. To do this, we needed those dollars."[43] Cox's lead actor in the film, Ed Harris (who had won critical acclaim a few years earlier playing astronaut John Glenn in the blockbuster hit *The Right Stuff*), helped a reluctant Cox get funding from the mega-studio Universal.

Cox was reluctant because he had had several bad experiences with that same studio when it financially backed *Repo Man* a few years earlier. Late in production of that film, the leadership at Universal changed, and executives who were allegedly out to undermine the work of the previous studio head tried to alter the film. "An inferior, fucked-up film would have resulted," Cox said. "By staying united behind our vision, the producers, director, and editor won the battle for control.... Creatively, the film was saved."[44] But financially, it was doomed. Universal gave the film limited release and pulled it from theaters after just one week. It was contractually obligated to release the film in other markets, but Cox said the marketing was lackluster at best and perhaps even sabotaged by those at Universal who wanted the film to fail for political reasons.[45] That certainly became the case a few years later with *Walker*, which upon its release was met with hostility by the largely pro-Reagan/anti-communist zeitgeist then rampant in the United States, including Hollywood. Universal only put the film out to limited release and quickly pulled it before it could make any money; the Hollywood establishment also made it clear that the "renegade" Cox was not welcome in its mainstream fold.[46]

Cox involuntarily became a DIY filmmaker. That came with curses and blessings. After *Walker*, the job of fundraising became more difficult and time-consuming, but also more grounded in a moral sense of artistic autonomy:

> I was blacklisted by the studios and haven't had a job offer from them or a project accepted by them since. So I was obliged to look for more creative/ innovative/desperate ways to make films. Pissing pretentious and obnoxious people off is always fun, but it's a by-product, not a goal.... The goal is the film itself — the work of art to which our labours, for a period of time, are dedicated. The film itself is what's important. And it's also important that

those involved are proud of their work, and that the film is properly sold, and honest accounts kept — because some films actually make money![47]

Cox's latest film, *Searchers 2.0*, cost a reported $172,000 to make[48] (thanks largely to Cox's use of low-cost video instead of film), and as with all of his films, Cox worked the film-festival circuit to get *Searchers 2.0* seen by those who enjoy his work and appreciate his decidedly anti-mainstream approach. But even though he isn't welcome (or really comfortable) in Hollywood, he readily acknowledges the necessary evil of dealing with some aspect of the power structures that trickle down from the mainstream, whether it involves finding a celebrity actor to play a lead that a talented upstart could perhaps portray just as well or spending time and money traveling to film festivals rather than working on the next project. As he stated:

> Filmmakers — mainly directors and actors — are used as a sales tool in the promotion of films when they're distributed. This has been happening since the Sixties. Prior to then, I think it was possible to be a low-key filmmaker. But now, whether you direct for the studio or for yourself, you are expected to get out there and promote that movie by going to festivals and giving interviews. If a film doesn't have a Hollywood movie star, and the director isn't available, many festivals — especially the larger ones — won't show it. And festivals can be of great value in generating reviews, word of mouth, and making sales. So you have to go.
>
> Even if you manage to play the part of the Recluse, as [Stanley] Kubrick did, you must be the Accessible Recluse — talking on the phone to *Time* and *Newsweek*, videoconferencing with studio heads, inviting Roger Ebert to dinner at your home ... could there be anything more ghastly?[49]

Sounds of Revolution: Making and Distributing Indie Music

Until fairly recently, that same kind of moral tension between artistic integrity and paying the bills also tormented those who worked in the various basements and lofts of the sprawling underground music scene. Like the DIY film world, the DIY music scene involves collaborations between esoteric artists and those who fund and distribute their recordings. For the latter, the moral dimensions of running a DIY record label present similar challenges regarding autonomy, anti-establishment leanings, and a dose of measured rebellion against the mainstream.

As with the other forms of entertainment media discussed in this chapter, the music industry is dominated by a handful of global corporations driven largely by profit motives. Among the largest are SONY Music Entertainment, EMI, Universal Music Group, and Warner Music Group, which together represent the most popular mainstream artists of the day, such as Coldplay, Rihanna, Gavin McGraw, and Kanye West. The major labels tend to be control-oriented, often fighting against music-file sharing, cracking down on unauthorized recording or use of their artists' work (such as bootleg recordings of concerts), and being embroiled in lawsuits over ownership rights to recordings (as in the famous 2005–07 lawsuit by the Beatles' Apple Records against EMI for alleged non-payment of royalties on sales of Beatles recordings).[50] More than anything, major-label music is about making as much money as possible.

In the DIY music business, making money is certainly a consideration, but not as big a consideration as distributing interesting, highly artistic music. According to indie musician Clint Takeda, bassist for the 18-year-old art-rock band Bardo Pond, the appeal of signing to a major label is obvious: "Mainstream acceptance could bring in funds that could make the creating of music easier, as in making time (not having to hold a job down) and bringing in gear (instruments and equipment)." But he said the perks of operating on the fringes outweigh the benefits: "Really, we are following the path that our music affords us.... The nice thing about being known on the scale that we are is that we are respected as musicians in our local community by other musicians, artists, and other like-minded people — people of our kin. We get respect for still doing what we do and not changing our aesthetics to try and sell more records or to become more well known."[51]

It's musicians who privilege artistic autonomy over mainstream success that encouraged Vinita Joshi to launch her small, London-based label, Rocket Girl Records, in 1997. The label's first release was a double-sided vinyl single featuring a new recording by the reformed '60s psychedelic band Silver Apples and, on the flip side, a song by the contemporary art-rock band Windy & Carl.[52] As with the fan-fiction writers mentioned earlier, Joshi at first had no intentions to turn her love for music into a full-time business. "It wasn't planned, it just started off as a hobby that grew," she said.[53] More than a decade after launching her DIY label, and after issuing more than four dozen records and CDs, Joshi is enjoying moderate success, both artistically and financially. "The benefit right now of filling a niche market is that the sales are not suffering," she wrote in an e-mail. "There are always going to be fans of music who are into the more specialist markets, and those sales do not appear to be suffering as much as the majors."[54]

A substantial part of an indie label's success, Joshi suggested, is a sense of fairness and loyalty toward the musicians she signs, even developing true friendships with them. Unlike the heavy-handed, top-down meddling of major media companies, Joshi said she tries to serve her musician partners' needs and respect their creative goals so that both they and she will benefit:

The nature of running a small indie does mean that one does mix business with pleasure.... Maybe being too involved with the artists to the point that it has jeopardized relationships. Generally though, it means that the bands are fully informed of how the release is being marketed and [how] we are all in it together.... For an indie, we want every release to work. We know that the career of each band is on our shoulders and we want it to work.... On a positive side, any band working with Rocket Girl will know that I am available 24/7. If I work with bands in USA, I can spend my evenings working and corresponding with them. They would not get that dedication, even from the bigger indies. I have the time and commitment, as it is my label.[55]

Like those who work in other DIY media, Rocket Girl often works against more powerful and influential power structures, particularly the larger conglomerations of previously "indie" labels that now combine the resources of major labels with the cultural "cred" of the true indies (an example being the Beggars Group company that parents mid-sized "hip" labels, such as Rough Trade and Matador). "It is very frustrating to be chasing a band and competing with the bigger indies," Joshi says. "I have been in the situation where maybe the band is being made an offer from Rough Trade and although my offer might be similar, I do not have the history of signing The Smiths or whomever, and that can be very frustrating. I do not spend much time worrying about the majors. I don't feel that they are my competitors."[56]

Like those participating in the Enlightenment movement three centuries ago who tapped into a powerful new communication tool — the printing press — today's DIY artists have at their disposal a relatively new mass medium, the Internet, that allows them to easily bypass existing power structures and to undermine the oppressive dominance of the mainstream media establishment. In terms of indie music, the Internet may make it more difficult for artists and labels to control the distribution of their work, but Joshi said that isn't necessarily a bad thing: "As far as the Internet is concerned, it does mean a lack of control over the music, but back in the day they were concerned that 'taping is killing music.' I do not believe that the Internet is killing music. It certainly has made music more freely available.... It is a great way of putting majors and indies on a more level playing field to promote bands."[57]

Takeda, the indie musician, said his band is even less concerned about controlling the recording and distribution of their music. Bardo Pond is known as a "taper-friendly" band, one that encourages fans to record live performances and then share (or sell) those recordings to other fans. "The philosophy is 'We play music, it goes into the air, then it is gone,'" Takeda says. "It's nice that good folks can catch what they can and maybe they can share it with us and we can enjoy what happened from a different place."[58]

Conclusion: The Revolution Will Be Right-Sized

It is that parallel between a philosophical movement and a new form of mass communication that is perhaps the most obvious link between the Enlightenment of three centuries ago and the DIY movement of today. The Enlightenment had the printing press, a means to mass-produce and distribute individual thought and circumvent and undermine the powers that be. The DIY movement has at its disposal digital communication, which allows anybody to make entertainment with affordable computer hardware, cheap and powerful software (from desktop publishing applications to sophisticated multimedia editing tools), and cheap or free Internet access.

Via the Internet, fan-fiction writers can easily and cheaply distribute their works to an eager marketplace, and that marketplace's ability to provide feedback provides those authors with inspiration and validation. The Internet gives DIY computer programmers an easy and cheap way to share their works with almost no overhead and seemingly limitless potential for distribution. The advances of digital movie-making dramatically reduces the costs of making feature films, giving indie filmmakers more time to focus on their work and less pressure to deal with nefarious "money people." And, as with Rocket Girl, the Internet makes it much easier for tiny record labels to work with obscure musicians, and for both to reach the niche audiences of esoteric styles of music.

In his memoir, Alex Cox alludes to the many ways in which the indie/DIY culture, from entertainment to political activity, is reviving not only the anti-establishment ideals of the Enlightenment, but also the revolutionary attitudes of that era:

> Today, an independent filmmaker is a revolutionary fighter, in a prolonged popular war. This is the same war that Free Software and GNU/Linux activists fight against Microsoft; that the Slow Food movement fights against McDonald's; that independent musicians fight against the RIAA ... and the Apple Music Store; that Fairtrade activists fight against WalMart and the WTO; that the Zapatistas fight against patriarchal systems of control in Mexico. There are no spoils to be had on this battlefield, and no prospect of a quick and easy victory. Yet, buoyed by belief, and by the lack of a sustainable or sane alternative, the guerrilla soldiers on.[59]

Cox's observation is not purely optimistic, as he also sees how the power structures replaced by the revolutions of the Enlightenment were replaced by new and more complicated power structures: huge corporations "and the politicians, academics and media who work for them."[60] That perhaps reflects the most enduring and difficult aspect of Enlightenment ethics, one that is faced by those who operate on the fringes of the mainstream: that a perennial principle of a free and independent society is to not only work against the power structures that be, but also to forever be on guard against the power structures to come.

NOTES

1. Kate Coyer, Tony Dowmunt and Alan Fountain, *The Alternative Media Handbook* (New York: Routledge, 2007), 1.

2. *Ibid.*, 1.

3. Amy Spencer, *DIY: The Rise of Lo-Fi Culture* (London: Marion Boyars, 2008), 11.

4. The idea that DIY culture is "growing" is based on the increasing popularity of low-budget, individualistic media distributed via the Internet: original videos on YouTube, shareware or freeware computer games, self-published works of fiction, self-released music files from bands, etc.

5. Stuart Hall, "Deconstructing 'The Popular,'" in Stephen Duncombe, ed., *Cultural Resistance Reader* (New York: Verso, 2002), 187.

6. *Ibid.*

7. *Ibid.*, 190.

8. Specifically, the 1970s song "Everybody's Happy Nowadays" by the punk band The Buzzcocks was featured in recent years in TV ads for the AARP, and the late-'70s song "Lust for Life" by the "Godfather of Punk," Iggy Pop, has been featured prominently in a Royal Caribbean Cruises commercial, mainstream TV shows, including *The Drew Carey Show*, and mainstream films, including *Desperately Seeking Susan*.

9. E-mail message to author, August 10, 2008.

10. Roger Ebert, "Irreversible," *Chicago Sun-Times* (March 14, 2003), http://rogerebert.suntimes.com/apps/pbcs.dll/article?AID=/20030314/REVIEWS/303140303/1023 (accessed July 2, 2008).

11. "Awards for 'Irreversible,'" Internet Movie Database, http://www.imdb.com/title/tt0290673/awards (accessed January 5, 2009).

12. Peter Travers, "Irreversible," *Rolling Stone* (February 20, 2003) http://www.rolling stone.com/reviews/movie/5949425/review/5949426/irreversible (accessed January 5, 2009).

13. These three approaches to interpreting media messages are outlined in Stuart Hall, "Encoding/Decoding," in Centre for Contemporary Cultural Studies, ed., *Culture, Media, Language: Working Papers in Cultural Studies, 1972–79* (London: Hutchinson, [1973] 1980), 128–38.

14. Robert Wolker, "Enlightenment, Continental," in *Encyclopedia of Philosophy*, ed. Edward Craig (London: Routledge, 1998), http://www.rep.routledge.com/article/DB025 (accessed July 31, 2008).

15. Robert V. Bellamy, "Film Industry," in *Encyclopedia of Communication and Information*, Vol. 1., ed. Jorge Reina Schement (New York: Macmillan Reference USA, 2002), 320–325.

16. Karl Hagstrom Miller, "Music Industry," *Dictionary of American History*, ed. Stanley I. Kutler. Vol. 5. [3rd ed.] (New York: Charles Scribner's Sons, 2003), 502–503.

17. "Book Publishing," in *Encyclopedia of Global Industries*, eds. Wendy H. Mason and Diane M. Sawinski, 4th ed. (Detroit: Gale, 2007), http://vlex.com/vid/book-publishing-5205 7955 (accessed May 27, 2009).

18. Entertainment Software Association, "Sales and Genre Data," http://www.theesa.com/facts/salesandgenre.asp (accessed August 16, 2008). Due to the control those console-makers have over their software, nearly all of the independent game-making is for home computers, and this author could find no reliable data on what portion of computer-game sales could be attributed to indie developers.

19. The number of DIY artists may be literally uncountable, given the autonomous and esoteric nature of their work and the ephemeral qualities of many DIY ventures.

20. Henry Jenkins, *Textual Poachers* (New York: Routledge, 1992).

21. The fan-tiction phenomenon is covered in Karen Hellekson and Kristina Busse, *Fan Fiction and Fan Communities in the Age of the Internet* (Jefferson, NC: McFarland, 2006).

22. E-mail message to author, August 12, 2008.

23. E-mail message to author, August 11, 2008.

24. E-mail message to author, August 11, 2008.

25. E-mail message to author, August 12, 2008.

26. E-mail message to author, August 12, 2008.

27. E-mail message to author, August 12, 2008.

28. E-mail message to author, August 12, 2008.

29. Søren Kierkegaard, "The Point of View of My Work as an Author," in *The Essential Kierkegaard*, ed. Howard V. and Edna H. Hong (Princeton, NJ: Princeton University Press, 2000).

30. Jeff Vogel, "Introduction to Shareware," Spiderweb Software Web site, http://www.spiderwebsoftware.com/shareware/intro.html (accessed July 31, 2008).

31. One reviewer wrote on www.macupdate.com, "Great game; graphics aren't super, but they're better than most other RPGs of this type (Decent character pics anyone?). This game gets a 5 for depth and flexibility. Play the demo for hours and hours, you'll see what I mean." Comment posted August 18, 2006 to http://www.macupdate.com/reviews.php?id =8189 (accessed July 31, 2008).

32. Vogel, "Introduction to Shareware."

33. E-mail message to author, August 12, 2008.

34. E-mail message to author, August 12, 2008.

35. E-mail message to author, August 14, 2008.

36. E-mail message to author, September 12, 2008.

37. Harold L. Vogel, *Entertainment Industry Economics: A Guide for Financial Analysis.* (Cambridge: Cambridge University Press, 2007), 53.

38. E-mail message to author, August 11, 2008.

39. E-mail message to author, August 11, 2008.

40. James Patrick Kelley ("You and Your Characters," in *Writing Science Fiction and Fantasy*, ed. Gardner Dozois (New York: St. Martin's, 1991), http://www.sfwa.org/writing/character.htm (accessed August 30, 2008) offers this useful definition of the term "unsympathetic character": "One whose motivations are suspect and whose feelings make us uncomfortable. The boundary between sympathetic and unsympathetic characterization is necessarily ill-defined."

41. Alex Cox, *X Films: True Confessions of a Radical Filmmaker* (Berkeley: Soft Skull, 2008), 36.

42. The illegality of the U.S. Iran-Contra affair is not in contention according to the "Tower Commission" report stemming from an official investigation of the matter. See: "The Iran-Contra Affair 20 Years On," The National Security Archive at George Washington University, http://www.gwu.edu/~nsarchiv/NSAEBB/NSAEBB210/index.htm (accessed August 20, 2008).

43. Cox, *X Films*, 140.

44. *Ibid.*, 72.

45. *Ibid.* 75–76.

46. Steven Paul Davies, *Alex Cox: Film Anarchist* (Somerset, England: Butler and Tanner, 2000), 104.

47. E-mail message to author, August 11, 2008.

48. "Box Office/business for Searchers 2.0," Internet Movie Database, accessed 25 August 2008 from http://www.imdb.com/title/tt0943982/business.

49. E-mail message to author, August 11, 2008.

50. "Beatles Settle EMI Royalties Row," BBC News online, April 12, 2007, http://news.bbc.co.uk/2/hi/entertainment/6548035.stm (accessed January 5, 2009).

51. E-mail message to author, September 12, 2008.

52. Assigning genre labels to some of the musicians named in this section would be an

effort in futility. Although all of them operate loosely under the genre of "psychedelic music," the musical styles range from breezy and spare acoustic instrumentals to distortion-drenched walls of sound intermixed with esoteric lyrics.

53. Keith Cameron, "About Rocketgirl," http://www.rocketgirl.co.uk/store/html_file/aboutrg.php (accessed August 28, 2008).
54. E-mail message to author, August 26, 2008.
55. E-mail message to author, August 26, 2008.
56. E-mail message to author, August 26, 2008.
57. E-mail message to author, August 26, 2008.
58. E-mail message to author, August 26, 2008.
59. Cox, *X Films*, 2.
60. *Ibid.*, 3.

WORKS CITED

BBC News online. "Beatles Settle EMI Royalties Row." April 12, 2007, http://news.bbc.co.uk/2/hi/entertainment/6548035.stm.

Bellamy, Robert V. "Film Industry." In Schement, Jorge Reina, *Encyclopedia of Communication and Information*, Vol. 1. New York: Macmillan Reference USA, 2002.

Cameron, Keith. "About Rocketgirl." http://www.rocketgirl.co.uk/store/html_file/about rg.php.

Cox, Alex. *X Films: True Confessions of a Radical Filmmaker*. Berkeley: Soft Skull, 2008.

Coyer, Kate, Tony Dowmunt, and Alan Fountain. *The Alternative Media Handbook* New York: Routledge, 2007.

Davies, Steven Paul. *Alex Cox: Film Anarchist*. Somerset, England: Butler and Tanner, 2000.

Ebert, Roger. "Irreversible." *Chicago Sun-Times*. March 14, 2003. http://rogerebert.suntimes.com/apps/pbcs.dll/article?AID=/20030314/REVIEWS/303140303/1023.

Entertainment Software Association, "Sales and Genre Data." http://www.theesa.com/facts/salesandgenre.asp.

Hall, Stuart. "Deconstructing 'The Popular.'" In Stephen Duncombe, ed. *Cultural Resistance Reader*. New York: Verso, 2002.

_____. "Encoding/Decoding." In Centre for Contemporary Cultural Studies, ed., *Culture, Media, Language: Working Papers in Cultural Studies, 1972–79* London: Hutchinson, [1973] 1980.

Hellekson, Karen, and Kristina Busse. *Fan Fiction and Fan Communities in the Age of the Internet*. Jefferson, N.C.: McFarland, 2006.

Internet Movie Database. "Awards for 'Irreversible.'" http://www.imdb.com/title/tt0290673/awards.

Jenkins, Henry. *Textual Poachers*. New York: Routledge, 1992.

Kelley, James Patrick. "You and Your Characters." In *Writing Science Fiction and Fantasy*, Gardner Dozois, ed. New York: St. Martin's, 1991.

Kierkegaard, Søren. "The Point of View of My Work as an Author." In *The Essential Kierkegaard*. Howard V. Honged and Edna H. Honged, eds. Princeton, NJ: Princeton University Press, 2000.

Mason, Wendy H., and Diane M. Sawinski. "Book Publishing." In *Encyclopedia of Global Industries*, 4th ed. Detroit: Gale, 2007. http://vlex.com/vid/book-publishing-52057955.

Miller, Karl Hagstrom. "Music Industry." In Stanley I. Kutler, ed., *Dictionary of American History*, Vol. 5. [3rd ed.] New York: Charles Scribner's Sons, 2003.

The National Security Archive at George Washington University. "The Iran-Contra Affair 20 Years On." http://www.gwu.edu/~nsarchiv/NSAEBB/NSAEBB210/index.htm.

Spencer, Amy. *DIY: The Rise of Lo-Fi Culture*. London: Marion Boyars, 2008.

Travers, Peter. "Irreversible." *Rolling Stone*. February 20, 2003. http://www.rollingstone.com/reviews/movie/5949425/review/5949426/irreversible.

Vogel, Harold L. *Entertainment Industry Economics: A Guide for Financial Analysis.* Cambridge: Cambridge University Press, 2007.

Vogel, Jeff. "Introduction to Shareware." Spiderweb Software Web site. http://www.spider websoftware.com/shareware/intro.html.

Wolker, Robert. "Enlightenment, Continental." In Edward Craig, ed. *Encyclopedia of Philosophy.* London: Routledge, 1998. http://www.rep.routledge.com/article/DB025.

Chapter 16

Fictionalized Torture:
Jack Bauer's War on Terrorism

K. Maja Krakowiak

Individuals around the world were shocked by reports of U.S. military officials abusing and torturing prisoners in the Abu Ghraib prison in Baghdad and the prisoner camp in Guantanamo Bay. What could have prompted interrogators and guards to use such tactics? How could they have been so seemingly proud of their handiwork, as suggested by their smiles and thumbs-up in numerous photographs depicting heinous prisoner abuse? These questions led to a more general debate about torture. Is it effective? Are there circumstances under which torture is an acceptable interrogation technique? What are the consequences of using torture?

The topic of torture was not limited to non-fiction during this time. In fact, depictions of torture in prime-time network television rose dramatically in the years preceding the Abu Ghraib reports, from 102 scenes of torture between 1996 and 2001 to 278 scenes in 2003.[1] The Fox Network's hit series, *24*, depicted torture scenes most frequently during this time.[2] As a *San Francisco Chronicle* reporter remarked about the show, "star Jack Bauer (Kiefer Sutherland) demonstrate[s] a ruthless penchant for torture and strategic murder."[3] Other news reports have suggested that "Bauer's means of gathering intel (grab terrorist's finger, snap, repeat) make *24* a weekly rationalization of the 'ticking time bomb' defense of torture."[4] Although fictional portrayals are not generally held up to the same ethical standards as non-fictional reports, the principles of utilitarianism — which are often used by characters on *24* to defend the use of torture — and the National Association of Broadcasters (NAB) Statement of Principles can both be used to assess the ethical ramifications of these portrayals.

Torture Defined

The topic of torture was in the forefront of the news after the Abu Ghraib prisoner abuse scandal and the release of Amnesty International's report on the human rights abuses in Guantanamo Bay. Initially, the public and media seemed outraged at photographs showing prisoners naked, chained, and hooded. Because such U.S.–inflicted atrocities have rarely been documented with photography and broadcast through the mainstream media, the public reaction was intense. Many were shocked that U.S. military officials sanctioned and participated in such degrading and inhumane treatment, especially because government officials had previously publicly denounced torture. Moreover, the international laws set forth by the Geneva Conventions prohibit the use of torture. Some of those defending torture suggested that these laws were not applicable to the United States, because Afghanistan was a failed state; as a result, individuals captured in Afghanistan could not be considered prisoners of war and would not have the same legal protections. Similar arguments were made about detainees at Guantanamo Bay. Some government officials also debated what specific acts (e.g., sleep deprivation, sensory overload, stress positions, etc.) could be defined as torture.

For the purpose of this chapter, the term "torture" will be defined by its dictionary definition: "something that causes agony or pain" or "the infliction of intense pain (as from burning, crushing, or wounding) to punish, coerce, or afford sadistic pleasure."[5] Although slight variations exist, the dictionary definition reflects the definitions by such organizations as the United Nations and Amnesty International. The United Nations states "the term 'torture' means any act by which severe pain or suffering, whether physical or mental, is intentionally inflicted on a person for such purposes as obtaining from him or a third person information or a confession."[6] Therefore, any act that causes severe suffering for the purposes of coercion will be considered "torture" for the purposes of this analysis.

The Ethics of Torture

Although most people believe torture is never acceptable, almost one-third of individuals worldwide support the use of torture in some circumstances.[7] Furthermore, some scholars have argued that torture can be ethically justified in some circumstances. In fact, philosopher Fritz Allhoff argues that all dominant moral theories, except for Kantianism, justify the use of torture.[8] Utilitarianism, in particular, is often used to defend the use of torture. This ethical framework is summed up with the phrase, "the greatest good for the greatest number," suggesting that ethical actions are those that produce the most positive outcomes for the most people. However, the rule of utility can be applied in different ways. Act utilitarianism suggests that the consequence of every action should be analyzed, and the action that produces the most happiness for the most individuals should be taken, whereas rule utilitarianism suggests that the right action is the one that complies with a *rule* that generally produces the most happiness.

Louis Pojman argues that aspects of both act and rule utilitarianism are present in the work of the most prominent utilitarian theorist, John Stuart Mill.[9] Nevertheless, Allhoff asserts that rule utilitarianism resembles deontology and is therefore not a "true" utilitarianism. He proposes that "true" utilitarianism (i.e., act utilitarianism) supports the use of torture if "the use of torture aims at acquisition of information, the captive is reasonably thought to have the relevant information, the information corresponds to a significant and imminent threat, and the information could likely lead to the prevention of the threat."[10] These conditions rely on a "reasonable expectation" that torturing a suspect would prevent an attack, rather than on certainty of such an outcome.

According to rule utilitarianism and deontology, there is a moral presumption against torture. From these perspectives, torture is one of the worst moral wrongs because it degrades and dehumanizes human beings, uses them as a means to an end, violates human rights, and destroys free will. Michael Davis argues that the use of torture is unethical because people are shocked by images of torture: "If morality requires us to treat each person as a person (and that, it seems to me, is relatively uncontroversial), then we do something (at least prima facie) morally wrong if we inflict on a person (against her will and without benefit to her) treatment we find shocking."[11] In addition, torture can have negative consequences for the torturer in that s/he can suffer emotional distress and regret. As a result, most individuals agree that torture is morally wrong; however, they disagree about whether its use can ever be justified.

Although most individuals agree that the use of torture is rarely, if ever, justifiable, there is less agreement about how torture should be portrayed in fictional content. According to utilitarianism, it is important to assess the probable outcomes of actions or behaviors when determining their ethicality. Therefore, when assessing the ethicality of torture scenes in entertainment, it is necessary to examine both the negative and positive consequences of such media depictions. Individuals may choose to watch certain programming because they enjoy doing so. Some media researchers suggest that individuals seek out mediated content to fulfill certain needs or desires, such as diversion, surveillance/information gathering, companionship, etc.[12] Individuals thus benefit from viewing certain content. After all, most individuals would not spend their time watching a show such as *24* if doing so weren't pleasurable on some level.

However, fictional content may also have other effects. Louis Althusser argued that the media are part of an "Ideological State Apparatus" that ultimately supports the ideology of the ruling class.[13] Likewise, Stuart Hall states, "The media's main sphere of operations is the production and transformation of ideologies."[14] The media accomplish this by articulating or connecting certain ideas to other ones, ordering them according to importance, and omitting divergent viewpoints. They thereby shape perceptions of what is acceptable and not acceptable in society. In addition, Hall argues that certain meanings may be determined from media texts and that these meanings often reflect class interests. It is thus possible that mediated depictions support the interests of those in power by normalizing certain behaviors while discrediting others.

According to cultivation theory, television viewers make assumptions about the world based on what they see on television. Because many television shows focus on law enforcement (e.g., CSI, Law & Order, Criminal Minds, etc.) and depict many scenes of violence, individuals who watch a lot of television are more likely to develop a "mean world syndrome" in that they perceive the world to be mean and dangerous.[15] Mary Beth Oliver and G. Blake Armstrong found that people get most of their information about law enforcement from television rather than from real-life experience.[16] Furthermore, television portrayals of law enforcement and crime often suggest appropriate responses to crime and social problems.[17] They suggest what should be done, which is problematic because some TV programs show law enforcement officials doing ethically questionable or illegal activities. This is particularly troubling because law enforcement officials hold positions of power and authority, and, as the infamous Milgram experiments showed, individuals often obey authority figures even when they are directed to do things against their own conscience.[18] Therefore, depictions that justify the use of unethical tactics by authority figures may be particularly effective at legitimizing these types of actions. In short, mediated portrayals of law enforcement have potential ideological consequences for society, in addition to possible psychological effects on individuals.

Some studies indicate that people may become desensitized to certain mediated content, especially violent acts, after repeated exposure.[19] Viewing certain acts for the first time may result in greater physical and psychological arousal, but these reactions may diminish with each subsequent viewing and can lead to the acceptance of such actions as natural or normal. Television shows may thus "provide models for identification, confer status on people and behavior, spell out norms, define new situations, provide stereotypes, set frameworks of anticipation and indicate levels of acceptability, tolerance and approval."[20] Depictions of violence may thus lead to serious social consequences, as certain actions can become legitimized for audience members.

As a result of these concerns, the NAB addressed in 1990 the issue of violence in its Statement of Principles:

> Violence, physical or psychological, should only be portrayed in a responsible manner and should not be used exploitatively. Where consistent with the creative intent, programs involving violence should present the consequences of violence to its victims and perpetrators. Presentation of the details of violence should avoid the excessive, the gratuitous and the instructional. The use of violence for its own sake and the detailed dwelling upon brutality or physical agony, by sight or by sound, should be avoided.[21]

For portrayals of violence to be ethical, according to this statement, they must show realistic consequences of violence and avoid excessively graphic or cruel depictions. In addition, according to utilitarian principles, the consequences of the portrayals should result in more positive than negative outcomes for the most individuals, including viewers, media producers, interrogators, criminal suspects, and others. One potential benefit of portraying torture realistically is that audience members may gain a better understanding of torture. Inaccurate portrayals, however, may lead to a misinformed public. Therefore, the accuracy of these portrayals will be an essential factor when considering their harms and benefits to all affected.

As previously mentioned, depictions of torture on prime-time television have increased dramatically in the last ten years. According to a content analysis by the Parents Television Council, there were no scenes of torture on prime-time network television in 1996 and 1997.[22] During the next few years, the number of torture scenes increased; between 2002 and 2005, 624 torture scenes were broadcast. Such shows as *Law & Order, Alias,* and *Lost* all depicted scenes of torture during this time, but none accounted for more torture scenes than *24.*[23]

Legitimizing Torture in the 24 Series

Drama series often depict situations that seem relevant to viewers, so it is no surprise that themes of terrorism and torture permeate a series such as *24.* The show first aired in November 2001 and began its seventh season in January 2009. The premise and main attraction of the show is that it is presented in real time. In other words, one minute on the show is equivalent to one minute of real time, and each episode takes place during one hour. One season consists of one day (24 hours) in the lives of the characters. As Celia Wren points out, "the program's 'real time' conceit enhances a virtual-reality experience,"[24] a factor that can potentially exacerbate the societal effects of its depictions.

The show revolves around Jack Bauer, played by Kiefer Sutherland. Jack, until the 2009 season, was a counterterrorist agent working for the Counter-Terrorist Unit (CTU) of Los Angeles. During the course of the day/season, Jack must save the world from imminent disaster caused by nuclear bombs, biological warfare, terrorist attacks on nuclear power plants, and so forth. He often works outside the law, disobeying orders from his superiors. But because he always comes out victorious, these unlawful acts appear right and justified.

The show has been successful since its premiere and has risen in popularity over the last eight years. The sixth season premiere was watched by an average of 15.7 million viewers.[25] The show also has received critical acclaim. It has won 17 Prime-time Emmy awards, including one for outstanding drama series and one for outstanding lead actor (Sutherland) in a drama series in 2006.[26] In addition, the show has received 12 Golden Globe nominations, winning twice — once for best television series drama in 2004 and once for best performance by an actor in a television series drama in 2002.[27]

Misrepresenting Torture

Due in large part to its subject matter and time constraints, interrogation techniques, including torture, have prevailed to varying degrees throughout the show's run. In the first season, Jack must save a presidential candidate and his own family from death. By the fourth season, he must save the country from nuclear power plant meltdowns, the president from a stealth missile, and the world from a nuclear bomb. It is easier for the series to justify the use of torture from a utilitarian perspective when millions of lives are at stake than when two family members are in danger, so the use of torture has steadily increased throughout the series' history. In fact, both the terrorists and government agents on the show rely on torture to get information quickly (terrorists torture Jack and other CTU agents on several occasions). However, the use of torture by government agents is particularly troubling because these acts are often portrayed as being effective, good, and necessary, whereas the torture used by terrorists is represented as being evil and damaging. For example, during the sixth season, one of the CTU agents is captured and tortured by terrorists until he helps them program a suitcase bomb. Thus when terrorists use torture on the show it is used to facilitate killing others, not save them. By distinguishing between the torture used by terrorists and that used by Jack and other CTU agents, 24 makes an act utilitarian argument that torture can be either morally reprehensible or morally acceptable depending on who is doing the torturing and why. However, according to rule utilitarianism or deontological ethics, torture is presumed to be morally wrong, regardless of who is doing the torturing or why they are doing it.

The torture employed by the government, namely Jack and other CTU agents, often occurs in a special interrogation room at the CTU complex. The room has concrete floors, walls, and ceilings, and one side of the room has a one-way mirror, which makes it possible for other CTU agents to watch, something they often do. Scenes of torture are generally disturbing. Showing the audience that it is okay for the agents to watch the torture sends the message that it is likewise okay for viewers to do so. In this way, viewers are invited to be complicit in the torture, which, in a symbolic sense, leads to sanctioning the torture through the act of viewing.

The typical scenario on *24* is that a suspect who may have vital information about some upcoming terrorist plot is captured and must quickly be forced to reveal the information to stop the attack. In most instances, Jack must do the interrogation. After the suspect refuses to answer a couple of questions, Jack resorts to torture, which may include breaking suspects' fingers, staging an execution of the suspect's family, and/or punching the face or stomach of the suspect. At other times, another special agent is called upon to exact a more precise form of torture, usually with the use of syringes and other devices, which he carries in a black case.

As Dónal P. O'Mathúna points out, the portrayals of torture on *24* exemplify the "ticking time bomb" defense of torture, which states that if a person is known to have information that could prevent the deaths or sufferings of many people, it would be appropriate to resort to torture to get the necessary information from that person.[28] This defense is based on act utilitarian principles and is often used by the protagonists on *24* to justify the use of torture. For example, in trying to persuade a supervisor that torture is necessary, one of the CTU agents says, "We don't have the luxury of time. Intel indicates that an attack is imminent — within an hour. Tens, maybe hundreds of thousands of Americans are at risk."[29] Therefore, *24* makes the arguments for using torture quite explicit, and these types of scenarios are presented frequently on the show. This may give viewers the impression that such situations are common when, in reality, interrogators are rarely certain that a specific individual has information that will prevent an imminent disaster. Although certainty is not a requirement for an act utilitarian analysis, interrogators must be reasonable in thinking that a suspect has information that would prevent many deaths to ethically resort to torture. Depicting situations of absolute certainty obsures the difficult struggle involved in arriving at such an expectation.

Torture is also presented as effective most of the time, especially when Jack Bauer is doing the torturing. The suspects usually give up information very quickly once Jack starts torturing them, and most often, Jack gets useful information that helps him save lives. For example, in a season six episode, Jack gets information about the location of a terrorist after cutting off a Russian consul's finger with a cigar cutter and threatening to shoot him.[30] These portrayals suggest that interrogators can be at least reasonably certain that torturing a suspect will produce reliable information, something that is necessary to justify torture using an act utilitarian framework. However, these portrayals misrepresent the effectiveness of torture because tortured suspects do not often provide reliable information to the ones who are torturing them.[31] Therefore, these portrayals give audience members an inaccurate view of the effectiveness of torture techniques when used on suspected terrorists.

Mistakes Without Consequences

The series has depicted several scenes of innocent individuals being tortured by Jack and other CTU agents. This shows a negative consequence of torture — that innocent individuals are sometimes mistakenly tortured. However, the torture techniques used on these individuals are nonetheless defended, and the consequences, ignored. For example, a CTU agent herself is tortured by other CTU agents, even though the audience is aware of her innocence throughout the interrogation. Despite her pleas, the torture begins with the use of an electric Tazer and continues for at least an hour (although only a few minutes are actually shown). The interrogation does not result in any helpful information, and the other CTU agents eventually recognize the mistake, but those who administered the torture are never penalized or even reprimanded. In explaining her behavior to the innocent suspect, the CTU agent who ordered the torture proclaims she "had no choice. You were identified as a threat to security, and I acted accordingly."[32] Torture is thus presented as a mandated part of the interrogator's job, something even the suspect understands when she agrees to go back to work for the agent who tortured her. This sends a dangerous message about what is acceptable. First, there seem to be no long-term effects, not even resentment on the part of the innocent suspect, even though the initial torture scene is horrendous— the suspect yells and her body shakes violently. Second, the guilt or innocence of the person being tortured is seemingly unimportant; what is important is following protocol, even if that means torturing an innocent person. Following protocol can be compatible with a rule utilitarian framework as long as that protocol, when generally followed, results in the greatest happiness for the most individuals. However, act utilitarianism cannot justify torturing innocent individuals because this action does not result in any positive outcomes.

On 24, the torture of innocent people is not limited to those who work for the government, as the son of the secretary of defense learns. The son is first subjected to a polygraph test, which he passes. The CTU agents clear him of any knowing involvement with the crime they are investigating. Nevertheless, because one of the results is inconclusive (i.e., he was not clearly lying or telling the truth), torture is the next logical step in the interrogation process. The torture specialist is called in to retrieve any information the son may be hiding, but one of the CTU agents has a change of heart and instead orders only "non-invasive" psychological torture known as "sensory disorientation." This interrogation once again proves to be fruitless, yet there seem to be no repercussions for the agents who ordered and performed the torture. On the contrary, when the defense secretary finds out about the torture, he orders another line of torture: "I am authorizing you to do whatever you feel is necessary to get this information out of my son. I love you, son. But I have a duty to my country."[33]

Therefore, torture, even of your own child, is presented as a duty, not a choice, and as something patriotic, rather than treasonous, which suggests a utilitarian framework. After two and a half hours of torture, the defense secretary apparently becomes convinced of his son's innocence and apologizes to his son by saying, "I'm sorry this had to happen ... but we had to make sure that you weren't withholding anything from us."[34] The father's apparent lack of intense remorse further legitimizes the use of torture. No alternative to torture is ever mentioned, and no character who works for CTU seems to have any difficulty ordering someone to torture a suspect, watching the suspect get tortured, or torturing the suspect himself. In the world of *24*, torture is a normal and frequent procedure. Furthermore, the criterion for using torture is not evidence of guilt, but a lack of clear evidence of innocence. Although no ethical framework can justify knowingly torturing innocent individuals, an act utilitarian framework may justify torturing someone if torture is reasonably likely to result in the prevention of an imminent attack that could harm many. However, the characters on *24* seem to routinely overestimate the chances that torture will have such a result, casually accepting the torture of innocent suspects as collateral damage in their race against the ticking bomb. Therefore, even an act utilitarian framework could not justify all of the acts of torture depicted on *24*.

Negative consequences of torture have been depicted on the show, but this mostly occurs when terrorists or antagonists are performing the torture. For example, Jack and his girlfriend are shown to be both emotionally and physically scarred after being tortured by the Chinese government. Likewise, a CTU agent who is tortured by terrorists is seen struggling with the fact that he revealed information to his captors. These depictions of the negative ramifications of torture give viewers a more realistic representation of torture and follow the NAB's guidelines about portraying the consequences of violence. However, these portrayals would be more ethically sound if the long-term consequences of torture were presented regardless of who was being tortured.

The effects of torture on torturers are likewise rarely portrayed. As previously mentioned, the interrogators who commit torture usually do not feel regret even when they have tortured innocent individuals. However, torture is portrayed as somewhat of a moral burden for Jack. He is conflicted at times, but refuses to let anything stop him from doing what must be done. He has made several attempts to leave the life of a CTU agent behind because of the toll it takes on him and his family, but always returns when he is needed. He is thus portrayed as a good man, who has to suffer being the bad guy for the good of the rest of society.

During the seventh season, *24* tried to address some of the criticisms levied against its portrayal of torture. In fact, at the beginning of the season, Jack Bauer is being questioned in a Senate hearing about his illegal use of torture, and the CTU has been disbanded for its use of questionable tactics. At first, it appears Jack may finally have to answer for his previous actions. However, an FBI agent who needs Jack's help in stopping an imminent terrorist attack interrupts the hearing. During the course of this season, Jack once again uses torture and justifies doing so with a crude act utilitarian argument. But, unlike in previous seasons, several main characters rebuke Jack's use of torture and provide strong arguments against the use of torture. Nevertheless, Jack continues to use torture and even convinces a skeptical FBI agent that his tactics are necessary, so much so that she herself tortures one suspect to retrieve information and another to avenge the murder of her boss. In the season finale, Jack admits to the agent that he is uncomfortable with breaking the law, but maintains that he has no regrets.

Dismissing Critics of Torture

Before the seventh season, arguments against the use of torture were routinely dismissed and mocked on *24*. For example, during the fourth season, the torture of one suspect is delayed because a lawyer representing an organization named Amnesty Global has a court order that states the lawyer must be present during the interrogation. As the name suggests, the organization is obviously meant to represent Amnesty International. The judge who signed the court order contends that he wants to protect the suspect's rights because he is a U.S. citizen with no prior criminal record. However, the CTU agents see it differently and mock the lawyer.

The discrediting of social and political protesters by the media is not new and has been studied extensively. Discrediting protesters limits the discussion of alternative viewpoints and may undermine the voice of minorities. Moreover, without an open discussion, it is possible to ignore counterarguments. By analyzing anti–Vietnam war movement coverage, Todd Gitlin identified several mechanisms by which the media showcase protesters' deviance.[35] First, the media trivialize protesters by making deprecating comments about their language, appearance, and goals. Second, the media focus on the most ideologically radical elements of the movement. Third, they ignore the movement's accomplishments. Although the framing of social pro-testers has mostly been studied in regards to news media, all of the above mechanisms described by Gitlin were present in *24*'s portrayal of the human rights advocate, his organization, and his cause.

The lawyer was trivialized by being called "slimy" and "prissy," and accused of preventing the CTU agents from "doing their jobs."[36] The human rights organization he represented was further discredited by the fact that the terrorist in charge of orchestrating several attacks against the United States was the one who contacted the organization and informed them that the sus-pect was being held at CTU headquarters. It is thus implied that the organ-ization is not only a nuisance, but also a supporter of terrorist activities because of its interference with the interrogation process. Lastly, no accom-plishments or positive aspects of the organization or its representative are presented, and in the end, the lawyer is completely ineffective at preventing Jack from torturing his client.

Since Jack is the hero of the show, he must find a way to torture the sus-pect despite the court order if he is to save the country from attack. He thus attempts to convince the suspect's lawyer, stating that he doesn't "want to bypass the Constitution, but these are extraordinary circumstances."[37] This suggests that the Constitution can be bypassed whenever a government official thinks it is appropriate. There is no uncertainty about what Jack plans to do with the suspect. When talking to the president, Jack clearly asks for permis-sion to torture the suspect: "If we want to procure any information from this suspect, we're going to have to do it behind closed doors." When the presi-dent asks whether Jack means that he will torture the suspect, Jack replies, "I'm talking about doing what is necessary." Although torture is not some-thing to be flaunted, it is portrayed as being the only means by which gov-ernment agents can do their jobs and stop a terrorist attack. This, however, is not accurate since other tactics may be equally, if not more effective, at stop-ping terrorist attacks. Furthermore, if these other tactics result in less harm to the suspect, interrogator, or others, torture cannot be justified even with act utilitarianism. Because almost all criticism of torture is discredited, and no alternative to torture is discussed, the act utilitarian justification that is used to justify torture on the show is severely flawed.

In the show, the president does not authorize the torture because he does not want to deal with the ramifications of breaking a court order, so Jack must find another means by which to be alone with the suspect. He decides to release the suspect from custody. Then, when the suspect's lawyer leaves, Jack attacks him, puts him in a car, and proceeds to break his fingers one at a time. When that doesn't work, Jack finally pulls out a knife and threatens to slit the suspect's throat. Jack's actions are portrayed as heroic; he cleverly bypasses the hurdles set forth by a human rights organization, a judge, and the president in order to get the job done. According to the act utilitarian arguments presented in *24*, in a world filled with terrorism, there is no time to ponder a suspect's rights, as national security always trumps personal rights.

Overall, on *24*, torture is misrepresented, and the justifications made for its use are flawed. Torture is presented as almost always effective, which is inaccurate. Furthermore, although the characters on the show often use act utilitarian arguments to justify their use of torture, these arguments are invalid because the interrogators on the show often lack even reasonable certainty about suspects' guilt. In addition, the consequences of torture are not portrayed and are thus not used to weigh the overall goodness or badness of the outcomes. Lastly, arguments against torture are discredited, and no alternatives to torture are explored, which makes it impossible to determine whether torture is, in fact, an ethically acceptable choice according to act utilitarianism. Therefore, *24* presents torture as an ethical option when it should not.

Does 24 Do More Harm Than Good?

Some people fear the real-world consequences of these portrayals. Dennis Broe concluded that although the first eight episodes of the show were produced before September 11, 2001, subsequent episodes have specifically supported the war on terrorism. "The conquest of time and space and the fetishization of entertainment, alternating with the embrace of global war as a continuation of the dominance of the global market, are written into the form and content of *24*."[38] Based on interviews with U.S. military interrogators, some human rights organizations argue that the depictions of torture on television are "having an undeniable impact on how interrogations are conducted in the field. U.S. soldiers are imitating the techniques they have seen on television — because they think such tactics work."[39] Presidential candidate Tom Tancredo seemed to believe in the effectiveness of the techniques he saw on *24* when he said during a Republican debate, "You say that nuclear devices have gone off in the United States, more are planned, and we're wondering about whether waterboarding would be a bad thing to do? I'm looking for Jack Bauer at that time!"[40] This indicates that the series may desensitize viewers to torture as a political and moral issue. By presenting torture as a given, *24* clears the way for it to be applied in the real world without great public concern or protest.

It is also worth noting that torture is addressed on the official Fox website for *24*. In his description of the *24* website, Bo Kampmann Walther points out that some of the pages on the site "constitute a more broadened knowledge resource for the cultural and political setting of *24*, which means that a number of the sub-sites exist in the grey area stuck between factual and fictional information."[41] Some of the content on the website is clearly fictional and advances the narrative of the television show. However, other parts of the site present real information that enhances the show's believability and applicability to current real-world situations. The "research files" section of the site contains definitions and descriptions of words, items, techniques, and so forth that appeared in each episode of the show. For example, the fourth season's "research files" contain information about the secretary of defense, hostage videos, traffic cameras, nitroglycerin, terrorist watchlists, fingerprint encryption, terrorist cells, stealth bombers, implanted tracking devices, and more. For the episode in which sensory deprivation was used on the son of the secretary of defense, the research files contained the following statement:

> Sensory deprivation and disorientation has been used in alternative medicine, for torture or punishment, and in psychological experimentation.... Although there is evidence of sensory deprivation in use in the prisons of Abu Ghraib — particularly the hoodings— it is still under debate whether these techniques constitute "severe pain or suffering" in violation of the article of the Geneva Convention on Prisoner torture.[42]

Although the truthfulness of that claim could be debated, the fact that this description is posted is telling in and of itself because it links the use of torture on the show to the prisoner abuse scandal. Furthermore, this statement legitimizes the use of sensory deprivation as an interrogation technique, both on the show and in real life, by questioning whether this technique should be defined as torture.

In 2006 the Heritage Foundation, a conservative research group, held a panel discussion entitled "*24* and America's Image in Fighting Terrorism: Fact, Fiction, or Does It Matter?" The guests included Rush Limbaugh and Michael Chertoff, the secretary of the U.S. Department of Homeland Security.[43] During his speech, Chertoff commented on the show's popularity and said the show reflects real life. "Typically ... the characters are presented with very difficult choices. Choices about whether to take drastic and even violent action against a threat and weighing that against the consequences of not taking the action and destruction that might otherwise ensue."[44]

Although *24* is a fictional program, it is taken seriously, even by those in positions of power in the government. In fact, the rhetoric used in the show to justify torture is similar to that used by the Bush administration to defend its use of certain interrogation methods. "Our nation recognizes that this new paradigm — ushered in not by us, but by terrorists— requires new thinking in the law of war."[45] This statement suggests that previous laws, such as those in the Constitution or the Geneva Convention, may hinder the war on terrorism and thus should be updated or changed. Furthermore, the Bush administration's use of interrogation manuals to blur traditional distinctions between regular interrogation and torture echoes *24*'s preoccupation with protocol. On *24*, an act that is considered to be part of protocol is automatically justified. Likewise, labeling an act as an interrogation technique, rather than torture, in a training manual gives that act legitimacy. Overall, the similarities between what occurs on *24* and what occurs in real life indicate that the show may legitimize, not only the use of torture in the future, but also the torture that has already been done.

Television writers and producers should be aware that the portrayals of torture could have significant consequences for the viewing public and strive to present torture in a more ethical way. Specifically, based on utilitarian principles, *24* and other shows would be more ethically sound if the benefits of their portrayals of torture outweighed the potential harms. This could be accomplished in several ways. First, torture should be represented more realistically. Television shows could portray the ineffectiveness of torture in most instances, as well as present alternatives to torture. Moreover, based on the NAB's own statement of principles, TV shows could show both the short- and long-term consequences of torture. Second, torture should be presented as an illegal act, and the perpetrators of torture should be punished. Third, though arguments for and against torture should be presented, the arguments should not misrepresent the ethicality of using torture. In other words, if an act utilitarian framework is suggested on the show, all aspects of that framework should be discussed, including reasonable certainty. If these changes were made, depictions of torture in entertainment content could result in a more informed public that would be more likely to question governmental policies that permit torture.

NOTES

1. Parents Television Council, "Scenes of Torture on Primetime Network Television 1995–2006," http://www.humanrightsfirst.org/us_law/etn/primetime/images/graph2.jpg, 1 (accessed August 6, 2008).

2. Martin Miller, "24" and "Lost" Get Symposium on Torture," *The Seattle Times*, February 14, 2007, http://seattletimes.nwsource.com/html/television/2003570697_tvtorture14.html, para. 7 (accessed August 6, 2008).

3. "'24' Meets 9 to 5," *The San Francisco Chronicle*, May 31, 2005, B6.

4. James Poniewozik, "The Evolution of Jack Bauer," *Time Magazine*, January 14, 2007, http://www.time.com/time/magazine/article/0,9171,1576853-1,00.html, para. 3 (accessed February 7, 2007).

5. Merriam-Webster Online (based on Merriam-Webster's Collegiate Dictionary, 10th ed.), http://www.m-w.com/ (accessed August 6, 2008).

6. United Nations Convention Against Torture and Other Cruel, Inhuman or Degrading Treatment or Punishment, http://www2.ohchr.org/english/law/declarationcat.htm, para. 1 (accessed February 7, 2007).

7. BBC News, "One-Third Support 'Some Torture,'" October 19, 2006, http://news.bbc.co.uk/2/hi/in_depth/6063386.stm, para. 1 (accessed August 6, 2008).

8. Fritz Allhoff, "A Defense of Torture: Separation of Cases, Ticking Time-Bombs, and Moral Justification," *International Journal of Applied Philosophy* 19 (2005): 243–264.

9. Louis P. Pojman, *Ethics: Discovering Right and Wrong* (Belmont, CA: Wadsworth, 1995), 115.

10. Fritz Allhoff, "Terrorism and Torture," *International Journal of Applied Philosophy* 17 (2003): 112.

11. Michael Davis, "The Moral Justifiability of Torture," *International Journal of Applied Philosophy*, 19 (2005): 168.

12. Elihu Katz, Jay J. Blumler, and Michael Gurevitch, "Utilization of Mass Communication by the Individual," in *The Uses of Mass Communications: Current Perspectives on Gratifications Research,* eds. Jay J. Blumler and Elihu Katz (Beverly Hills, CA: Sage, 1974), 19–32.

13. Louis Althusser, "Ideology and Ideological State Apparatuses" in *Lenin and Philosophy and other Essays,* trans. Ben Brewster (New York: Monthly Review, 1971), 127–186.

14. Stuart Hall, "The Whites of Their Eyes: Racist Ideologies and the Media," in *Gender, Race, and Class in Media: A Text-Reader,* eds. Gail Dines and Jean McMahon Humez (Thousand Oaks, CA: Sage, 2004), 89.

15. See Michael Morgan, James Shanahan, and Nancy Signorielli, "Growing Up with Television: Cultivation Processes" in *Media Effects: Advances in Theory and Research,* eds. Jennings Bryant and Mary Beth Oliver (Mahwah, NJ: Lawrence Erlbaum, 2008), 34–49.

16. Mary Beth Oliver and G. Blake Armstrong, "The Color of Crime: Perceptions of Caucasians' and African Americans' Involvement in Crime," in *Entertaining Crime: Television Reality Programs,* eds. Mark Fishman and Gray Cavender (New York: Aldine De Gruyter, 1998), 95–116.

17. Ray Surrette, *Media, Crime, and Criminal Justice: Images and Realities* (Pacific Grove, CA: Brooks/Cole, 1998), 155–193.

18. Stanley Milgram, "Behavioral Study of Obedience," *Journal of Abnormal Social Psychology* 67 (1963): 371–378.

19. Hans Eysenck and D. K. B. Nias, "Desensitization, Violence and the Media," in *Media Studies: A Reader,* eds. Paul Marris and Sue Thornham (New York: New York University Press, 2000), 425–432.

20. James D. Halloran, "On the Social Effects of Television," in *Media Studies: A Reader,* eds. Paul Marris and Sue Thornham (New York: New York University Press, 2000), 434.

21. The Board of Directors of the National Association of Broadcasters, "Statement of Principles," http://www.nab.org/AM/Template.cfm?Section=Search&template=/CM/HTML Display.cfm&ContentID=3377, para. 10–12 (accessed February 7, 2007).

22. Parents Television Council, "Scenes of Torture," 1.

23. Miller, "24" and "Lost" Get Symposium," para. 7.

24. Celia Wren, "The Longest Day," *Commonweal* 129 (2002): 21.

25. Colin Mahan, "Ratings: Jack Bauer vs. The Globes," TV.com, January 16, 2007, http://www.tv.com/24/show/3866/story/8132.html?tag=story_list;title;6, para. 1 (accessed March 29, 2009).

26. Academy of Television Arts and Sciences, "Advanced Primetime Awards Search," http://www.emmys.tv/awards/awardsearch.php (accessed August 6, 2008).

27. Hollywood Foreign Press Association. "Search," http://www.hfpa.org/browse/film/23452 (accessed August 6, 2008).

28. Dónal P. O'Mathúna, "The Ethics of Torture in '24': Shockingly Banal," in *"24" and Philosophy: The World According to Jack,* eds. Jennifer Hart Weed, Richard Davis and Ronald Weed (Malden, MA: Blackwell, 2008), 91–104.

29. *24.* Episode no. 111, first broadcast 27 March 2006 by Fox. Directed by Jon Cassar and written by David Ehrman.

30. *24.* Episode no. 132, first broadcast 5 March 2007 by Fox. Directed by Tim Lacofano and written by David Fury, Howard Gordon, Evan Katz.

31. Evan Thomas, "'24' Versus the Real World, *Newsweek*, September 20, 2006, http://www.newsweek.com/id/45788/page/1, para. 5 (accessed August 6, 2008).

32. *24.* Episode no. 82, first broadcast 21 February 2005 by Fox. Directed by Brad Turner and written by Stephen Kronish and Peter M. Lenkov.

33. *24.* Episode no. 78, first broadcast 31 January 2005 by Fox. Directed by Jon Cassar and written by Matt Michnovetz.

34. *24.* Episode no. 79, first broadcast 7 February 2005 by Fox. Directed by Ken Girotti and written by Joel Surnow and Michael Loceff.

35. Todd Gitlin, *The Whole World Is Watching: Mass Media and the Making and Unmaking of the New Left* (Berkeley: University of California Press, 1980), 27–28.

36. *24.* Episode no. 78, first broadcast 31 January 2005 by Fox. Directed by Jon Cassar and written by Matt Michnovetz.

37. *24.* Episode no. 78, first broadcast 31 January 2005 by Fox. Directed by Jon Cassar and written by Matt Michnovetz.

38. Dennis Broe, "Fox and its Friends: Global Commodification and the New Cold War," *Cinema Journal* 43 (2004):100.

39. Human Rights First, "The Impact: Soldiers Imitate What They See on TV," http://www.humanrightsfirst.org/us_law/etn/primetime/index.asp, para. 5 (accessed August 6, 2008).

40. Quoted in Joe Kovac's, "'Jack Bauer' Called on at Republican Debate,'" WorldNetDaily, May 16, 2007, http://www.worldnetdaily.com/news/article.asp?ARTICLE_ID=55722, para. 2 (accessed August 6, 2008).

41. Bo Kampmann Walther, "A Hard Day's Work: Reflections on the Interfacing of Transmedialisation and Speed in '24,'" in *Interface://Politics. The World Wide Web as Democratic Resource and Cultural Form*, ed. Klaus Bruhn Jensen (Copenhagen, Denmark: Sam fundslitteratur, 2005), 208.

42. Fox Broadcasting Company, "'24' Official Site: Research Files (Sensory Disorientation)," http://www.fox.com/24/research (accessed February 7, 2007).

43. Allesandra Stanley, "Suicide Bombers Strike, and America is in Turmoil. It's Just Another Day in the Life of Jack Bauer," *The New York Times*, January 12, 2007, http://query.nytimes.com/gst/fullpage.html?res=9503E3D61230F931A25752C0A9619C8B63&sec=&spon=&pagewanted=2, para. 2 (accessed February 7, 2007).

44. Quoted in Digby's "TV Politics" Hullabaloo, posted June 9, 2007, http://digbysblog.blogspot.com/2007/06/tv-politics-by-digby-so-even-though-we.html, para. 18 (accessed August 6, 2008).

45. Quoted in Mike Allen and Susan Schmidt's, "Memo on Interrogation is Disavowed," *The Washington Post*, June 23, 2004, A01.

WORKS CITED

Academy of Television Arts and Sciences. "Advanced Primetime Awards Search." http://www.emmys.tv/awards/awardsearch.php (accessed August 6, 2008).

Allen, Mike, and Susan Schmidt. "Memo on Interrogation Is Disavowed." *The Washington Post*, June 23, 2004, A01.

Allhoff, Fritz. "A Defense of Torture: Separation of Cases, Ticking Time-Bombs, and Moral Justification." *International Journal of Applied Philosophy* 19 (2005): 243–264.

_____. "Terrorism and Torture." *International Journal of Applied Philosophy* 17 (2003): 105–118.

Althusser, Louis. "Ideology and Ideological State Apparatuses." In *Lenin and Philosophy and Other Essays*, translated by Ben Brewster, 127–186. New York: Monthly Review, 1971.

BBC News. "One-Third Support 'Some Torture.'" October 19, 2006, http://news.bbc.co.uk/2/hi/in_depth/6063386.stm (accessed August 6, 2008).

Board of Directors of the National Association of Broadcasters. "Statement of Principles."

http://www.nab.org/AM/Template.cfm?Section=Search&template=/CM/HTMLDisplay.cfm&ContentID=3377 (accessed February 7, 2007).

Broe, Dennis. "Fox and its Friends: Global Commodification and the New Cold War." *Cinema Journal* 43 (2004): 97–102.

Davis, Michael. "The Moral Justifiability of Torture." *International Journal of Applied Philosophy* 19 (2005): 161–178.

Digby. "TV Politics." Hullabaloo, posted June 9, 2007, http://digbysblog.blogspot.com/2007/06/tv-politics-by-digby-so-even-though-we.html (accessed August 6, 2008).

Eysenck, Hans, and D.K.B. Nias, "Desensitization, Violence and the Media." In *Media Studies: A Reader,* edited by Paul Marris and Sue Thornham, 425–432. New York: New York University Press, 2000.

Fox Broadcasting Company. "'24' Official Site: Research Files (Sensory Disorientation)." http://www.fox.com/24/research (accessed February 7, 2007).

Gitlin, Todd. *The Whole World Is Watching: Mass Media and the Making and Unmaking of the New Left.* Berkeley: University of California Press, 1980.

Hall, Stuart. "The Whites of Their Eyes: Racist Ideologies and the Media." In *Gender, Race, and Class in Media: A Text-Reader,* edited by Gail Dines and Jean McMahon Humez, 89–93. Thousand Oaks, CA: Sage, 2004.

Halloran, James D. "On the Social Effects of Television." In *Media Studies: A Reader,* edited by Paul Marris and Sue Thornham, 433–437. New York: New York University Press, 2000.

Hollywood Foreign Press Association. "Search." http://www.hfpa.org/browse/film/23452 (accessed August 6, 2008).

Human Rights First. "The Impact: Soldiers Imitate What They See on TV." http://www.humanrightsfirst.org/us_law/etn/primetime/index.asp (accessed August 6, 2008).

Katz, Elihu, Jay J. Blumler, and Michael Gurevitch. "Utilization of Mass Communication by the Individual." In *The Uses of Mass Communications: Current Perspectives on Gratifications Research,* edited by Jay J. Blumler and Elihu Katz, 19–32. Beverly Hills, CA: Sage, 1974.

Kovac, Joe. "'Jack Bauer' Called on at Republican Debate.'" *WorldNetDaily,* May 16, 2007, http://www.worldnetdaily.com/news/article.asp?ARTICLE_ID=55722 (accessed August 6, 2008).

Mahan, Colin. "Ratings: Jack Bauer vs. The Globes." TV.com, January 16, 2007, http://www.tv.com/24/show/3866/story/8132.html?tag=story_list;title;6 (accessed March 29, 2009).

Milgram, Stanley. "Behavioral Study of Obedience." *Journal of Abnormal Social Psychology* 67 (1963): 371–378.

Miller, Martin. "'24' and 'Lost' Get Symposium on Torture." *The Seattle Times,* February 14, 2007, http://seattletimes.nwsource.com/html/television/2003570697_tvtorture14.html (accessed August 6, 2008).

Morgan, Michael, James Shanahan, and Nancy Signorielli. "Growing Up with Television: Cultivation Processes." In *Media Effects: Advances in Theory and Research,* edited by Jennings Bryant and Mary Beth Oliver, 34–49. Mahwah, NJ: Lawrence Erlbaum, 2008.

Oliver, Mary Beth, and G. Blake Armstrong. "The Color of Crime: Perceptions of Caucasians' and African Americans' Involvement in Crime." In *Entertaining Crime: Television Reality Programs,* edited by Mark Fishman and Gray Cavender, 95–116. New York: Aldine De Gruyter, 1998.

O'Mathúna, Dónal P. "The Ethics of Torture in '24': Shockingly Banal." In *"24" and Philosophy: The World According to Jack,* edited by Jennifer Hart Weed, Richard Davis, and Ronald Weed, 91–104. Malden, MA: Blackwell, 2008.

Parents Television Council. "Scenes of Torture on Primetime Network Television 1995–2006." http://www.humanrightsfirst.org/us_law/etn/primetime/images/graph2.jpg (accessed August 6, 2008).

Pojman, Louis P. *Ethics: Discovering Right and Wrong.* Belmont, CA: Wadsworth, 1995.

Poniewozik, James. "The Evolution of Jack Bauer." *Time Magazine,* January 14, 2007, http://www.time.com/time/magazine/article/0,9171,1576853-1,00.html (accessed February 7, 2007).

Stanley, Allesandra. "Suicide Bombers Strike, and America is in Turmoil. It's Just Another Day in the Life of Jack Bauer." *The New York Times*, January 12, 2007, http://query.ny times.com/gst/fullpage.html?res=9503E3D61230F931A25752C0A9619C8B63&sec=&spo n=&pagewanted=2 (accessed February 7, 2007).

Surrette, Ray. *Media, Crime, and Criminal Justice: Images and Realities*. Pacific Grove, CA: Brooks/Cole, 1998.

Thomas, Evan. "'24' Versus the Real World." *Newsweek*, September 20, 2006, http://www.news week.com/id/45788/page/1 (accessed August 6, 2008).

24. Episode no. 78, first broadcast 31 January 2005 by Fox. Directed by Jon Cassar and written by Matt Michnovetz.

24. Episode no. 79, first broadcast 7 February 2005 by Fox. Directed by Ken Girotti and written by Joel Surnow and Michael Loceff.

24. Episode no. 82, first broadcast 21 February 2005 by Fox. Directed by Brad Turner and written by Stephen Kronish and Peter M. Lenkov.

24. Episode no. 111, first broadcast 27 March 2006 by Fox. Directed by Jon Cassar and written by David Ehrman.

24. Episode no. 132, first broadcast 5 March 2007 by Fox. Directed by Tim Lacofano and written by David Fury, Howard Gordon, and Evan Katz.

"'24' Meets 9 to 5." *The San Francisco Chronicle*, May 31, 2005, B6.

United Nations. Convention Against Torture and Other Cruel, Inhuman or Degrading Treatment or Punishment. http://www2.ohchr.org/english/law/declarationcat.htm (accessed February 7, 2007).

Walther, Bo Kampmann. "A Hard Day's Work: Reflections on the Interfacing of Transmedialisation and Speed in '24.'" In *Interface://Politics. The World Wide Web as Democratic Resource and Cultural Form*, edited by Klaus Bruhn Jensen, 205–240. Copenhagen, Denmark: Samfundslitteratur, 2005.

Wren, Celia. "The Longest Day." *Commonweal* 129 (2002): 21–22.

CHAPTER 17

Hillbilly Stereotypes and Humor: Entertaining Ourselves at the Expense of the Other[1]

Elizabeth K. Hansen *and*
Angela F. Cooke-Jackson

The conversation taking place at a professional conference had been going smoothly until the well-dressed college student revealed she was from Kentucky.

"But you're wearing shoes," the man teased.

While disheartening for the young woman, the man's stereotypical comment is characteristic of what our students at Eastern Kentucky University often experience when they venture outside the state. As professors at a university in Appalachia,[2] we're a bit surprised he didn't also ask her if she were pregnant and dating her uncle or check her mouth to see if she were toothless. Our students regularly report being teased about their Appalachian roots when they encounter people from other regions. Whether it's the students' accents or their statements of origin that invite the hillbilly label, they have to deal with stereotypes that are perpetuated by television, movies, cartoons, and other media.

Some portrayals of hillbillies are undoubtedly humorous and entertaining, but they also have the potential to harm. Reality television shows may cause harm by poking fun at the characteristics of real people for the sake of a laugh, while programs featuring fictional characters may do harm by assigning characteristics of a few individuals to the larger group. As professors, all too often we see the impact on our students of these false stereotypes depicting Appalachians as lazy, barefoot and pregnant, toothless simpletons who might also be moonshiners on the side. Although our students are deeply rooted in their communities and proud of their heritage,[3] these stereotypes often cause them to question their ability to contribute to the larger society. Unfortunately, Appalachian — and perhaps to a lesser extent Ozark Mountain — stereotypes, such as toothlessness, ignorance, and maladjustment, have their roots in serious economic, social, and health issues. Also, the perpetuation of the hillbilly stereotype permits dominant culture, as represented by the mass media, to justify the marginalization of Appalachians in society.

Whether fact or fiction, entertainment that perpetuates stereotypical portrayals of Appalachians and other mountain dwellers creates ethical dilemmas for producers of entertainment media. Although use of stereotypes cannot be avoided completely in entertainment media, we suggest use of some stereotypes is unethical while others are less problematic. In this chapter, we first examine the media's stereotyping of Appalachians and its ethical implications. Next, we explore how ethical guidelines drawn from Emmanuel Levinas and Immanuel Kant can be used to analyze Appalachian stereotypes in entertainment media. Finally, we illustrate how a decision tree[4] we developed can aid producers of entertainment media in making ethical decisions for both reality programming and fictional works.

Appalachian Stereotypes in the Media

Stereotypical images of Appalachians abound in the media, appearing in both non-fiction and fiction. The idea that mountain dwellers are strange, peculiar, and potentially dangerous dates back many centuries, although the image of the hillbilly did not develop until the twentieth century.[5] The hillbilly first appeared in print in the *New York Journal* on April 23, 1900. A "hillbillie" was defined as a "free and untrammeled white citizen of Alabama, who lives in the hills, has no means to speak of, dresses as he can, talks as he pleases, drinks whiskey when he gets it, and fires off his revolver as the fancy takes him."[6] By 1915, the word "hillbilly" had begun to appear in print and movies, with the first visual depiction of what is now the stereotypical hillbilly appearing in the 1926 film *Rainbow Riley*. The film depicts a reporter sent to cover a feud in eastern Kentucky. The men he encounters match the image of the hillbilly now recognizable worldwide: "a lanky, black-bearded, white male who lives in a cabin in the mountains with an outhouse out back. He wears a battered slouch hat, totes a shotgun and a jug of moonshine, and holds little regard for the law, work, cleanliness, or book learning. He has loose morals and is decidedly dangerous."[7] Such cartoon strips as *Li'l Abner* and *Barney Google and Snuffy Smith* solidified the image. Television in the 1950s and 1960s was populated with shows (i.e., *The Beverly Hillbillies*, *The Real McCoys*, *The Andy Griffith Show*, *The Dukes of Hazzard*, and *Hee Haw*) that featured hillbillies and rednecks and added to the stereotypes of Appalachians. These television programs, as well as movies such as *Deliverance* and *Thunder Road*, represented mountain and country people as simple, backwards moonshiners outside the dominant culture's acceptance of normal. Writer Bill Bryson's humorous account of hiking the Appalachian Trail listed hillbillies among the dangers awaiting those who venture into the mountains: "The woods were full of peril — rattlesnakes and water moccasins and nests of copperheads; bobcats, bear, coyotes, wolves, and wild boar: loony hillbillies destabilized by gross quantities of impure corn liquor and generations of profoundly unbiblical sex; rabies-crazed skunks, raccoons, and squirrels...."[8] The list continued, but the message was clear: Hillbillies are incestuous moonshiners and, based on the company they keep on this list, less than human. Even documentaries that supposedly depict real people and situations, such as the CBS special *Christmas in Appalachia* and the more recent ABC *20/20* episode, *A Hidden America: Children of the Mountains*, don't accurately reflect the region.

When CBS proposed a reality television program called *The Real Beverly Hillbillies* in 2002, the program would have been the latest in a long line of entertainments that have used poor white Appalachians as targets of humor and ridicule. The program would have transplanted a poor Appalachian family to California — much as *The Beverly Hillbillies* followed the adventures of a fictional Ozark family in Beverly Hills decades earlier. To cast the show, CBS launched what critics labeled a "hick hunt" throughout the South.[9] Fliers circulated in several of Kentucky's poorest counties offered a $1,000 reward for tips leading to a suitable family. "The flier also offered as much as $500,000 to a multigenerational family willing to move into a Beverly Hills mansion for a year: 'Parents in their 40s with children ages 17–25. Grandparents and other kin invited.'"[10]

Unlike the sitcom *Beverly Hillbillies*, *The Real Beverly Hillbillies* sparked an immediate outcry from Appalachians and others. Given the popularity of earlier portrayals of poor Southern whites, why the negative response to *The Real Beverly Hillbillies*? Perhaps this particular stereotypical depiction of Appalachian whites was the proverbial "straw that broke the camel's back" in the long string of hillbilly images created by the media. It's more likely, however, this protest sprang from the fact this show, like almost all reality television, was going to feature "real people," not actors. "These 'real people' that they're talking about would be chosen because they're poor, rural, uneducated, and haven't traveled far from home. The network would put them in this televised fishbowl for America's entertainment," Dee Davis, president of the Center for Rural Strategies in Whitesburg, Kentucky, told *The Los Angeles Times*. "Reality TV is pretty much humiliation TV."[11]

Another work that relies on stereotyping Appalachians is Robert

Schenkkan's 1992 Pulitzer Prize-winning play, *The Kentucky Cycle*. Appalachian scholars were not content to let Schenkkan's play perpetuate stereotypes. The result was *Back Talk from Appalachia: Confronting Stereotypes*.[12] In the foreword to the book, Ronald D. Eller wrote: "An epic tragedy about violence and greed, *The Kentucky Cycle* seeks to recast the American myth as a story of repeated failure and poverty, the failure of the American spirit, and the poverty of the American soul. No other region quite symbolizes this countervailing image of America as does Appalachia. With its stereotypical feuds, moonshine stills, mine wars, environmental destruction, joblessness, and human depredation, Appalachia was the place where the American dream had failed, and that idea for Mr. Schenkkan made it 'quintessentially American.'"[13]

Appalachian writer Gurney Norman, an editor of *Back Talk from Appalachia*, criticized Schenkkan for "tromping on real people and the real facts of their history." Outraged by the portrayal of Appalachians, Norman told another Kentucky writer, Bobby Ann Mason, "America needs hillbillies.... Mountain people are the last group in America it is acceptable to ridicule. No one would stand for it for a minute if you took any other group — Native Americans, African Americans, Hispanics, women — and held it up as an example of everything that is low and brutal and mean. But somehow it's OK to do that with hillbillies."[14]

Stereotyping and Harm

Stereotyping is not a new phenomenon, nor is it one invented by the media, although modern media have tremendous power to create and perpetuate stereotypes. Stereotypes have been defined as "a fixed mental image of a group that is frequently applied to all its members."[15]

Although stereotypes are normally viewed from a negative perspective, they are necessary because they allow people to manage the vast amounts of information with which they are bombarded in the modern world. Walter Lippmann addressed the role of stereotypes in his 1922 book *Public Opinion*: "[T]he attempt to see all things freshly and in detail, rather than as types and generalities, is exhausting, and among busy affairs practically out of the question.... Instead, we notice a trait which marks a well known type, and fill in the rest of the picture by means of the stereotypes we carry around in our heads."[16]

Stereotyping is automatic to the extent people use short cuts to arrive at their perception and categorizations of others. This automaticity involves the spontaneous activation of some well-learned set of associations or responses a person has developed through repeated activation in memory (e.g., semantic groupings or social categorizations).[17] As a result, stereotypes and prejudice are insidious and inevitable even for the well-intentioned.

Although stereotyping is inevitable, when media producers erroneously attribute characteristics of a few individual members of a group to the whole group, stereotyping becomes problematic. Stereotypes usually fail to reflect the richness of the subculture and ignore the realities from which the images come. Besides being untruthful, such stereotypes can result in social injustices for individuals who make up that subculture. Many Appalachian stereotypes, for example, stem from accurate depictions of a few people in the subculture. Appalachian people do have less access to dental care and have more oral health needs than their urban counterparts,[18] and the region's educational attainment level lags behind much of the country.[19] However, negative stereotypes based on these facts may ignore the realities and challenges facing the group. Hillbilly stereotypes are often based on characteristics of Appalachians that are beyond their control because of the poverty and isolation of the region. When groups internalize negative stereotypes, it becomes difficult for their members to value themselves or the unique aspects of their culture.[20] One study[21] that investigated identity formation among minorities found African Americans, Asian Americans, Hispanics, and Native Americans who were exposed to negative stereotypes from dominant American culture denigrated those aspects of their ethnic culture in which they once took pride. Such stereotyping of cultures is one ideological tactic dominant cultures use to implement control.[22]

Despite such ethically questionable aspects, stereotypes play a role in creating humor. In a 1988 anthology of national humor, Don and Alleen Nilsen identified three major traditional types of prejudice responsible for most stereotype humor in the United States: "prejudice against people of color, prejudice against newly arrived immigrants, and prejudice against regional, peripheral groups."[23] Among those regional groups, according to Leon Rappoport, are New England Yankees, Swedes and Norwegians in Minnesota, Texans, Southerners in general, and Appalachian hill dwellers.[24] Rappoport argued that use of regional and ethnic stereotypes in humor is more prevalent than ever, but is less offensive because of public sophistication. "We laugh at ethnic humor based on stereotypes today precisely because we know they are essentially false yet contain enough residual grains of truth to raise the tension necessary for laughter."[25]

While all humor takes a target, that does not place humor above moral considerations. There are boundaries to what is acceptable humor.[26] Humor that belittles Appalachians or members of other subcultures is often used against the group and at the group's expense. Such humor located in the marginalization, misrepresentation, and targeting of poor Appalachians may be an ethical violation, unlike humor produced by members of the group itself (i.e., Appalachians), which may be less destructive. This reality is reflected by writer Rod Dreher's comment: "[T]here's something to be said for the unwritten rule of joke telling that says I can talk about my kind, but don't you dare."[27]

Ethical Principles and Portrayal of Appalachians

In portraying Appalachians, media producers cannot entirely abandon stereotypical images because, unfortunately, some of those images are accurate. Also, as media scholar Tom Brislin notes, "Sometimes because of space or time limitations, sometimes out of ingrained insensitivity, they (media producers) trade the completeness and context that gives meaning for the shorthand code words and images that perpetuate stereotypes."[28] In addition, people who are presented with certain images of individuals automatically stereotype them. As a result of the interplay of truth and stereotypes, portraying Appalachian culture may create ethical dilemmas for producers of entertainment media. The theories of Emmanuel Levinas and Immanuel Kant provide a framework for examining the ethical issues associated with stereotypical portrayals of Appalachians and other subcultures. We use both the reality show and the sitcom *Beverly Hillbillies* as illustrations.

Levinas and Stereotyping of Appalachians

Levinas' ethical theory seems particularly appropriate for examining the use of stereotypes in entertainment media. For Levinas, ethics stems from the relationship of the self to the "other."[29] Levinas' relational ethics begins with the other person rather than with the decision maker. In other words, Levinas' ethics begins with the subjects being portrayed and asks what those subjects want.

If we attempt to define another person, what is projected onto the other comes from our own definition of ourselves. In trying to define the other, we lose parts of who that person is. We only see of the other what that person has revealed, not all aspects of that person. In attempting to define another person, we place limits on the person.[30] For Levinas, trying to define or represent another person negates that person. The other person resists any attempt to box him/her in by imposition of a definition or a stereotype. Because there is much that we cannot know about another person, if we act as if we have the power to be able to know and define the other, we violate that person. Representations in the media may be inevitable, but Levinas suggests that media content producers have a responsibility to let those they portray have a say in *how* they are represented.

Levinas saw the struggle to define the other leading to what he termed an "epiphany."[31] The experience of trying to define another and meeting resistance leads rational people to the realization that defining the other is not only impossible, but also unethical. Levinas would argue that people who present others (e.g., real people cast in reality television shows) to others (e.g., an audience) have a responsibility to let those real people define themselves. Media content producers who have an epiphany recognize that they cannot define other people and to try to do so is wrong.

When the creators of *The Real Beverly Hillbillies* began searching for real people to cast in their show, they already had in mind the characteristics they wanted those people to exhibit. Outrage from Appalachians may have come in part from the producers' efforts to define in stereotypical terms the real people who would have been cast for the show. After CBS announced the program was on hold while it searched for the "right" family, Sen. Zell Miller of Georgia, whose state lies partly in Appalachia, wrote to the *Atlanta Journal-Constitution*: "Seems they are having a hard time finding the family they had in mind: toothless illiterates with hookworms and an old man who has impregnated his barefoot, teenage daughter."[32] Some may argue that reality television, by its very nature, allows participants to define themselves, and, therefore, the producers who create those shows are not imposing stereotypes on them. However, the creators of reality television shows film hours of material and then edit those hours to create 30-, 60-, 90-, or 120-minute programs. By selecting materials for the show, the content producer is indeed imposing his/her own definitions or stereotypes on individuals included in the production. The problem is not limited to reality programs. Producers of fact-based documentaries also face the challenge of choosing what to include. And even if the individual is allowed to define himself, that representation may not match reality.

Kant and Stereotyping of Appalachians

Kant would argue that human beings deserve respect: "Act so that you treat humanity, whether in your own person or in that of another, always as an end and never as a means only."[33] Kant's principles are particularly useful for producers of reality television. "Reality television as a genre must face up to Kant's claim that each person should be valued, no one should be treated as fodder for another's exploitation. To violate this principle is ... to put human relationships in jeopardy."[34] Kant would not have approved of *The Real Beverly Hillbillies* or other reality programs that treat human beings as objects for others' entertainment and as a means to line the wallets of media producers and others associated with entertainment programming.

Among the real people outraged by *The Real Beverly Hillbillies* were mine workers from West Virginia and Kentucky. They took their protest of *The Real Beverly Hillbillies* to CBS's parent company in May 2003. "We're tired of the negative image of the Appalachian people," Tom Manuel, an underground electrician from Fairmont, West Virginia, said outside Viacom's Manhattan headquarters. Manuel told the *Toronto Star* that CBS has "been on what we call a 'hick hunt,' trying to find somebody that will take money and go to Beverly Hills to live in a mansion so that our entire country can make fun of them. We think that's practicing bigotry ... it's hurtful and painful. It's discrimination of an entire segment of our society."[35] Manuel added, "Every state of the union has people who are illiterate and culturally backward, but for some reason everybody thinks all Appalachian people are like that. We're not. It's a very rich heritage, and we resent the way we're presented on national media."[36]

Although they did not use Kant's terminology, Manuel and others who objected to *The Real Beverly Hillbillies* echoed Kant's categorical imperative: "Act only according to that maxim by which you can at the same time will that it should become universal law."[37] For example, writing for *National Review* Online, Dreher labeled *The Real Beverly Hillbillies* a "minstrel show" and observed that poor Southern whites are "the only ethnic group in the country that it is permissible to mock in polite company."[38] Morris Dees, chief trial counsel for the Southern Poverty Law Center, likewise told *The Los Angeles Times* that *The Real Beverly Hillbillies* illustrated a form of classism. It's still acceptable in some quarters to make fun of poor white Southerners, he said. "If they were to take a poor, uneducated black family from rural Mississippi or rural Alabama, that had never left the area, and moved them to Beverly Hills, that would serve the same CBS purpose of getting people to laugh at them, but I don't think they'd do that," Dees said. "The NAACP would go through the roof."[39]

As these critics of *The Real Beverly Hillbillies* pointed out, poor white Southerners—Appalachians, hillbillies, and rednecks—are among the few subcultures or minority groups it is acceptable to make fun of in polite company. According to Kant, singling out members of a subculture for such treatment would be a violation of the categorical imperative. Media content producers have not suggested transplanting an African-American or Hispanic family to Beverly Hills so that people may gawk at their adjustment to upper-class life. If media producers find it unacceptable to use stereotyped portrayals of other subcultures and minority groups, then they also should find such portrayals of real or fictional Appalachians unacceptable. Perhaps more significantly, though, *The Real Beverly Hillbillies* and other reality television shows have the potential to violate Kant's edict that people always should be treated as ends rather than as merely a means to an end.

Producers often defend their treatment of reality show stars by arguing participants have given their consent. But permission does not free media content producers from their ethical obligation to treat subjects of their work with respect — even if those individuals willingly accept stereotyping as the price for celebrity. Also, although individuals may have given consent, other members of the stereotyped group have not, nor have they been compensated with fame or money.

Analyzing the Ethics of Stereotypes in Entertainment Media

It would be unrealistic to expect media content producers to abandon stereotypes or ignore their bottom lines. Stereotypes make it possible for media consumers to manage the vast amounts of information they encounter in the modern world. Although stereotypes are not always true of everyone in a subculture, their use allows media producers to convey large amounts of information succinctly. For example, without using stereotypes, it would be difficult, if not impossible, for cartoonists to convey a message in three or four frames of a cartoon strip.

We recognize that a major obstacle to ethical actions on the part of media producers is the profit motive fueling the entertainment industry. As Clifford Christians and his associates noted: "Entertainment media in America are 90% business and 10% public service.... Only the most unrepentant idealist would argue that social responsibility is a major consideration in most entertainment media decisions."[40] However, those profit-driven decisions made by media producers have tremendous impact.

In examining ethical issues created by portrayals of Appalachians, fiction and non-fiction works must be dealt with separately. Differing ethical obligations are associated with producing fiction and reality programming, although both can have harmful effects. Stereotypes used by the producers of fiction may harm the members of the subculture as a whole, but do not target individuals as directly as a reality television show that exploits an Appalachian family (i.e., *The Real Beverly Hillbillies*) or a documentary that focuses on identifiable children whose poverty is beyond their control (i.e., *Christmas in Appalachia* and *Hidden America: Children of the Mountains*). In a non-fiction work, media producers are also bound by the ethical obligation to tell the truth. When Diane Sawyer turned the cameras of ABC's *20/20* on three children in Appalachia in 2009, the reaction was mostly negative. Many criticized the report for focusing on the worst stereotypes of mountain people, including toothlessness (in part attributed to high consumption of Mountain Dew soft drinks), poverty, and drug addiction while not exploring the causes of the problems or offering solutions.[41] "It seemed like Diane Sawyer said, 'You know the stereotypes, and just in case you don't, watch while I reinforce all of them for you,'" observed Derek Mullins, chair of the executive board of Appalshop, an arts and education center in Whitesburg, Kentucky. "The camera doesn't lie, but it also doesn't tell the whole story."[42]

One of the developers of *The Real Beverly Hillbillies*, Appalachian documentary filmmaker Dub Cornett, told the *Washington Post* he expected the joke to be on folks in Beverly Hills (as it often was in the original sitcom, *The Beverly Hillbillies*). Dreher, the writer, scoffed at the remark: "It's true that literature has long made use of the fool to reveal the folly of the high and mighty, and that's what *The Beverly Hillbillies* did, to an extent. But that's fiction; those scenes can be manipulated by the artist for morally instructive effect. Nonfiction is not amenable to this kind of shading."[43]

Creators of both fiction and non-fiction works have an ethical duty to individuals they portray, the larger subculture they represent, and audiences who view their work. The usefulness of stereotypes and the desire for a robust bottom line do not remove this responsibility.

Using an Ethical Decision Tree

The works of Levinas and Kant are useful not only in identifying and analyzing ethical problems arising from stereotyping, but also in developing a decision tree to guide producers of entertainment media.[44] Media producers can ask themselves a series of questions to guide their decision-making about stereotypes. These questions vary depending on the nature of the media text and can be adapted for use with other subcultures. Although the decision tree is based on the premise that all stereotypes are harmful, there are circumstances (satire, trivial references, etc.) where media producers may use stereotypes without necessarily acting unethically.

In using the decision tree, a starting point for media content producers is to determine if the work in question depicts Appalachians or another subculture. If the answer is yes, additional questions to guide media producers include:

> I. *Are the people portrayed fictional characters or real people?*
> If a **fictional character**, then:

>> 1. *Does the portrayal rely on one or more stereotypes?*
>> If no, then no analysis may be needed. If yes, then ask:

>> 2. *Does the stereotype misrepresent the subculture as a whole?*
>> If it does, use of the stereotype may be unethical.

>> 3. *Is the stereotype being used for the primary purpose of humiliating, embarrassing, or exploiting members of the subculture?*
>> If so, use of the stereotype may be unethical.

4. Does a character display traits that are stereotypical, but
nonetheless accurate descriptors of the character?
If yes, this may be an ethical use of a stereotype.

5. Is a stereotype used primarily as a shorthand to move the story
forward, rather than for the primary purpose of humiliating,
embarrassing, or exploiting members of a subculture?
If yes, this may be an ethical use of a stereotype.

II. *Are the people portrayed fictional characters or real people?*
If **real people,** then:

1. Does the portrayal rely on one or more stereotypes?
If no, then no analysis may be needed. If yes, then ask:

2. Is a stereotypical description applied to the people being depicted?
If so, use of the stereotype may be unethical.

3. Does a person or group used in an entertainment medium
display characteristics that have become stereotypes,
but are nonetheless true for those depicted?
If so, this may be an ethical portrayal. However, the larger
context would also need to be considered (e.g., even if the
portrayal is accurate, the context in which the person
or group is presented may raise ethical issues).

4. Does the stereotyping define the individual primarily
to serve the media producer's purposes (i.e., is the
person being treated merely as a means to an end)?
If so, use of the stereotype may be unethical.

A decision tree of this sort provides media content producers with a reasonable way to examine their use of stereotypes and offers a framework within
which they can analyze and improve their representation of Appalachians and
other subcultures. We recommend it be used in tandem with the moral guidance offered by Levinas and Kant.

What would have happened had the producers of *The Real Beverly Hillbillies* used such a framework? What if the decision tree had been used to analyze the television sitcom, *The Beverly Hillbillies,* which was set in the Ozarks,
not Appalachia, but relied on many stereotypes commonly applied to people
from both regions? Let's see.

The Beverly Hillbillies, which ran on CBS from 1962 to 1971, depicted a
fictional family from the Ozarks transplanted to Hollywood after striking oil
on their land back in the hills. Its main characters were the honest, gun-tot-
ing father, Jed Clampett, moonshining Granny, barefoot Elly May, and sim-
ple-minded Jethro. All of the characterizations relied on stereotypes and
clearly misrepresented the subculture as a whole (since there were no Ozark
characters in the cast who did not fit the stereotypes). One of the authors of
this chapter (Hansen) was a teenager growing up in the Ozarks at the time
the show was on the air. Although she and her family and friends recognized

the show was fiction, they nonetheless felt somewhat violated by the stereo-typical portrayal of their subculture being presented to the rest of the coun-try.

The producers of *The Beverly Hillbillies* made fun of "mountain people," but they also used the stories to make fun of and point out the foibles of the rich city folks the Clampetts encountered and to extol the family's core val-ues. Although some of the descriptors of the Clampetts were authentic rep-resentations of some members of Ozark families, they were not true for most, including the author's own. Clearly, using stereotypes allowed the show's producers to move the story forward at times; in other episodes it appeared the primary purpose of the stereotypes was to make fun of members of the subculture. While the hillbillies were not always the target of the humor, we have concerns about the harm the show may have done in terms of perpet-uating stereotypes about mountain residents and damaging the self-esteem of those who grew up in the region, such as Kentucky native Fenton John-son, who wrote that *The Beverly Hillbillies* taught him to despise himself more than any source.[45]

Even more problematic from our perspective was the proposed *The Real Beverly Hillbillies*. It's unlikely the producers of the show would have embarked on a "hick hunt" to find a family for the show had they applied our decision tree and the ethical principles of Levinas and Kant. The "hick hunt" was aimed at finding a poor Appalachian family that matched the media producer's stereotypical view of the subculture. Although *The Real Beverly Hillbillies* was never produced, using the producers' own description and Fen-ton Johnson's predictions about the family, it's easy to imagine what those characters would have looked like and the types of story lines the shows might have featured. Writing in the *Los Angeles Times*, Johnson predicted the fam-ily would be white, speak with a strong accent, and have little or no educa-tion. They would have been from the country — probably Kentucky, as that would most perfectly fit the stereotype. Finally, they would be desperate enough to sacrifice self-respect for money and would be willing to live in a Beverly Hills mansion wired with cameras so that audiences could watch and ridicule their every move. [46]

Applying the decision tree to this "real" family, it's obvious the portrayal would have relied on stereotypes and the participants would have been selected because they fit the media producer's stereotyped image. While the characteristics may have been true for the family selected, the context in which the family was presented would have raised ethical concerns. As John-son wrote: "The producers know, as the family they select cannot, that these people's lives will be unalterably changed, possibly destroyed by this experi-ence. It's one thing for an educated, prosperous suburbanite to choose to participate in such humiliation; it's another matter entirely for a rich and powerful institution to set out deliberately to locate a family characterized by its vulnerability."[47] Finally, an Appalachian family was being recruited to benefit the media producer, not necessarily the family. Johnson concludes: "[E]very human being has a story that is worth telling well. The producers of *The Real Beverly Hillbillies* are not interested, though, in telling their subjects' stories well. They are interested in making money, which is their story."[48]

Using the decision tree, it becomes apparent that searching for people to fit or be labeled with the negative stereotypical image of Appalachians and then holding them up to ridicule for the purpose of making a profit is unethical. Eventually, it was the outrage of Appalachians that kept *The Real Beverly Hillbillies* off the air. Using a newspaper advertising campaign, the Internet, and word of mouth, advocacy groups and individuals fought to keep CBS from going forward with the program.

Conclusion

Is stereotyping a subculture in entertainment media inherently unethical? No, but as this chapter has suggested, perhaps no one ethical theory is adequate to deal with the ethics of stereotyping subcultures, although at least two theories are useful in guiding media producers in making justifiable decisions. This chapter has examined the relationship between the media content producer and his/her subjects or characters through the work of Levinas and Kant. Media content producers' tendency to stereotypically define the other, the subject of their work, on their own terms without consideration for how these subjects see themselves is an ethical violation. According to Levinas, one can never define the other and should not attempt to. Rather than saying to their subjects, "This is how you are," media content producers should explore how their subjects see themselves and present themselves to the world. Despite its appeal, Levinas' approach presents some practical obstacles for media producers because both communication and the way individuals relate to the world are dependent to a degree on stereotypes. Furthermore, it is unclear whether individuals can, in fact, accurately define or represent themselves.

Kant's emphasis on treating persons as ends, rather than merely as means to an end, indicates many media portrayals are, in fact, exploitive. Kant provides guidance for treating individuals with dignity and respect.

Producers of both fiction and non-fiction works must be cognizant of the ethical implications of their actions. While their primary focus may be on the bottom line, they must not ignore the power of media to affect the people and the subcultures they portray. Our decision tree and the ethical principles that underlie it provide guidance for media content producers as they portray Appalachians or members of other subcultures. Permission from individuals participating in a reality program does not free media content producers from their ethical obligation to treat the subjects of their work with respect. Nor does it give them permission to portray those individuals as representative of the subculture or apply characteristics of the individual to the larger subculture.

Ironically, a year after CBS abandoned plans for *The Real Beverly Hillbillies*, NBC shot a pilot for a television series tentatively titled *The High Life*. However, NBC quickly shelved the program, which would have followed a family transported from backwoods Appalachia to ritzy life in a Beverly Hills mansion.[49] NBC must have been aware of CBS's experience with *The Real Beverly Hillbillies*, but apparently chose to initially ignore it in hopes of making a profit from a reality television show built on stereotyped images of Appalachians.

The power of media producers to perpetuate negative stereotypes and violate the people and subcultures they portray makes it essential that they adhere to high ethical standards. To do less wrongs not only Appalachians, but also society as a whole. In a groundbreaking exploration of Appalachian stereotyping and media content producers' ethical obligations, filmmaker Elizabeth Barret recounted the story of Canadian filmmaker Hugh O'Connor, who went to Letcher County, Kentucky, in 1967 to show the contrast between miners' lives and the American dream. As O'Connor filmed a coal miner (with permission) playing with his child on the porch of a ramshackle rental house, the owner of the property, Hobert Ison, shot and killed O'Connor. Two decades later, filmmaker Barret, herself a Letcher County native, explored the relationship between media content producers and their subjects in her award-winning documentary, *Stranger with a Camera*.[50] "Media images can bring out powerful emotions," Barret says in the film. "What are the responsibilities of any of us who take the images of other people and put them to our own uses? Who does get to tell the community's stories and what are the storytellers' responsibilities?" Acknowledging O'Connor's positive motives, Barret raised an important question about the dilemma facing media content producers who accurately portray poor Appalachians: "Can filmmakers show poverty without shaming the people we portray?" Her conclusion: "I came to see there is a complex relationship between social action and social embarrassment."[51]

Just as Barret questioned the role and responsibilities of filmmakers in producing truthful representations of subcultures, so, too, must media producers examine their purposes and ethical responsibilities in using stereotypes to represent Appalachians or other subcultures in both fiction and nonfiction works.

NOTES

1. Portions of this chapter were previously published in Angela Cooke-Jackson and Elizabeth K. Hansen, "Appalachian Culture and Reality TV: The Ethical Dilemma of Stereotyping Others," *Journal of Mass Media Ethics: Exploring Questions of Media Morality* 23.3 (July 2008): 183–200 and are reprinted with permission of the publisher (Taylor & Francis, http://www.informaworld.com). Both authors contributed equally to this chapter. The authors wish to thank James Grady of the Vanderbilt University Philosophy Department for his assistance in unpacking Levinas.

2. According to the Appalachian Regional Commission, Appalachia is a 200,000-square-mile region that follows the spine of the Appalachian Mountains from southern New York to northern Mississippi. It includes all of West Virginia and parts of 12 other states: Alabama, Georgia, Kentucky, Maryland, Mississippi, New York, North Carolina, Ohio, Pennsylvania, South Carolina, Tennessee, and Virginia. Twenty-three million people live in the 420 counties of the Appalachian region; 42 percent of the region's population is rural, compared with 20 percent of the national population.

3. The negative stereotypes of Appalachia usually don't capture the strong value system of people living there. Loyal Jones, an Appalachian scholar and co-founder of the Berea College Appalachian Center, enumerated those values, which include individualism, self-reliance, pride, religion, familism, and love of place. See Loyal Jones, *Appalachian Values* (Ashland, KY: Jesse Stuart Foundation, 1994.)

4. See Cooke-Jackson and Hansen, "Appalachian Culture and Reality TV," 183–200.

5. Jean Haskell, "Hillbilly," in *Encyclopedia of Appalachia,* eds. Rudy Abramson and Jean Haskell (Knoxville: University of Tennessee Press, 2006), 216–218.

6. Julian Hawthorne, "Mountain Votes Spoil Huntington's Revenge," *The Journal* (April 23, 1900), 2, quoted in Anthony Harkins, *Hillbilly: A Cultural History of an American Icon* (New York: Oxford University Press, 2004), 49.

7. Haskell, "Hillbilly," 216.

8. Bill Bryson, *A Walk in the Woods* (New York: Broadway, 1998), 5.

9. Meg James, "'Beverly Hillbillies'? CBS Has Struck Crude, Appalachia Says," *Los Angeles Times,* February 11, 2003, http://www.commondreams.org/headlines03/0211-03.htm (accessed March 31, 2007), 18.

10. *Ibid.*, 17.

11. *Ibid.*, 7, 12.

12. Dwight D. Billings, Gurney Norman, and Katherine Ledford, eds., *Back Talk from Appalachia: Confronting Stereotypes,* with a forward by Ronald D. Eller and an introduction by Dwight B. Billings (Lexington: University of Kentucky Press, 1999).

13. Ronald D. Eller, forward to *Back Talk from Appalachia: Confronting Stereotypes,* eds. Dwight D. Billings, Gurney Norman and Katherine Ledford (Lexington: University of Kentucky Press, 1999), ix.

14. Dwight B. Billings, introduction to *Back Talk from Appalachia: Confronting Stereotypes,* eds. Dwight D. Billings, Gurney Norman and Katherine Ledford (Lexington: University of Kentucky Press, 1999), 9.

15. Charles Zastrow and Karen K. Kirst-Ashman, *Understanding Human Behavior and the Social Environment* (Chicago: Nelson-Hall, 1987), 556.

16. Walter Lippmann, *Public Opinion* (New York: Macmillan, 1922), 88–89.

17. For a more comprehensive overview of this research, see John A. Bargh, Mark Chen, and Lara Burrows, "Automaticity of Social Behavior: Direct Effects of Trait Construct and Stereotype Activation on Action," *Journal of Personality and Social Psychology* 71 (1996): 230–244; John A. Bargh, "The Cognitive Monster: The Case Against the Controllability of Automatic Stereotype Effects," in *Dual-Process Theories in Social Psychology,* eds. Shelly Chaiken and Yaacov Trope (New York: Guilford, 1999), 361–382; Patricia G. Devine, "Stereotypes and Prejudice: Their Automatic and Controlled Components," *Journal of Personality and Social Psychology* 56 (1989): 5–18.

18. Clemencia M. Vargas, Cynthia R. Ronzio, and Krall L. Hayes, "Oral Health Status of Children and Adolescents by Rural Residence, United States," *The Journal of Rural Health* 19.3 (2003): 260–268; Ian Urbina, "In Kentucky's Teeth, Toll of Poverty and Neglect," *New York Times,* December 24, 2007, http://www.nytimes.com (accessed December 24, 2007).

19. Appalachian Regional Commission, "Education — High School and College Completion Rates in Appalachia, 2000," http://www.arc.gov/search/LoadQueryData.do?queryId =16 (accessed August 21, 2008).

20. Sharon L. Sullivan, "Refusing Stereotypes: Princess Pocahontas and the Blue Spots," 2004, http://www.womenstudies.ku.edu/graduate_certificate_research/ (accessed February 5, 2008).

21. Jean S. Phinney, "Ethnic Identity in Adolescents and Adults: Review Of Research," *Psychological Bulletin* 108 (1990): 499–514.

22. Christine Ballengee-Morris, "Hillbilly: An Image of a Culture" (paper presented at the annual conference of the Women of Appalachia: Their Heritage and Accomplishments, Zanesville, Ohio, October 26–28, 2000).

23. Don L.F. Nilsen and Alleen Pace Nilsen, with Ken Donelson, "Humor in the United States," in *National Styles of Humor,* ed. Avner Ziv (New York: Greenwood, 1988, 157–188), cited in Leon Rappoport, *Punchlines: The Case for Racial, Ethnic, and Gender Humor.* (Westport, CT: Praeger, 2005), 58.

24. Rappoport, *Punchlines,* 60.

25. Rappoport, *Punchlines,* 126.

26. Clifford G. Christians, Kim B. Rotzoll, Mark Fackler, Kathy B. McKee, and Robert H. Woods, Jr., *Media Ethics: Cases and Moral Reasoning,* 7th ed. (Boston: Pearson Education, 2005), 276.

27. Rod Dreher, "Minstrel Show," *National Review Online,* August 30, 2002, http://www.nationalreview.com/dreher/dreher083002.asp (accessed March 31, 2007).

28. Tom Brislin, "Media Stereotypes and Code Words: Let's Call Media to Task for Promoting Stereotypes," *The Honolulu Advertiser,* February 23, 1997, http://www2.hawaii.edu/_ tbrislin/stereo.html (accessed September 21, 2007).

29. Emmanuel Levinas, *Totality and Infinity: An Essay on Exteriority,* trans. Alphonso Lingis (Pittsburgh: Duquesne University Press, 1961/1969).

30. *Ibid.*

31. *Ibid.,* 197–199.

32. James, "'Beverly Hillbillies'?" 21.

33. Immanuel Kant, (1959). *Foundations of the Metaphysics of Morals,* trans. Lewis White Beck (Indianapolis and New York: Bobbs-Merrill, 1785/1959), 429.

34. Christians, et al., 278.

35. Ula Ilnytzky "Rural Folks Protest Hillbilly Show," *Toronto Star,* May 22, 2003, A35, http://www.thestar.com/ (accessed March 31, 2007).

36. *Ibid.,* A35.

37. Kant, *Foundations of the Metaphysics of Morals,* 421.

38. Dreher, "Minstrel Show," 3.

39. James, "'Beverly Hillbillies'?" 22, 23.

40. Christians, et al., *Media Ethics,* 257.

41. Mary Meehan and Rich Copley, "Appalachia's Story a Hard One to Tell: '20/20' Report Upsets Many in Mountains," *Lexington Herald-Leader,* Feb. 18, 2009, A1, A8.

42. *Ibid.,* A8.

43. Dreher, "Minstrel Show," 8, 12.

44. See Cooke-Jackson and Hansen, "Appalachian Culture and Reality TV," 194–196. Our decision tree for producers of entertainment media was influenced by a utilitarian decision tree developed by Deni Elliott. See Deni Elliott, "Getting Mill Right," *Journal of Mass Media Ethics* 22.2/3 (2007): 100–112.

45. Fenton Johnson, "Gold in Them Thar Hillbillies," *Los Angeles Times,* January 26, 2003, http://www.ruralstrategies.org/campaign/fenton.html (accessed March 21, 2009), 3.

46. *Ibid.*, 3, 4.
47. *Ibid.*, 5.
48. *Ibid.*, 6.
49. "Congressman Rogers: NBC Backs Away from 'Hillbilly' Reality Program," Center for Rural Strategies press release, May 7, 2004, http://www.ruralstrategies.org/campaign/highlife.html (accessed September 19, 2007).
50. Elizabeth Barret, *Stranger with a Camera* (Whitesburg, KY: Appalshop, 2000).
51. Barret, *Stranger with a Camera.*

WORKS CITED

Appalachian Regional Commission. "Education — High School and College Completion Rates in Appalachia, 2000." http://www.arc.gov/search/LoadQueryData.do?queryId=16 (accessed August 21, 2008).

Ballengee-Morris, Christine. "Hillbilly: An Image of a Culture." Paper presented at the annual conference of the Women of Appalachia: Their Heritage and Accomplishments, Zanesville, Ohio, October 26–28, 2000.

Bargh, John A. "The Cognitive Monster: The Case Against the Controllability of Automatic Stereotype Effects." In *Dual-Process Theories in Social Psychology*, edited by Shelly Chaiken and Yaacov Trope, 361–382. New York: Guilford, 1999.

_____, Mark Chen, and Lara Burrows. "Automaticity of Social Behavior: Direct Effects of Trait Construct and Stereotype Activation on Action." *Journal of Personality and Social Psychology* 71 (1996): 230–244.

Barret, Elizabeth. *Stranger with a Camera.* Whitesburg, KY: Appalshop, 2000.

Billings, Dwight B. Introduction to *Back Talk from Appalachia: Confronting Stereotypes*, edited by Dwight B. Billings, Gurney Norman, and Katherine Ledford, 3–20. Lexington: University of Kentucky Press, 1999.

_____, Gurney Norman, and Katherine Ledford, ed. *Back Talk from Appalachia: Confronting Stereotypes*, with a foreword by Ronald D. Eller and an introduction by Dwight B. Billings. Lexington: University of Kentucky Press, 1999.

Brislin, Tom. "Media Stereotypes and Code Words: Let's Call Media to Task for Promoting Stereotypes." *The Honolulu Advertiser*, February 23, 1997. http://www2.hawaii.edu/_tbrislin/stereo.html (accessed September 21, 2007).

Bryson, Bill. *A Walk in the Woods.* New York: Broadway, 1998.

Christians, Clifford G., Kim B. Rotzoll, Mark Fackler, Kathy B. McKee, and Robert H. Woods, Jr. *Media Ethics: Cases and Moral Reasoning*, 7th ed. Boston: Pearson Education, 2005.

"Congressman Rogers: NBC Backs Away from 'Hillbilly' Reality Program." Center for Rural Strategies press release, May 7, 2004. http://www.ruralstrategies.org/campaign/highlife.html (accessed September 19, 2007).

Cooke-Jackson, Angela, and Elizabeth K. Hansen. "Appalachian Culture and Reality TV: The Ethical Dilemma of Stereotyping Others." *Journal of Mass Media Ethics* 23, no. 3 (July 2008): 183–200.

Devine, Patricia G. "Stereotypes and Prejudice: Their Automatic and Controlled Components." *Journal of Personality and Social Psychology* 56 (1989): 5–18.

Dreher, Rod. "Minstrel Show." *National Review Online*, August 30, 2002. http://www.nationalreview.com/dreher/dreher083002.asp (accessed March 31, 2007).

Eller, Ronald D. Foreword to *Back Talk from Appalachia: Confronting Stereotypes*, edited by Dwight B. Billings, Gurney Norman, and Katherine Ledford, ix–xi. Lexington: University of Kentucky Press, 1999.

Elliott, Deni. "Getting Mill Right." *Journal of Mass Media Ethics* 22, no. 2/3 (2007): 100–112.

Haskell, Jean. "Hillbilly." In *Encyclopedia of Appalachia*, edited by Rudy Abramson and Jean Haskell, 216–218. Knoxville: University of Tennessee Press, 2006.

Hawthorne, Julian. "Mountain Votes Spoil Huntington's Revenge." *The Journal*, April 23,

1900, 2. Quoted in Anthony Harkins. *Hillbilly: A Cultural History of an American Icon*, 49. New York: Oxford University Press, 2004.

Ilnytzky, Ula. "Rural Folks Protest Hillbilly Show." *Toronto Star*, May 22, 2003, A35. http://www.thestar.com/ (accessed March 31, 2007).

James, Meg. "'Beverly Hillbillies'? CBS Has Struck Crude, Appalachia Says." *Los Angeles Times*, February 11, 2003, 18. http://www.commondreams.org/headlines03/0211-03.htm (accessed March 31, 2007).

Johnson, Fenton. "Gold in Them Thar Hillbillies." *Los Angeles Times*, January 26, 2003, 3. http://www.ruralstrategies.org/campaign/fenton.html (accessed March 21, 2009).

Jones, Loyal. *Appalachian Values*. Ashland, KY: Jesse Stuart Foundation, 1994.

Kant, Immanuel. *Foundations of the Metaphysics of Morals*. Translated by Lewis White Beck. Indianapolis and New York: Bobbs-Merrill, 1785/1959.

Levinas, Emmanuel. *Totality and Infinity: An Essay on Exteriority*. Translated by Alphonso Lingis. Pittsburgh: Duquesne University Press, 1961.

Lippmann, Walter. *Public Opinion*. New York: Macmillan, 1922.

Meehan, Mary, and Rich Copley. "Appalachia's Story a Hard One to Tell: '20/20' Report Upsets Many in Mountains." *Lexington Herald-Leader*, February 18, 2009, A1, A8.

Nilsen, Don L.F., and Alleen Pace Nilsen, with Ken Donelson. "Humor in the United States." In *National Styles of Humor,* edited by Avner Ziv, 157–188. New York: Greenwood, 1988. Cited in Leon Rappoport. *Punchlines: The Case for Racial, Ethnic, and Gender Humor*, 58. Westport, CT: Praeger, 2005.

Phinney, Jean S. "Ethnic Identity in Adolescents and Adults: Review of Research." *Psychological Bulletin* 108 (1990): 499–514.

Sullivan, Sharon L. "Refusing Stereotypes: Princess Pocahontas and the Blue Spots," 2004. http://www.womenstudies.ku.edu/graduate_certificate_research/ (accessed February 5, 2008).

Urbina, Ian. "In Kentucky's Teeth, Toll of Poverty and Neglect." *New York Times*, December 24, 2007. http://www.nytimes.com (accessed December 24, 2007).

Vargas, Clemencia M., Cynthia R. Ronzio, and Krall L. Hayes. "Oral Health Status of Children and Adolescents by Rural Residence, United States." *The Journal of Rural Health* 19, no. 3 (2003): 260–268.

Zastrow, Charles, and Karen K. Kirst-Ashman. *Understanding Human Behavior and the Social Environment*. Chicago: Nelson-Hall, 1987.

CHAPTER 18

Epistemic Freedom, Science Fiction, and Ethical Deliberation

Trin Turner *and* Joshua D. Upson

While admittedly "out of this world," science fiction is more than mere escapism. Sci-fi offers an advantage for ethical deliberation and analysis not found in other popular genres. Sci-fi grants *epistemic freedom*—that is, it allows audiences to confront ethical dilemmas head-on without the overly complex and constraining details often present in everyday discussions of ethical issues. Therefore, science fiction can be used to illustrate the core of ethical dilemmas.[1]

This essay will explore the analytical possibilities the genre affords by suggesting that sci-fi be read as ethical *thought experiments* devoted to enhancing core concepts in moral debates. We begin by describing the key characteristics of the sci-fi genre for our purposes; we then discuss thought experiments and their role as devices for elucidating central concepts in both science and ethics; and, finally, we discuss examples of sci-fi as ethical thought experiments with respect to abortion and gay-friendly schools.

What Is This Thing Called Sci-Fi?

What is it that makes a piece of fiction properly categorized as "science" fiction? When one thinks of sci-fi, one's mind typically wanders to the well-worn tropes of the genre. Little green men and ray guns are so common in science fiction that often their presence is taken to be what categorizes a story as sci-fi rather than some other form of fantasy fiction. However, we claim that what makes a story as properly belonging to the sci-fi genre lies in the speculative nature of the fiction itself—that is, in the way it invites readers to imagine a different world or set of circumstances outside of the ordinary world they inhabit.

The so-called "mother of science fiction," Judith Merril, a former *SF* editor and writer, noted the sci-fi genre's roots lie in its "what if" nature. Merril, who often used the term "speculative fiction" when referring to the genre, defined sci-fi as follows:

> I use the term "speculative fiction" here specifically to describe the mode which makes use of the traditional "scientific method" (observation, hypothesis, experimentation) to examine some postulated approximation of reality, by introducing a set of changes—imaginary or inventive—into the common background of "known facts," creating an environment in which the response and the perceptions of the characters will reveal something about the inventions, the characters, or both.[2]

Merril views the genre as a literary scientific experiment of sorts. The piece of fiction is essentially the "experimental group" where subjects are introduced to variables in their environment and then "observed" to see what results these variations have on their behavior. Merril specifically notes that the worlds of sci-fi typically take the form of "some postulated approximation of reality" that share a common background of "known facts" with our own world. Her word choice suggests that this connection between the fictional world and the real world encourages the audience to draw analogies between the (sometimes literally) alien world of fiction and their own. Or, to put it another way, the sci-fi world and its inhabitants are seen as an "experimental group" with the real world as a control. Merril's definition appears to allow for the possibility of exploring real-world consequences of scientific innovations or discoveries through carefully "designed" sci-fi stories.

An example of how such a real-world exploration might come from sci-fi can be found in the 1997 film *Gattaca*. In it, progress in the field of genetics has brought forth a society where "natural" births are unheard of; children's genetic codes are manipulated *in vitro* in order to select for traits of the parents' choosing. While fantastic in terms of the current state of genetic research, the fact that it has a basis in contemporary scientific theory lends the postulated "set of changes" a plausibility that allows audiences to draw important parallels between this fictional world and their own. Audience members are faced with the question of what such advances might mean in the real world and how they might deal with them if that time ever comes.

There is something special about the way in which "sci-fi" poses such interesting "what if" scenarios that sets it apart from other genres. John W. Campbell, Jr., former editor of *Astounding Science Fiction*, directly compares sci-fi to the fantasy genre in an attempt to capture the definitive characteristics of the former:

The major distinction between fantasy and science fiction is, simply, that science fiction uses one, or a very, very few new postulates, and develops the rigidly consistent logical consequences of these limited postulates. Fantasy makes its rules as it goes along.... The basic nature of fantasy is "The only rule is, make up a new rule any time you need one!" The basic rule of science fiction is "Set up a basic proposition — then develop its consistent, logical consequences."[3]

It is worth noting that while Campbell's take on sci-fi differs from Merril's, it echoes the idea that science fiction involves exploring the logical consequences that follow from a certain set of "changes" or "postulates." This odd mixture of creativity and constraint seems to be a defining characteristic of sci-fi. The sci-fi world is notably different from our own, but the creator is expected to play by the rules posited at the outset of the story.

Certain key features of sci-fi become apparent when we look at Merril and Campbell's respective takes on the genre. The first feature involves the genre's reliance on introducing a "set of changes" or "new postulates." Such changes often challenge the audience to ask "what if?" The changes introduced are, therefore, typically not up for question. The audience isn't challenged to ask if the real world is *actually* like this— if, for example, there are *actually* humanlike A.I.'s walking around — but to take these as settled matters and explore the logical consequences that follow from them.

The second feature is the idea that the sci-fi world is, in some way, relatable to the reader. The "unchanged" portions of the world allow the audience to find connections between the fictional world and their own. Sometimes what happens in sci-fi may have real-world analogues, and the audience is invited to find these.

The above two features make sci-fi structurally similar to thought experiments. Both thought experiments and sci-fi introduce novel changes to some situation in order to aid our thinking on a given topic. Just as important, however, both sci-fi and thought experiments introduce only changes that make explicit the analogical similarities between real life and the modeled situation. In fact, we would go so far as to say that a foundational characteristic of sci-fi is the creation and maintenance of the epistemic freedom so sought after by those who construct thought experiments.

The Structure of Thought Experiments

Thought experiments are tools for speculating about our beliefs concerning reality.[4] Albert Einstein famously used thought experiments throughout his theoretical work on gravitation and acceleration. *Einstein's Elevator* is a thought experiment he used to prove his equivalence principle (that the force of gravity is nothing more than constant uniform acceleration). Einstein asks us to imagine two windowless elevators, one sitting motionless on the ground while the other is suspended by an enormous crane in outer space that is pulling the elevator "upwards" at the constant rate of 9.8 mps².[5] Now imagine that each elevator has one occupant and that the occupants are unaware as to which elevator they occupy. Einstein's point is that, from each occupant's perspective, it's impossible to deduce which elevator one is occupying based on one's physical experiences of the elevator's interior. If the occupants were to jump inside either elevator, things would appear identical: They would jump the same height with no floating around. If they had coins in their pockets and threw them to the ground, the coins would behave in identical ways. Hence, Einstein concluded that gravity was in fact no different than uniform acceleration.

Thought experiments, while unquestionably valuable for the theoretical physicist, are also invaluable for the morally minded sci-fi writer. Interestingly, the structure of the thought experiment does not dramatically change whether you're thinking about the physics of four-dimensional space-time or about the moral permissibility of torture. We think it helps to think about thought experiments in terms of five related structural components, all of which play a significant role in fostering the notion of epistemic freedom we find to be so important to the nature of thought experiments within sci-fi.

First, thought experiments attempt to elucidate the core concepts that are significant to a given situation. Second, thought experiment typically highlight the central claims and/or theoretical commitments that are explicitly or implicitly attached to a situation. The reason that these components are so important is because they tend to remove unnecessary distractions from the real-life situation, which is the third structural component of thought experiments. Fourth, in removing the unnecessary distractions, thought experiments are often used to draw attention to factors that influence judgment in illicit ways, bring to light contradictions and inconsistencies within a set of beliefs, or undermine a closely held assumption about some situation. Fifth, thought experiments typically involve analogical reasoning, a component that will be developed in more detail later in the essay.

With respect to elucidating core concepts, thought experiments are typically structured in one of two broad ways. Sometimes it is necessary to reduce the number and/or type of active variables in a given situation. We call these *reductive-type* thought experiments. *Einstein's Elevator* is an excellent example of a reductive experiment; he consciously abstracted away all the tedious factors that might bog down any computation of gravitational/acceleration values. By reducing the number of active variables, he was able to focus on just two physical forces, pretending for the sake of argument that there were only two forces in the universe: gravitation and acceleration. This allowed him to conclude that there was no physical difference between the two.[6]

The reduction of relevant variables is only the first step in elucidating the core concepts, however. The second step is that a few variables are then given prominence. Looking again at Einstein's example, he was able to display both gravitation and acceleration as the significant variables precisely because he intentionally ignored the other causal forces that affect the behavior of the elevators and the objects they contained.

Another prominent characteristic of reductive-type thought experiments involves delineating the method of observation. Einstein places constraints on how the occupants can acquire knowledge about their environment by making the elevator windowless and by allowing only simple physical experiments (jumping up and down, tossing coins, e.g.). Defining the method of observation is an important component in elucidating core concepts and theoretical commitments involved in a real-life situation as well.[7] Some thought experiments require that the method of observation be exactly as it would be in the real-life situation, yet others elucidate core concepts precisely by altering our usual method of observation.

Altering the method of observation is sometimes necessary to pinpoint closely held beliefs about certain situations. In *Mary's Room*, a thought experiment from Frank Jackson, we are to imagine that Mary is a brilliant scientist who was placed at birth in a black-and-white room and forced to study the world without any sense-experience of color. This thought experiment draws attention to a commonly held assumption in science — that knowledge about any object is reducible to a set of empirical facts, typically written in the language of physics. We are supposed to imagine that Mary has studied all there is to know about the laws of optics, including the behavior of wavelengths of light, and she is also well versed in neuroscience research on sensation and perception. Jackson then asks whether Mary knows all there is to know about the experience of seeing the color red. She has access to all of the physical facts about the behavior of light and the physico-chemical reactions in the brain that capture sensory stimuli and produce a sensory experience, but has never seen color of any sort. Jackson has two points he wishes to make with *Mary's Room*. First, he wishes to draw attention to deficiencies in the method of observation employed by scientists in Mary's world, since that method has obviously missed a significant component in defining what it means to have an experience of seeing color. Second, he criticizes the widely accepted assumption that all knowledge is reducible to scientific facts.[8]

Unlike *Einstein's Elevator*, *Mary's Room* adds details and complex variables to the situation. Whereas *Einstein's Elevator* reduces the very strange to the very familiar (reducing four-dimensional space-time to a situation involving two elevators and two occupants), *Mary's Room* takes us from the very familiar to the very strange (our beliefs about color experience to a woman forced to live in a room with no access to color). Apart from being an excellent example of a *constructive-type* thought experiment, *Mary's Room* is also an example of thought experiments testing basic assumptions and bringing to light inconsistencies in our beliefs— this time an inconsistency between our beliefs about the best means of studying the natural world and our beliefs about what constitutes knowledge about the world.

In sum, thought experiments assist in the contemplation of "uncrystallized issues" with the hope of attaining reflective equilibrium between our theoretical principles and our practical judgments.[9] This can occur either by reducing the number of variables involved and focusing on a few significant concepts or by developing an elaborate imaginary world to test our most basic assumptions. As we have seen, thought experiments are excellent devices for *freeing up* central issues from seemingly intractable real-life situations. This is exactly what our notion of epistemic freedom is all about: freeing our thinking about difficult issues from extraneous beliefs that have become attached to complex real-life situations. For instance, the debate about the proper characterization of sensory beliefs is, on the face of it, a hugely complicated matter involving physics, biochemistry, and neuroscience, yet when placed within the artificial confines of *Mary's Room*, it becomes easy to decide the matter.

For the rest of this essay, we will be concerned with thought experiments that clarify our moral beliefs along the same lines as those used in scientific theorizing— that is, by elucidating the key concepts involved, highlighting relevant theoretical commitments, removing irrelevant distractions, and drawing out factors that illicitly affect our judgments.[10] Science fiction, as it turns out, offers up many such thought experiments.

Science Fiction as Thought Experiment

In the following two sections, respectively titled "*Battlestar Galactica* and the Problem of Abortion," and "*New X-Men*, Gay-Friendly High Schools, and the Xavier Institute," we intend to show how sci-fi can itself be a thought experiment on a particular moral situation. Our strategy for doing this is to explicitly lay out the *argument-isomorphism* between the sci-fi literature and a morally significant real-life analogue situation. We think that the two cases discussed below (a television series and a comic book, respectively) are best seen as explicit explorations of morally significant situations presented in a sci-fi setting, a situation that we call *argument-isomorphism* since a specific debate within moral philosophy is being explored within that setting. As with all good sci-fi, these two presentations are accompanied by the requisite structured changes to the real-life situation discussed in the section detailing the structure of thought experiments in general. It is our belief that these two instances of argument-isomorphism in sci-fi perform admirably in showing how the genre can be a great source for explicitly elucidating core issues in larger moral debates.

Battlestar Galactica and the Problem of Abortion

The issue of abortion is incredibly complex. Apart from sociopolitical issues, there are ethical considerations attached to abortion debates. Two of the most significant ethical issues related to abortion concerns the moral status of the fetus and the reproductive rights of women. *Battlestar Galactica* (*BSG*, henceforth), a television series which ran on the Sci-Fi Channel from December 2003 to March 2009, provides an opportunity to explore the core issues related to the question of the moral permissibility of abortion, one that attempts to detach that question from our anthropomorphic conception of personhood, from the relation between personhood and moral status, and from the question of women's reproductive rights. In the next few paragraphs, we'll introduce the *BSG* universe and follow that by a discussion of the thought experiment devoted to separating the abortion question from both the rights question and the personhood question.

In the *BSG* universe, humans have developed a race of technologically advanced, artificially intelligent robots designed to be nothing more than subservient laborers, denied status as moral and political entities. This class of slave robots, called cylons, rebelled from their human masters and, after a prolonged conflict, emigrated to a distant part of the galaxy, presumably never to be heard from again. However, some forty years later, the cylons return to confront their human creators, only now they have evolved beyond mere robot-slaves to sentient organic beings capable of abstract thought and in possession of a sophisticated theology, yet without the capability to genetically reproduce. The cylons require their human creators for reproduction, not by performing the reproduction in a laboratory, but by actually playing a role in the reproductive act. And here's where we get to start asking the really interesting questions, such as "Are there any conditions under which abortion should be permissible?" and "What happens when the mother of a cylon/human hybrid wishes to get an abortion?" and, relatedly, "What is the moral status of a hybrid fetus?" All these questions are asked in a story arc that spans episodes titled "The Captain's Hand" and "Downloaded."[11]

In "The Captain's Hand," a young Gemenese citizen, Rya Kibby, seeks political asylum from the military's highest-ranking officer, Admiral William Adama, also the commander of the battlestar *Galactica*. On Gemenon, one of the Twelve Colonies of Kobol, abortion is illegal for religious reasons and, further, children under the age of 18 are considered to be the property of their parents. Rya, who is only 17 years old, seeks to circumvent both her parents' wishes and Gemenese law by obtaining asylum under the Articles of Colonization (the constitution of the Twelve Colonies that establishes and protects the basic rights of its citizens) in order to procure a legal abortion.

It is at this point that the traditional abortion debate takes on a uniquely sci-fi twist, given that the Twelve Colonies of Kobol, once with a population of millions of humans, has been reduced by the returning cylon armada to a population of roughly 49,000 humans. This disastrously low population number troubles many of the remaining humans, all of whom share a worry about repopulating the human population before the species goes extinct. In fact, one of President Laura Roslin's first official statements after being sworn in soon after the near-annihilation of the Twelve Colonies was, "We need to concentrate on having babies." This sentiment gains scientific backing when Dr. Gaius Baltar confirms, via mathematical population models, that the minimum viable population size is alarmingly close to their current population size, which means that each and every reproductively capable human will play an invaluable role in repopulating the human race. This worry is wonderfully dramatized by Roslin keeping track on a whiteboard in her office of the number of remaining humans by recording both births and deaths as they occur.

Here the constructive-type thought experiment is obvious and powerful: Imagine that the human population were tragically reduced and were facing extinction due to the effects of a genetic bottleneck (where lack of adequate genetic variance reduces the number of possible viable mates within a population). That premise is expounded throughout the early part of the series and comes to a head when Roslin must make the difficult choice of whether or not to ban abortion, given the Colonies' dire circumstances. Roslin has long been an activist for women's reproductive rights who, presumably, believes in the right to abortion on those grounds. Yet now her situation is different; she is the democratic leader of a population of humans beings threatened with extinction unless, as she so endearingly says, "People start having babies." But requiring people to start having babies is clearly at odds with the right to have an abortion. She recognizes that there is a logical conflict between these related commitments and must, in essence, choose between the two for the good of the population *as a whole.*

Separating the rights question from the abortion question provides the ethical deliberator the epistemic freedom to explore her thoughts concerning abortion apart from her thoughts concerning an individual's rights. This separation shows that the two concepts are unique, though related, and allows for an unencumbered exploration of both. It also allows for an analysis of the separation via a critique of Roslin's decision-making procedure — that is, the thought experiment allows for an examination as to whether the abortion question *should* be separated from the rights question in the first place or whether the abortion question is in some way logically dependent on the rights question.

Sci-fi in general, and *BSG* in particular, allows us to explore the implications of granting moral status to, say, non-human, non-biological entities, thus removing the question of moral status from the volatile situation it often gets attached to in real-life situations. For instance, arguments regarding the moral permissibility of abortion are often cast in terms of general moral theories that define personhood in such a way that either allows or does not allow for fetuses to be considered as persons. This either allows the fetuses status as moral entities or excludes fetuses from moral status. The question whether fetuses count as moral entities is highly significant for the debate about the permissibility of abortion: If the fetus is defined as a person, then there are several persuasive arguments suggesting that the fetus has a strong claim to the right to life and, as such, that any abdication of that right (e.g., an abortion) is tantamount to murder. Murder, of course, is a clear violation of moral principles that underwrite many moral theories, religious and otherwise. Likewise, if the fetus is excluded from personhood, the fetus does not have a strong claim to the right to life, and, therefore, an abortion is not to be considered a murderous act.

In trying to decide what sorts of entities count as persons, many different sets of characteristics have been proposed as *the* defining characteristics of personhood, including the ability to feel pain or to engage in reflective thought. The problem, of course, is to define personhood in such a way that the definition includes just the entities we think it should include while neither excluding entities that ought to be included (infants or young children) nor including entities that should not be included (a toaster oven or a graphing calculator). But contemporary literature devoted to defining personhood in moral philosophy is replete with inconsistent sets of characteristics, none of which has been agreed upon by a majority of the moral community.

In the case of the *BSG* universe, however, we are faced with a constructive-type thought experiment that invokes the question, "Which sorts of entities are to be given moral status?" in an entirely new light, one that proposes the question in lieu of the "fact" that there exists a population of seemingly sentient non-biological entities who possess many of the characteristics that traditionally define personhood. As the series progresses, it is clear that the evolved cylons have the full range of functional equivalents to human emotions[12] and, further, that they seem to experience pain similarly to humans. The cylons also have evolved to look just like humans (some even think they are human!) and are fully organic beings that may or may not be conscious (they believe they are conscious).[13]

So no longer is the question about personhood bogged down by the complicating factors orbiting the abortion debate in the real world. Now the question can be explored for precisely what it is: a philosophical query into the nature of a moral entity. Within the *BSG* universe, one does not have to worry about being pro-choice or pro-life and allowing those commitments to pre-determine how one thinks about the nature of moral entities. Within the thought experiment one is able to weigh how important consciousness is in granting moral status without worrying what that means for the abortion clinic down the street. One is able to adjudicate the philosophical justification of limiting moral status solely to human beings without being forced to also worry about whether this commits one to accepting that women do not have full rights over their bodies. Similarly, within the *BSG* universe one is able to examine how well one's intuitions on abortion mesh with the hypothetical scenario involving the proposed abortion of non-human, non-biological organisms in order to gain a more thorough understanding about those intu-itions—again, without contemporaneously worrying about what this means for cases like *Roe v. Wade*.

We are not suggesting that these thoughts have no bearing on the real-life situation. In fact, we believe that these thoughts have a direct bearing on the real-life situation being modeled. The beauty of sci-fi is that it provides a unique forum for thinking about these topics in a way that allows for unusual clarity.

New X-Men, Gay-Friendly High Schools, and the Xavier Institute

Problems facing lesbian, bisexual, gay, and transgender (LBGT) students in Chicago, ranging from an extremely high dropout rate to physical attacks, have led school officials to propose the establishment of a "gay-friendly" high school.[14] The proposed School for Social Justice Pride Campus is similar to another "gay-friendly" high school, Harvey Milk High School, in New York City. The idea is that "gay-friendly" schools would offer LBGT students a place to learn without the fear of persecution or bullying from their peers. Such schools are not open *exclusively* to LBGT students—any other so-called "at-risk" students are welcome—but it is no secret that the problems facing LBGT youths have acted as the impetus behind the proposal of the Chicago school and the establishment of Harvey Milk High School.

The concept of "gay-friendly" schools has been met with controversy. Some LBGT advocates fear that such schools inadvertently establish a form of morally unjustifiable segregation. The worry is that establishing such schools does not deal with the real problem of prejudice found within cur-rent schools and sets up an inherently unequal and unethical educational sys-tem. Some claim that this will foster a feeling of inferiority among LBGT students, regardless of the content of courses taught within the school.[15]

Another worry is that such schools make these students easier targets for discrimination by providing objectors with a highly visible public location that could act as a stage for protests and, more troubling, acts of violence against the students. Still, others oppose such institutions because they think that special treatment for LBGT students implicitly legitimizes what they see as an immoral lifestyle.

There are two questions to be addressed, but too often they are mistaken for one. The first is whether establishing a special school is a morally justifiable way to confront problems faced by persecuted students. All but extremists desire a school system that provides a safe learning environment for students. However, there remain serious questions about the appropriateness of establishing separate schools as a strategy to accomplish this goal. The second question is whether the students' LBGT status is morally relevant to granting them *any* special protections, be it the establishment of separate schools or the codification of rules that expressly prohibit harassment related to a student's LBGT status. For those who claim sexual orientation is a choice, particularly those who find it to be an immoral choice, this latter question may overshadow the first. It is hard to clearly deliberate on these questions separately, but such a deliberation is just what this real-world situation requires.

The difficulty in confronting the relevant moral questions often stems from an inability to explore either question in isolation. Sexuality is a controversial subject, and the controversy too often distracts from clear deliberation. However, a recent sci-fi narrative provides an opportunity for just such deliberation. Grant Morrison's work on the comic book *New X-Men*, particularly his work in the storyline "Riot at Xavier's," sets up a constructive-type thought experiment that explores the question, "Is the establishment of a separate school for persecuted groups morally justifiable?"[16] While the text itself does not provide a definitive answer, it does allow for a framework in which to explore the core concepts related to the school-establishment question in isolation from the sexuality question.

In the *X-Men* universe, there exists a persecuted group known as "mutants." Mutants are carriers of a special "X-gene" that, around the time of puberty, causes the carrier to manifest a special genetic mutation. Sometimes this is in the form of a power; sometimes it is simply a noticeable physical change. Mutants face prejudice due to a genetic makeup that they do not control. Note that there are many parallels to the sexuality issue, particularly the "mutation" appearing at puberty. However, within the sci-fi narrative the "fact" postulated is that the reason for the persecution, the mutation in this case, is beyond the control of the students. In other words, there is no question of whether or not "being a mutant" is a morally problematic choice. It isn't a choice at all in this fictional world. One of the postulations of this sci-fi narrative is that there exist these mutants and that they face persecution from the general public. Hence, one does not have to dwell on the matter of whether there is something morally problematic about the group that is being persecuted, only if the means for dealing with the persecution are morally justifiable.

In Morrison's *New X-Men*, Charles Xavier (Professor X), the headmaster of an institution known as the Xavier Institute for Higher Learning, announces to the world that he is a mutant.[17] By announcing that he is a member of this persecuted group, he also informs the world that his school is a school for mutants, a place of refuge for mutant youths.[18] This announcement soon brings about a number of changes to not only the Professor's life, but to the lives of his students as well. "Riot at Xavier's" takes place shortly after the professor's announcement. In the story, the professor decides to open the school to not only mutants, but to any student who seeks refuge from persecution. The admittance of these non-mutant students is to take place on "Open Day," and much of the storyline involves the days leading up to the "Open Day Celebration."

"Riot at Xavier's" seems to have a real-world analogue in the "gay-friendly" school debate. Xavier wants to provide a safe learning environment: a school initially established for a particular persecuted group, but now accepting any students who feel the need for a different learning environment. The intent appears to be analogous to the impetus behind the proposal of "gay-friendly" high schools, but since readers need not bring along the epistemic baggage of the "sexuality debate," they are free to explore the specific issue of whether the establishment/continuation of such a school for persecuted youths is a morally acceptable strategy to deal with persecution.

But the story presents analogues to the real-world debate over gay-friendly high schools in more ways. Analogous to the worry that "gay-friendly" high schools may make easy targets of their students, the initial announcement that the Xavier Institute is a mutant-friendly school draws a large amount of negative attention. The school soon finds its students confronted with mobs of protesters outside its gates sporting signs that read "God hates mutants" and other hateful epithets.[19] The imagery is striking; protesters peer into the zoo-like gates of the school, while teachers stand guard in the school's courtyard, fists clenched, ready to protect their students.[20] One professor, Hank McCoy (aka Beast), notes that the school is "turning into a fortress under siege."[21] Added to this is the imagery of the students in the courtyard. Their slumped shoulders and pained faces suggest the negative psychological consequence of being singled out for attendance at the Xavier Institute.[22]

These scenes question whether establishing a separate school for persecuted groups is an effective way to combat public prejudice. The imagery of students "behind bars" suggests that the school itself is an instrument in stereotyping the students as "freaks." a group to be kept separate from the general public. These types of questions are sometimes overlooked in the real-world debate regarding "gay-friendly high schools" because so much attention is paid to the controversy surrounding sexuality rather than to the possible consequences *any* such school may hold in store for its students. This story, when read as a thought experiment, explores some potential consequences that could befall students at such schools.

However, the narrative is not one-sided. The imagery used to depict school life paints a different picture.[23] Hallways are filled with all types of students, grinning and laughing. Furthermore, many students seem excited at the prospect of "Open Day" and what it means to be a part of the school. Students are shown working on presentations and displays to formally announce the school's purpose to the world.[24] Professor X expresses to his students that the purpose of the "Open Day" is not to endanger anyone, but rather is part of an effort to "heal the split between humans and mutants."[25] These scenes suggest that the schools could provide persecuted groups with a healthy environment in which they can build supportive communities. Surely, this is the hope many advocates of "gay-friendly" high schools have as well.

While we have argued that the sci-fi narrative in question simplifies the matter, we do not believe it does so at the cost of oversimplifying the moral question regarding the strategy of establishing schools specifically geared toward persecuted student populations. By postulating that "being a mutant" is not itself a moral matter, the reader is invited to explore the general question of whether establishing a "persecuted-group friendly" school is morally justifiable. The sci-fi narrative allows for epistemic freedom in thinking about the situation. It brings to the forefront many of the core issues involved in the debate over "gay-friendly" high schools, allowing one to discuss these issues without being bogged down by the separate sexuality question.

Conclusion

To summarize, we think that sci-fi is an effective intellectual tool for enhancing the quality of our moral deliberations, whether or not a work of science fiction intentionally elucidates some core concepts in a moral debate. In the first section, we showed how sci-fi allows us to explore the implications of changes to our reality and our judgments about these changes. In the second section, we discussed a time-honored philosophical tool — the thought experiment — and endeavored to show how strikingly similar the structure of thought experiments is to the sci-fi genre as a whole. We also articulated the methods by which thought experiments can be constructed so that they can provide epistemic freedom from the factors that complicate moral deliberation in the real world.

The epistemic freedom that sci-fi provides has practical benefits. Simply put, discussion of morally touchy subjects can be facilitated by the use of sci-fi narratives. It is sometimes easier for people to discuss such issues when discussing them as happening in a far-off galaxy than in their own backyard. This could provide a pedagogical benefit to ethics instructors across the curriculum in getting their students to engage the hard questions while leaving some of their epistemic baggage at the door.

Outside the classroom, being conscious of this possible interpretation of sci-fi narratives also has benefits. The narratives can get us to think about significant moral concepts in novel ways. Sci-fi is not merely some form of escapism; it has the potential to be a sophisticated tool for investigating some of our most deeply held beliefs and assumptions. When we allow ourselves to get lost in these fictional worlds, we can find out a lot about our own.

NOTES

1. Furthermore, the genre offers a unique pedagogical opportunity that can facilitate rational discussion of controversial topics that students may be initially reluctant to explore.

2. Vivian Carol Sobchack, *Screening Space: The American Science Fiction Film,* 2nd ed. (New York: Ungar, 1991), 19.

3. John W. Campbell, Jr., ed., Introduction to *Analog 6* (Garden City, NY: Doubleday, 1968), xiv–xv.

4. Roy Sorensen, *Thought Experiments* (New York: Oxford University Press, 1992), 7.

5. 9.8 mps^2 is the traditional value given to calculate the gravitational force objects have on one another.

6. There is one more provision that is required to draw that conclusion, and it is that Einstein states that the occupants' method of observation remains unchanged.

7. Sometimes this means fixing or getting rid of theoretical principles in favor of intuitions; sometimes, however, it means getting rid of our intuitions in favor of our theoretical principles. See, for instance, pp. 34 and 83 of Sorensen (*Thought Experiments,* 1992) for more details.

8. Jackson, in his "Epiphenomenal Qualia," (1982) and "What Mary Didn't Know," (1986) criticizes the assumption by showing how it is undermined by embracing the very method of observation recommended by its proponents. Once we accept that assumption, Jackson goes on to show how that view leads to a consequence that is very difficult to accept. In this case we are forced to accept the conclusion that there is nothing substantially different between knowing all of the physical facts about color perception and the actual color perception itself as it takes place inside the mind of the perceiver, a conclusion that is thoroughly at odds with our intuitions about this issue. Frank Jackson, "Epiphenomenal Qualia," *Philosophical Quarterly* 32 (1982): pp. 127–36; Frank Jackson, "What Mary Didn't Know," *Journal of Philosophy* 83 (1986): pp. 291–295.

9. For Einstein, the point of the thought experiment was to demonstrate that the experiences in both elevators is identical from the perspective of physics; hence, no amount of physical experimentation will be able to justify positing gravity as a separate physical force in the universe. Physics is typically seen as a reductive enterprise, and any hypothesis that reduces numerous forces to a single force is highly prized. *Einstein's Elevator,* by reducing two forces to a single force, was highly prized for that fact.

10. Some thought experiments can shed light on the conditions that constitute morality itself. However, we are interested, much like the experiments of moral psychology, in furthering our means of making explicit which, if any, moral beliefs we actually have and, just as importantly, which sort of beliefs play a role in our everyday moral deliberations.

11. *Battlestar Galactica,* season 2, episodes 30 and 31.

12. It is impossible to say whether they actually have the same set of emotions found within humans. What we can say is that the cylons typically behave in ways strikingly similar to humans in similar emotionally significant situations.

13. Whatever we may think of their status as moral entities, however, it is clear that many of the humans in the *BSG* universe certainly do not grant them full status. Popular racial epithets used by humans to denigrate cylons are "toaster" and "skin-job"—one to remind the cylons of their previous status as mere machines used for menial tasks such as making toast and the other, to remind them that their human appearance is a mere artifice.

14. Mallory Simon, "Chicago May Get 'Gay-Friendly' High School." CNN.com, October 13, 2008, http://www.cnn.com/2008/US/10/13/gay.friendly.school/index.html (accessed November 13, 2009).

15. Randy Hedlun, "Segregation by Any Other Name: Harvey Milk High School," *The Journal of Law & Education* 33, no. 2 (2004): 425–430.

16. Grant Morrison (w), *New X-Men* Issues 114 to 154 (New York: Marvel Comics), 2001–2004. "Riot at Xavier's" consists of the story arc running through Issues 134 to 138.

17. *Ibid.,* Issue 116, 23.

18. This is not explicitly noted in the comic, as we state. However, in the following issue, no. 117, the public protests outside the school's gates are a clear indication that Xavier let the world know about the school and the reader is meant to "fill in the blanks" regarding why there are suddenly protests outside the school.

19. Morrison, *New X-Men,* Issue 117, 4. While not explicitly part of the "Riot at Xavier's" storyline, this image portrays the public reaction to the "mutant-friendly" announcement preceding the official "Open Day" celebration. The protest signs' slogan is an interesting, and possibly intentional, parallel to the "God Hates Fags" protest signs popularized by Fred Phelps' Westboro Baptist Church groups, best known for picketing military funerals. The "mutant as gay" metaphor is also suggested in the words of Morrison's character Henry "Beast" McCoy, who notes the parallels between mutant persecution and the persecution of the LBGT community.

20. *Ibid.,* 5–6.

21. *Ibid.,* 6.

22. *Ibid.,* 5–6.

23. *Ibid.,* 5–6.

24. Morrison, *New X-Men,* Issue 134, 14.

25. Morrison, *New X-Men,* Issue 135, 5.

WORKS CITED

Battlestar Galactica. Episode no. 30, "The Captain's Hand," first broadcast 17 February 2006 by Sci-Fi. Directed by Sergio Mimica-Gezzan and written by Jeff Vlaming.

Battlestar Galactica. Episode no. 31, "Downloaded," first broadcast 24 February 2006 by Sci-Fi. Directed by Jeff Woolnough and written by Bradley Thompson and David Weddle.

Campbell, John, Jr., ed. *Analog 6.* Garden City, NY: Doubleday, 1968.

Hedlun, Randy. "Segregation by Any Other Name: Harvey Milk High School." *The Journal of Law & Education* 22 no. 2 (2004): 425–430.

Jackson, Frank. "Epiphenomenal Qualia." *Philosophical Quarterly* 32 (1982): 127–136.

_____. "What Mary Didn't Know." *Journal of Philosophy* 83, (1986): 291–295.

Morrison, Grant. *New X-Men* no. 114–154. New York: Marvel Comics, 2001–2004.

Simon, Mallory. "Chicago May Get 'Gay-Friendly' High School." CNN.com, October 13,

2008, http://www.cnn.com/2008/US/10/13/gay.friendly.school/index.html (accessed November 13, 2009).

Sobchack, Vivian Carol. *Screening Space: The American Science Fiction Film*, 2nd ed. New York: Ungar, 1991.

Sorenson, Roy. *Thought Experiments*. New York: Oxford University Press, 1992.

CHAPTER 19

Weight Watching:
The Ethics of Commodifying
Appearance for Profit

Berrin A. Beasley

All media institutions, of course, have the economic function "to attract and hold large audiences for advertisers," but that is irrelevant to a discussion in the moral realm. That is, economic realities don't provide justification for causing people to suffer harms.

— Deni Elliott

Kirstie Alley's TV comeback via Jenny Craig ads. Same for Valerie Bertinelli. Denise Richards' return to pre-baby weight just six weeks after giving birth to baby number two. Demi Moore's marriage to a man 15 years her junior, and the $400,000 in plastic surgery it took to get him. These sound like tabloid stories because they are, but the stories aren't just limited to tabs anymore. They're the mainstay of celebrity journalism, and they're all centered on celebrities' appearance. Page after page of such celebrity magazines as *In Touch* and *Life & Style* dissect celebrities' choice of dress, coat, shoes, and bag, comparing two celebrities in similar outfits to see who looked better. We're obsessed with weight, and we objectify anyone and everyone famous who dares step outside the privacy of her home.

Our national obsession with appearance goes beyond celebrity magazines. Television is fraught with reality shows in which people are physically altered for ratings. *The Biggest Loser, Bulging Brides, Celebrity Fit Club, Weighing In, Shaq's Big Challenge, Extreme Makeover,* and *The Swan* are all examples of the bogus philosophy that an improved appearance equals an improved life. The shows run the gamut of television outlets, from NBC to VH1 to The Food Network. What they teach media consumers—in conjunction with such entertainment news shows as *Extra, Hard Copy,* and *Entertainment Tonight,* and such celebrity magazines as *People, OK,* and *Us Weekly*— is that how you look is far more important than who you are.

People are learning the lesson all too well. For example, 80 percent of American women don't like the way they look,[1] and 75 percent of normal-weight women think they're overweight.[2] Eighty-one percent of girls as young as 10 are afraid of getting fat,[3] and the number one wish for girls ages 11–17 is to be thin.[4] Not fame, fortune, or health. Not even world peace, but to be thin. And this isn't just a female issue. An estimated 1 million men and boys in the United States suffer from eating disorders.[5] Specific documentation on the rate of body image disorders growth among males is limited, but a 2007 study by Harvard University Medical School revealed that of the 3,000 men and women surveyed, 25 percent of adults with eating disorders were male, as were 40 percent of the self-reported binge eaters.[6]

Using media to convince Americans that their appearance is unacceptable is an unethical practice because, according to a basic, commonly accepted ethical principle, every person, regardless of his or her physical characteristics, is entitled to respect and to being treated as something more than a means to a profitable end. This chapter looks at the ethical issues associated with the media's relentless commodification of appearance to sell programs, products, and services, and it examines the ways in which consumers, particularly women, may be negatively affected by the media's obsession with celebrities and their bodies.

The Ethics of Body Image Exploitation for Profit

For the average media consumer, the relentless message that one's worth is defined by one's appearance is impossible to ignore. It's everywhere every day. In addition to the reality weight-loss and surgical makeover shows, the celebrity magazines that push diet secrets of the stars and the stars themselves who sell the diet products, there are dozens of television shows dedicated to hair, makeup, and clothing makeovers, and thousands of television shows, films, music videos, and websites devoted to telling stories with images of young, thin, busty — and primarily white — women who epitomize the physical ideal of beauty, even if that beauty has been artificially achieved. Research indicates that the viewing of such media can and does affect our perceptions of reality.[7] Endlessly surrounded by mediated images of supposed perfection, we begin to think that's the way all women should look, a groomed size 0 or 2 with unnaturally large breasts. This effect is explained by George Gerbner, a social psychologist, as the cultivation effect. The narrow, standardized message of ideal female beauty that is continuously repeated in the media cultivates an attitude in consumers that this message is correct because it's almost always the only message we see.

Never mind that we rarely encounter this idealized image in the real world. We have so internalized the media's messages regarding the norm for women's appearances that we automatically rate every real woman we see as either ideal or not, and very few real women meet the ideal threshold. Advertisers and producers tell those who don't measure up to eat less, exercise more, highlight their hair, whiten their teeth, change their makeup, and buy new clothes, or breasts, whatever the case may be, so they'll be worthy of love and attention.

This is a dangerous and damning way to live, and that is at the heart of the ethical dilemma created by the commodification of appearance for profit purposes. Whether or not the creators of body image entertainment intentionally construct programming that distorts consumers' views of reality, as advertisers do, is irrelevant. Literally thousands of research studies tell us that the media can and do have negative effects, even if those effects are unintended, and creators of media products have an ethical responsibility to guard against those effects because of their potential harm to media consumers. For example, one study revealed that reading magazines correlated with body image dissatisfaction among teenage girls.[8] In another study, researchers found that teenage girls who watched TV commercials featuring women with the ideal female form felt angrier, less confident, and more dissatisfied with their weight and appearance.[9] If girls as young as 10 are afraid of getting fat, there's clearly a negative association made with weight gain, and one way girls can acquire that association is by heavily consuming media that focus on appearance.

Scholars explain the field of ethics as the search for the best or *right* way to solve an ethical dilemma. Ethics is frequently defined using two characteristics: as providing mutual aid and refraining from inflicting harm. From there we can allow that people don't want to be harmed without their consent and that, unfortunately, people often do harm others without the others' consent.[10] It's this contradictory environment that makes the study of ethics so important, especially for those who work in the media. We expect, or at least we should expect, people who work in such social organizations as the media to behave ethically.

Deontology, or duty ethics, is an ethics system that requires the moral agent to make a decision based on his or her duty to others, regardless of the results of the decision. One frequently cited framework for moral decision-making was proposed by eighteenth-century German philosopher Immanuel Kant, who theorized that ethical decisions should be made out of a sense of duty, because it's the right thing to do, not because the consequences of the action would be favorable to the person making the decision. According to Kant, ethical duties include respecting others and promoting their good health.

Kant also based his ethical framework on the idea that the moral force resides in the act, not in the moral agent, meaning that people can act morally from a sense of duty, even though the act may run counter to their natural inclinations. So for media professionals, while they may be driven by a desire to accumulate wealth or increase ratings or simply come up with a memorable ad, they can choose to act ethically in the pursuit of those goals by creating media that aid others rather than harm them. Of Kant's three categorical imperatives, his second, to view individuals as an end in and of themselves and never as a means only, is the one that most media content producers violate on a daily basis. They treat audiences as merely a means to making money, thereby placing economic interests above their moral obligations. Yes, the commercial media in American exist to make money, but the need for profits doesn't justify causing people harm.

What Is Normal?

The average American woman weighs 140 pounds and stands 5 foot 4 inches tall.[11] Compare that to the average model that weighs 117 pounds and stands 5 foot 11.[12] Based on those statistics alone, there's no way the average woman will ever achieve the ideal female form. You can't add inches to your height any more than you can take years off your age. And now is a good time to point out that, according to medical charts that list the desirable weight range for a person's height, the average model is seriously underweight. According to the Metropolitan Life Insurance Company's Ideal Weight chart, women ages 25 to 59 who are 5 foot 11 should weigh between 135 and 176 pounds to be at a healthy weight. At an average of 117 pounds, that's 14 percent under the *lowest* reported healthy weight for women of that height.[13]

So what passes for ideal in American society is a woman who is taller than 95 percent of all American women and unhealthily thin for her height. But that's not what most women see when they look at mediated images of models. They see the ideal. Coupled with ad messages laden with psychological appeals designed to make women feel bad about their bodies, these images influence Americans to spend $40 billion annually on dieting and diet products alone.[14] To paraphrase body image expert Jean Kilbourne, we live in a toxic media environment, one specifically created to make us feel bad about ourselves so we'll buy sham products and services to try to make ourselves feel better.[15]

Academic scholars have amassed a large body of evidence since the 1970s that demonstrates a relationship between media exposure to the ideal female form and an increase in dissatisfaction of personal body image, which is defined as negative feelings toward physical attributes, such as weight, height, hair, face, and upper-, mid-, and lower-torso,[16] and feelings of frustration,[17] depression, anger, and anxiety towards one's body.[18] Evidence of the success of advertisers' messages of inferiority, combined with the relentless images of the ideal beauty on television shows, in magazines, and online, is that normal-weight women are convinced there is something wrong with them that needs to be changed. This message is so engrained in some people that they turn to the Internet's pro-anorexia websites for tips on becoming a more successful anorexic. Ethics scholars Elaine Englehardt and Ralph Barney write that Kantian philosophy defines the mass media, and their employees, as moral agents who have the *duty* to create socially responsible products.[19] The "moral law implicit within the First Amendment protections of the media requires that" media place a priority on "making better social participants of their viewers."[20]

But perhaps what's most frightening is that "weight" has become a morality issue in the United States, especially in the media, so that being overweight implies a person is lazy, self-indulgent, or lacks self-control. One example of this attitude can be found in the supposedly family-friendly animated Pixar film *Wall-E*, where an adorable little trash compactor spends his days packing trash into tiny cubes on Earth, now devoid of human life. It seems the humans are too fat and lazy to do anything for themselves. Instead they rely on robotics to survive, riding around in hovering recliners, sipping their meals instead of eating them out of pure laziness. Pixar's message is that fat people are responsible for the end of mankind — a brutally biased message for children to consume. Study after study shows that failing to meet ideal standards of appearance have tangible effects on people, such as being perceived as less active, less hardworking, less intelligent, less athletic, less successful, and less popular than thin people.[21] Perhaps even more revealing about society's prejudice against those who fail to meet ideal weight expectations is the finding that college students would prefer to marry an embezzler, cocaine user, or shoplifter than an overweight person.[22]

Wanted by Advertisers: Women Who Hate the Way They Look

Throughout Western European history, physical female beauty has been defined in varying ways. From the generously rounded tummies and thighs of the fifteenth-century Rubenesque beauties to the 97-pound, ultra-thin 1960s British model Twiggy, the ideals of feminine beauty have changed according to the social and cultural norms of the times. But one axiom has remained unchanged: Beauty is in the eye of the beholder.

Never has that phrase been more true than in the twenty-first century, though not perhaps in the way originally intended. Today's American woman does not see beauty when she looks at herself in the mirror; she sees crow's feet, sagging eyelids, graying or thinning hair, too-small breasts and too-large hips. She's convinced these physical attributes define her not as beautiful, but as old and ugly — as far from the modern cultural ideal of beauty as possible. The statistics are alarming:

- 1 out of every 2 American women is on a diet at any given time.[23]
- 42 percent of girls ages 6 to 9 want to be thinner.[24]
- 33 percent of American female teens begin smoking cigarettes to help control their appetite.[25]

True to the capitalistic way of life, for every problem, there is a product or service that promises to "fix it." Got wrinkles? Use this brand of face cream to reduce fine lines. Got yellow teeth? Use this brand of whitener for brighter, whiter teeth in just seven days. Carrying some extra weight? Try this diet/fitness product or plastic surgery procedure to get rid of it.

Also, according to the capitalist model, to sell products, there must be a perceived need for the product, either a real need or a created one. Hence, the unethical practices of advertisers who create the perception of beauty problems — such as gray hair, yellow teeth, a few extra pounds — to sell products to people who are, for the most part, simply experiencing the signs of natural aging based on varying genetic traits. One notable exception to this rule is the case of Dove's Campaign for Real Beauty.[26] Launched in 2004, the campaign features real women, not models, of various ages, sizes, and colors to sell its products in advertisements. The brand's campaign goal, as stated on its website, is to "provoke discussion and debate about today's typecast beauty images." Dove's mission of widening the definition of beauty may be a clever marketing ploy to profit from consumers' dissatisfaction with traditional advertising tactics, but when compared to Kant's imperative to treat individuals as an end, not a means only, it's advertising that is ethically executed and apparently economically successful, as it's still in practice all these years later. Whether the creators of the "Real Beauty" campaign consciously chose that approach for the betterment of society is debatable, but the campaign does meet the ethical requirements of meeting institutional duties toward society despite economic pressures.[27]

But to place the blame on all advertisers save Dove would be unethical in and of itself, for all forms of media are responsible for perpetuating the post–Twiggy ideal female form: young, tall, thin, large bust, tiny waist, narrow hips, and predominately Caucasian. Look around you. This is the modern mass-mediated version of female beauty, and many times it's not even real. The beautiful woman you see on the billboard or magazine cover probably had her wrinkles digitally removed, or she may even be the digital compilation of one woman's face, another's body. But one thing is for certain: she's everywhere we look, with a few notable exceptions, and so she skews our understanding of what "normal" women should look like.

Also distorted is the hyper-sexualization of women via pornography. What was once relegated to the back of the book stand or video store is now highly profitable and widely available on the Internet. Pornography often depicts female sexuality as something for men to consume for their pleasure, thereby reducing women to saleable objects valued solely for their sex appeal. This is yet another example of the media's violation of Kant's categorical imperative to treat humans with respect. Documented negative effects of this media form are troubling. Research indicates that male viewers of sexually explicit films find less satisfaction with the "affection, physical appearance, sexual curiosity, and sexual performance of their real-life partners."[28]

Baring Your Body (and Soul) on National Television

Advertisers aren't the only media players that exploit the notion of ideal beauty for profit. In the past few years we've seen a glut of television shows, both broadcast and cable, focusing on transforming "unappealing" bodies into bodies worthy of "value." NBC's *The Biggest Loser*, VH1's *Celebrity Fit Club*, and The Food Network's *Weighing In*, all focus on the slimming down of overweight or morbidly obese Americans with the help of registered dieticians and certified physical trainers. The participants are under the supervision of medical doctors and free from the constraints of real-world responsibilities, such as work and family obligations. In truth, any ethical person associated with the health industry will tell you that the extreme conditions under which the weight is lost — isolation, highly restricted food intake, hours of intense daily exercise — are unhealthy. These aren't conditions that facilitate a slow, healthy weight reduction for the necessary long-term maintenance of weight loss. And they're conditions that can't be emulated by the average American. These reality weight-loss shows aren't real at all. They're highly structured and heavily edited to provide audiences with a select view of reality.

Then there are the cosmetic surgery shows, such as ABC's *Extreme Makeover*, which describes its multiple-surgical-procedure-in-one-sitting approach as a "once in a lifetime chance to be given a truly 'Cinderella-like' experience." Other recent shows in this category include Fox's *The Swan*, which used multiple plastic surgery procedures to change the ugly duckling into the beautiful woman, and E's *Dr. 90210*, MTV's *I Want a Famous Face*, Discovery Health's *Plastic Surgery: Before and After*, and Bravo's *Miami Slice*. While each of these shows tout surgery as a simple, acceptable cure-all for physical features one may dislike, they gloss over the dangerous and potentially deadly side effects of cosmetic surgery, creating the idea that surgery is safe and worth the physical and financial stresses it entails. Research also tells us that viewing these shows increases viewers' interest in plastic surgery.[29]

In 2006 nearly 11 million cosmetic surgery procedures were performed in the United States, an increase of 7 percent from 2005, according to the American Society of Plastic Surgeons.[30] Even more frightening is the fact that breast augmentation surgeries for teens, meaning females 18 years of age and younger, rose nearly 500 percent between 1997 and 2007.[31] That's a two-thirds increase over the 300 percent increase in breast augmentation surgery among all age groups reported for the same 10-year period.[32] Breast augmentation is the most popular cosmetic surgery performed in the United States, accounting for approximately 20 percent of all surgical procedures, according to the plastic surgeons' society.[33] Clearly, women have internalized the media's message of what the ideal female form looks like, which includes large breasts à la Pamela Anderson or Carmen Electra, both of whom have had elective breast augmentation.

At first glance, diet and makeover shows appear to be ethically responsible by helping people improve their appearance, albeit for profit, keeping in mind that the profit motive is not unethical in and of itself. Harming people in the pursuit of profit is. Both types of shows teach viewers that physical appearance is a person's most important trait, and that extreme measures to alter appearance are acceptable as long as the result brings one closer to the culture's physical ideal. It's unethical of producers to cultivate these attitudes among viewers because it creates a mentality that demeans human dignity by reducing personal worth to outer appearance. It's no accident the commercial breaks on these shows are filled with ads for weight loss products; the goal of the programs is to provide advertisers with audiences from whom profits may be wrung, a direct violation of Kant's directive to treat others as autonomous individuals worthy of respect.

Celebrities and Beauty

Celebrities understand the power of beauty only too well, especially those who fall outside the ideal. Stars have hair stylists, makeup artists, personal trainers, personal chefs, clothes stylists—all for the sole purpose of bringing their appearance as close to the ideal as possible. Some celebrities have seen their stars rise because of their appearance, not their talent, and some celebrities have seen their stars fall for the very same reasons.

Take Kirstie Alley, the self-titled "fat actress." Known for starring in the TV shows *Cheers* and *Veronica's Closet* and the *Look Who's Talking* film series, she became more famous in the current decade as tabloid fodder because of her weight gain. At first she tried to confront the issue head-on by creating and starring in a series on Showtime about a fat actress trying to lose weight and revive her Hollywood career. Unfortunately for her, the show only lasted seven episodes. But within months, Alley had secured a new way to revive a career stalled by appearance problems. She became the celebrity spokesperson for the Jenny Craig weight-loss program. Over the next three years she lost 75 pounds and kept the weight off for a year. In early 2008, she severed her contract with Jenny Craig, but not before she published a self-help autobiography titled *How to Lose Your Ass and Regain Your Life: Reluctant Confessions of a Big-Butted Star* in 2005. In 2007 she starred in a made-for-TV movie titled *Write & Wrong* and in a new TV series pilot for FOX called *The Minister of Divine*. Most recently, she played a supporting role in the film *Nailed*, which at press time was in post-production.[34]

Impressed by the media attention paid Alley for her weight-loss work, another former television star jumped on the weight-loss bandwagon to revive her flagging career. Valerie Bertinelli, best known for her work on the 1970s television series *One Day at a Time*, and later *Touched by an Angel*, joined Alley as a celebrity spokesperson for Jenny Craig in April 2007. Since then, she's lost a total of 40 pounds and found a wealth of fame, turning Hollywood's pressure to be thin into a money-making venture that's resulted in an autobiography, two made-for-TV movies, and a gig as a correspondent for the Rachel Ray daytime TV show.

Other formerly famous people reaching for the limelight by hawking diet products are music, film, and television star Queen Latifah (Jenny Craig), film actress Kristie Swanson and soap star Genie Francis (MediFast), supermodel Rachel Hunter (Slimfast), musician-actress Marie Osmond, and football quarterback Dan Marino (NutriSystem). They've each found a way to take the media's emphasis on appearance and turn a perceived negative into a career positive. But that still doesn't thwart the underlying message conveyed by their endless rounds of advertisements: How you look is more important than any talent you may have or any work you've done in the past. Faced with this constant barrage of messages pushing the importance of appearance, why shouldn't Americans buy diet products and fitness services in an effort to lose weight? After all, they clearly see the positives associated with weight loss (supportive media attention and a return to some level of fame and adoration) and the negatives associated with weight gain (celebrities are derided in magazines and on TV shows, and the Internet for their unglamorous appearance and their lack of self-control).

"Best & Worst Beach Bodies": Read All About Them in Celebrity Magazines

Consider the following headlines, taken directly from stories in several recent celebrity magazines: "Britney's Super Bad Week: Busted, Bloated & Banned," "10 Best & Worst (Celebrity) Body Makeovers," "Knifestyles of the Rich & Famous: Kathie Lee Gifford — A New Face?" and "Diets That Work! How Stars Get Skinny & Sexy for Summer." Such celebrity magazines as *Us*, *Life & Style*, and *Star*, where all five of those headlines were found, along with *People*, *In Touch*, and *OK!*, make their fortunes by mining celebrities' appearances for stories. What could make the average American woman buy a glossy, photo-laden magazine? Images of stars, the people who supposedly have it all, looking less than perfect. Another means to an end, another violation of Kant's second categorical imperative. If celebrities are the ideal in terms of appearance, then to see them move away from that ideal is a guilty pleasure for most, and one worth paying for. Magazine editors know this, so they give us page after page of celebrity physical failings. Or at least the speculation of failings. In many cases, the items are simply digitally edited photographs that deliberately make the celebrity look bad, or even photographs taken from unflattering angles.

Such was the case with *Ghost Whisperer's* Jennifer Love Hewitt. In November 2007 several photos of her wearing a bikini were taken from unflattering angles while she was vacationing in Hawaii. They were quickly published on the Internet with captions touting how fat she was. Hewitt, who is a size 2, decried the criticism of her body by posting on her blog that "A size 2 is not fat! Nor will it ever be. And being a size 0 doesn't make you beautiful.... To all girls with butts, boobs, hips and a waist, put on a bikini — put it on and stay strong."[35] While a beautiful sentiment, and a much-needed one, it wasn't enough to combat the thousands of images that consumers of these magazines see every week that either praise a celebrity for her slim appearance or mock a celebrity for her "trouble" area. By focusing on celebrities' appearances, these magazines convey the same messages as the reality weight-loss and plastic surgery shows — that appearance determines human worth.

Ethically Responsible Media

Kant believed that humans have a duty to respect others' dignity and to promote virtue in others, both of which can be done in conjunction with the pursuit of profits. Media ethicist Louis Alvin Day wrote there's nothing "inherently immoral" in pursuing wealth. Instead, he wrote, "self-interest can be the servant of the public's interest, because the pursuit of profits can work to benefit society at large. The issue, in any given situation, is how to balance economic pressures against individual or institutional duties to others."[36]

One appearance-oriented television show is doing just that by attempting to have positive effects on viewers' body image satisfaction levels. *How to Look Good Naked*'s eight first-season, 30-minute episodes in 2008 were so successful, it began its second season on Lifetime as a one-hour program. Clearly, viewers and advertisers alike responded to its ethically appropriate goal of promoting virtue and good health in others. Instead of pushing weight-loss products or plastic surgery, host Carson Kressley helps women learn to accept and even appreciate their bodies. Each episode has real men and women making positive comments (explained in the show as unscripted and unrehearsed) about the figures of the women featured, after which Kressley teaches the women how to dress to flatter their figures. The point of the show is to teach women that all body sizes and shapes are beautiful, not just the size 0 or 2 we see on TV, in magazines, and on the Internet and billboards. Successful with both viewers and advertisers, *How to Look Good Naked* epitomizes how institutional duties toward others can be ethically achieved by the media without abandoning its economic interests.

How to Look Good Naked is just a drop in the bucket compared to the thousands of appearance-related pictures, stories, and ads Americans face every day in the media. As long as media content creators push an unattainable standard of ideal beauty, Americans will continue to experience body image dissatisfaction and a prejudice against people who don't conform to that standard. Positive change will only occur when media producers accept responsibility for their actions and treat audience members with respect, and not simply as a means to a profitable end.

NOTES

1. National Eating Disorders Association, June 2, 2009, http://nationaleatingidsorders.org/p.asp?WebPage_ID=286&Profile_ID=41138.

2. *Ibid.*

3. *Ibid.*

4. Jean Kilbourne, *Slim Hopes: Advertising and the Obsession with Thinness*, documentary, Northampton, MA: Media Education Foundation, 1995.

5. National Eating Disorders Association, June 2, 2009, http://nationaleatingdisorders.org/p.asp?WebPage_ID=320&Profile_ID=41138.

6. James I. Hudson, Eva Hiripi, Harrison Pope, and Ronald Kessler, "The Prevalence and Correlates of Eating Disorders in the National Comorbidity Survey Replication," *Biological Psychiatry* 61(3) February 2007: 348–358.

7. Kristen Harrison and Joanne J. Cantor, "The Relationship Between Media Consumption and Eating Disorders. *Journal of Communication* 47.1 (1997): 40–67.

8. Linda Hofschire and Bradley S. Greenberg, "Media's Impact on Adolescents' Body Dissatisfaction," In Jane Delano Brown, Jeanne R. Steele, and Kim Walsh-Childers, eds., *Sexual Teens, Sexual Media Mahwah*, NJ: Lawrence Earlbaum, 2002), 125–149.

9. Duane Hargreaves, "Idealized Women in TV Ads Make Girls Feel Bad," *Journal of Social and Clinical Psychology* 21 (2002): 287–308.

10. Elaine E. Englehardt and Ralph D. Barney, *Media and Ethics: Principles for Moral Decisions* (Belmont, CA: Wadsworth/Thompson, 2002) 35–59.

11. National Eating Disorders Association, June 2, 2009, http://www.nationaleatingdisorders.org/p.asp?WebPage_ID=320&Profile_ID=41138.

12. *Ibid.*

13. Metlife, May 1, 2008, http://www.metlife.com/Lifeadvice/Tools/Heightnweight/Docs/women.html.

14. National Eating Disorders Association, June 2, 2009, http://www.nationaleatingdisorders.org/p.asp?WebPage_ID=320&Profile_ID=41138.

15. Kilbourne, *Slim Hopes.*

16. Thomas Cash and Patricia E. Henry, "Women's Body Images: The Results of a National Survey in the U.S.A." *Sex Roles*, 33 1/2 (1995): 19–28.

17. Sherry Turner, Heather Hamilton, Meija Jacobs, Laurie. M. Angood, and Deanne Hovde Dwyer, "The Influence of Fashion Magazines on the Body Image Satisfaction of College Women: An Exploratory Analysis," *Adolescence* 32.127 (1997): 603–614.

18. Leslie Heinberg and Joel Kevin Thompson, "Body Image and Televised Images of Thinness and Attractiveness: A Controlled Laboratory Investigation," *Journal of Social and Clinical Psychology* 14.4 (1995): 325–338.

19. Englehardt and Barney, *Media and Ethics,* 14–15.

20. *Ibid.*

21. Mary Harris, Richard Harris, and Stephen Bochner, "Fat, Four-Eyed and Female: Stereotypes of Obesity, Glass, and Gender," *Journal of Applied Social Psychology* 12 (1982): 503–516.

22. Arthur Vener, Lawrence Krupka and R.J. Gerard, "Overweight/Obese Patients: An Overview," *The Practitioner* 226 (1982): 1102–1109.

23. *Ibid.* 1104.

24. *Ibid.* 1105

25. Kilbourne, *Slim Hopes,*

26. Campaign for Real Beauty, June 2, 2009, http://www.campaignforrealbeauty.com.

27. Louis A. Day, *Ethics in Media Communications: Cases and Controversies*, 5th ed. (Scarborough, Ontario, Canada: Thompson Wadsworth, 2006), 26.

28. Dolf Zillman and Jennings Bryant, "Pornography's Impact on Sexual Satisfaction," *Journal of Applied Psychology*, 18 (1988): 438–453. Dolf Zillman and Jennings Bryant, "Effects of Prolonged Consumption of Pornography on Family Values," *Journal of Family Issues* (1988): 518–544.

29. Richard Crockett, Thomas Pruzinsky, and John Persing, "The Influence of Plastic Surgery 'Realty TV' on Cosmetic Surgery Patient Expectations and Decision Making," *Journal of Plastic and Reconstructive Surgery* 120 (1) July 2007: 316–324.

30. Melanie Lefkowitz and Beth Whitehouse, "More Teens Getting Breast-Augmentation," *The Times-Union*, March 31, 2008, C-4.

31. *Ibid.*

32. *Ibid.*

33. *Ibid.*

34. Internet Movie Database, June 2, 2009, http://imbd/name/nm0000263.

35. People.com, June 2, 2009, http://www.people.com/people/article/0,,20163862,00.html.

36. Day, *Ethics in Media Communications*, 24.

Works Cited

Campaign for Real Beauty. (June 2, 2009), http://www.campaignforrealbeauty.com.

Cash, Thomas, and Patricia E. Henry. "Women's Body Images: The Results of a National Survey in the U.S.A." *Sex Roles*, 33 no. 1/2 (1995): 19–28.

Crockett, Richard, Thomas Pruzinsky, and John Persing. "The Influence of Plastic Surgery 'Reality TV' on Cosmetic Surgery Patient Expectations and Decision Making." *Journal of Plastic and Reconstructive Surgery*, 120 no. 1 (July 2007): 316–324.

Day, Louis A. *Ethics in Media Communications: Cases and Controversies,* 5th ed. Scarborough, Ontario, Canada: Thompson/Wadsworth, 2006.

Englehardt, Elaine E., and Ralph D. Barney. *Media and Ethics: Principles for Moral Decisions.* Belmont, CA: Wadsworth/Thompson, 2002.

Hargreaves, Duane. "Idealized Women in TV Ads Make Girls Feel Bad." *Journal of Social and Clinical Psychology,* 21 (2002): 287–308.

Harris, Mary, Richard Harris, and Stephen Bochner. "Fat, Four-Eyed and Female: Stereotypes of Obesity, Glasses, and Gender." *Journal of Applied Social Psychology* 12 (1982): 503–516.

Harrison, Kristen, and Joanne J. Cantor. "The Relationship Between Media Consumption and Eating Disorders." *Journal of Communication,* 47 no. 1 (1997) 40: 67.

Heinberg, Leslie, and Joel Kevin Thompson. "Body Image and Televised Images of Thinness and Attractiveness: A Controlled Laboratory Investigation." *Journal of Social and Clinical Psychology,* 14 no. 4 (1995): 325–338.

Hofschire, Linda, and Bradley S. Greenberg. "Media's Impact on Adolescents' Body Dissatisfaction." In Jane Delano Brown, Jeanne R. Steele, and Kim Walsh-Childers, eds., *Sexual Teens, Sexual Media: Investigating Media's Influence on Adolescent Sexuality.* Mahwah, N.J.: Lawrence Earlbaum, 2002: 125–149.

Hudson, James I., Eva Hiripi, Harrison Pope, and Ronald Kessler. "The Prevalence and Correlates of Eating Disorders in the National Comorbidity Survey Replication." *Biological Psychiatry* 61 no. 3 (February 2007): 348: 358.

Internet Movie Database. (June 2, 2009), http://imdb/name/nm0000263.

Kilbourne, Jean. *Slim Hopes: Advertising and the Obsession with Thinness* (documentary). Northampton, MA: Media Education Foundation, 1995.

Lefkowitz, Melanie, and Beth Whitehouse. "More Teens Getting Breast Augmentation." *The Florida Times-Union,* March 31, 2008, C-4.

Metlife. (May 1, 2008), http://www.metlife.com/Lifeadvice/Tools/Heightnweight/Docs/women.html.

National Eating Disorders Association. (June 2, 2009), http://nationaleatingdisorders.org/p.asp?WebPage_ID286&Profile_=41138.

People Magazine Online. (June 2, 2009), http://people.com/people/article/0,,20163862,00.html.

Turner, Sherry, Heather Hamilton, Meija Jacobs, Laurie M. Angood, and Deanne Hovde Dwyer. "The Influence of Fashion Magazines on the Body Image Satisfaction of College Women: An Exploratory Analysis." *Adolescence,* 32 no. 127 (1997): 603–614.

Vener, Arthur, Lawrence Krupka, and R.J. Gerard. "Overweight/Obese Patients: An Overview." *The Practitioner* 226 (1982): 1102–1109.

Zillman, Dolf, and Jennings Bryant. "Effects of Prolonged Consumption of Pornography on Family Values." *Journal of Family Issues* (1988): 518–544.

_____, and _____. "Pornography's Impact on Sexual Satisfaction." *Journal of Applied Psychology* 18 (1988): 438–453.

Contributors

Berrin A. Beasley is an associate professor of journalism and a senior fellow for the Blue Cross Blue Shield Center for Ethics, Public Policy and the Professions at the University of North Florida. Her research areas include journalism ethics and the portrayal of women in the media, and her research has been published in *Mass Media and Society*, the *Newspaper Research Journal*, the *Journal of Radio Studies*, the *Southwestern Mass Communication Journal*, and the *Florida Communication Journal*. She has a chapter on *Wag the Dog* in *Journalism Ethics Goes to the Movies* (Rowman & Littlefield, 2008), edited by Howard Good.

Sandra L. Borden is a professor in the School of Communication at Western Michigan University, where she also co-directs the Center for the Study of Ethics in Society. Her work has been published in several scholarly books and journals, including *The Handbook of Mass Media Ethics*, the *Journal of Mass Media Ethics* and *Communication Monographs*. Her book, *Journalism as Practice: MacIntyre, Virtue Ethics and the Press*, won the 2008 Clifford G. Christians Ethics Research Award and the National Communication Association's 2008 top book award in applied ethics. Borden, who teaches ethics and media criticism, is associate editor of the journal *Teaching Ethics*.

Jack Breslin is an associate professor of mass communication at Iona College, with a doctorate from the University of Minnesota. Breslin was a reporter for the *Daily Freeman* in Kingston, New York, and has written free-lance articles for numerous newspapers and magazines. As a publicist, manager, and director at NBC and Fox, he publicized the premieres of *Late Night with David Letterman, America's Most Wanted,* and *COPS.* He wrote the Harper paperback *"America's Most Wanted": How TV Catches Crooks.*

Kristie Bunton is a professor in and the chair of the Department of Communication and Journalism at the University of St. Thomas, where she teaches communication ethics. She completed her Ph.D. at Indiana University and has published in *Journal of Mass Media Ethics, Journalism and Mass Communication Educator,* and *Public Integrity.*

John Chapin is an associate professor of communications at Penn State University, with a Ph.D. from Rutgers University. He conducts applied community-based research in violence prevention education. He is the recipient of the Stephen Schafer National Research Award for significant contributions to the field of crime victim rights from the National Organization for Victim Assistance and the Governor's Victim Service Pathfinder Allied Professional Award from Pennsylvania Governor Rendell.

David Charlton studies philosophy as a graduate student at Western Michigan University. He has worked with the university's Center for the Study of Ethics in Society and has helped coach WMU's Intercollegiate Ethics Bowl team for several years. He earned his M.A. at Western Michigan University in comparative religion in 2007, focusing on Chinese philosophy and religion in American education.

Angela F. Cooke-Jackson, who holds a Ph.D. in health communication and behavioral science, is completing her M.P.H. in health behavior and epidemiology from the University of Kentucky. She was an assistant professor at Eastern Kentucky University before joining the faculty at Emerson College. An article she co-wrote with Elizabeth K. Hansen was published in the *Journal of Mass Media Ethics.*

Thomas F. Corrigan is a Ph.D. candidate in Penn State's College of Communications and a research assistant for the College's John Curley Center for Sports Journalism. His research interests include the political economy of sports and media, online sports communities, and media and democracy.

Mike Dillon is an associate professor in the Department of Journalism and Multimedia Arts at Duquesne University, where he has been recognized for excellence in teaching and scholarship. Dillon, who received his Ph.D. from Penn State, has published extensively in the areas of media history and media ethics, including a co-authored book with Howard Good, *Media Ethics Goes to the Movies* (Praeger, 2003). A former award-winning newspaper and magazine journalist, his free-lance work has appeared in *New York Newsday,* the *Dallas Morning News,* the *Pittsburgh Post-Gazette,* and numerous other publications.

Deni Elliott holds the Poynter Jamison Chair in Media Ethics and Press Policy at the University of South Florida. She is the author or co-author of seven books and more than 100 book chapters, journal articles, and periodical pieces.

Howard Good is a professor in the Communication and Media Department at the State University of New York at New Paltz, where he originated the course in media ethics. Among his many books are *Acquainted with the Night, Outcasts, The Journalist as Autobiographer, Diamonds in the Dark, Girl Reporter, The Drunken Journalist, Media Ethics Goes to the Movies* (with Mike Dillon), *Educated Guess,* and *The Theory of Oz.* He is also the author of twelve poetry chapbooks and a full-length collection of poetry, *Lovesick* (Poetry Press/Press Americana, 2009). His poetry has been nominated four times for a Pushcart Prize and five times for the Best of the Net anthology.

Elizabeth K. Hansen is a Foundation Professor in the Department of Communication at Eastern Kentucky University, where she teaches media ethics, community journalism, writing and reporting, media law, and magazine free-lancing. Her research interests include community journalism, ethics, law, and media effects. She serves on the national Ethics Committee and the Board of Directors of the Society of Professional Journalists. Hansen has worked for newspapers in Arkansas, Louisiana and Kentucky.

Marie Hardin is an associate professor of journalism in the College of Communications at Penn State University and associate director for research in the John Curley

Center for Sports Journalism. Her work has appeared in the *Sociology of Sport Journal, Electronic News, International Journal of Sport Communication,* and *Communication, Culture and Critique.*

Joseph C. Harry is an associate professor in the Department of Communication at Slippery Rock University of Pennsylvania, with a Ph.D. from Michigan State University. His research interests include rhetoric, semiotics, political-economy, and sociolinguistics as applied to the study of journalism, film, and television. His more recent research has been published in *Journalism and Mass Communication Quarterly,* the *Journal of Communication Inquiry,* and the scholarly volume *Journalism Ethics Goes to the Movies* (Rowman & Littlefield, 2008), edited by Howard Good.

Keisha L. Hoerrner is the chair of the Department of First-Year Programs and an associate professor of communication at Kennesaw State University. She is also co-editor of the *Journal of Learning Communities Research,* a peer-reviewed scholarly publication she helped launch in 2006. She has published journal articles and book chapters related to mass media issues in *Journalism and Mass Communication Quarterly, Women's Studies in Communication,* and *Mass Communication and Society.*

Cynthia M. King is the director of the Center for Entertainment and Tourism Studies and a professor of communications at California State University, Fullerton. As center director, she oversees academic and industry partnerships in education, research, and policy development in the fields of entertainment and tourism. Her published research focuses on emerging trends and effects of entertainment and commercial media. She is co-author (with Shay Sayre) of *Entertainment and Society: Influences, Impacts and Trends.*

K. Maja Krakowiak, who received her Ph.D. from Penn State University in 2008, is an assistant professor in the Department of Communication at the University of Colorado at Colorado Springs. Her recent research focuses on individuals' responses to morally ambiguous characters in entertainment media. Her work has appeared in *Media Effects: Advances in Theory and Research* and *Encyclopedia of Children, Adolescents, and the Media.*

Steve Lipkin teaches film study, and film and video production in Western Michigan University's School of Communication. His recent work extends the lines of inquiry he began in his book, *Real Emotional Logic: Film and Television Docudrama as Persuasive Practice* (2002). He has presented his research at the Society of Cinema and Media Studies, the University Film and Video Association, Film and History, and Visible Evidence conferences, and has published essays in *Quarterly Review of Film and Video, Cinema Journal,* the *Journal of Film and Video,* and *Jump Cut.*

Bill Reader is an assistant professor in the E.W. Scripps School of Journalism at Ohio University, where he teaches courses in media ethics, mass media and society, news editing and management, and community journalism. He is co-author (with Steven Knowlton) of *Moral Reasoning for Journalists,* 2nd ed. (Praeger, 2008).

Kyle F. Reinson is an assistant professor at St. John Fisher College in Rochester, New York. Reinson has contributed book reviews to the *Journal of Communication Inquiry, American Journalism* and the *Democratic Communiqué,* the journal of the Union for Democratic Communications. He continues his national public relations consulting following more than 15 years as a corporate and agency executive.

Erin L. Ryan is an assistant professor in the Department of Telecommunication and Film in the College of Communication and Information Sciences at the University of Alabama, Tuscaloosa. Her research centers on children and the electronic media, primarily in the effects tradition. She has published in *Mass Communication and Society* and has articles in press at *Communication Research* and *The Journal of Broadcasting and Electronic Media*.

Janel S. Schuh is a Provost's Doctoral Fellow at the University of Southern California's Annenberg School for Communication. Her research focuses on adolescents and young adults' involvement with celebrities.

Trin Turner is a doctoral student in the philosophy of evolutionary biology at Indiana University's Department of History and Philosophy of Science.

Joshua D. Upson, who received his M.A. in philosophy from Western Michigan University, teaches philosophy as a part-time instructor at various institutions, including Western Michigan University.

Nikki Usher is a doctoral student at the University of Southern California's Annenberg School for Communication. She has been a Wallace Annenberg Fellow for the Center for Journalism and Democracy and a Knight Digital Media Center research assistant. As part of her graduate work, she is engaged in researching the connection between new technology, mass media, journalism practice, and organizational change.

Wendy N. Wyatt is an associate professor in the Department of Communication and Journalism at the University of St. Thomas. Her research interests include communication ethics, press criticism, and media literacy. She is the author of *Critical Conversations: A Theory of Press Criticism* (Hampton, 2007) and book review editor for the *Journal of Mass Media Ethics*. Her work has been published in the *International Journal of Applied Philosophy*, the *Journal of Mass Media Ethics*, and *Journalism and Mass Communication Quarterly,* as well as several communication ethics texts.

Index